Shojo Beat

Millennium Snow

A Thousandth Snow

Vol. 1 Story & Art by **Bisco Hatori**

Table of Contents

First Snow 3

Second Snow 45

Third Snow 87

Fourth Snow 119

A Romance of One Moment 161

Egoistic Club 201

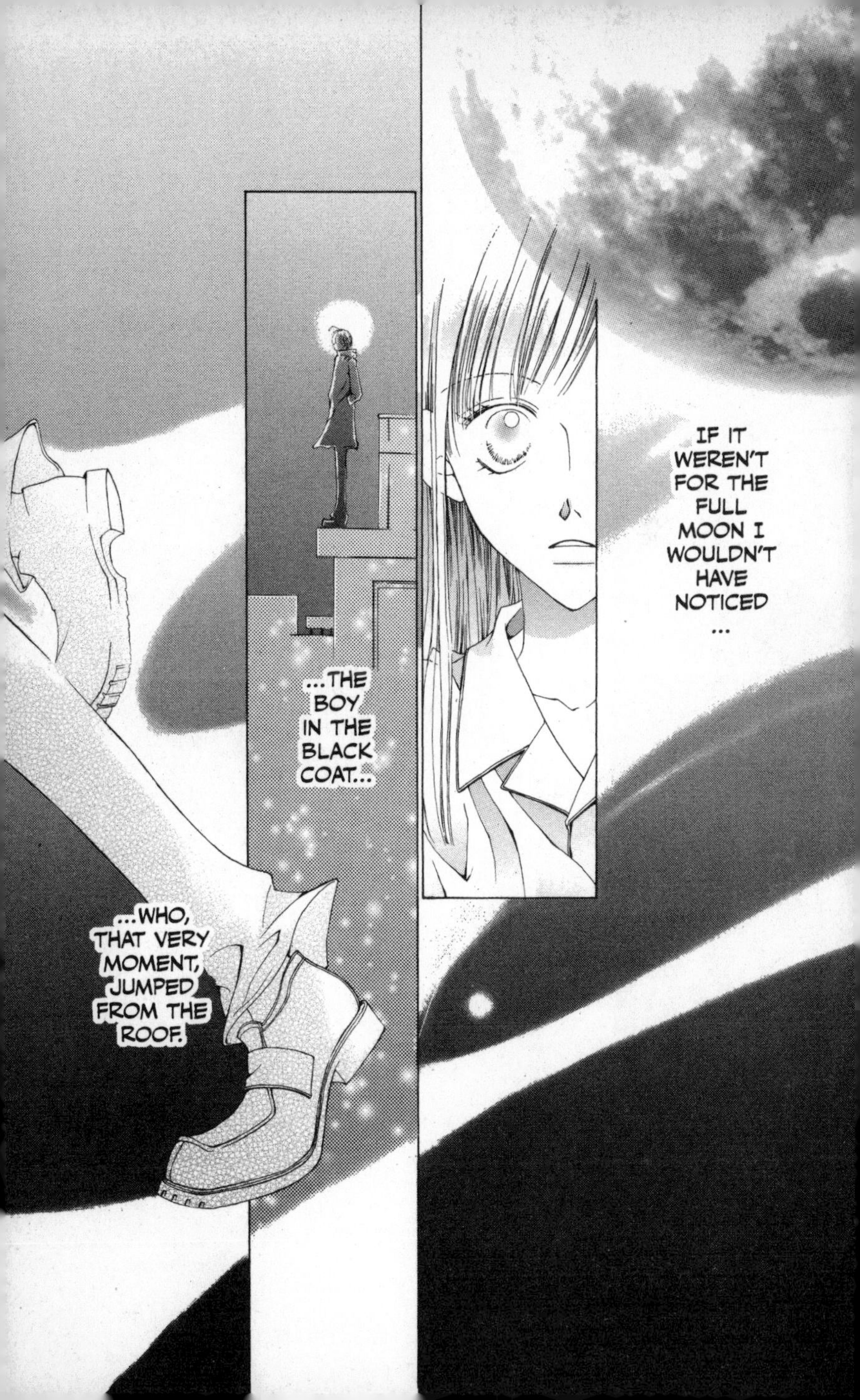
IF IT WEREN'T FOR THE FULL MOON I WOULDN'T HAVE NOTICED ...
...THE BOY IN THE BLACK COAT...
...WHO, THAT VERY MOMENT, JUMPED FROM THE ROOF.

Millennium Snow

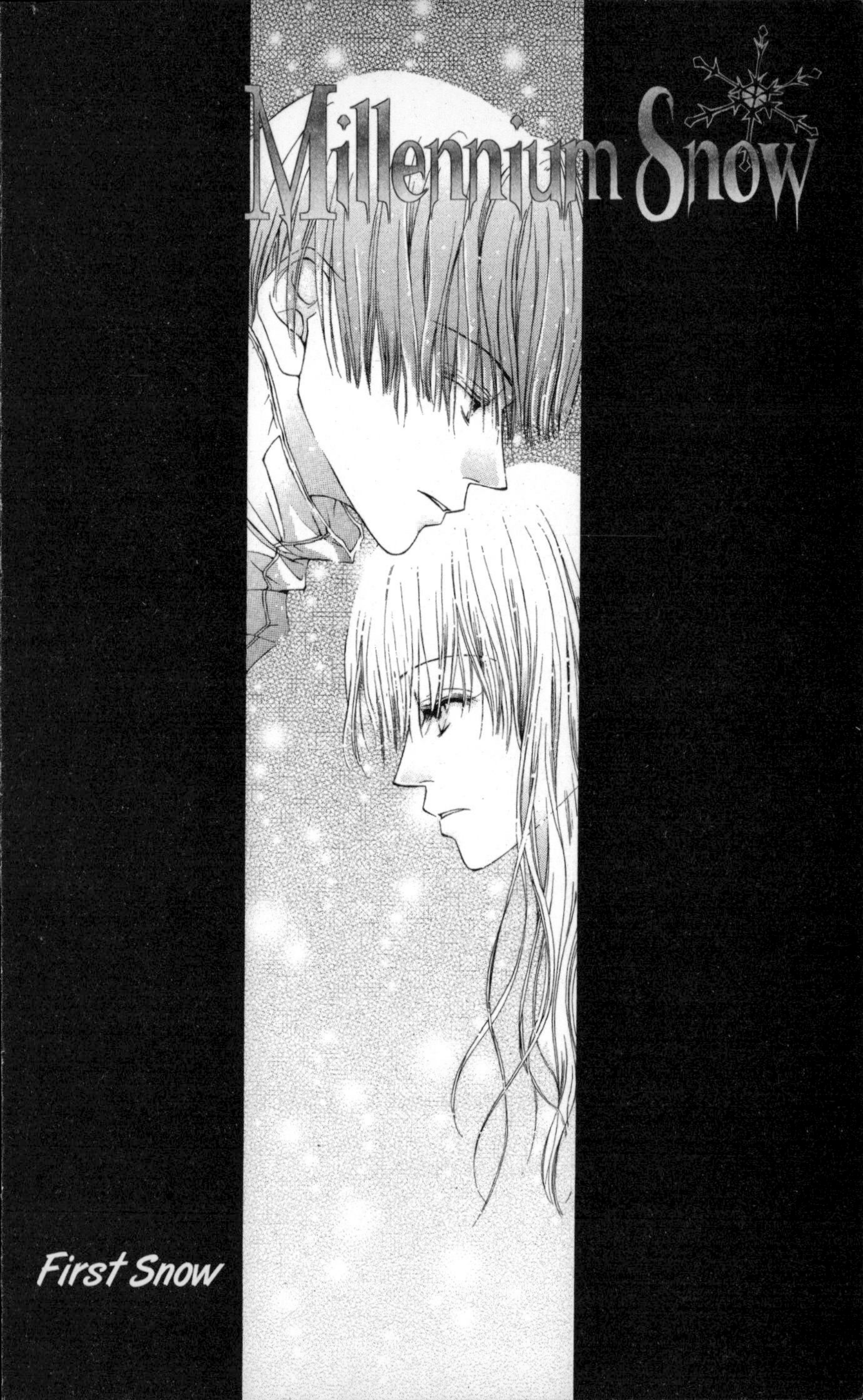

First Snow

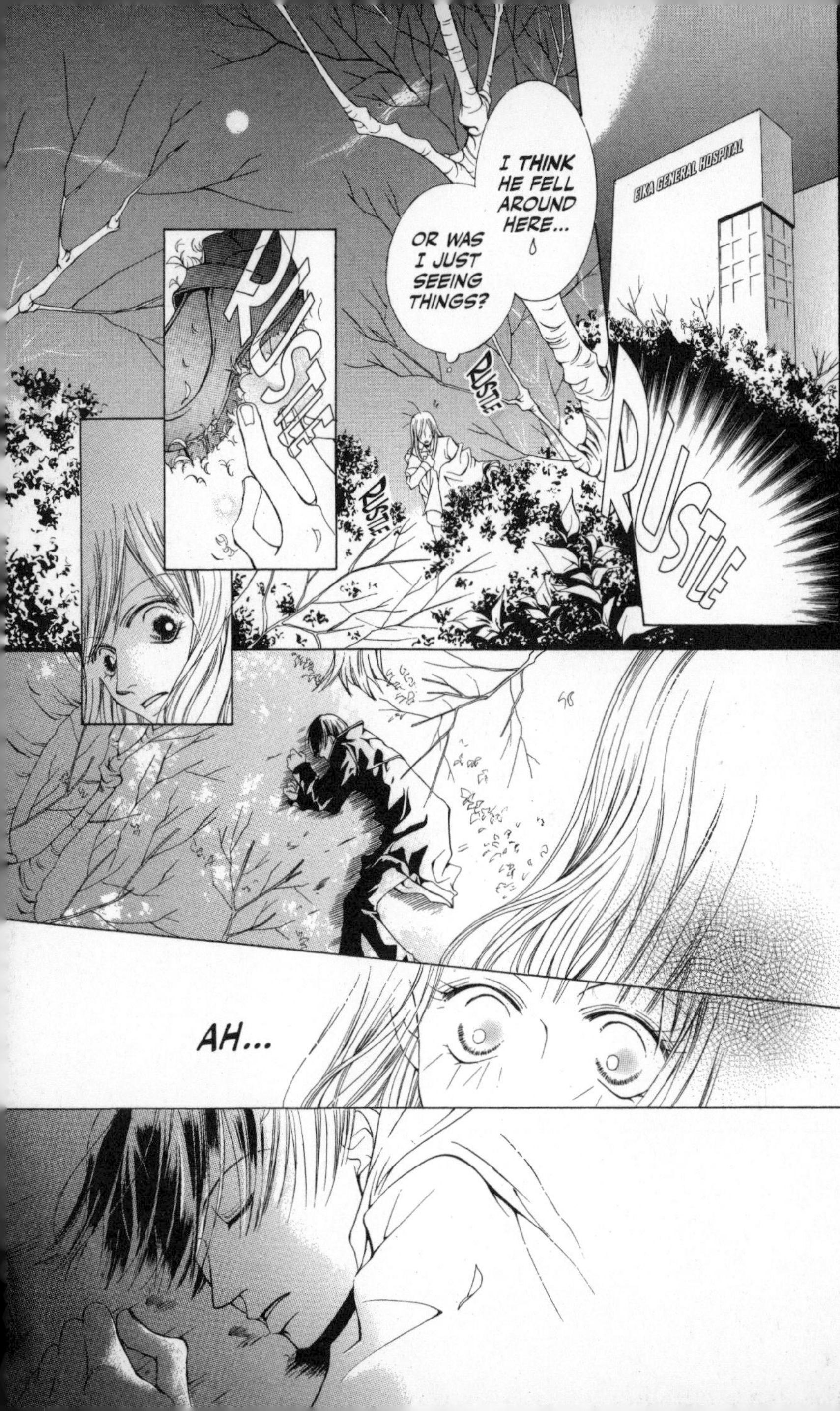
EIKA GENERAL HOSPITAL
I THINK HE FELL AROUND HERE...
OR WAS I JUST SEEING THINGS?
RUSTLE
RUSTLE
RUSTLE
RUSTLE
AH...

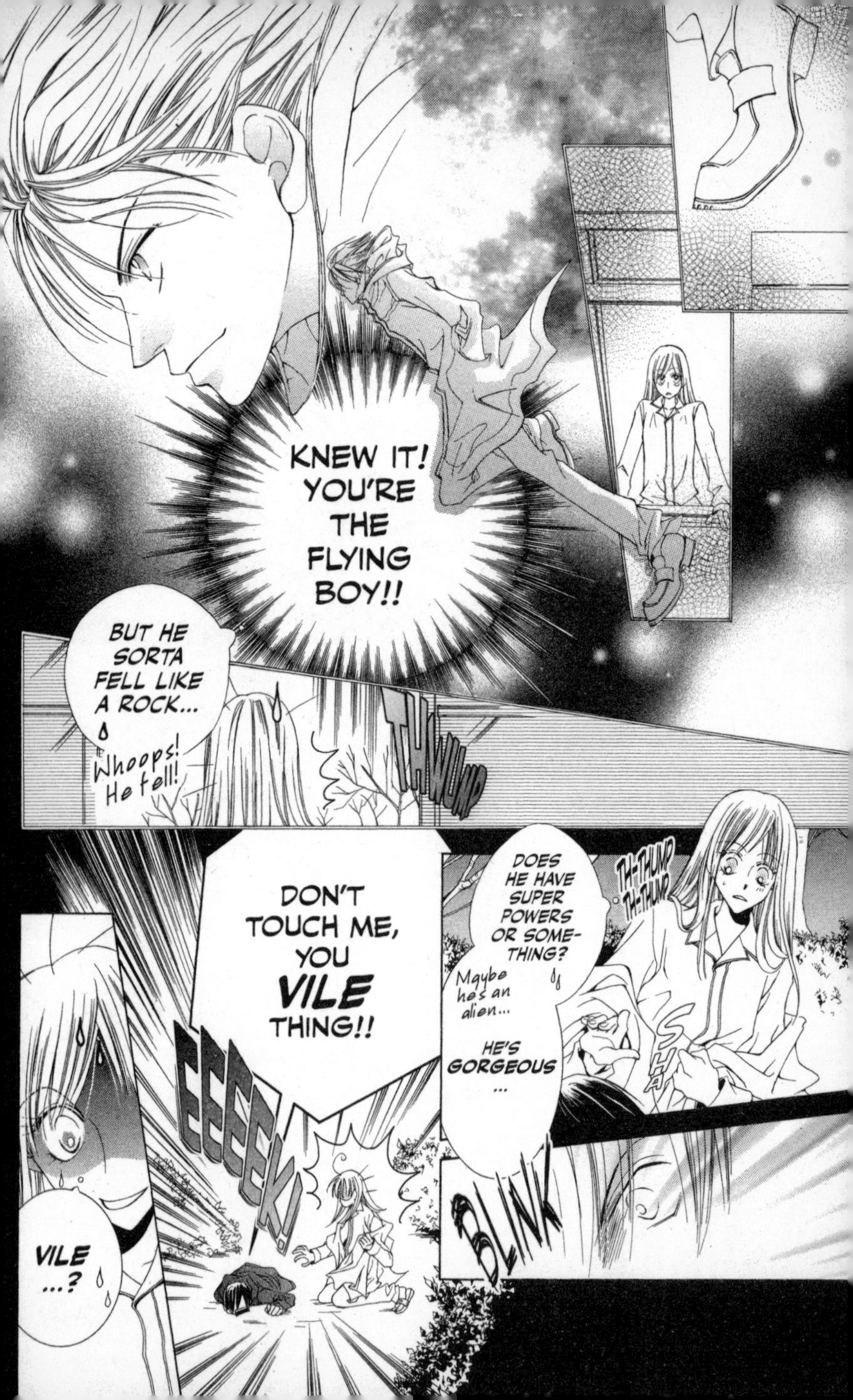
KNEW IT! YOU'RE THE FLYING BOY!!
BUT HE SORTA FELL LIKE A ROCK...
Whoops! He fell!
THWUMP
TH-THUMP TH-THUMP
DOES HE HAVE SUPER POWERS OR SOME-THING?
Maybe he's an alien...
HE'S GORGEOUS...
SHA
BLINK
DON'T TOUCH ME, YOU ***VILE*** THING!!
EEEEK!
VILE...?

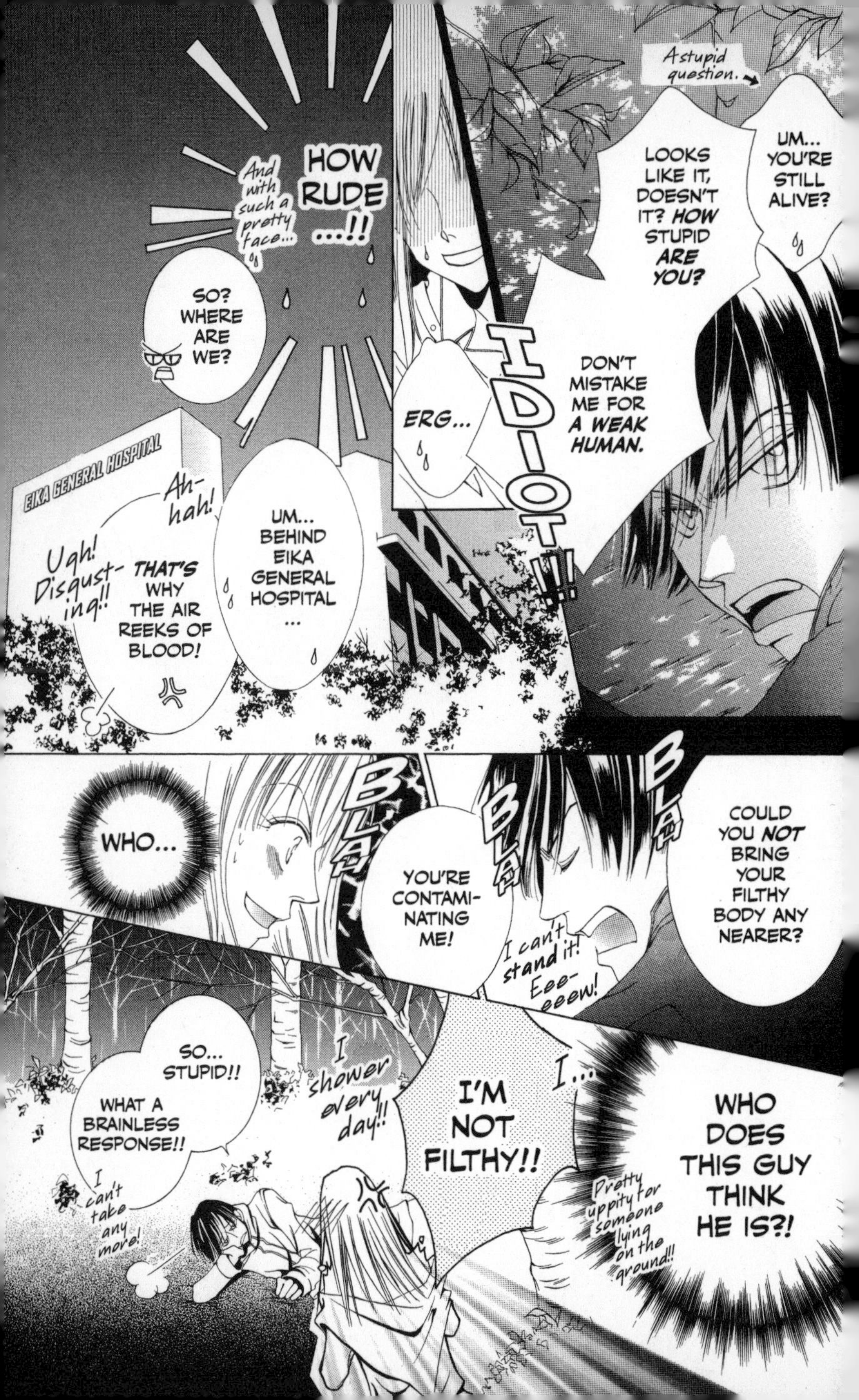
A stupid question.
UM... YOU'RE STILL ALIVE?
LOOKS LIKE IT, DOESN'T IT? HOW STUPID ARE YOU?
DON'T MISTAKE ME FOR A WEAK HUMAN.
IDIOT!!
ERG...
HOW RUDE...!!
And with such a pretty face...
SO? WHERE ARE WE?
UM... BEHIND EIKA GENERAL HOSPITAL...
EIKA GENERAL HOSPITAL
Ah-hah! THAT'S WHY THE AIR REEKS OF BLOOD!
Ugh! Disgusting!!
BLA
BLA
BLA
COULD YOU NOT BRING YOUR FILTHY BODY ANY NEARER?
YOU'RE CONTAMINATING ME!
I can't stand it! Eeeeeew!
WHO...
I...
WHO DOES THIS GUY THINK HE IS?!
Pretty uppity for someone lying on the ground!!
I'M NOT FILTHY!!
I shower every day!!
SO... STUPID!!
WHAT A BRAINLESS RESPONSE!!
I can't take any more!

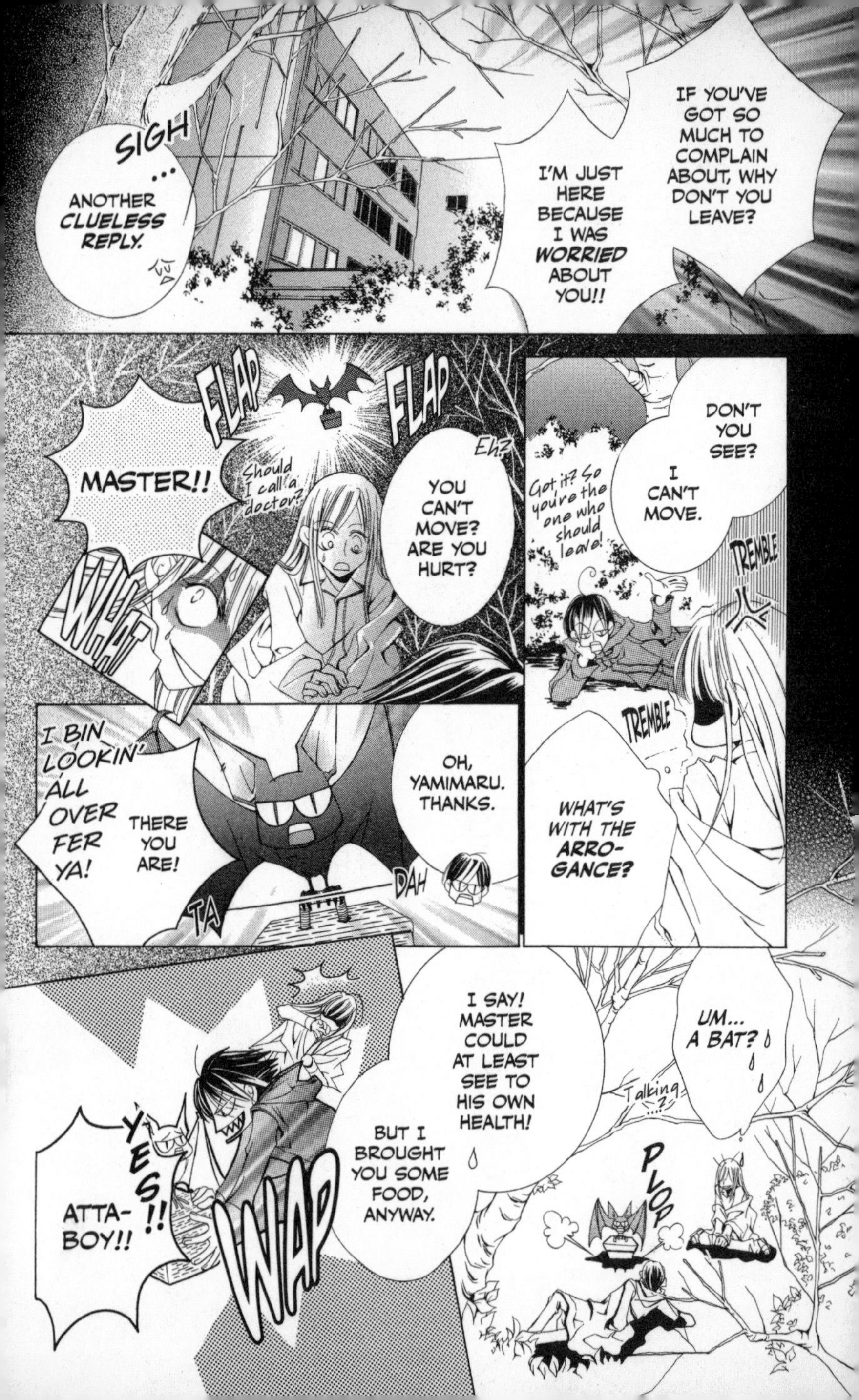
IF YOU'VE GOT SO MUCH TO COMPLAIN ABOUT, WHY DON'T YOU LEAVE?
I'M JUST HERE BECAUSE I WAS WORRIED ABOUT YOU!!
SIGH...
ANOTHER CLUELESS REPLY.
DON'T YOU SEE?
I CAN'T MOVE.
Got it? So you're the one who should leave!
TREMBLE
Eh?
YOU CAN'T MOVE? ARE YOU HURT?
Should I call a doctor?
FLAP
FLAP
MASTER!!
WHAT
TREMBLE
WHAT'S WITH THE ARROGANCE?
OH, YAMIMARU. THANKS.
DAH
THERE YOU ARE!
I BIN LOOKIN' ALL OVER FER YA!
TA
UM... A BAT?
Talking...?
PLOP
I SAY! MASTER COULD AT LEAST SEE TO HIS OWN HEALTH!
BUT I BROUGHT YOU SOME FOOD, ANYWAY.
WAP
YES!!
ATTA-BOY!!

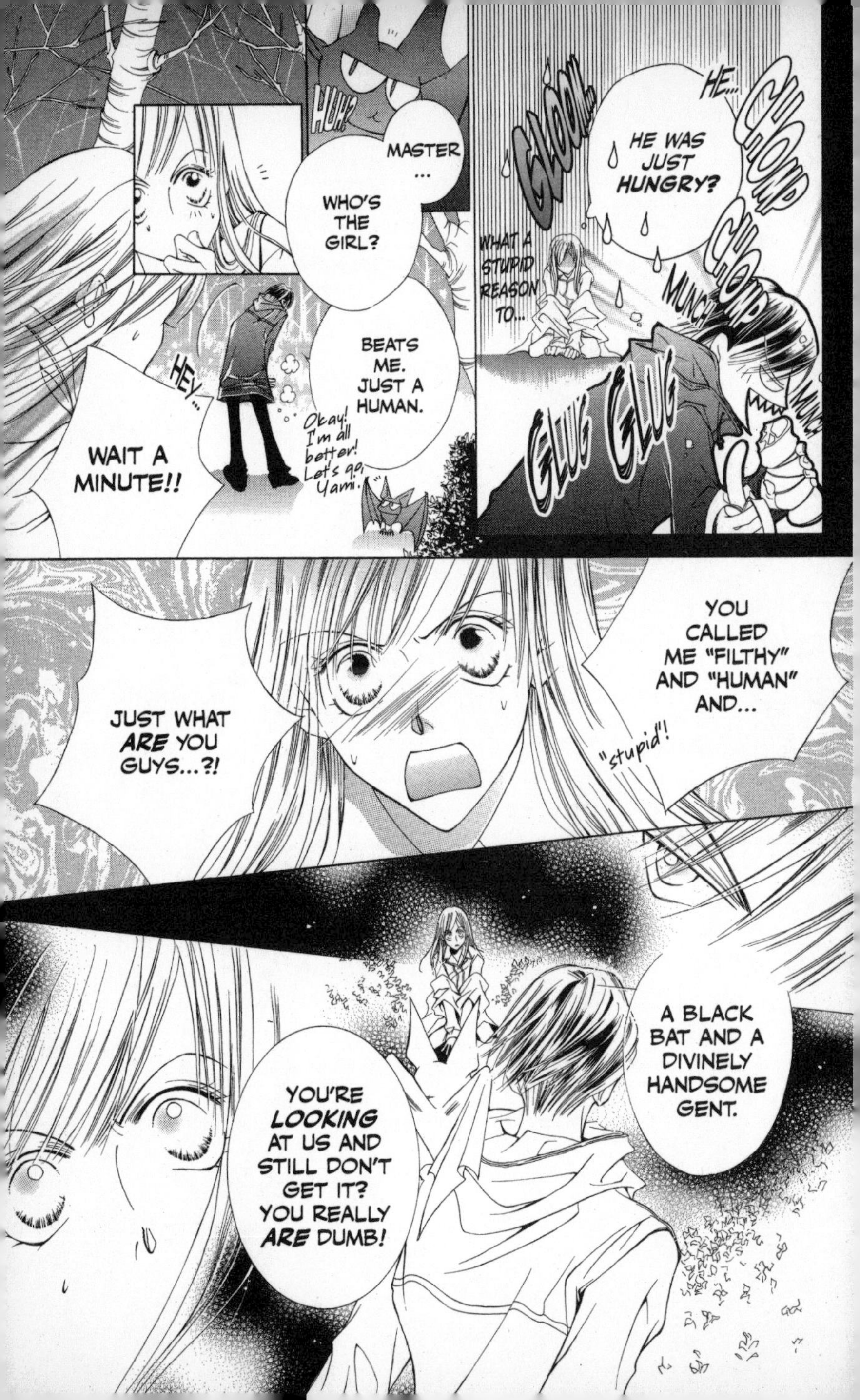
HE... HE WAS JUST HUNGRY?
CHOMP
CHOMP
GLOOM...
WHAT A STUPID REASON TO...
MUNCH
MUNCH
GLUG GLUG
HUH?
MASTER ... WHO'S THE GIRL?
BEATS ME. JUST A HUMAN.
Okay! I'm all better! Let's go, Yami.
HEY...
WAIT A MINUTE!!
YOU CALLED ME "FILTHY" AND "HUMAN" AND...
"stupid"!
JUST WHAT ARE YOU GUYS...?!
A BLACK BAT AND A DIVINELY HANDSOME GENT.
YOU'RE LOOKING AT US AND STILL DON'T GET IT? YOU REALLY ARE DUMB!

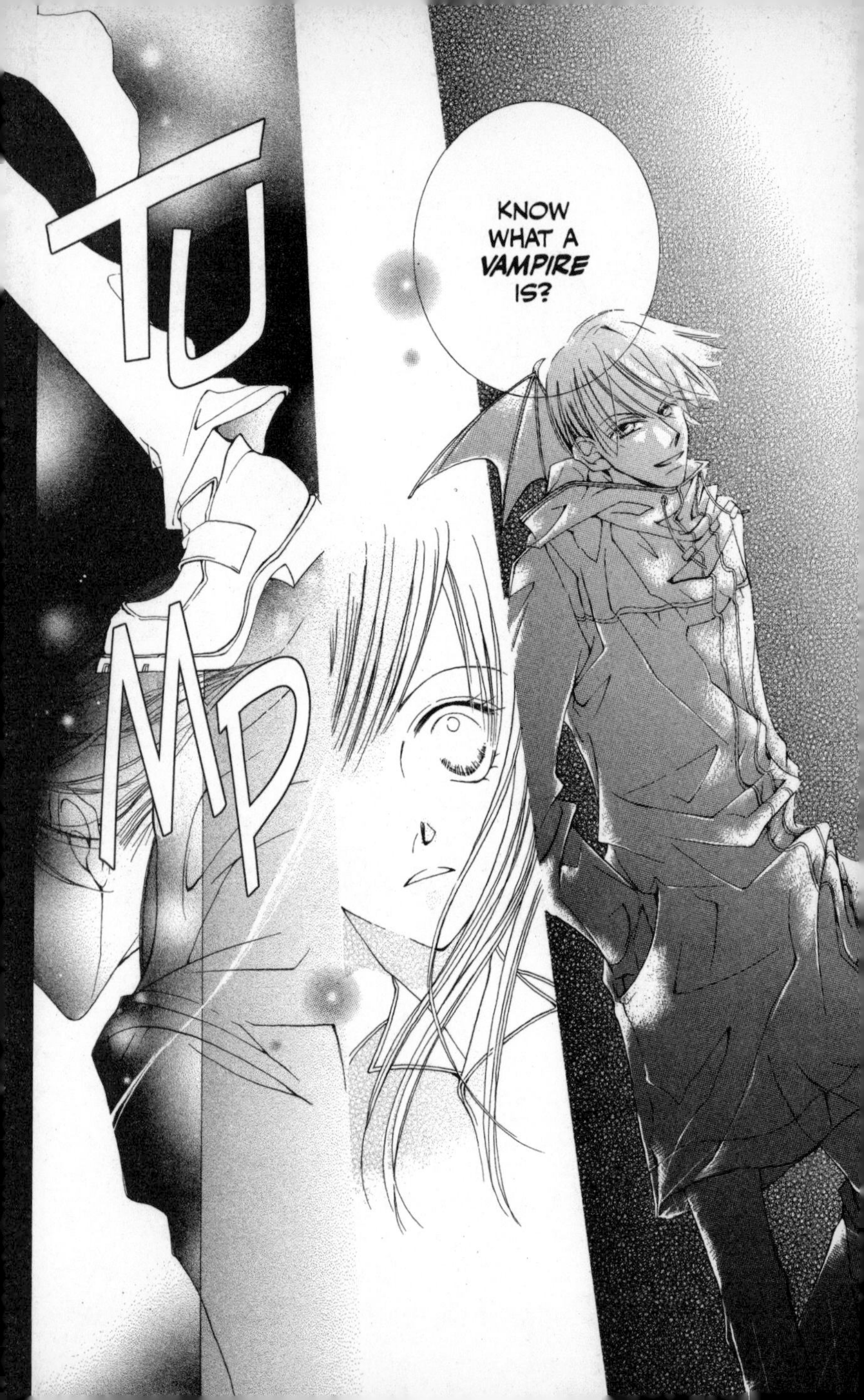
KNOW WHAT A VAMPIRE IS?
TUMP

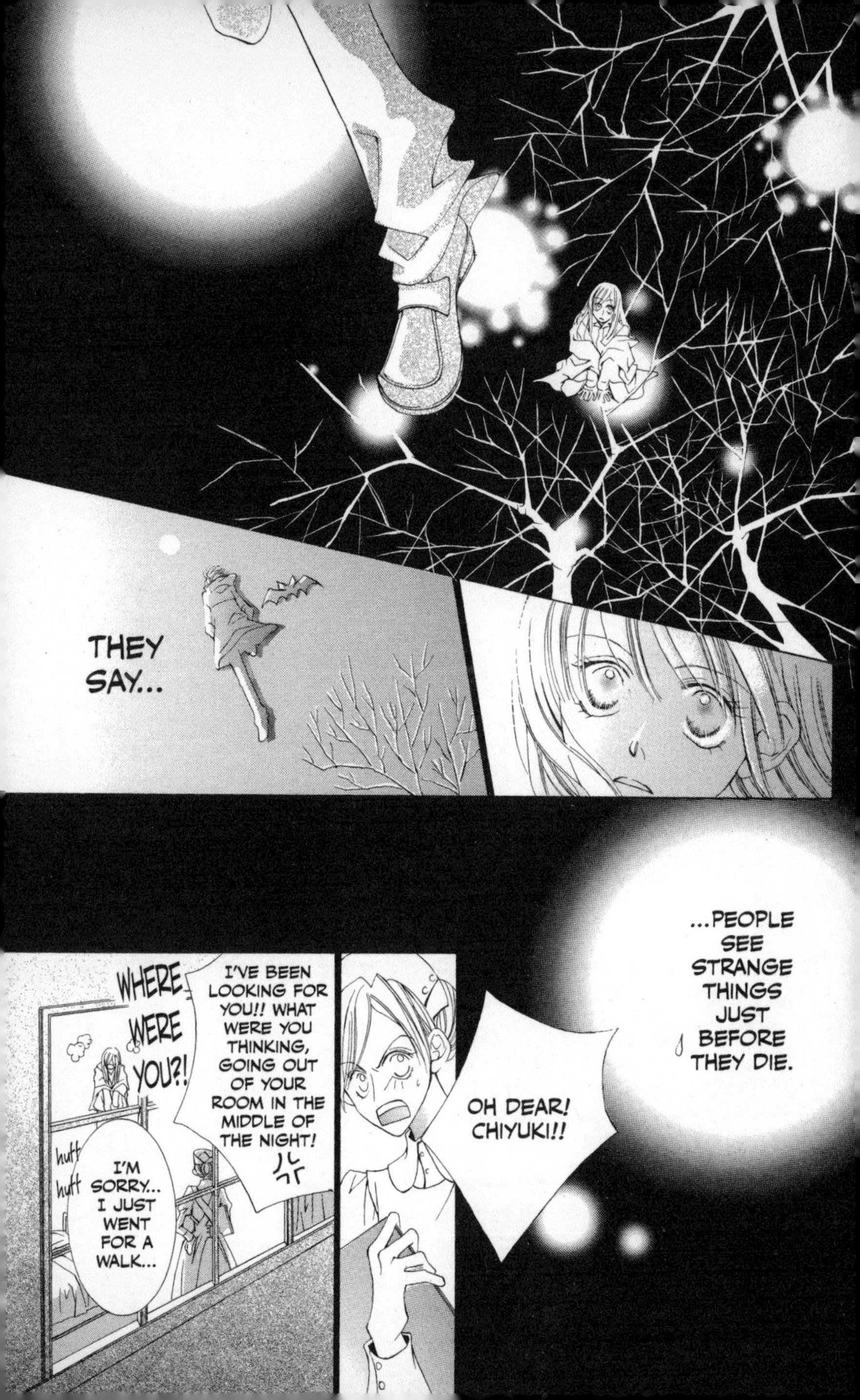
THEY SAY...
...PEOPLE SEE STRANGE THINGS JUST BEFORE THEY DIE.
OH DEAR! CHIYUKI!!
WHERE WERE YOU?!
I'VE BEEN LOOKING FOR YOU!! WHAT WERE YOU THINKING, GOING OUT OF YOUR ROOM IN THE MIDDLE OF THE NIGHT!
huff huff
I'M SORRY... I JUST WENT FOR A WALK...

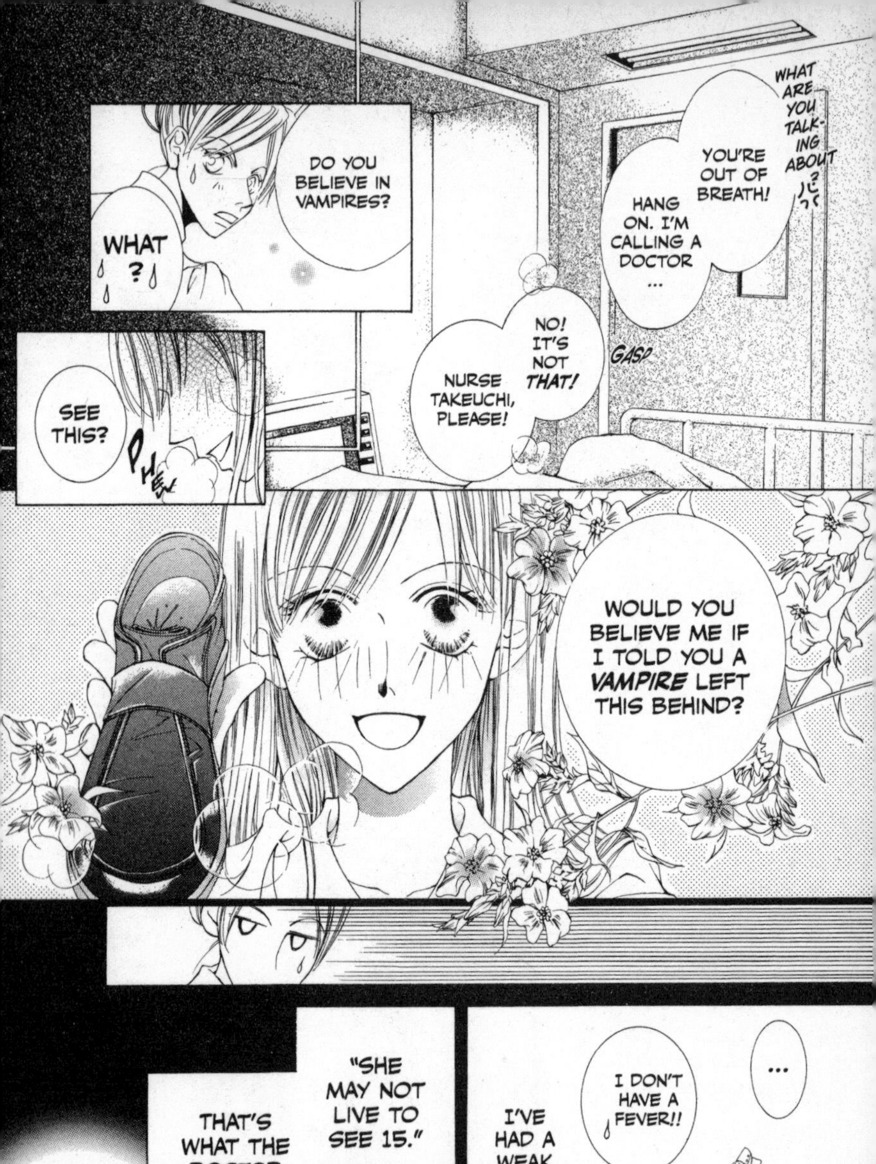
WHAT ARE YOU TALKING ABOUT?
YOU'RE OUT OF BREATH!
HANG ON. I'M CALLING A DOCTOR ...
GASP
NO! IT'S NOT *THAT!*
NURSE TAKEUCHI, PLEASE!
DO YOU BELIEVE IN VAMPIRES?
WHAT?
SEE THIS?
PHEW
WOULD YOU BELIEVE ME IF I TOLD YOU A *VAMPIRE* LEFT THIS BEHIND?
...
I DON'T HAVE A FEVER!!
I'VE HAD A WEAK HEART EVER SINCE I WAS BORN.
"SHE MAY NOT LIVE TO SEE 15."
THAT'S WHAT THE DOCTOR SAID WHEN I WAS BORN.
LISTEN, CHIYUKI...

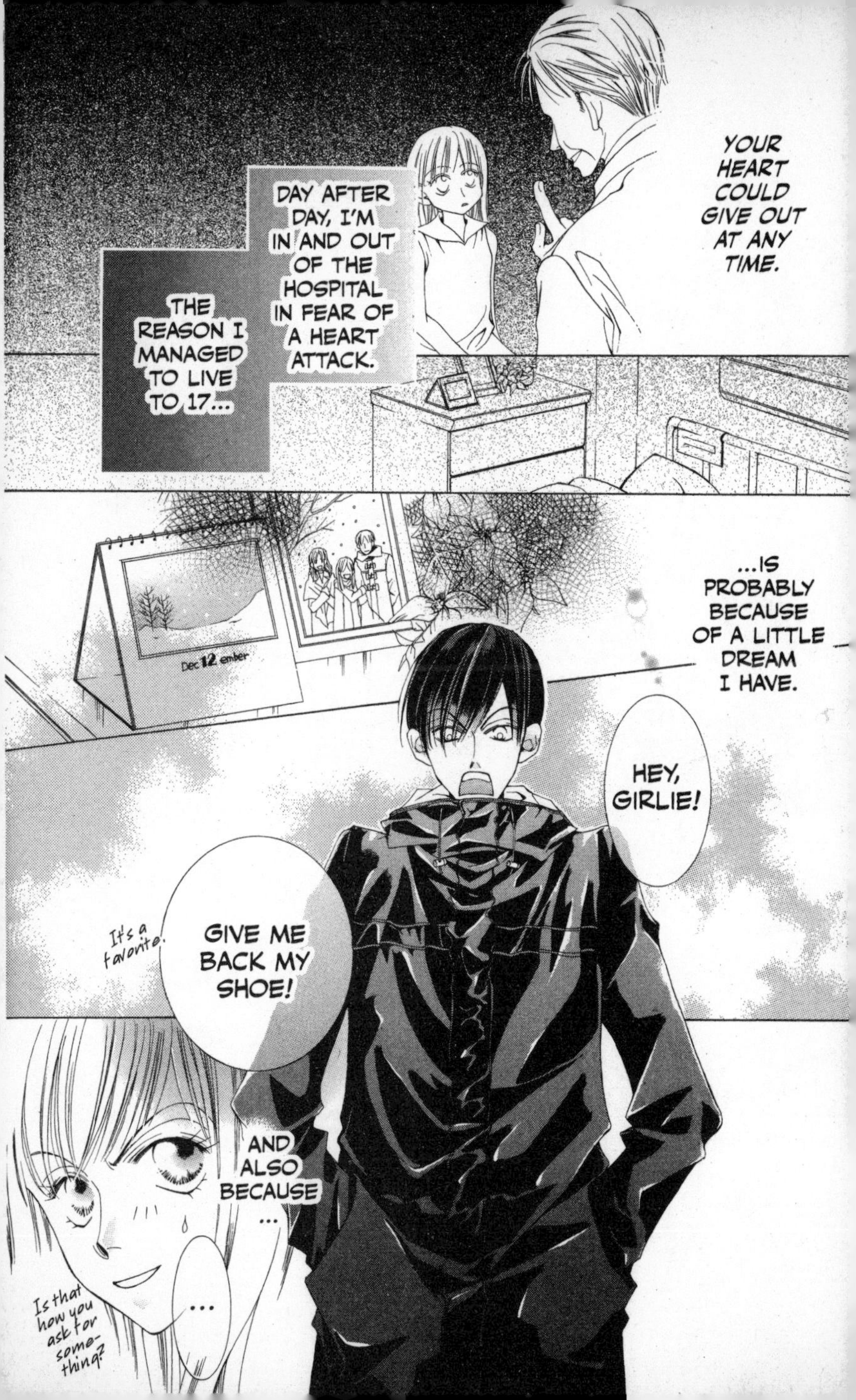
YOUR HEART COULD GIVE OUT AT ANY TIME.
DAY AFTER DAY, I'M IN AND OUT OF THE HOSPITAL IN FEAR OF A HEART ATTACK.
THE REASON I MANAGED TO LIVE TO 17...
...IS PROBABLY BECAUSE OF A LITTLE DREAM I HAVE.
Dec 12 ember
HEY, GIRLIE!
GIVE ME BACK MY SHOE!
It's a favorite.
AND ALSO BECAUSE ...
...
Is that how you ask for some-thing?

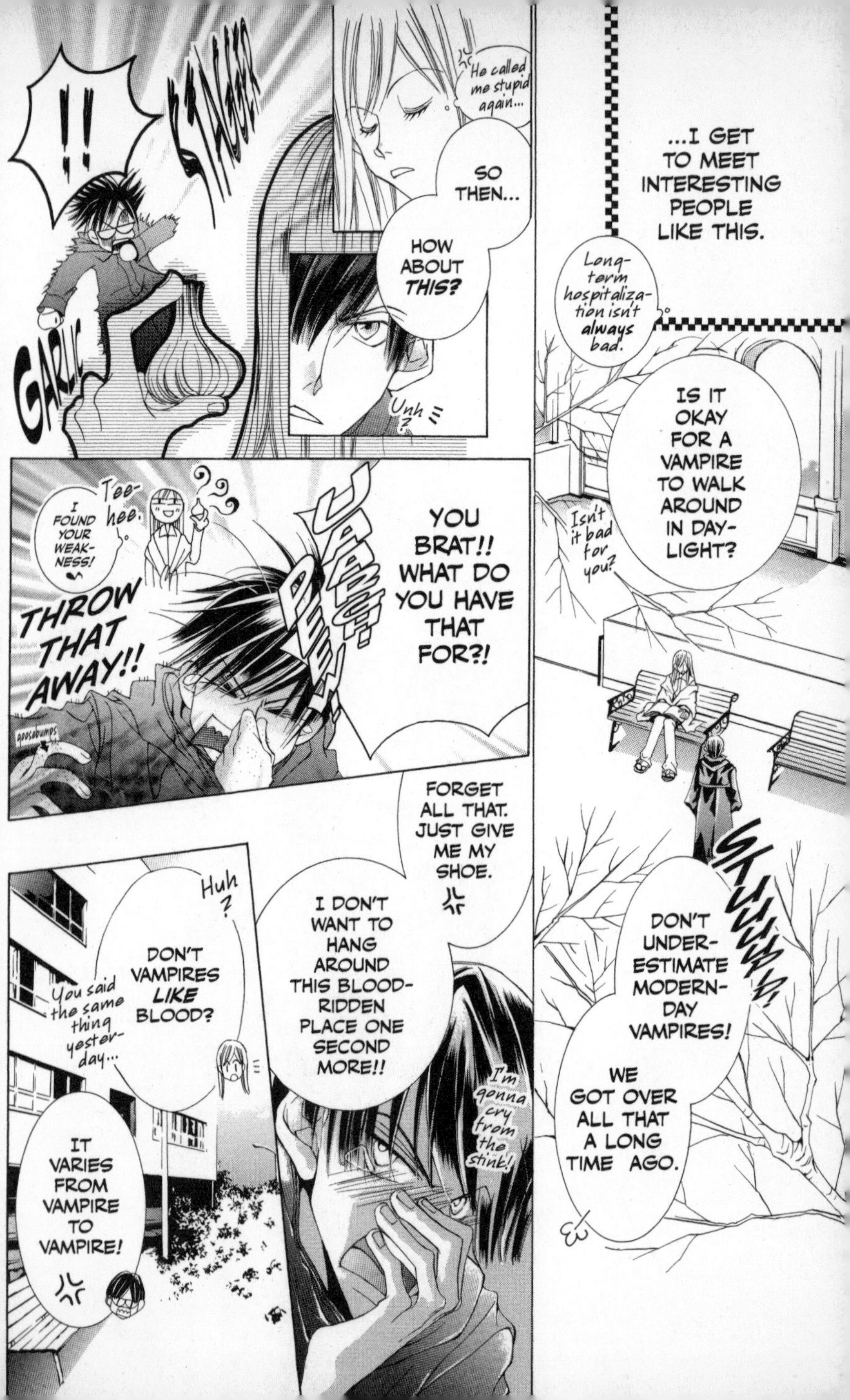
...I GET TO MEET INTERESTING PEOPLE LIKE THIS.
Long-term hospitalization isn't always bad.
IS IT OKAY FOR A VAMPIRE TO WALK AROUND IN DAYLIGHT?
Isn't it bad for you?
DON'T UNDERESTIMATE MODERN-DAY VAMPIRES!
WE GOT OVER ALL THAT A LONG TIME AGO.
He called me stupid again...
SO THEN...
HOW ABOUT *THIS?*
Unh?
!!
GARLIC
YOU BRAT!! WHAT DO YOU HAVE THAT FOR?!
Tee-hee.
I FOUND YOUR WEAKNESS!
THROW THAT AWAY!!
goosebumps
FORGET ALL THAT. JUST GIVE ME MY SHOE.
I DON'T WANT TO HANG AROUND THIS BLOOD-RIDDEN PLACE ONE SECOND MORE!!
I'm gonna cry from the stink!
Huh?
DON'T VAMPIRES *LIKE* BLOOD?
You said the same thing yesterday...
IT VARIES FROM VAMPIRE TO VAMPIRE!

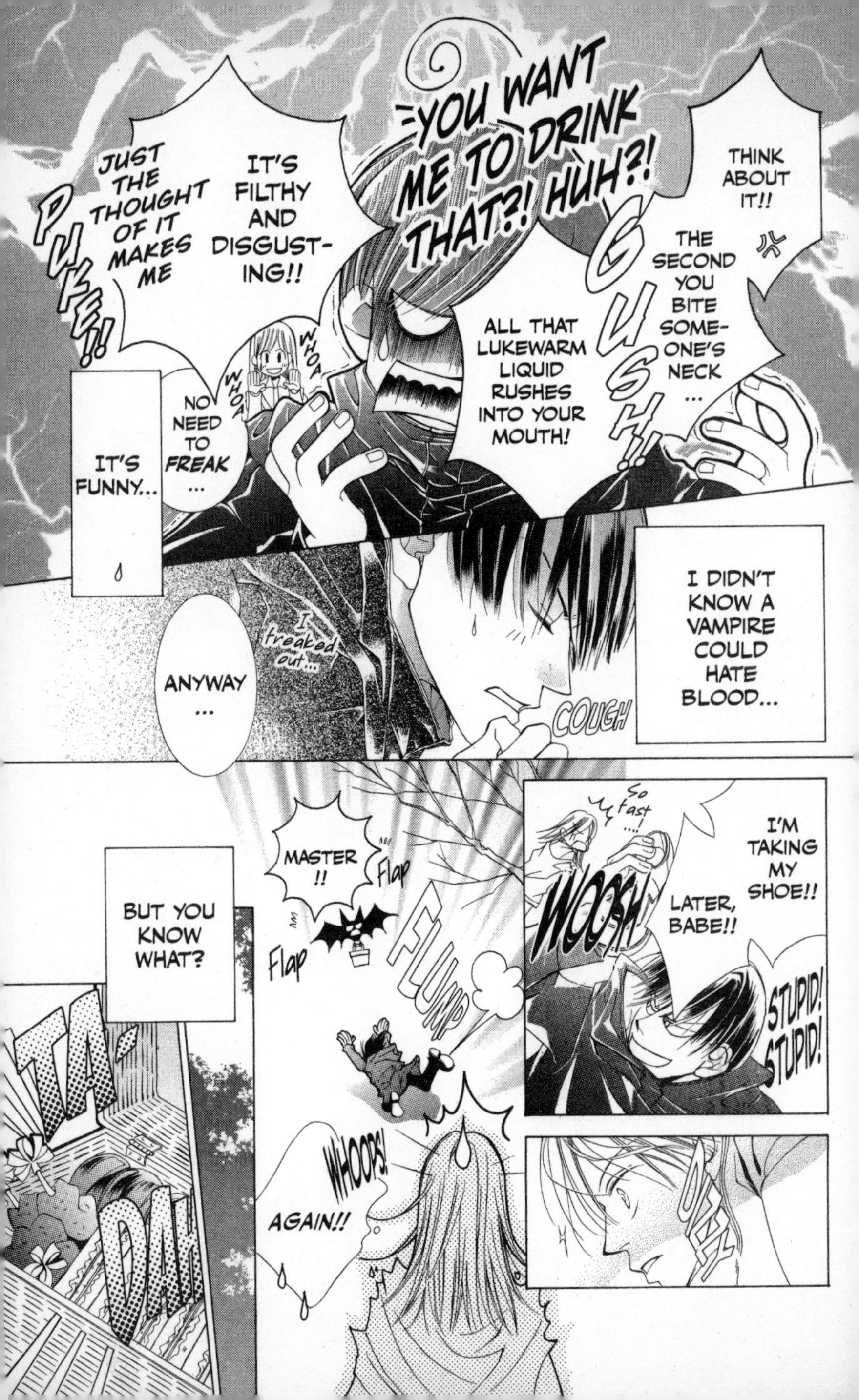
THINK ABOUT IT!!
THE SECOND YOU BITE SOME-ONE'S NECK...
GUSH!!
ALL THAT LUKEWARM LIQUID RUSHES INTO YOUR MOUTH!
YOU WANT ME TO DRINK THAT?! HUH?!
IT'S FILTHY AND DISGUST-ING!!
JUST THE THOUGHT OF IT MAKES ME
PUKE!!
WHOA WHOA
NO NEED TO FREAK...
IT'S FUNNY...
I DIDN'T KNOW A VAMPIRE COULD HATE BLOOD...
COUGH
I freaked out...
ANYWAY...
I'M TAKING MY SHOE!!
So fast...!
WOOSH
LATER, BABE!!
STUPID! STUPID!
MASTER!!
Flap
Flap
FLUMP
BUT YOU KNOW WHAT?
WHOOPS!
AGAIN!!
TA-DAH

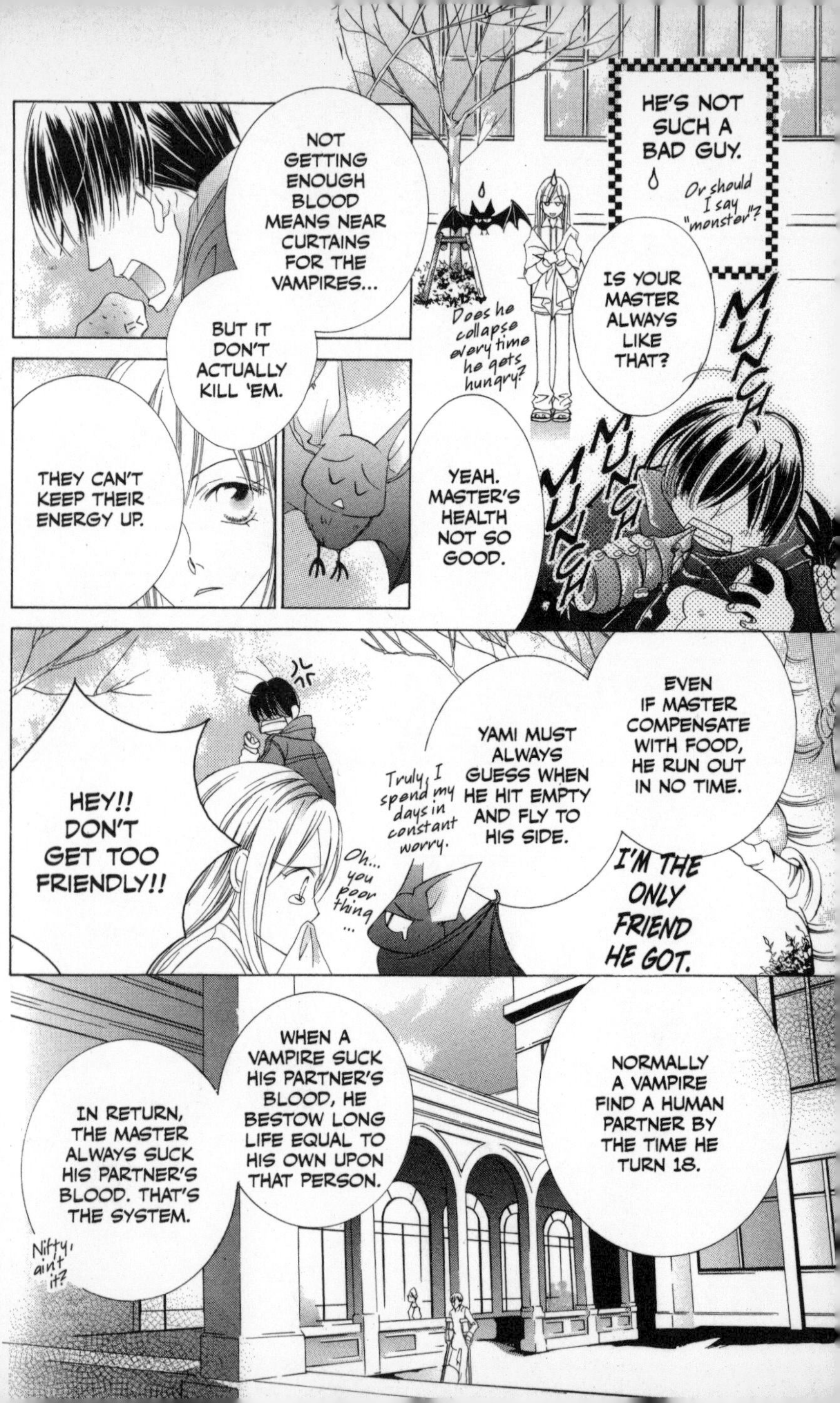
HE'S NOT SUCH A BAD GUY.
Or should I say "monster"?
IS YOUR MASTER ALWAYS LIKE THAT?
Does he collapse every time he gets hungry?
MUNCH MUNCH MUNCH
YEAH. MASTER'S HEALTH NOT SO GOOD.
NOT GETTING ENOUGH BLOOD MEANS NEAR CURTAINS FOR THE VAMPIRES...
BUT IT DON'T ACTUALLY KILL 'EM.
THEY CAN'T KEEP THEIR ENERGY UP.
EVEN IF MASTER COMPENSATE WITH FOOD, HE RUN OUT IN NO TIME.
YAMI MUST ALWAYS GUESS WHEN HE HIT EMPTY AND FLY TO HIS SIDE.
Truly, I spend my days in constant worry.
I'M THE ONLY FRIEND HE GOT.
Oh... you poor thing...
HEY!! DON'T GET TOO FRIENDLY!!
NORMALLY A VAMPIRE FIND A HUMAN PARTNER BY THE TIME HE TURN 18.
WHEN A VAMPIRE SUCK HIS PARTNER'S BLOOD, HE BESTOW LONG LIFE EQUAL TO HIS OWN UPON THAT PERSON.
IN RETURN, THE MASTER ALWAYS SUCK HIS PARTNER'S BLOOD. THAT'S THE SYSTEM.
Nifty, ain't it?

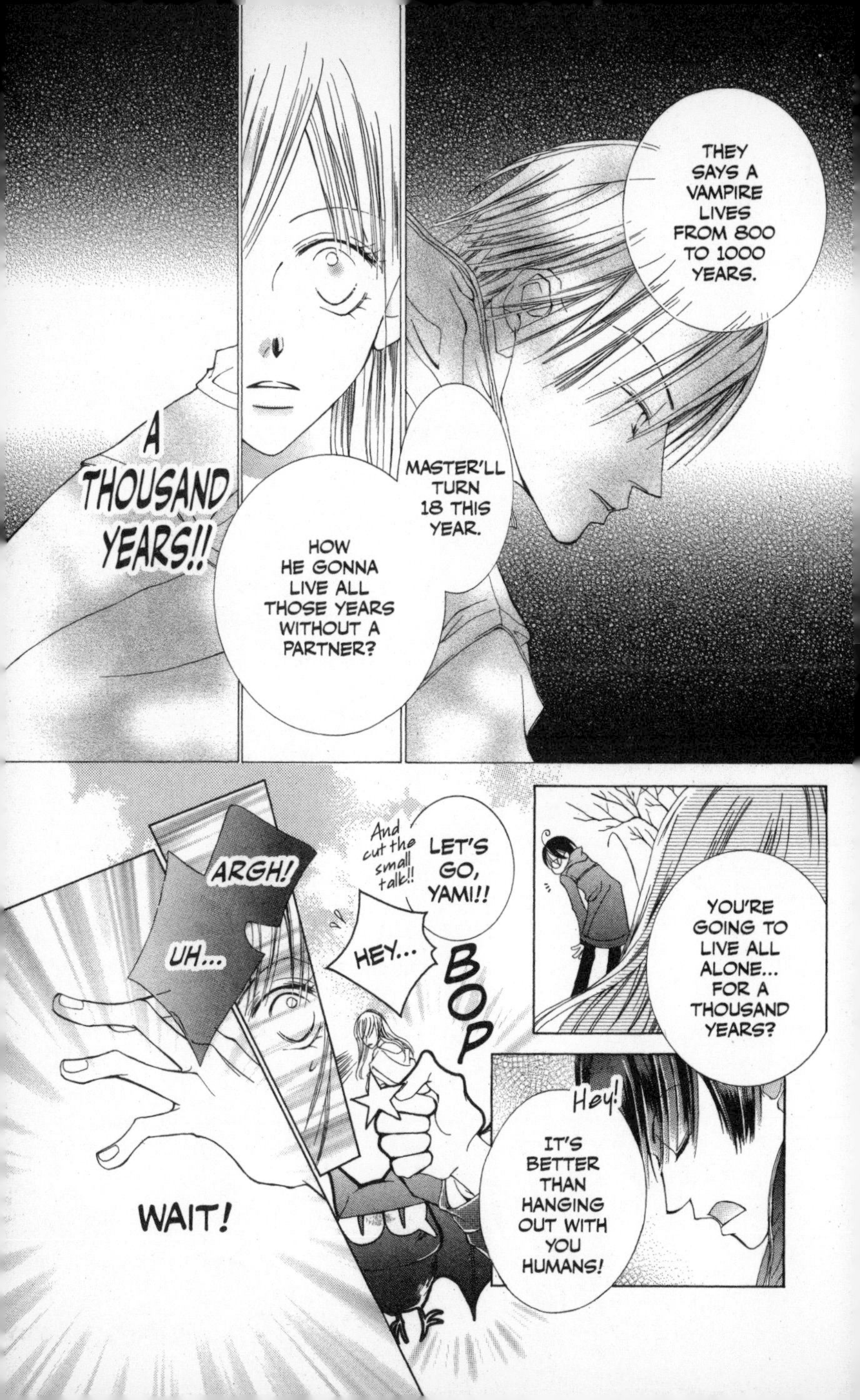
THEY SAYS A VAMPIRE LIVES FROM 800 TO 1000 YEARS.
MASTER'LL TURN 18 THIS YEAR.
HOW HE GONNA LIVE ALL THOSE YEARS WITHOUT A PARTNER?
A THOUSAND YEARS!!
YOU'RE GOING TO LIVE ALL ALONE... FOR A THOUSAND YEARS?
Hey!
IT'S BETTER THAN HANGING OUT WITH YOU HUMANS!
LET'S GO, YAMI!!
And cut the small talk!!
HEY...
BOP
ARGH!
UH...
WAIT!

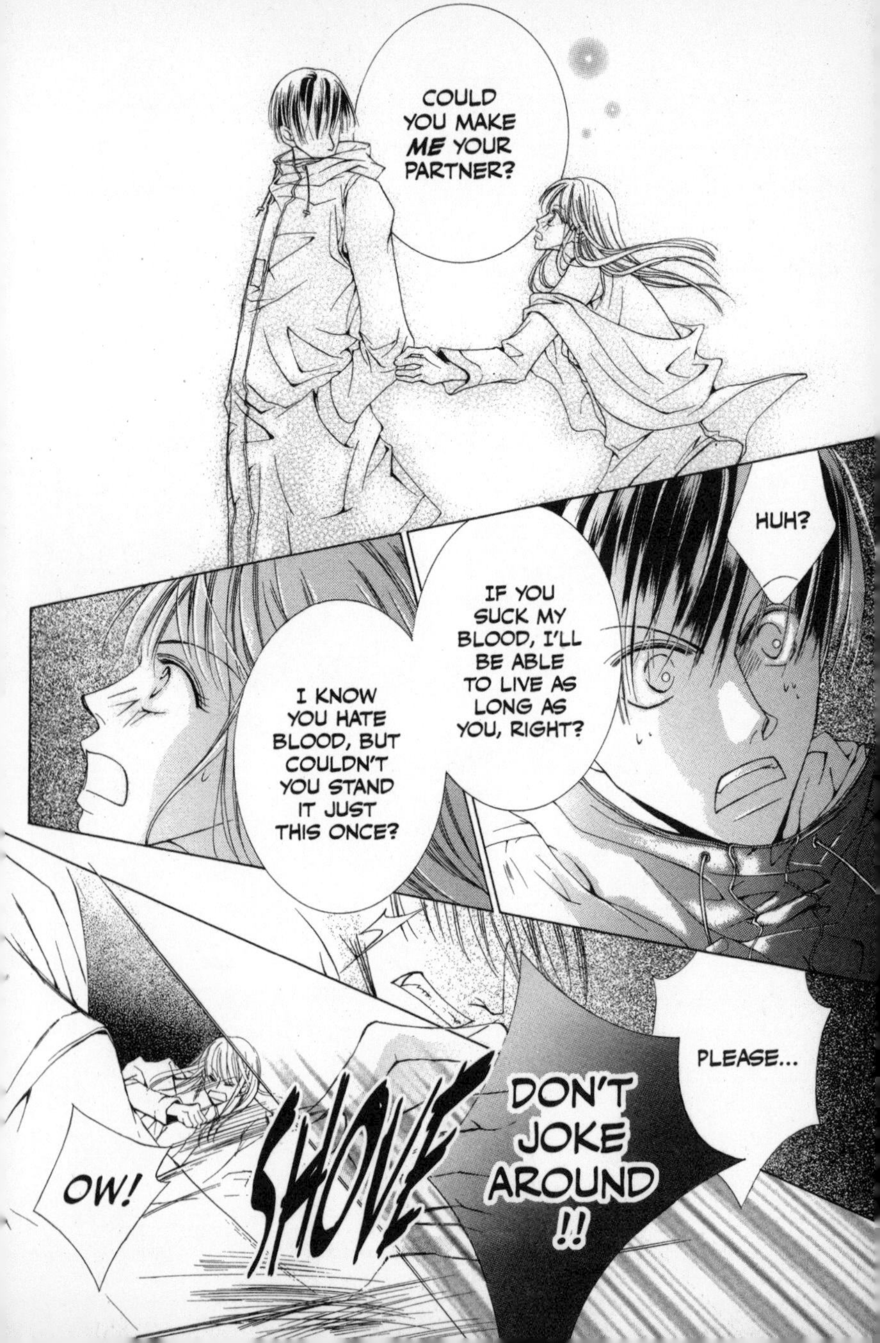
COULD YOU MAKE *ME* YOUR PARTNER?
HUH?
IF YOU SUCK MY BLOOD, I'LL BE ABLE TO LIVE AS LONG AS YOU, RIGHT?
I KNOW YOU HATE BLOOD, BUT COULDN'T YOU STAND IT JUST THIS ONCE?
PLEASE...
DON'T JOKE AROUND!!
SHOVE
OW!

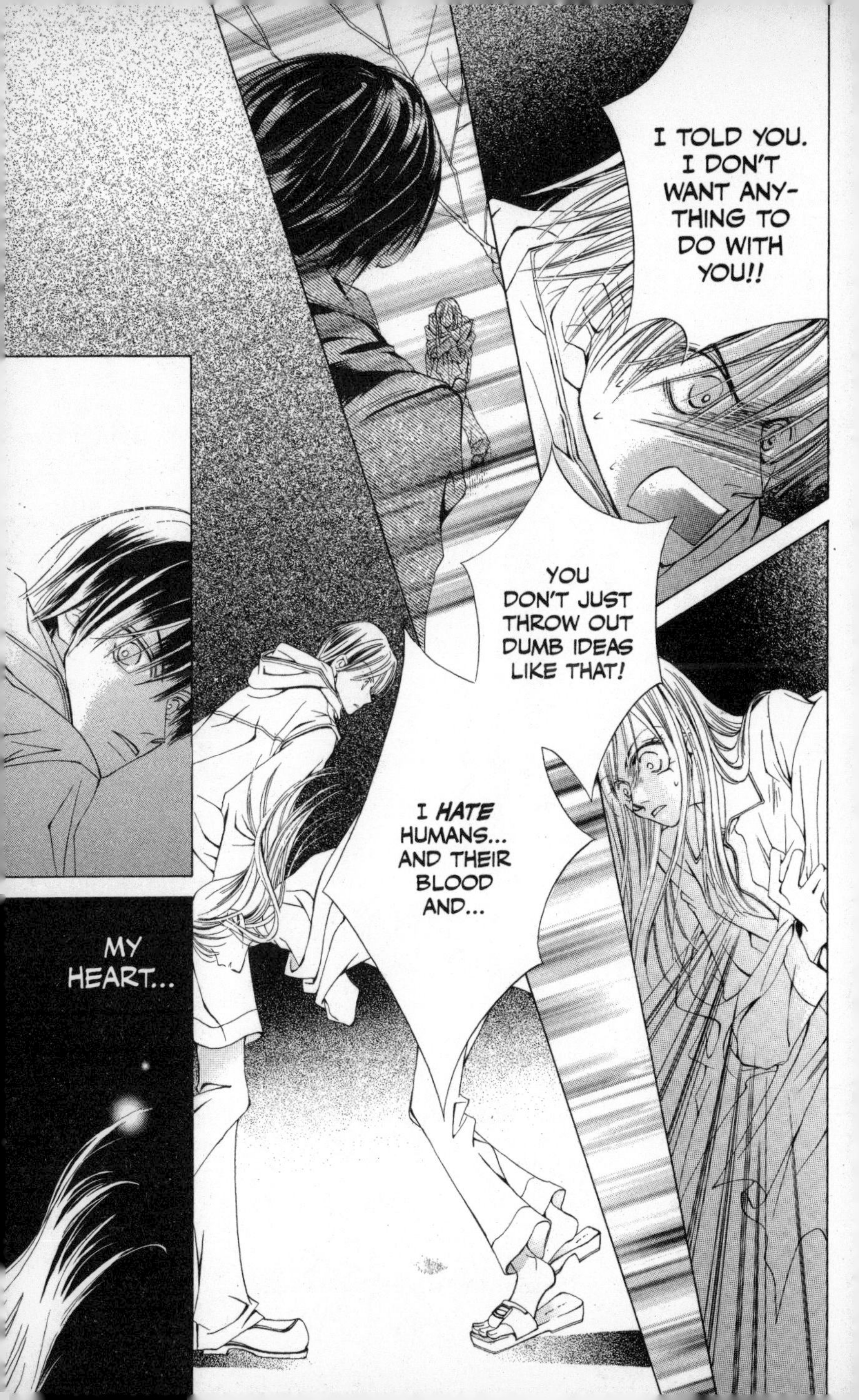
I TOLD YOU. I DON'T WANT ANYTHING TO DO WITH YOU!!
YOU DON'T JUST THROW OUT DUMB IDEAS LIKE THAT!
I *HATE* HUMANS... AND THEIR BLOOD AND...
MY HEART...

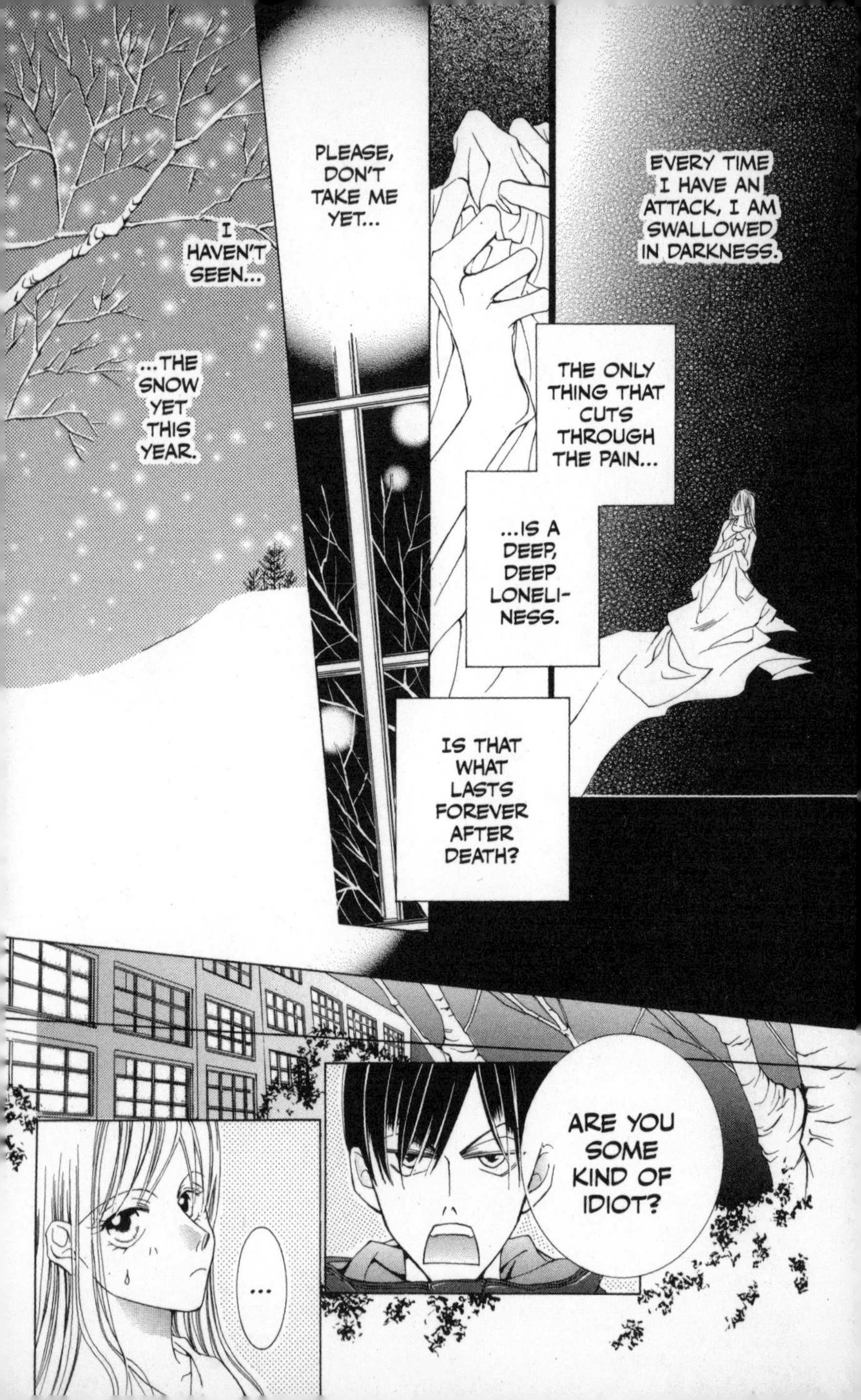
EVERY TIME I HAVE AN ATTACK, I AM SWALLOWED IN DARKNESS.
THE ONLY THING THAT CUTS THROUGH THE PAIN...
...IS A DEEP, DEEP LONELI-NESS.
IS THAT WHAT LASTS FOREVER AFTER DEATH?
PLEASE, DON'T TAKE ME YET...
I HAVEN'T SEEN...
...THE SNOW YET THIS YEAR.
ARE YOU SOME KIND OF IDIOT?
...

01

THANK YOU VERY MUCH FOR PICKING UP MY FIRST MANGA.

MILLENNIUM SNOW WAS FIRST PUBLISHED AS A STAND-ALONE AND THEN SERIALIZED A HALF A YEAR LATER.

WHEN I LOOK BACK NOW, MY DRAWINGS HAVE CHANGED A LOT... SORRY ABOUT THAT! (SWEAT)

THAT'S BECAUSE OF MY INEXPERIENCE, BUT I HOPE YOU WILL ENJOY THE MANGA—ALONG WITH ITS CHANGES—ALL THE WAY TO THE END.

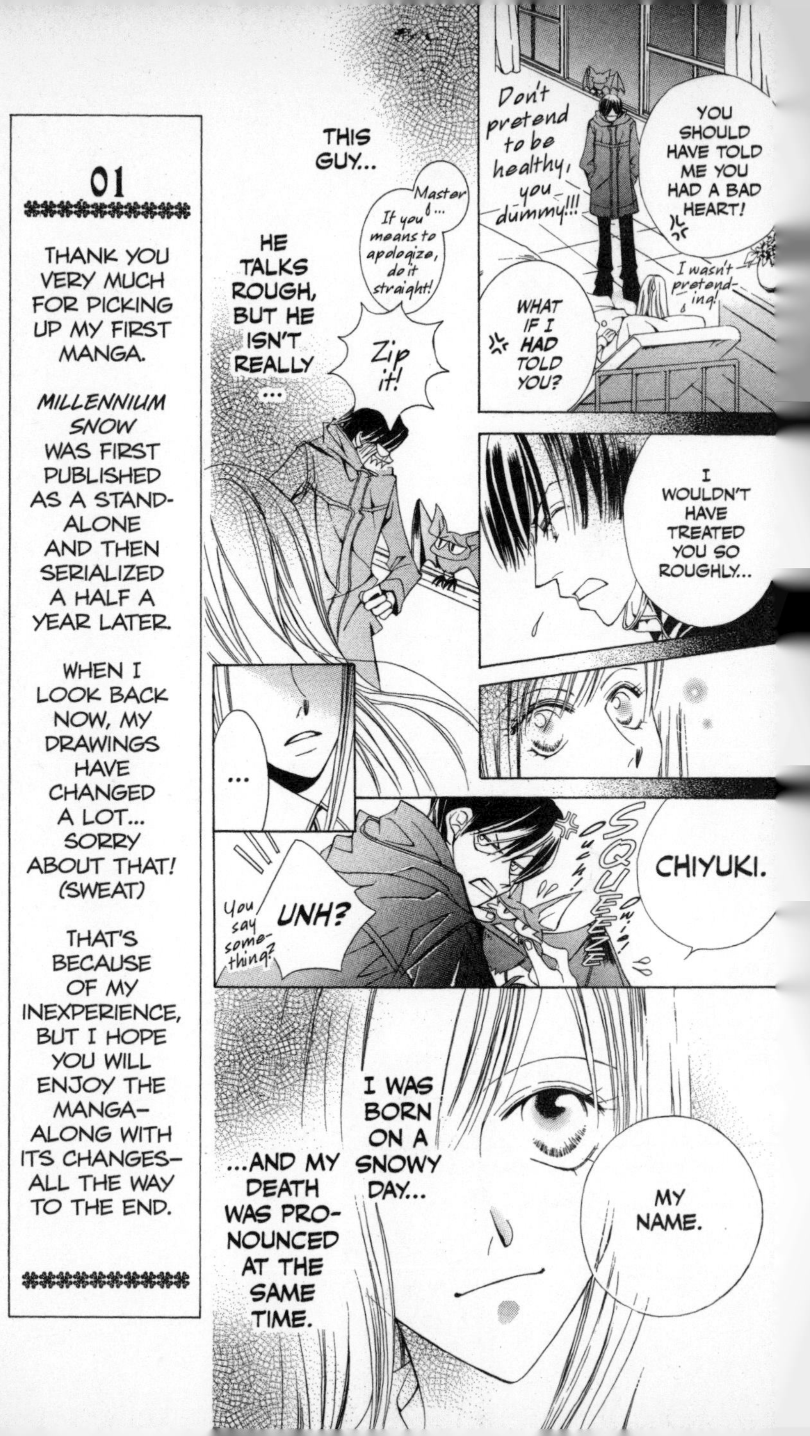

YOU SHOULD HAVE TOLD ME YOU HAD A BAD HEART!
Don't pretend to be healthy, you dummy!!!
I wasn't pretending!
WHAT IF I HAD TOLD YOU?
THIS GUY...
Master... If you means to apologize, do it straight!
Zip it!
HE TALKS ROUGH, BUT HE ISN'T REALLY ...
I WOULDN'T HAVE TREATED YOU SO ROUGHLY...
...
CHIYUKI.
SQUEEZE
Ouch!
Ow!!
UNH?
You say something?
MY NAME.
I WAS BORN ON A SNOWY DAY...
...AND MY DEATH WAS PRONOUNCED AT THE SAME TIME.

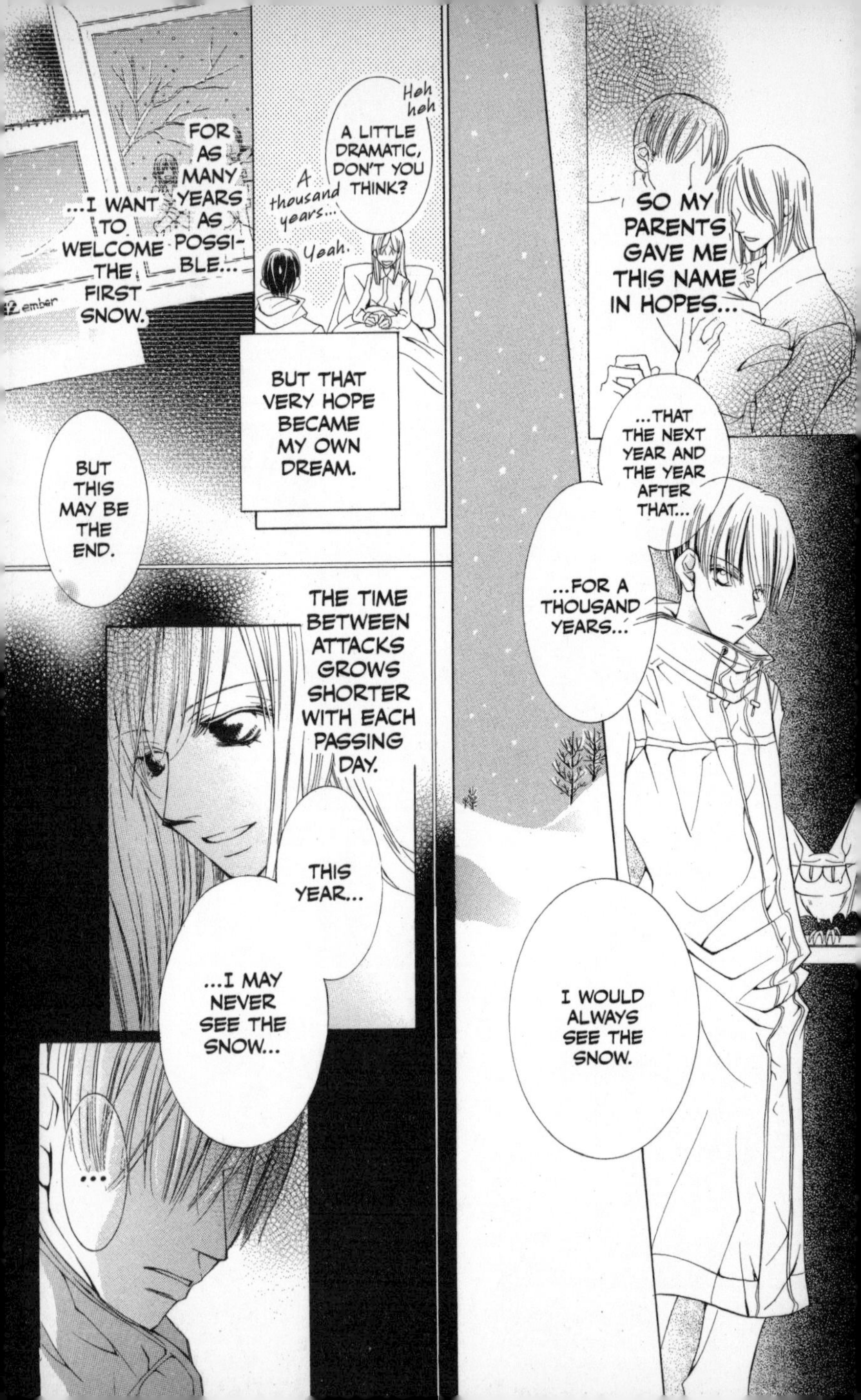
SO MY PARENTS GAVE ME THIS NAME IN HOPES...
...THAT THE NEXT YEAR AND THE YEAR AFTER THAT...
...FOR A THOUSAND YEARS...
I WOULD ALWAYS SEE THE SNOW.
Heh heh
A LITTLE DRAMATIC, DON'T YOU THINK?
A thousand years...
Yeah.
FOR AS MANY YEARS AS POSSIBLE...
...I WANT TO WELCOME THE FIRST SNOW.
BUT THAT VERY HOPE BECAME MY OWN DREAM.
BUT THIS MAY BE THE END.
THE TIME BETWEEN ATTACKS GROWS SHORTER WITH EACH PASSING DAY.
THIS YEAR...
...I MAY NEVER SEE THE SNOW...
...

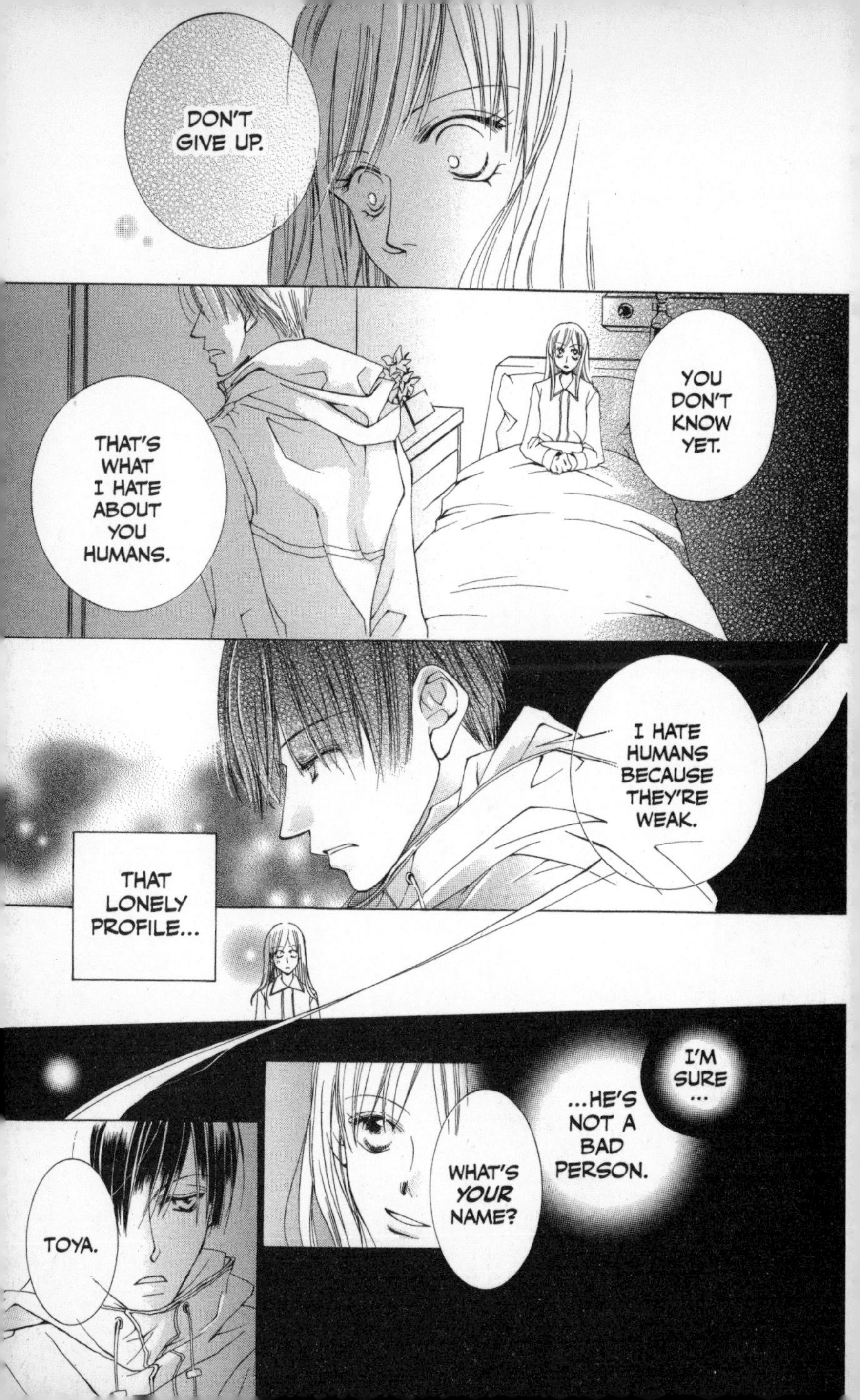
DON'T GIVE UP.
YOU DON'T KNOW YET.
THAT'S WHAT I HATE ABOUT YOU HUMANS.
I HATE HUMANS BECAUSE THEY'RE WEAK.
THAT LONELY PROFILE...
I'M SURE...
...HE'S NOT A BAD PERSON.
WHAT'S *YOUR* NAME?
TOYA.

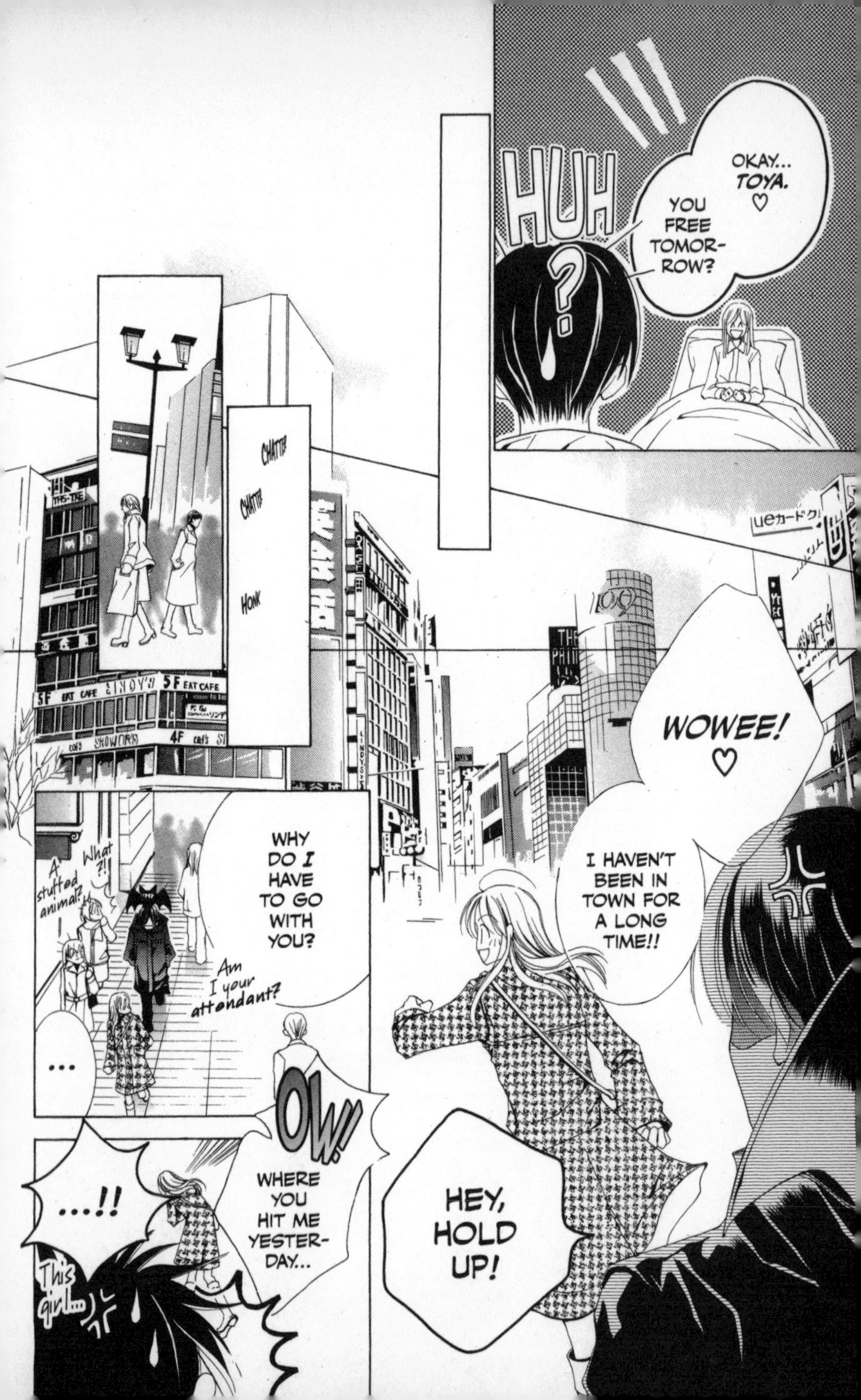
OKAY... TOYA. ♡
YOU FREE TOMORROW?
HUH ?
WOWEE! ♡
I HAVEN'T BEEN IN TOWN FOR A LONG TIME!!
HEY, HOLD UP!
CHATTER
CHATTER
HONK
WHY DO I HAVE TO GO WITH YOU?
What?!
A stuffed animal?
Am I your attendant?
...
OW!
WHERE YOU HIT ME YESTERDAY...
...!!
This girl...

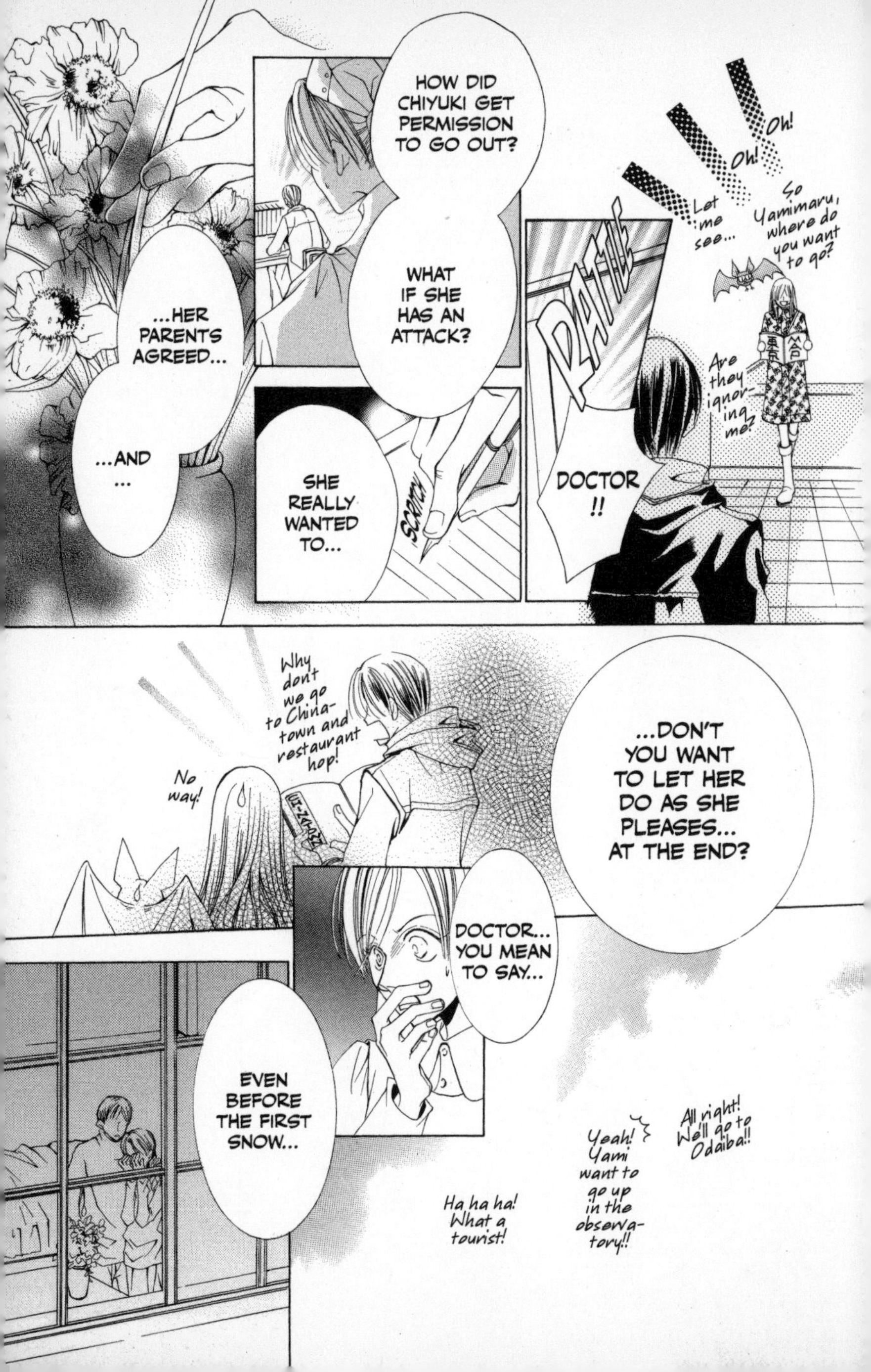
So Yamimaru, where do you want to go?
Let me see...
Oh!
Oh!
Are they ignoring me?
RATTLE
DOCTOR !!
HOW DID CHIYUKI GET PERMISSION TO GO OUT?
WHAT IF SHE HAS AN ATTACK?
SHE REALLY WANTED TO...
SCRITCH
...HER PARENTS AGREED...
...AND ...
...DON'T YOU WANT TO LET HER DO AS SHE PLEASES... AT THE END?
Why don't we go to China-town and restaurant hop!
No way!
DOCTOR... YOU MEAN TO SAY...
EVEN BEFORE THE FIRST SNOW...
All right! We'll go to Odaiba!!
Yeah! Yami want to go up in the observa-tory!!
Ha ha ha! What a tourist!

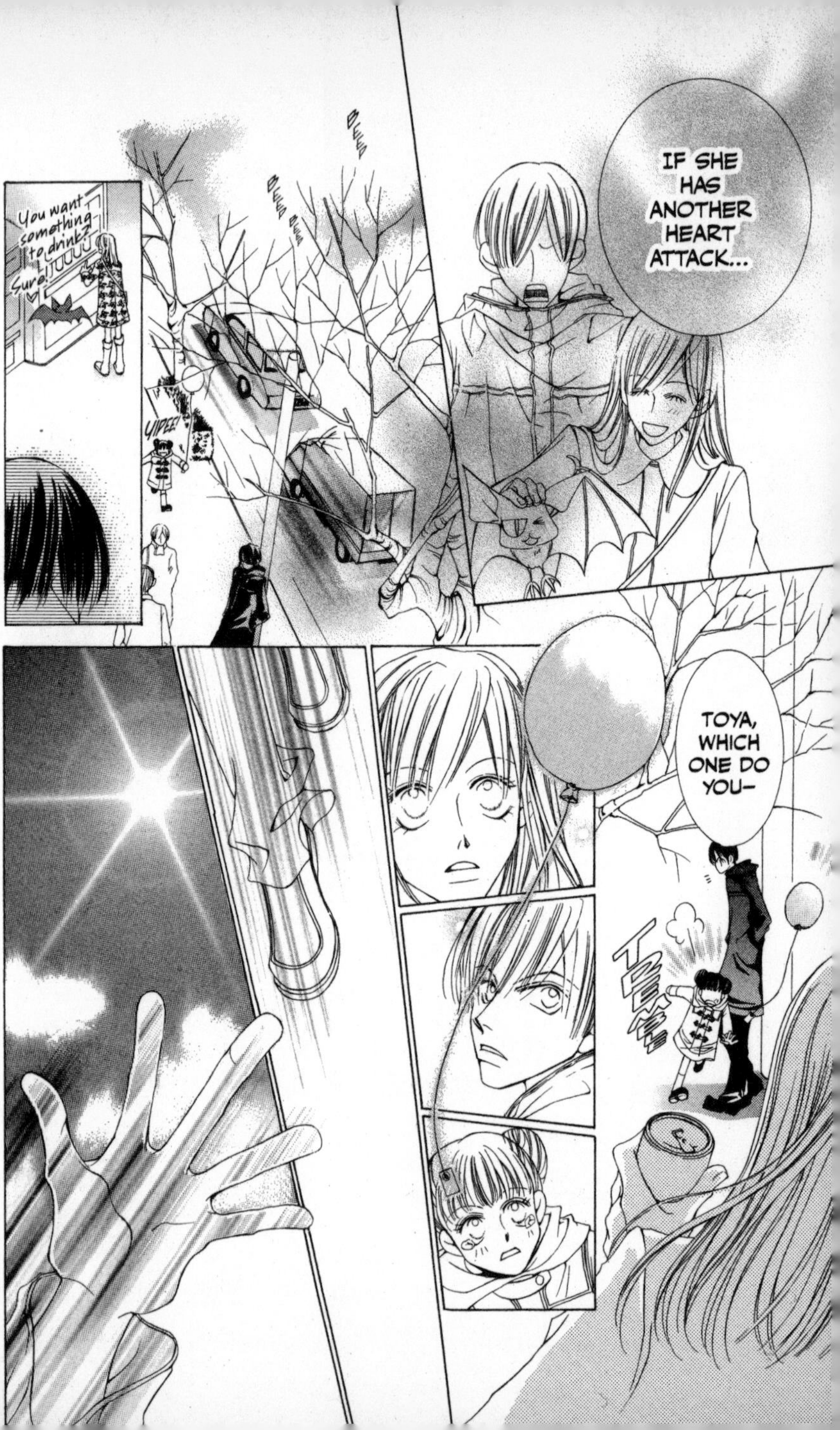
IF SHE HAS ANOTHER HEART ATTACK...
You want something to drink?
Sure! ♥
TOYA, WHICH ONE DO YOU–

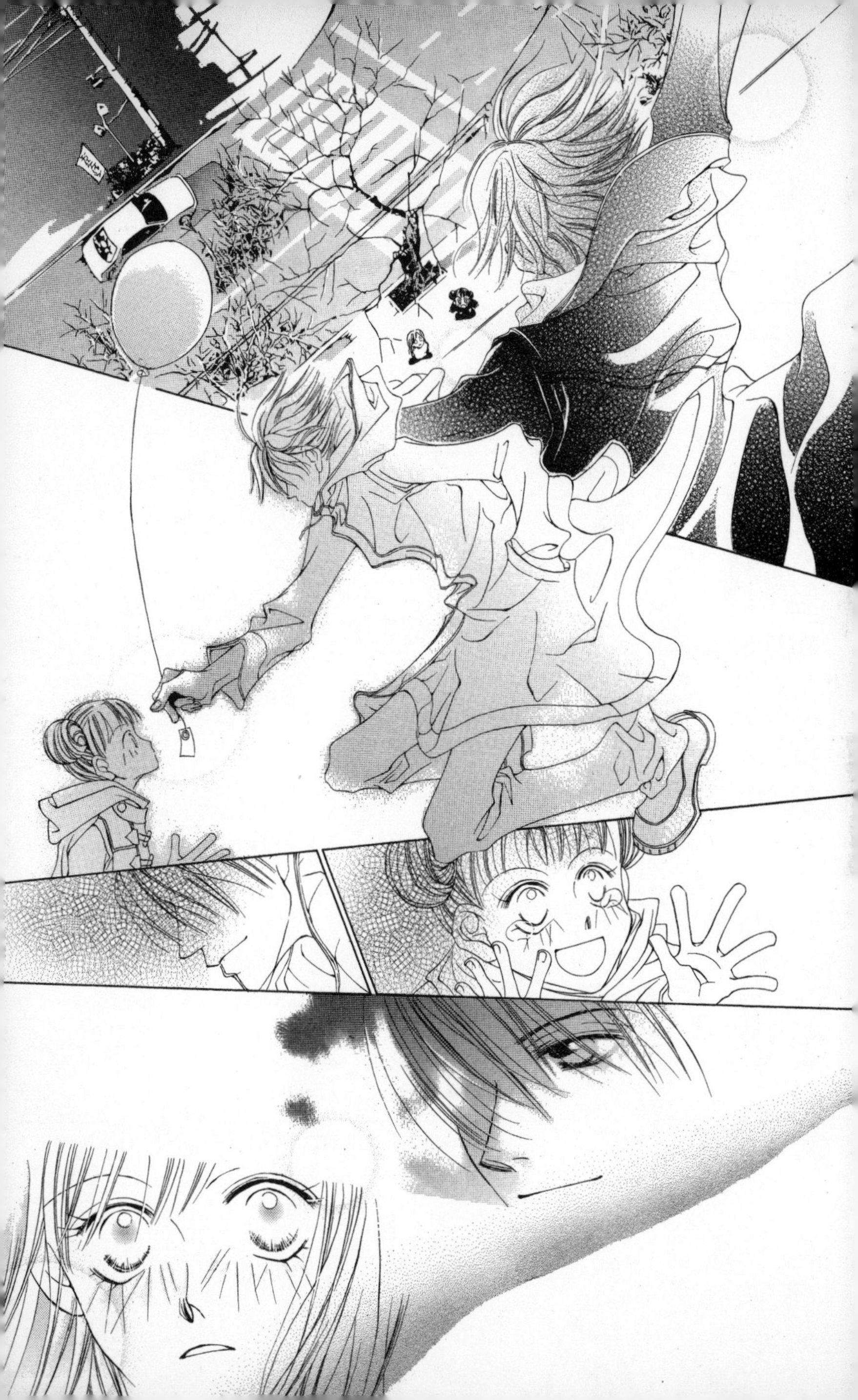

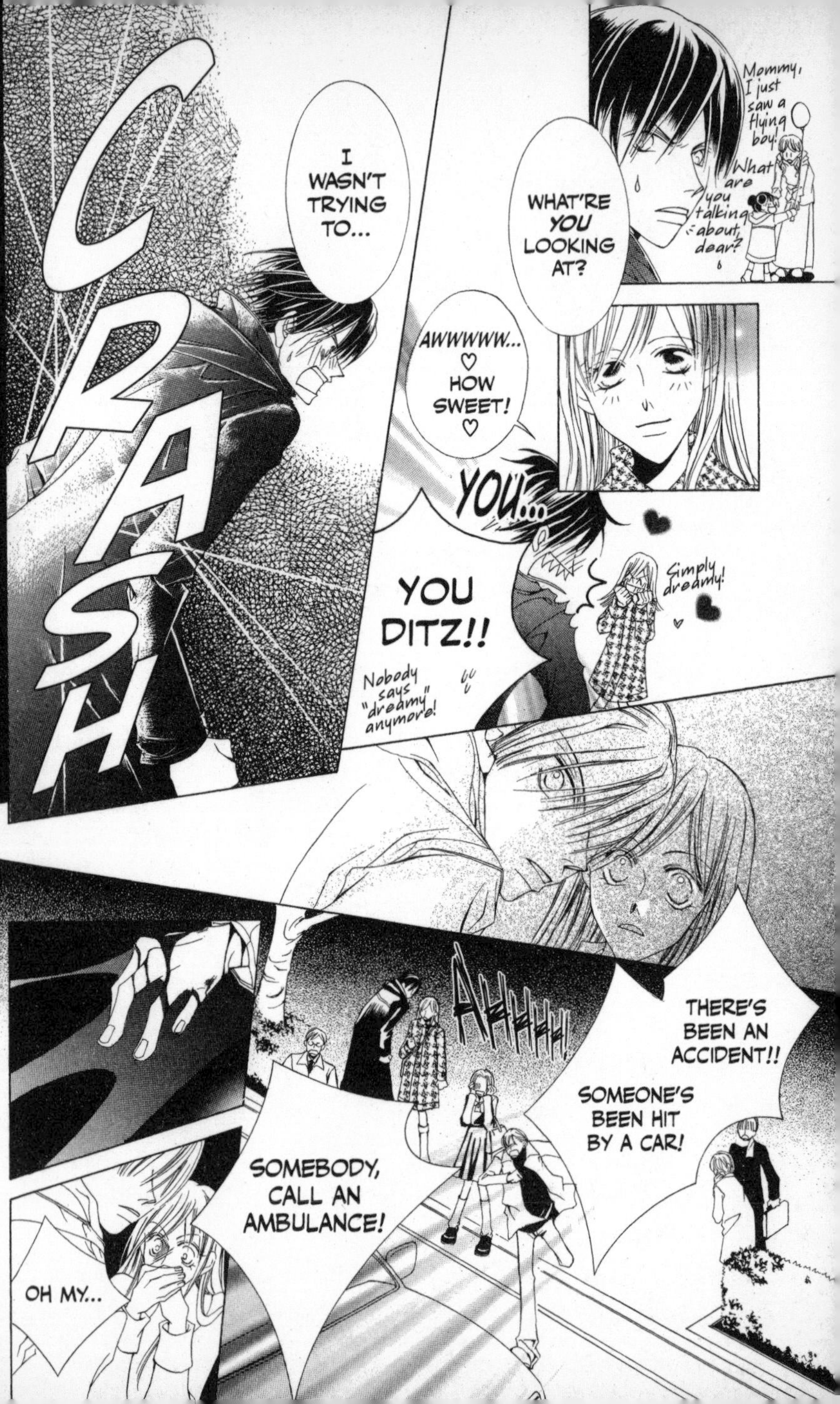
WHAT'RE YOU LOOKING AT?
Mommy, I just saw a flying boy!
What are you talking about, dear?
AWWWWW... ♡ HOW SWEET! ♡
YOU...
YOU DITZ!!
Simply dreamy!
Nobody says "dreamy" anymore!
I WASN'T TRYING TO...
CRASH
AHHHH
THERE'S BEEN AN ACCIDENT!!
SOMEONE'S BEEN HIT BY A CAR!
SOMEBODY, CALL AN AMBULANCE!
OH MY...

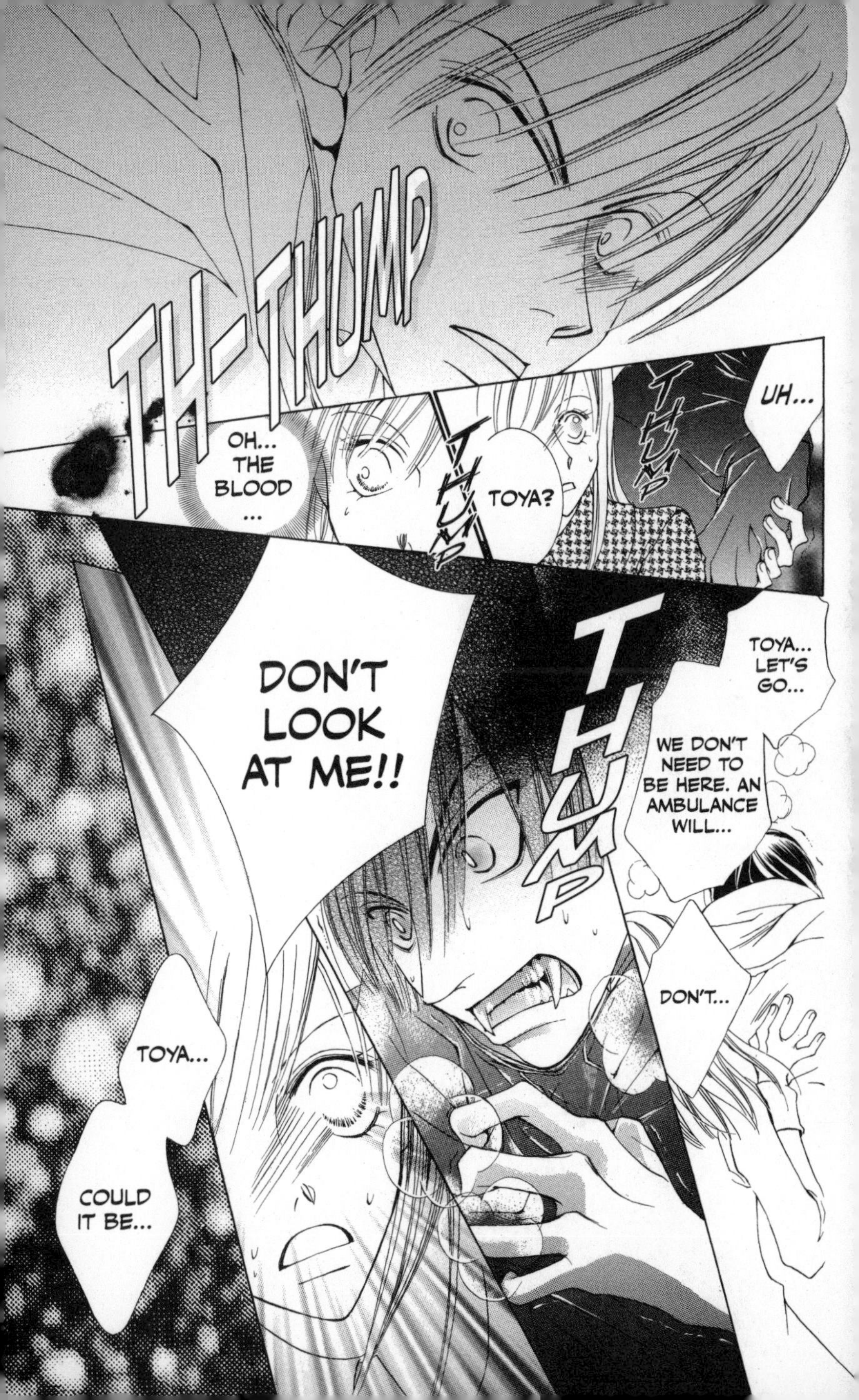
TH-THUMP
UH...
THUMP THUMP
TOYA?
THUMP
OH... THE BLOOD ...
TOYA... LET'S GO...
THUMP THUMP
DON'T LOOK AT ME!!
WE DON'T NEED TO BE HERE. AN AMBULANCE WILL...
DON'T...
TOYA...
COULD IT BE...

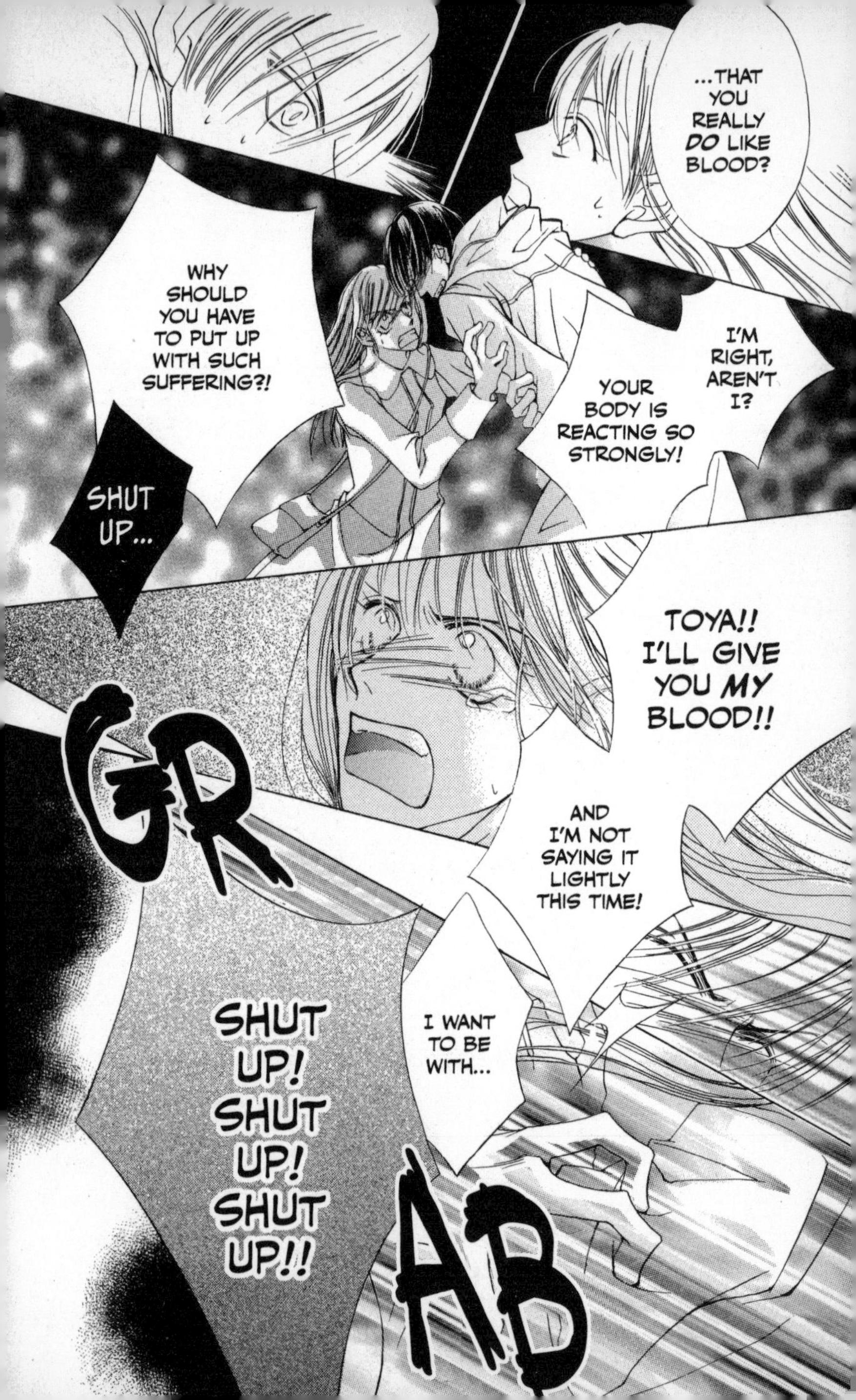
...THAT YOU REALLY *DO* LIKE BLOOD?
I'M RIGHT, AREN'T I?
YOUR BODY IS REACTING SO STRONGLY!
WHY SHOULD YOU HAVE TO PUT UP WITH SUCH SUFFERING?!
SHUT UP...
TOYA!! I'LL GIVE YOU *MY* BLOOD!!
AND I'M NOT SAYING IT LIGHTLY THIS TIME!
GR
I WANT TO BE WITH...
SHUT UP! SHUT UP! SHUT UP!!
AB

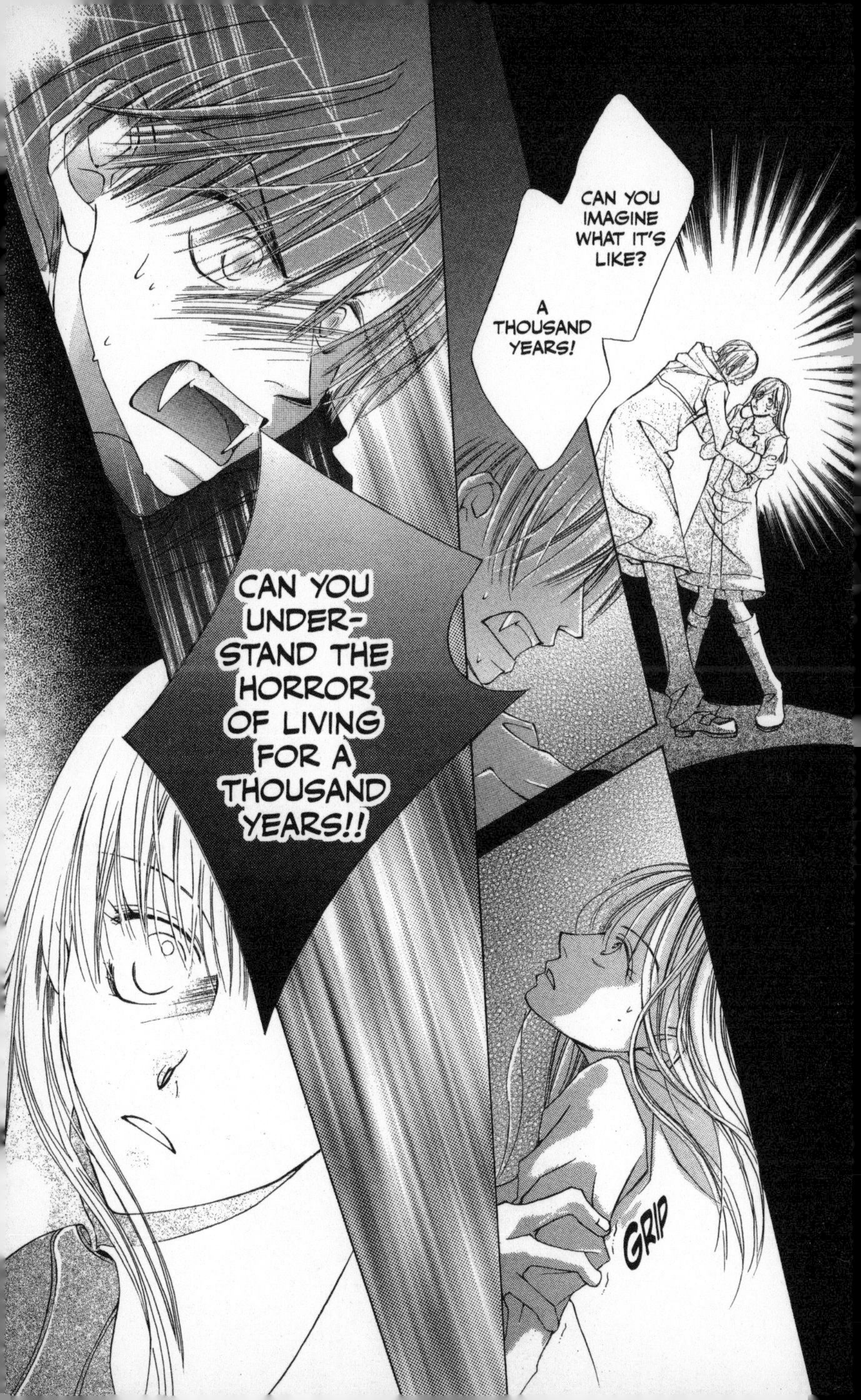
CAN YOU IMAGINE WHAT IT'S LIKE?
A THOUSAND YEARS!
CAN YOU UNDER-STAND THE HORROR OF LIVING FOR A THOUSAND YEARS!!
GRIP

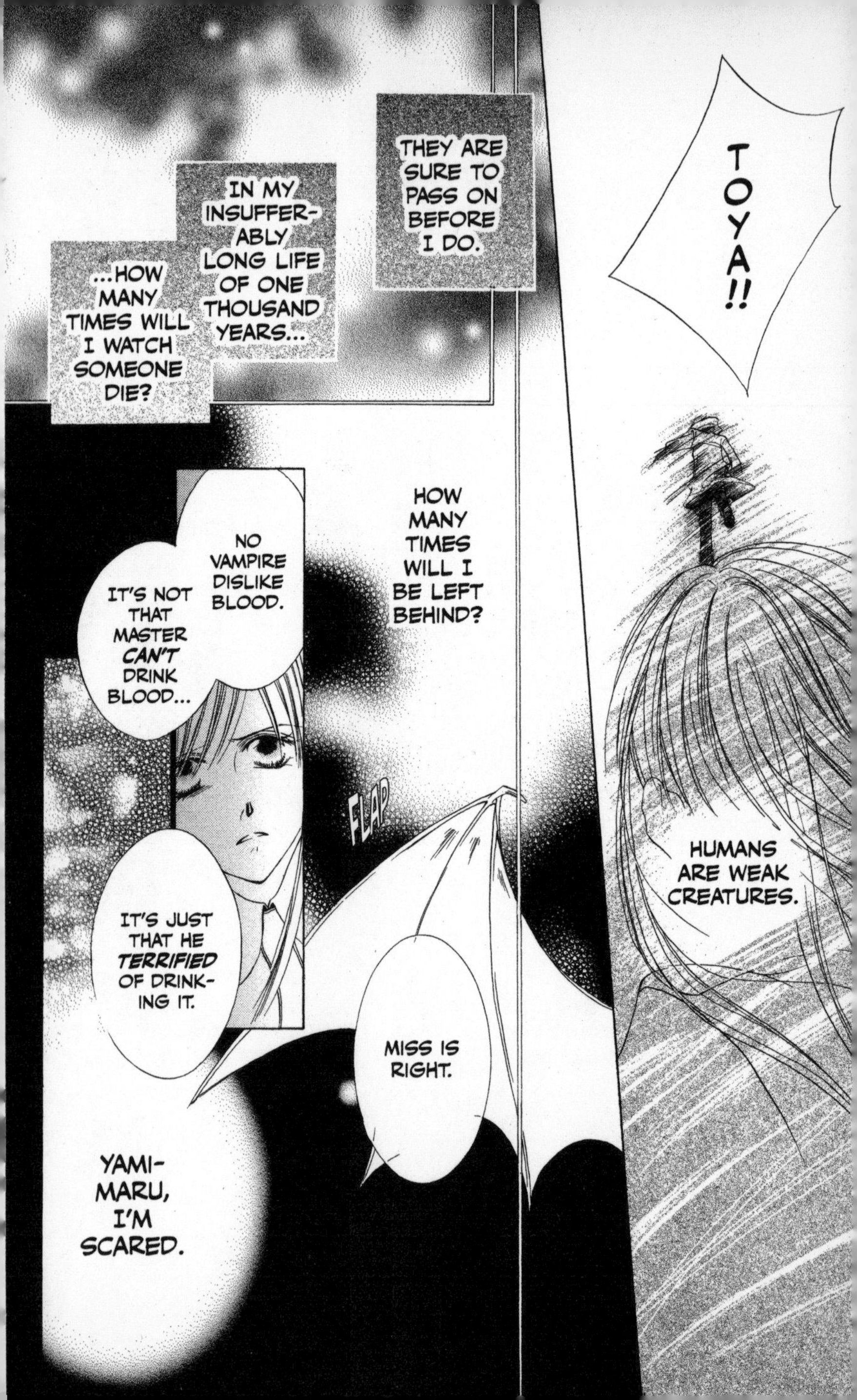
TOYA!!
HUMANS ARE WEAK CREATURES.
THEY ARE SURE TO PASS ON BEFORE I DO.
IN MY INSUFFER-ABLY LONG LIFE OF ONE THOUSAND YEARS...
...HOW MANY TIMES WILL I WATCH SOMEONE DIE?
HOW MANY TIMES WILL I BE LEFT BEHIND?
NO VAMPIRE DISLIKE BLOOD.
IT'S NOT THAT MASTER *CAN'T* DRINK BLOOD...
FLAP
IT'S JUST THAT HE ***TERRIFIED*** OF DRINK-ING IT.
MISS IS RIGHT.
YAMI-MARU, I'M SCARED.

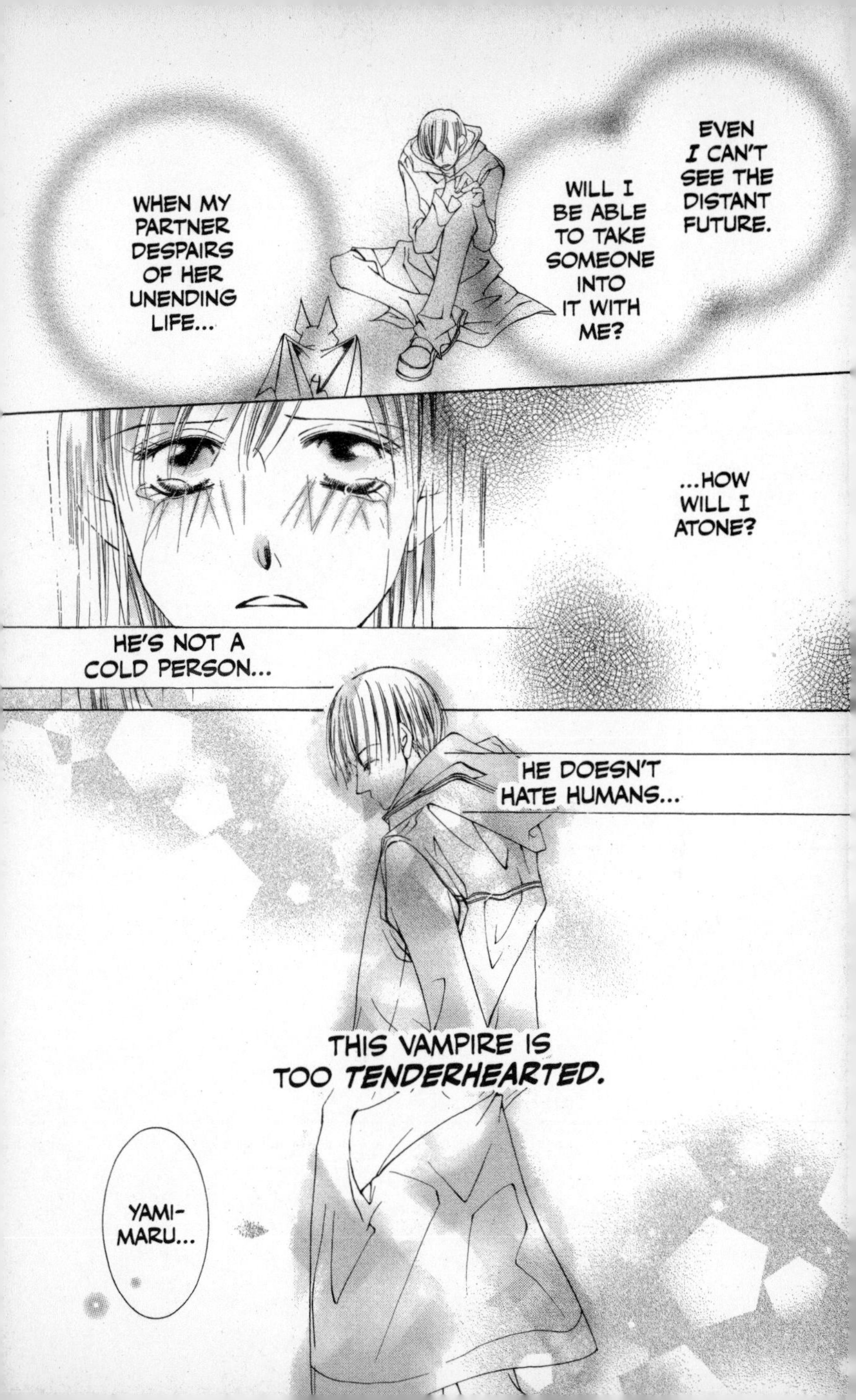
EVEN *I* CAN'T SEE THE DISTANT FUTURE.
WILL I BE ABLE TO TAKE SOMEONE INTO IT WITH ME?
WHEN MY PARTNER DESPAIRS OF HER UNENDING LIFE...
...HOW WILL I ATONE?
HE'S NOT A COLD PERSON...
HE DOESN'T HATE HUMANS...
THIS VAMPIRE IS TOO *TENDERHEARTED.*
YAMI-MARU...

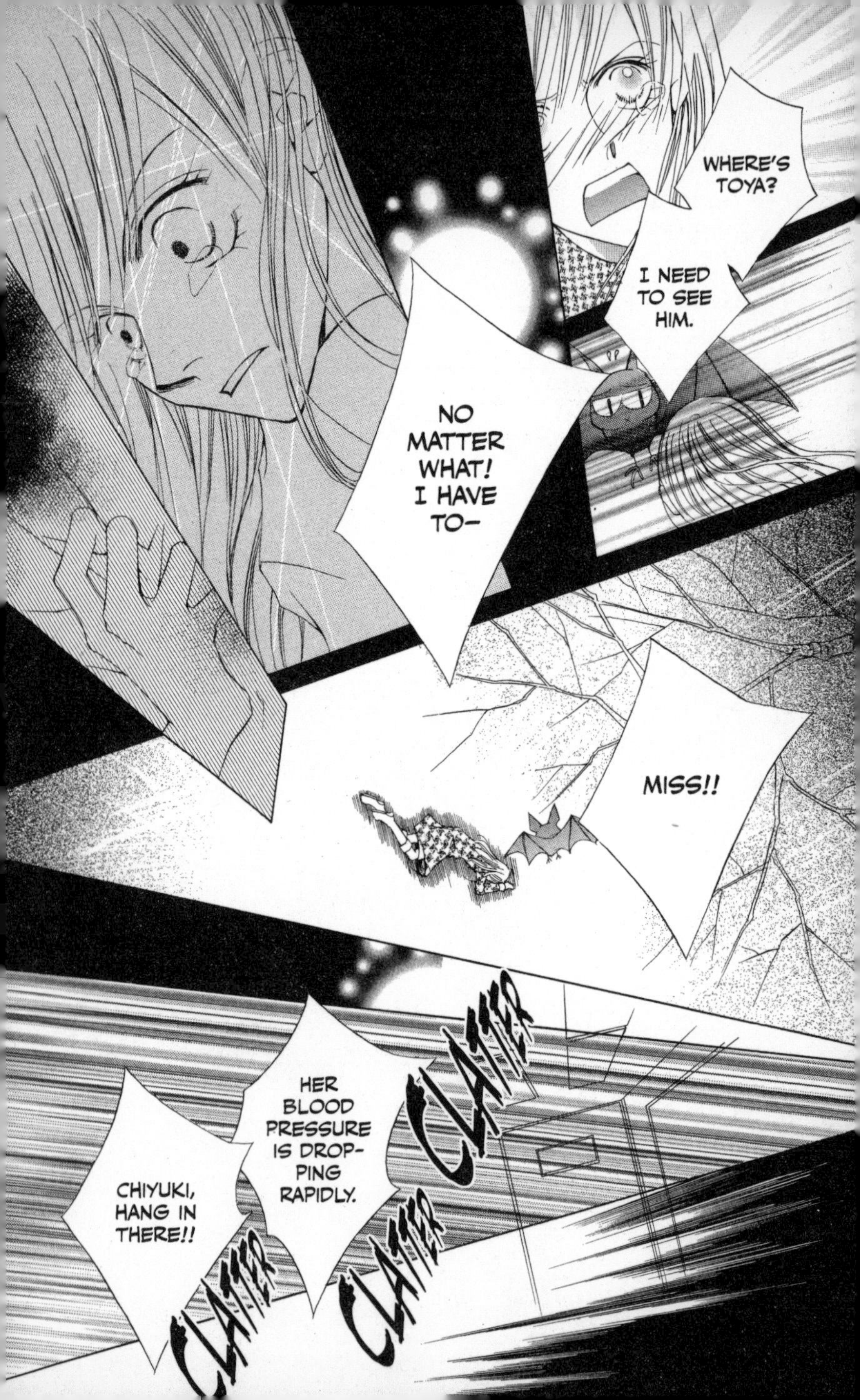
WHERE'S TOYA?
I NEED TO SEE HIM.
NO MATTER WHAT! I HAVE TO—
MISS!!
CLATTER
HER BLOOD PRESSURE IS DROP-PING RAPIDLY.
CHIYUKI, HANG IN THERE!!
CLATTER
CLATTER

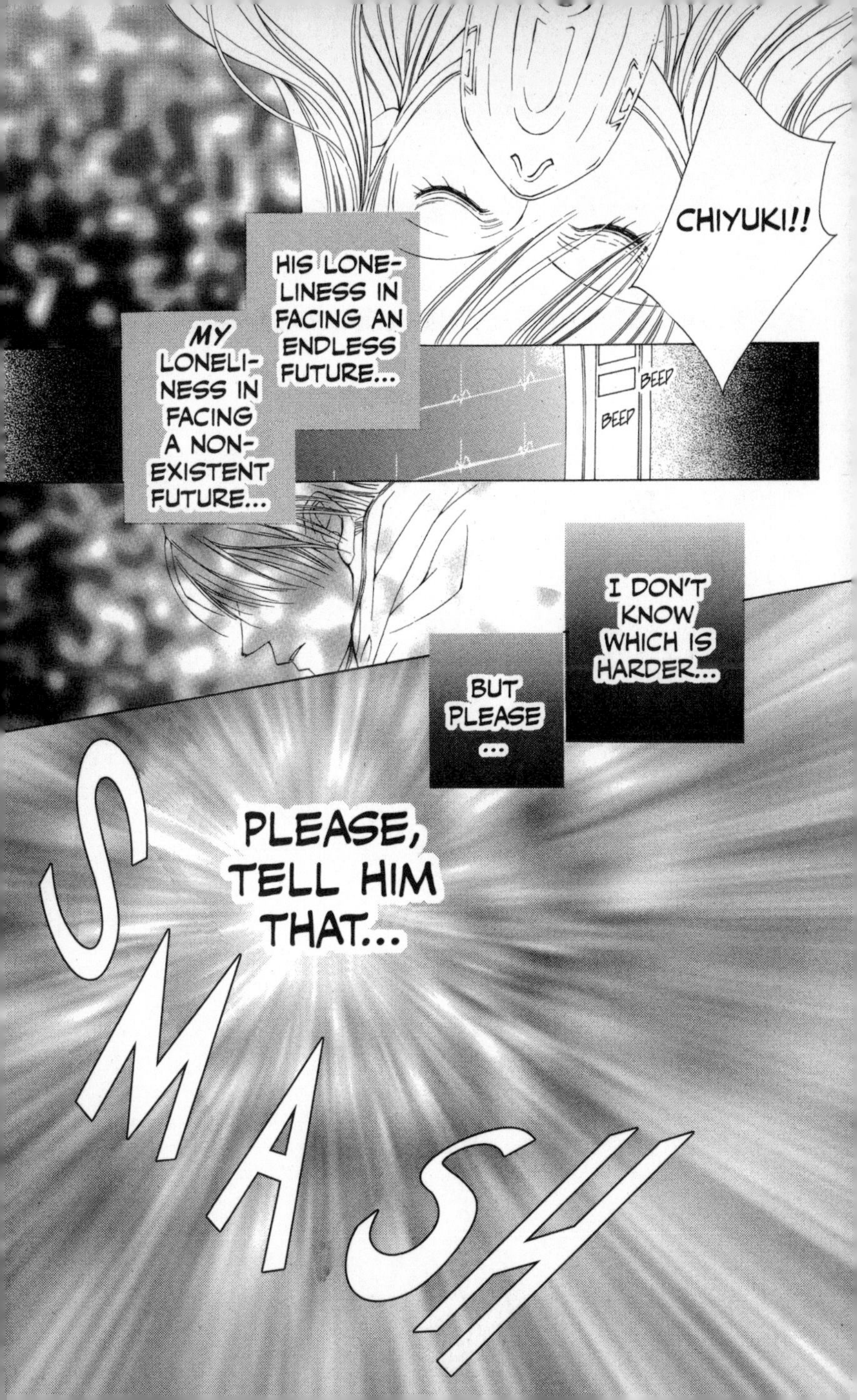
CHIYUKI!!
HIS LONE-LINESS IN FACING AN ENDLESS FUTURE...
MY LONELI-NESS IN FACING A NON-EXISTENT FUTURE...
BEEP
BEEP
I DON'T KNOW WHICH IS HARDER...
BUT PLEASE...
PLEASE, TELL HIM THAT...
SMASH

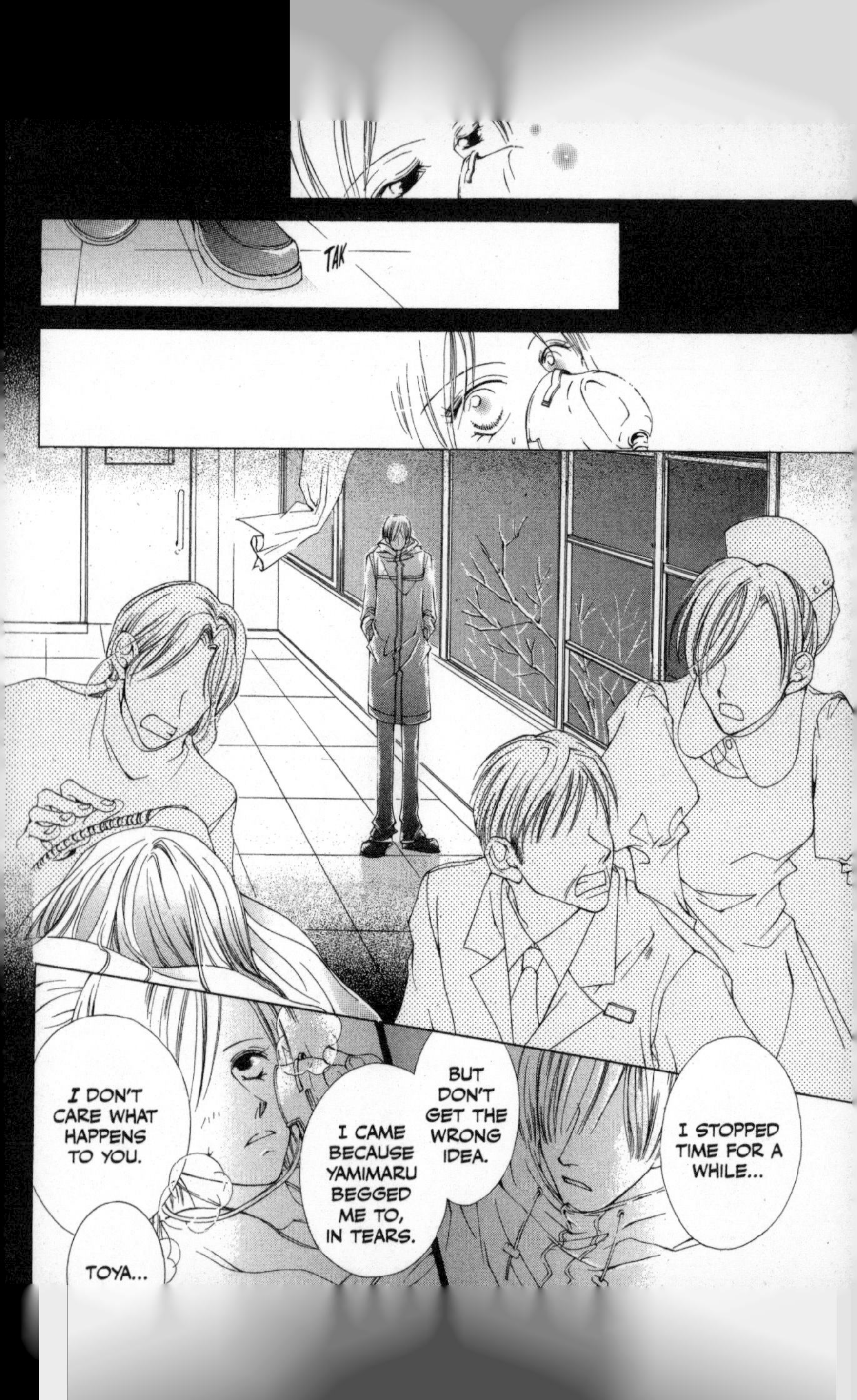
TAK
I STOPPED TIME FOR A WHILE...
BUT DON'T GET THE WRONG IDEA.
I CAME BECAUSE YAMIMARU BEGGED ME TO, IN TEARS.
I DON'T CARE WHAT HAPPENS TO YOU.
TOYA...

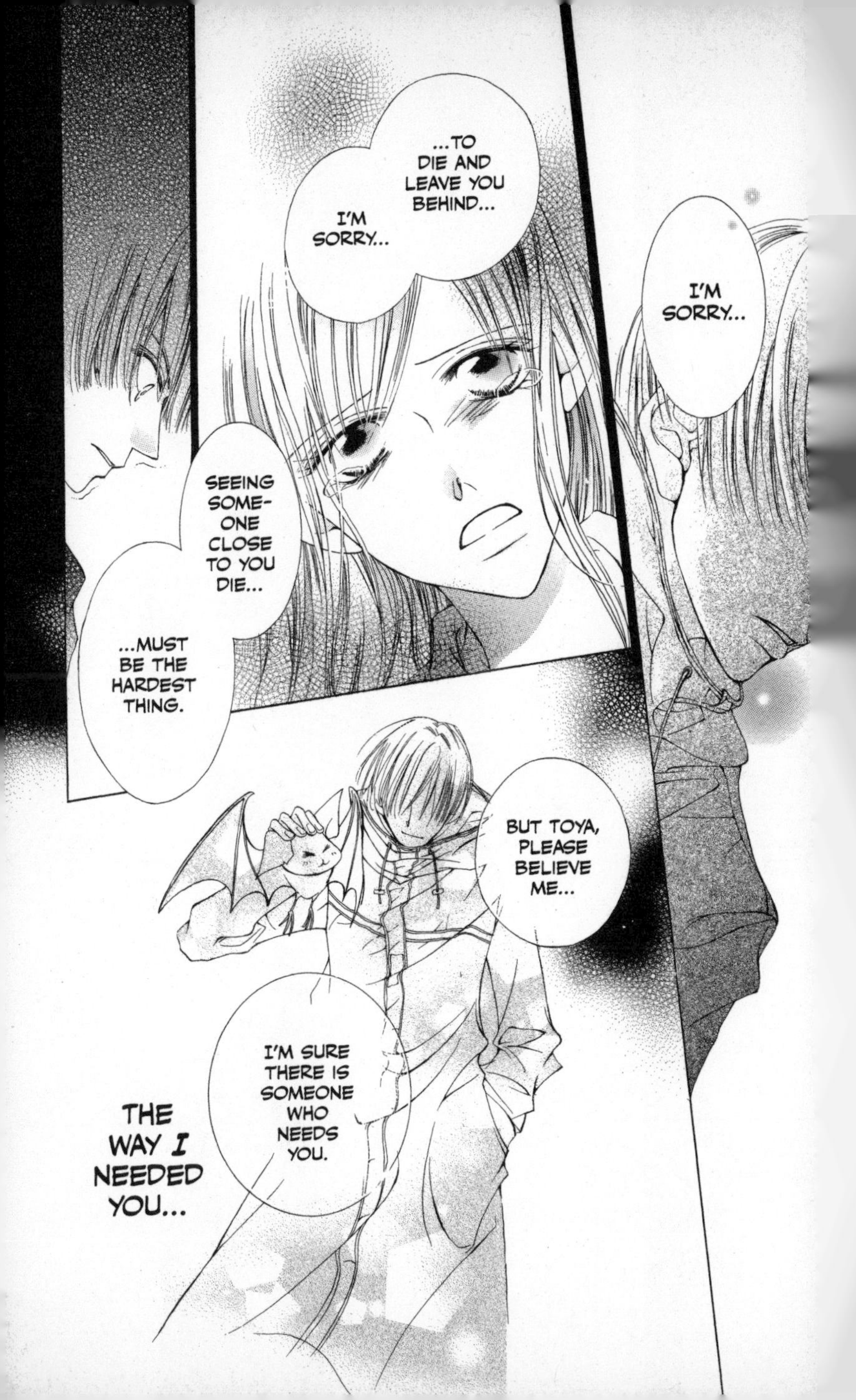

I'M SORRY...
I'M SORRY...
...TO DIE AND LEAVE YOU BEHIND...
SEEING SOMEONE CLOSE TO YOU DIE...
...MUST BE THE HARDEST THING.
BUT TOYA, PLEASE BELIEVE ME...
I'M SURE THERE IS SOMEONE WHO NEEDS YOU.
THE WAY *I* NEEDED YOU...

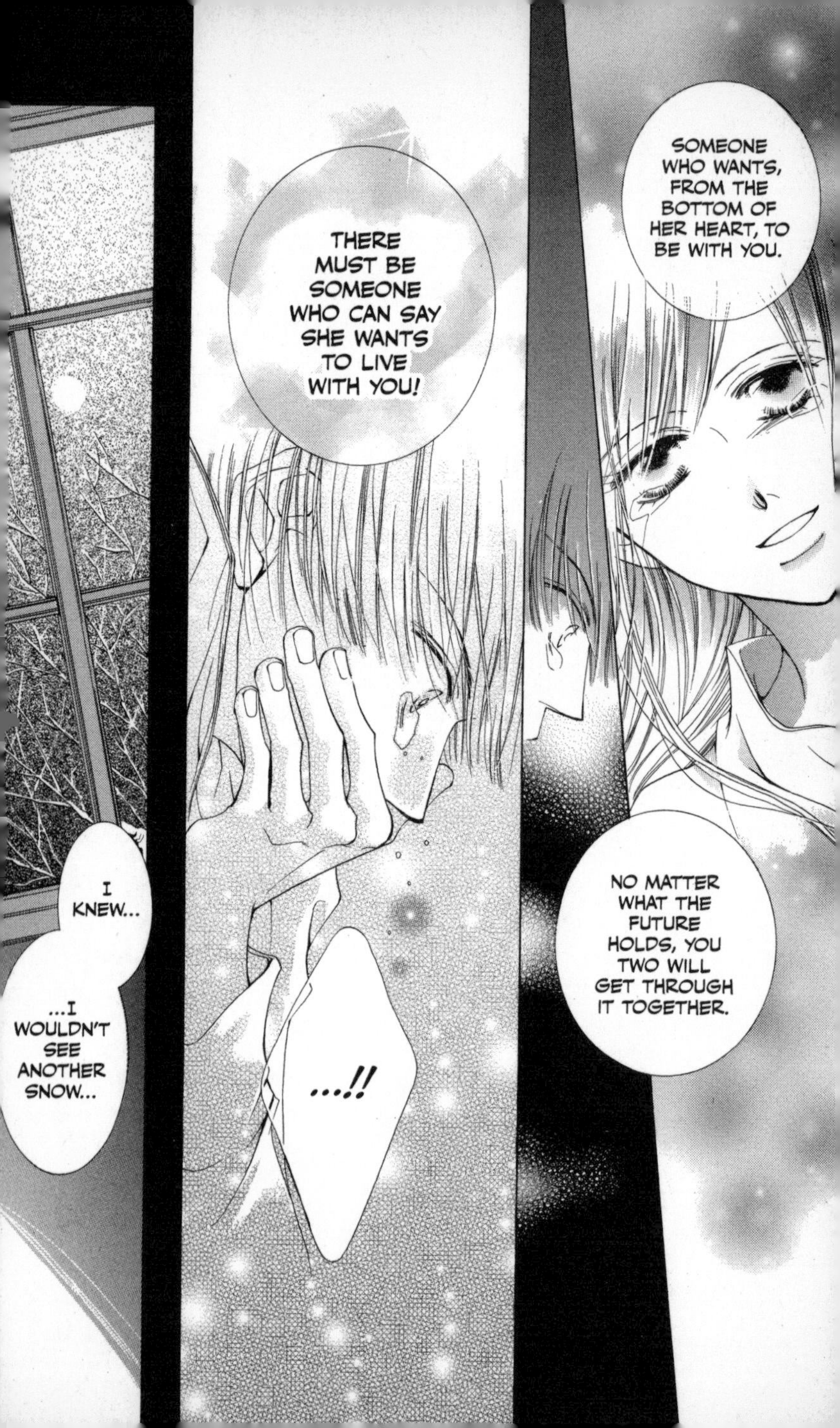
SOMEONE WHO WANTS, FROM THE BOTTOM OF HER HEART, TO BE WITH YOU.
NO MATTER WHAT THE FUTURE HOLDS, YOU TWO WILL GET THROUGH IT TOGETHER.
THERE MUST BE SOMEONE WHO CAN SAY SHE WANTS TO LIVE WITH YOU!
...!!
I KNEW...
...I WOULDN'T SEE ANOTHER SNOW...

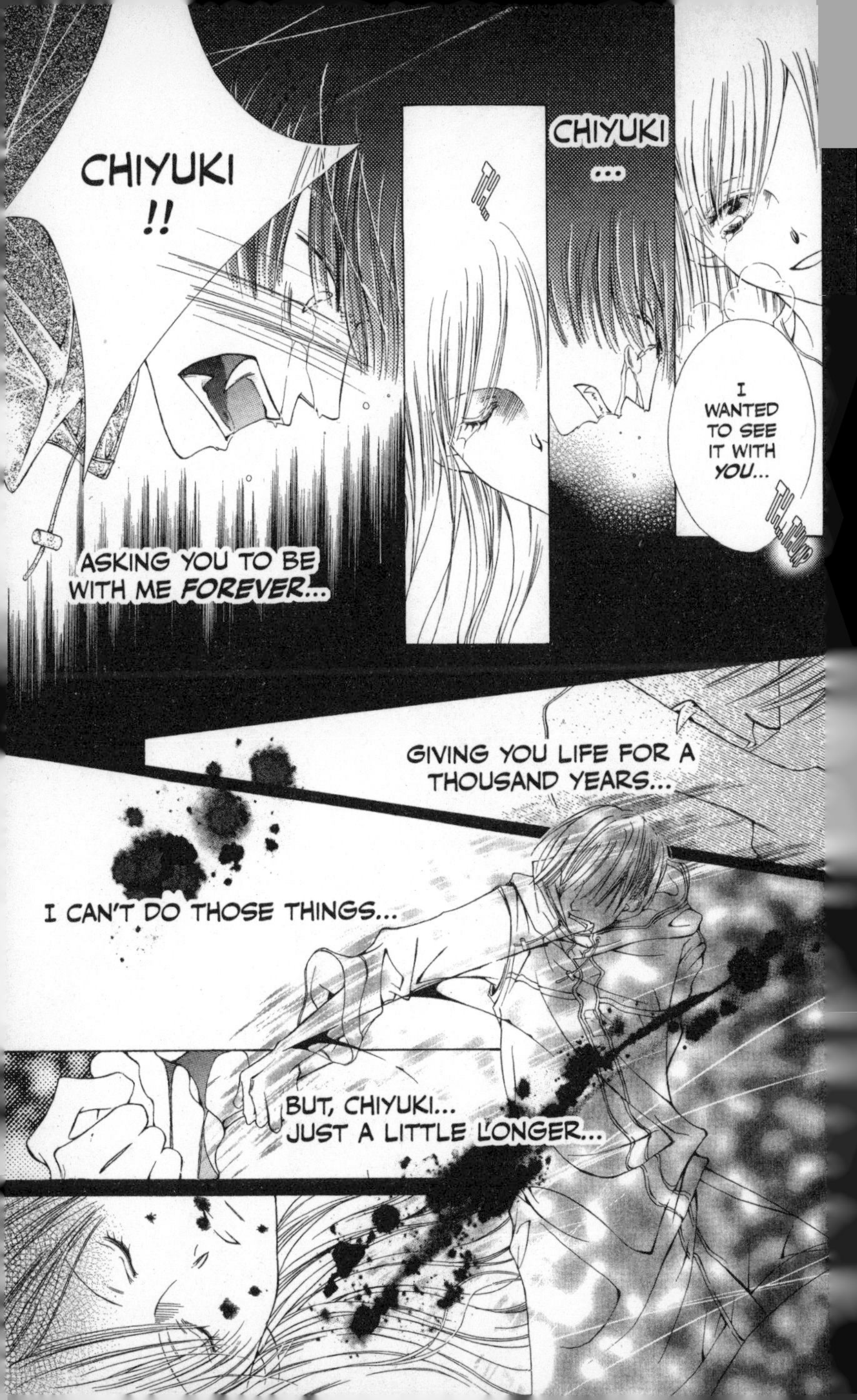
I WANTED TO SEE IT WITH YOU...
CHIYUKI ...
CHIYUKI !!
ASKING YOU TO BE WITH ME FOREVER...
GIVING YOU LIFE FOR A THOUSAND YEARS...
I CAN'T DO THOSE THINGS...
BUT, CHIYUKI... JUST A LITTLE LONGER...

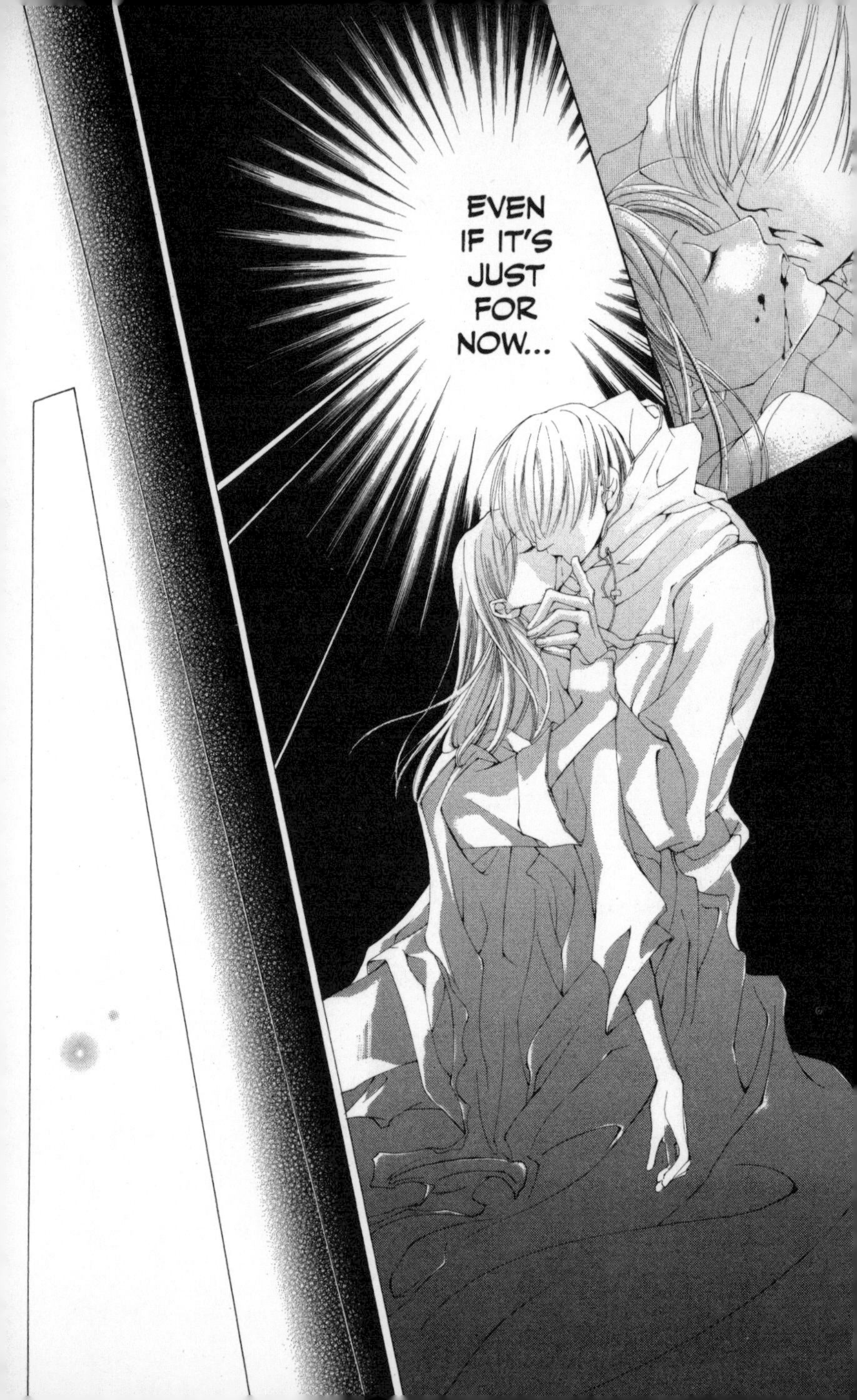
EVEN IF IT'S JUST FOR NOW...

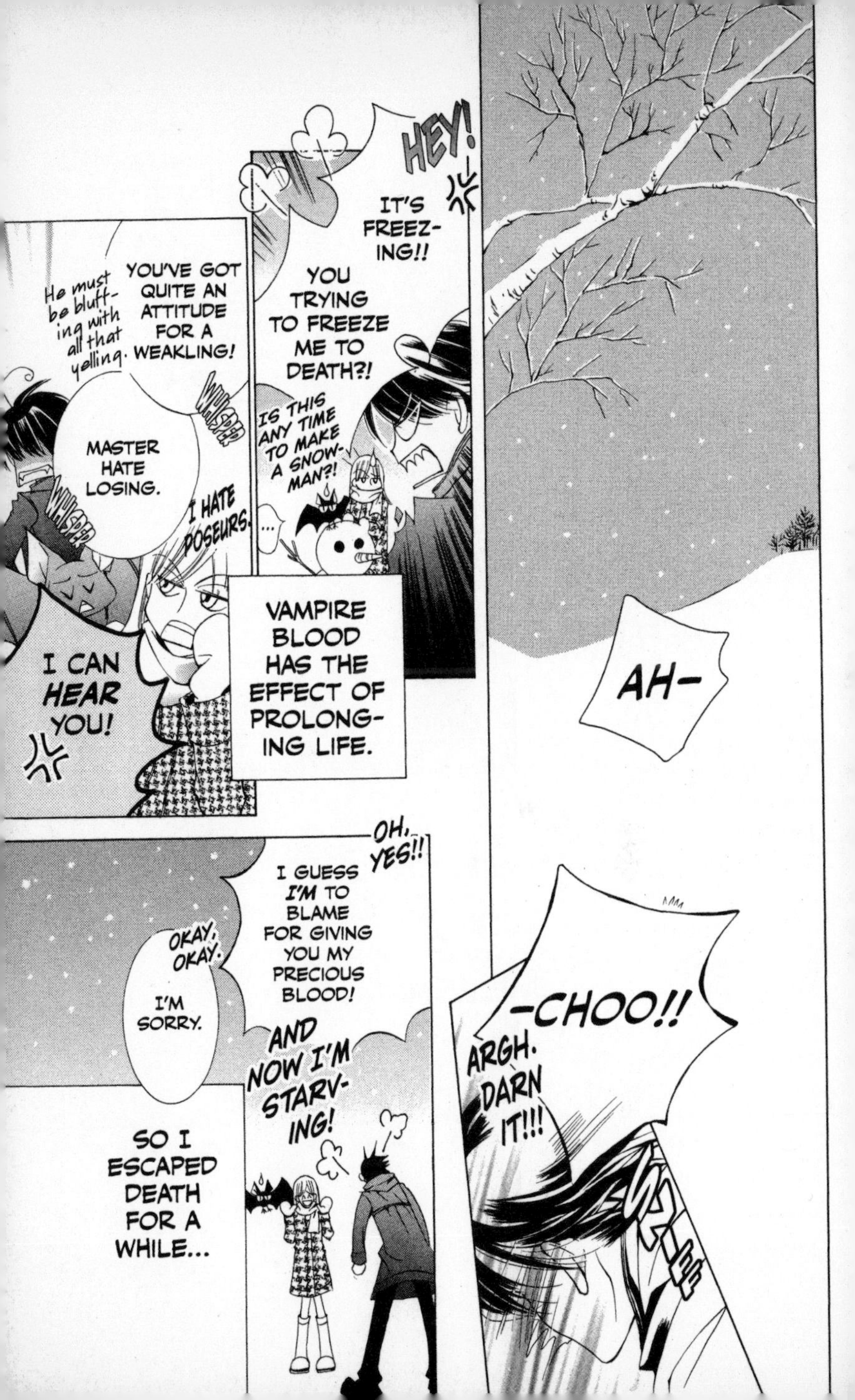
AH-
-CHOO!!
ARGH. DARN IT!!!
HEY!
IT'S FREEZING!!
YOU TRYING TO FREEZE ME TO DEATH?!
IS THIS ANY TIME TO MAKE A SNOWMAN?!
...
YOU'VE GOT QUITE AN ATTITUDE FOR A WEAKLING!
He must be bluffing with all that yelling.
MASTER HATE LOSING.
WHISPER
WHISPER
I HATE POSEURS.
I CAN HEAR YOU!
VAMPIRE BLOOD HAS THE EFFECT OF PROLONGING LIFE.
OH, YES!!
I GUESS I'M TO BLAME FOR GIVING YOU MY PRECIOUS BLOOD!
AND NOW I'M STARVING!
OKAY, OKAY.
I'M SORRY.
SO I ESCAPED DEATH FOR A WHILE...

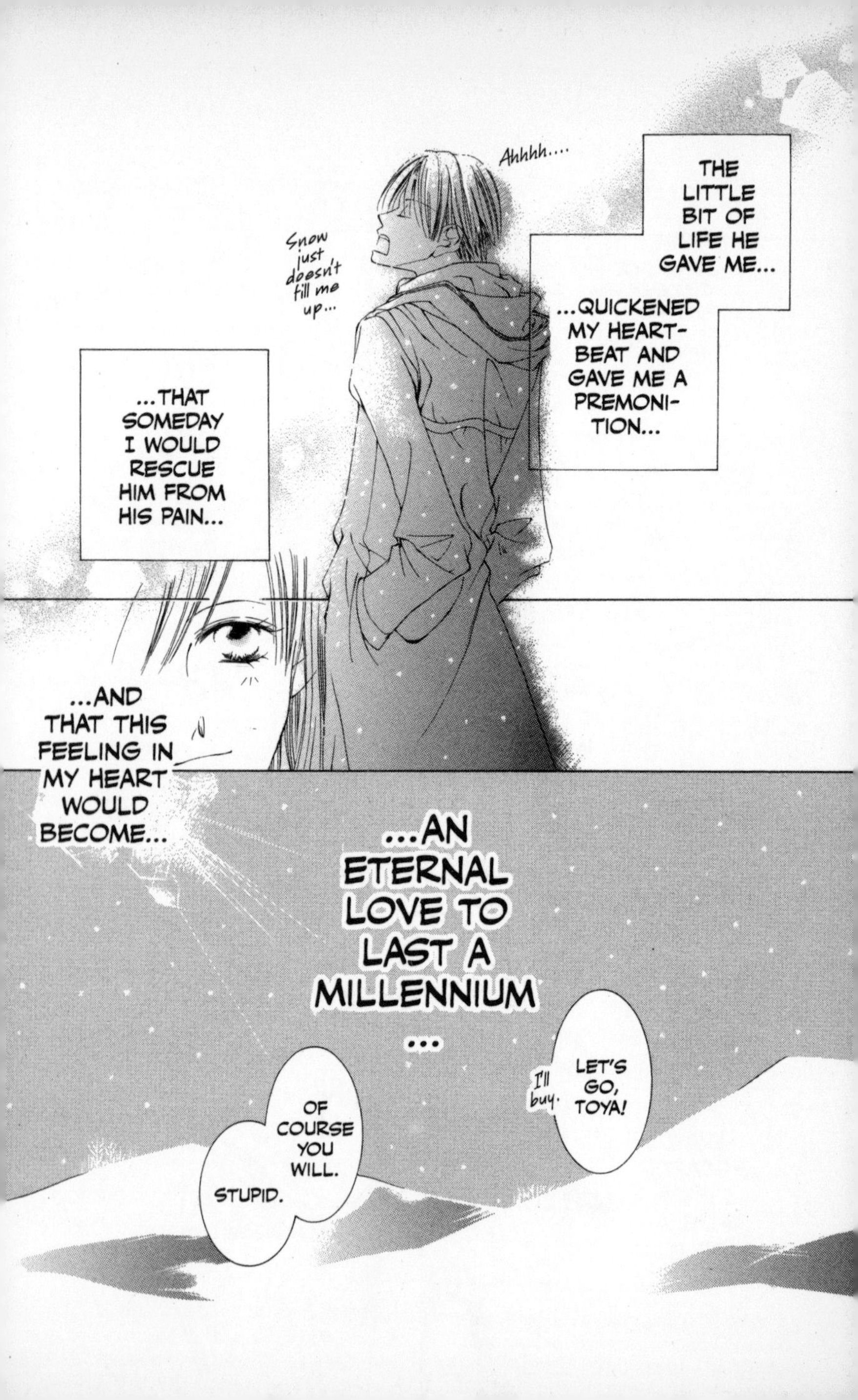
THE LITTLE BIT OF LIFE HE GAVE ME...
...QUICKENED MY HEART-BEAT AND GAVE ME A PREMONITION...
Ahhhh....
Snow just doesn't fill me up...
...THAT SOMEDAY I WOULD RESCUE HIM FROM HIS PAIN...
...AND THAT THIS FEELING IN MY HEART WOULD BECOME...
...AN ETERNAL LOVE TO LAST A MILLENNIUM ...
LET'S GO, TOYA!
I'll buy.
OF COURSE YOU WILL.
STUPID.

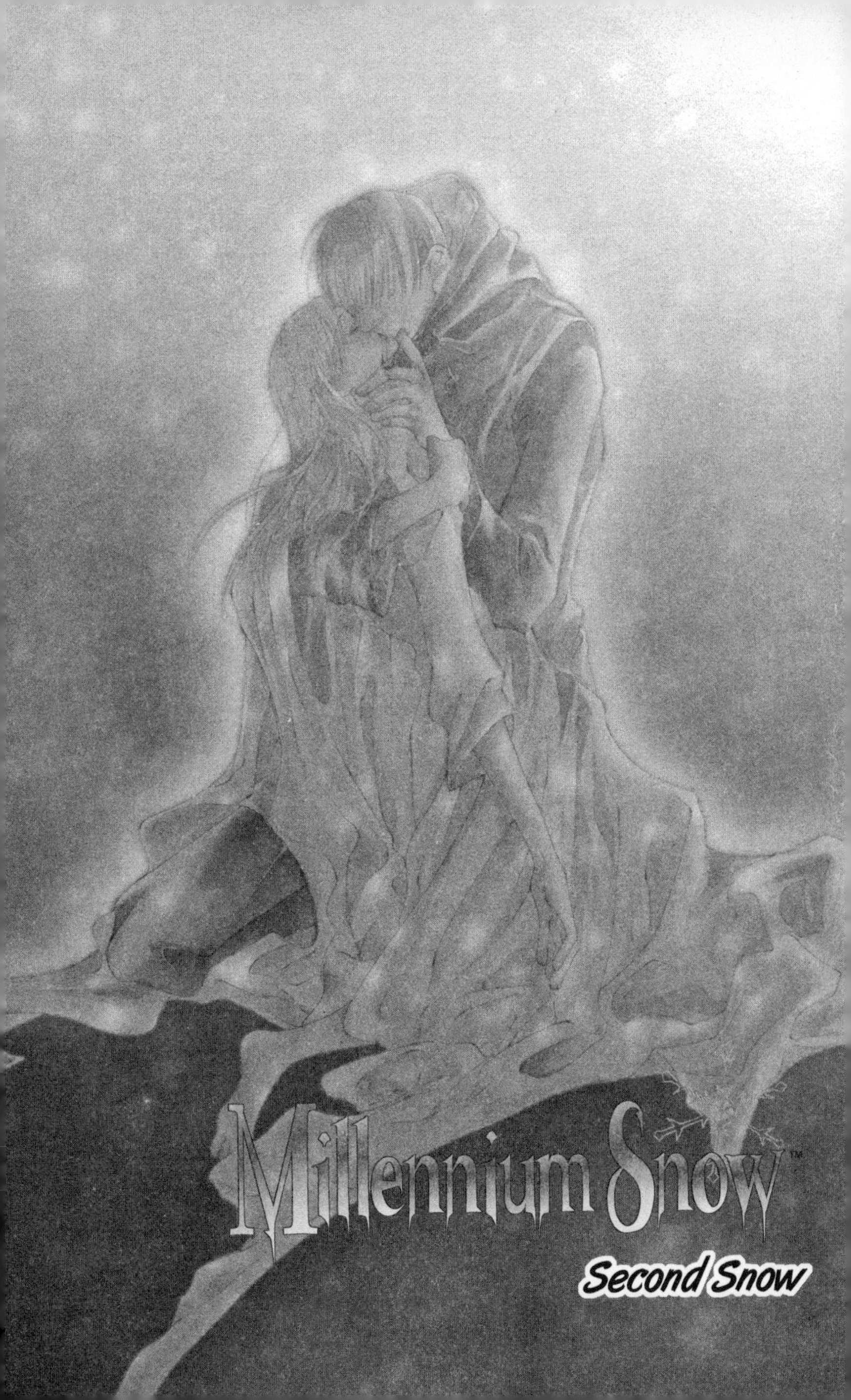
Millennium Snow™
Second Snow

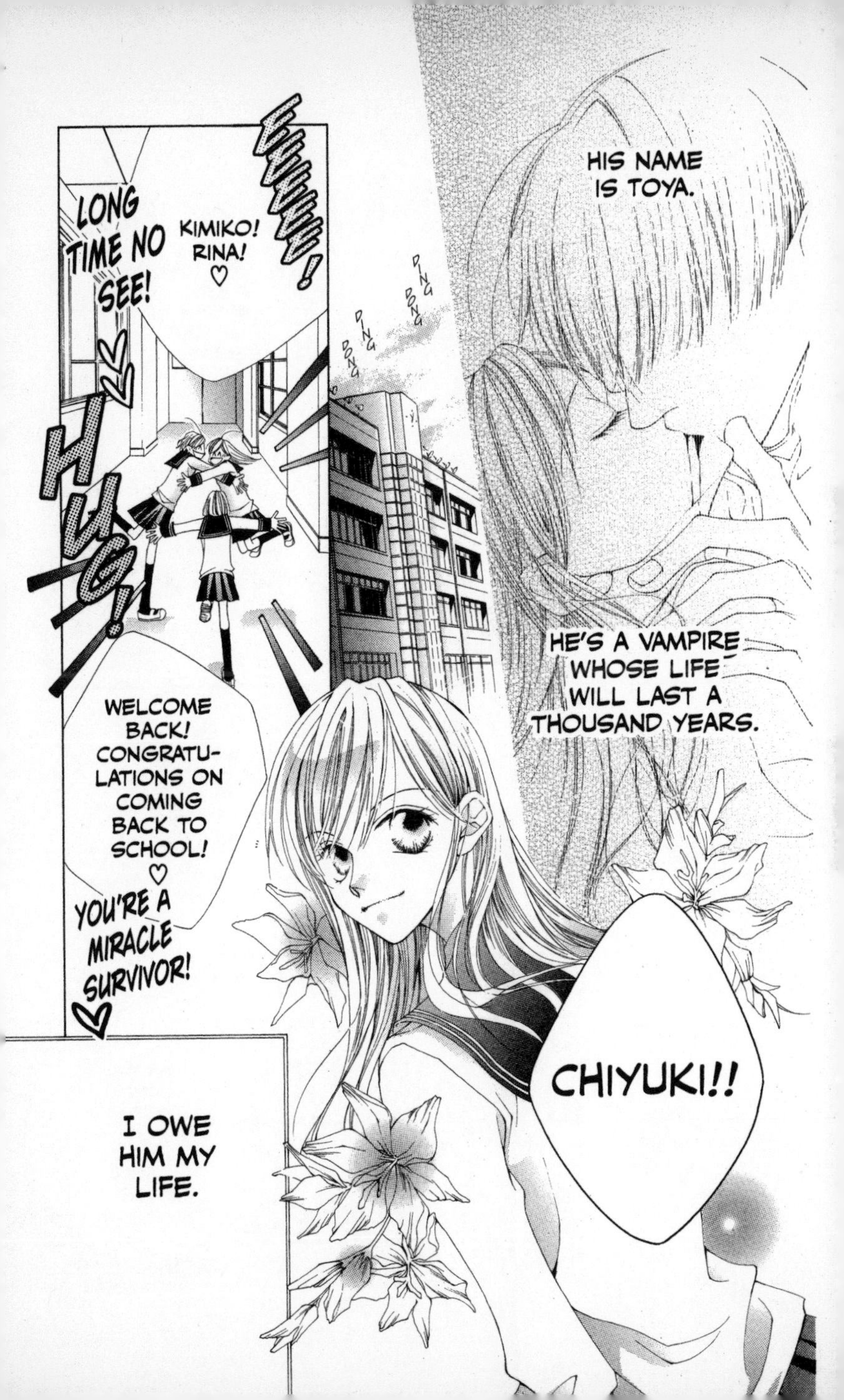
HIS NAME IS TOYA.
HE'S A VAMPIRE WHOSE LIFE WILL LAST A THOUSAND YEARS.
DING DONG DING DONG
EEEEEEE!
KIMIKO! RINA! ♡
LONG TIME NO SEE! ♡
HUG!
WELCOME BACK! CONGRATU-LATIONS ON COMING BACK TO SCHOOL! ♡
YOU'RE A MIRACLE SURVIVOR! ♡
CHIYUKI!!
I OWE HIM MY LIFE.

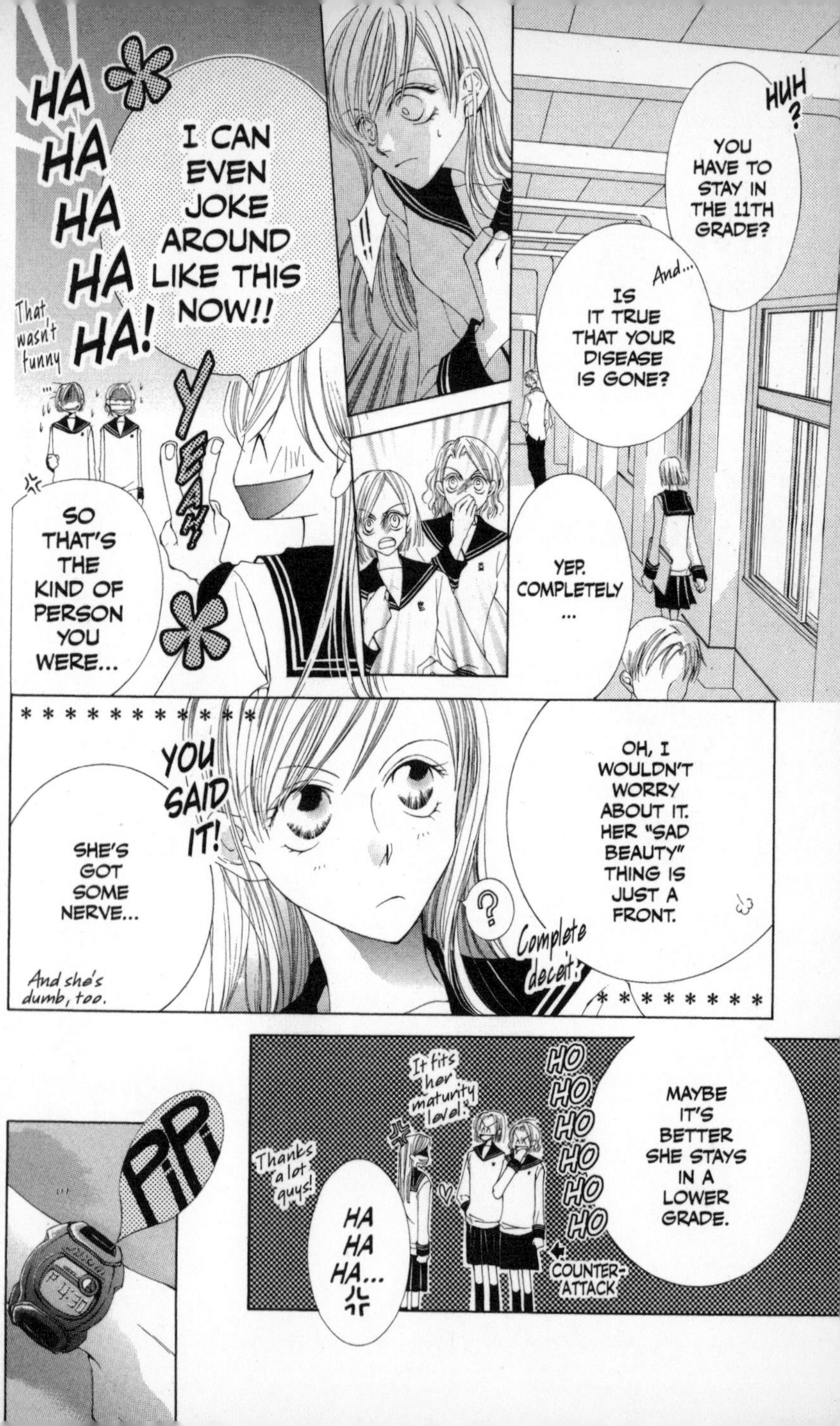
HUH?
YOU HAVE TO STAY IN THE 11TH GRADE?
And...
IS IT TRUE THAT YOUR DISEASE IS GONE?
YEP. COMPLETELY ...
!!
HA HA HA HA HA!
I CAN EVEN JOKE AROUND LIKE THIS NOW!!
YEAH
That wasn't funny
...
SO THAT'S THE KIND OF PERSON YOU WERE...
OH, I WOULDN'T WORRY ABOUT IT. HER "SAD BEAUTY" THING IS JUST A FRONT.
Complete deceit.
?
YOU SAID IT!
SHE'S GOT SOME NERVE...
And she's dumb, too.
MAYBE IT'S BETTER SHE STAYS IN A LOWER GRADE.
HO HO HO HO HO HO
COUNTER-ATTACK
It fits her maturity level.
Thanks a lot guys!
HA HA HA...
PiPi

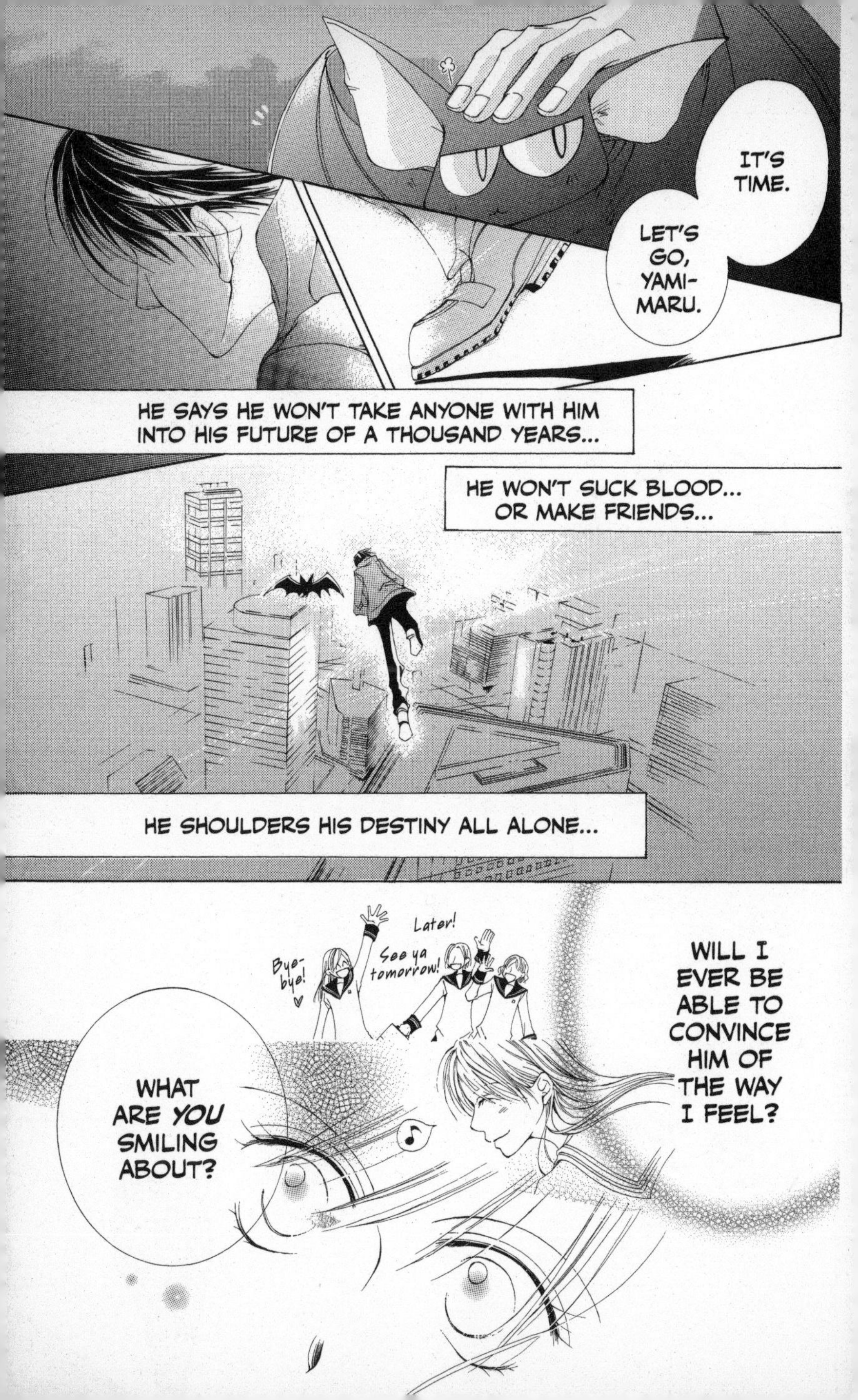
IT'S TIME.
LET'S GO, YAMI-MARU.
HE SAYS HE WON'T TAKE ANYONE WITH HIM INTO HIS FUTURE OF A THOUSAND YEARS...
HE WON'T SUCK BLOOD... OR MAKE FRIENDS...
HE SHOULDERS HIS DESTINY ALL ALONE...
WILL I EVER BE ABLE TO CONVINCE HIM OF THE WAY I FEEL?
Later!
See ya tomorrow!
Bye-bye!
WHAT ARE *YOU* SMILING ABOUT?

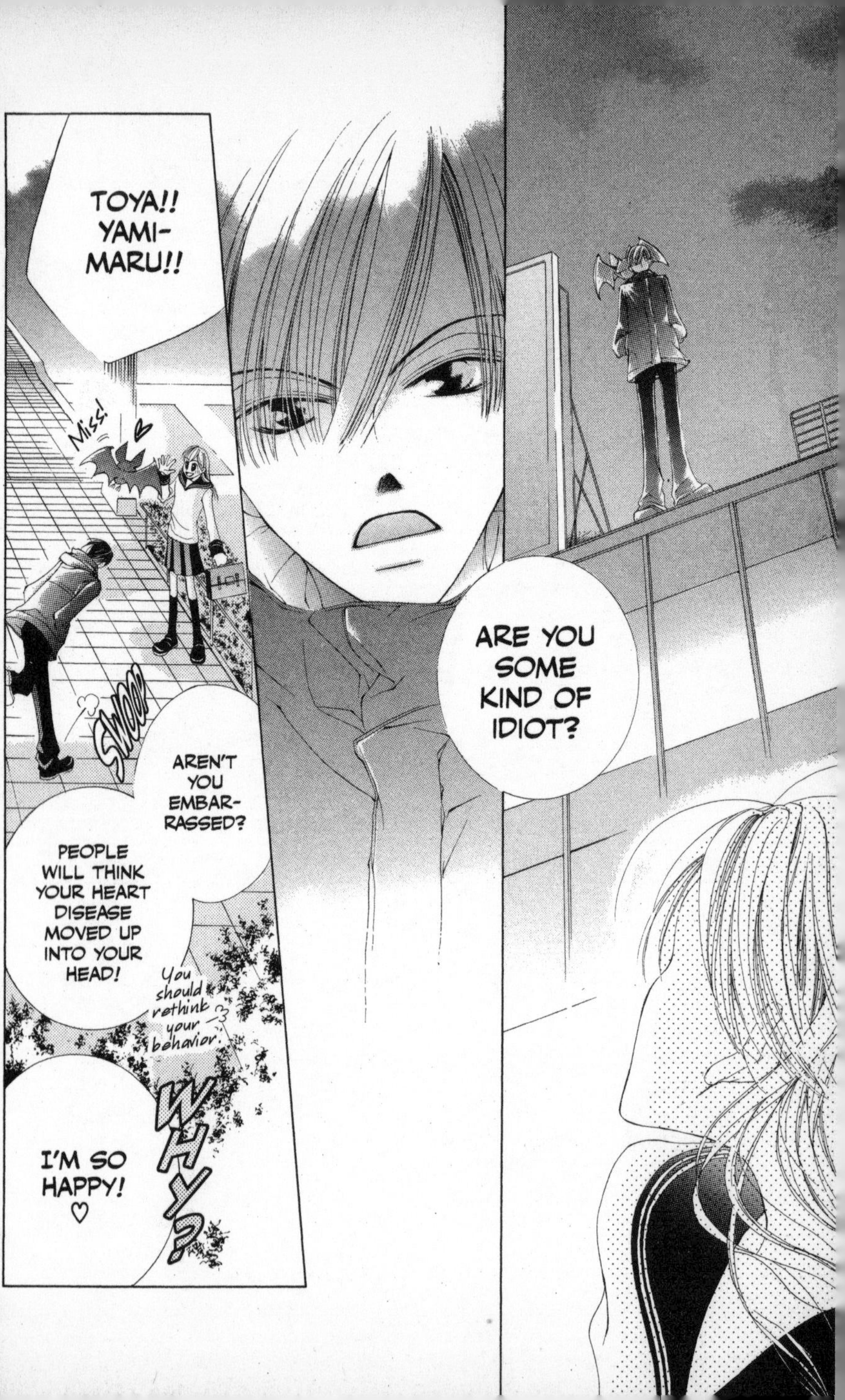
ARE YOU SOME KIND OF IDIOT?
TOYA!! YAMI-MARU!!
Miss!
SWOOP
AREN'T YOU EMBARRASSED?
PEOPLE WILL THINK YOUR HEART DISEASE MOVED UP INTO YOUR HEAD!
You should rethink your behavior.
I'M SO HAPPY! ♡
WHY?

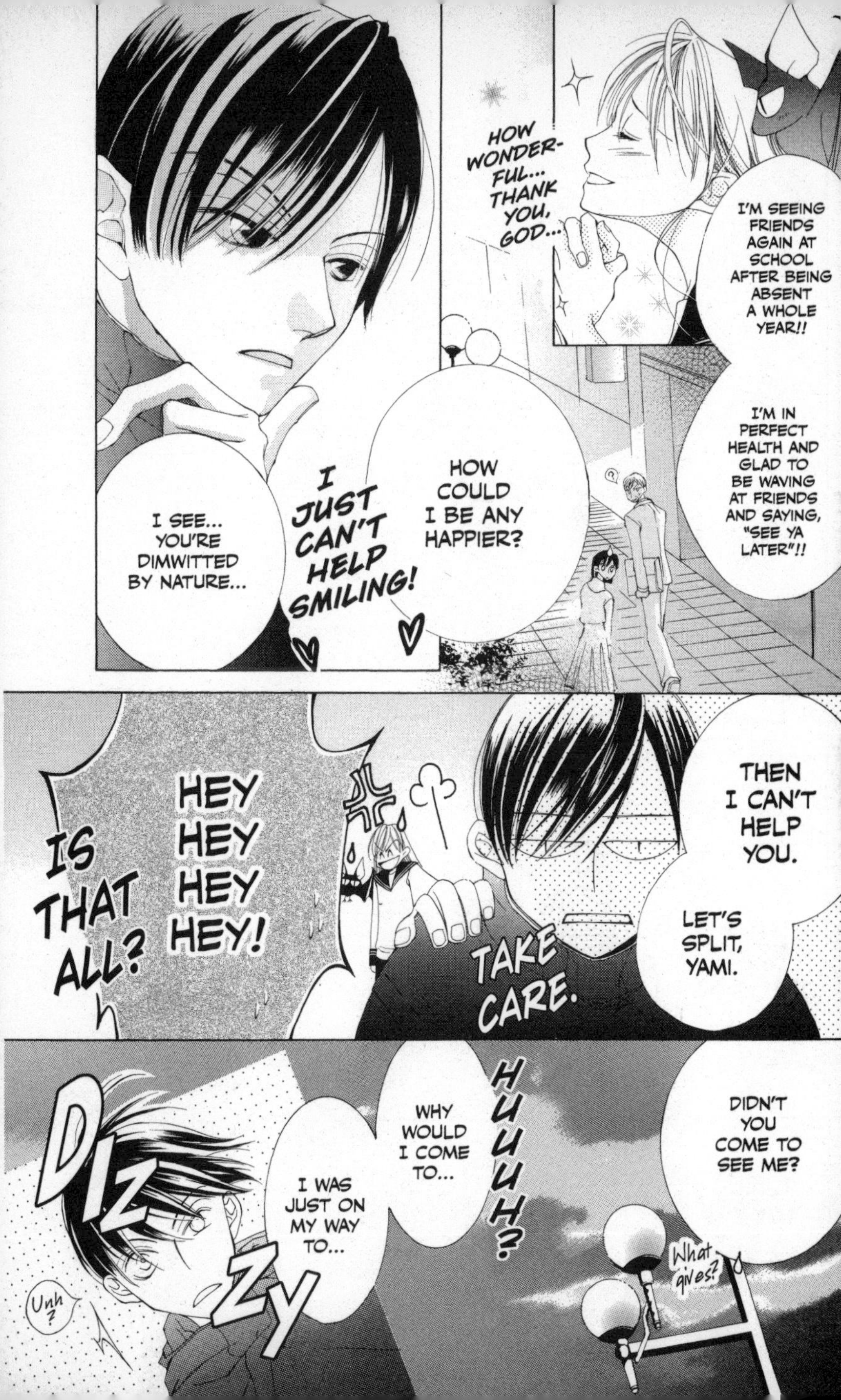
I'M SEEING FRIENDS AGAIN AT SCHOOL AFTER BEING ABSENT A WHOLE YEAR!!
HOW WONDERFUL... THANK YOU, GOD...
I'M IN PERFECT HEALTH AND GLAD TO BE WAVING AT FRIENDS AND SAYING, "SEE YA LATER"!!
HOW COULD I BE ANY HAPPIER?
I JUST CAN'T HELP SMILING!
I SEE... YOU'RE DIMWITTED BY NATURE...
THEN I CAN'T HELP YOU.
LET'S SPLIT, YAMI.
TAKE CARE.
HEY HEY HEY HEY!
IS THAT ALL?
DIDN'T YOU COME TO SEE ME?
What gives?
HUUUH?
WHY WOULD I COME TO...
I WAS JUST ON MY WAY TO...
DIZZY
Unh?

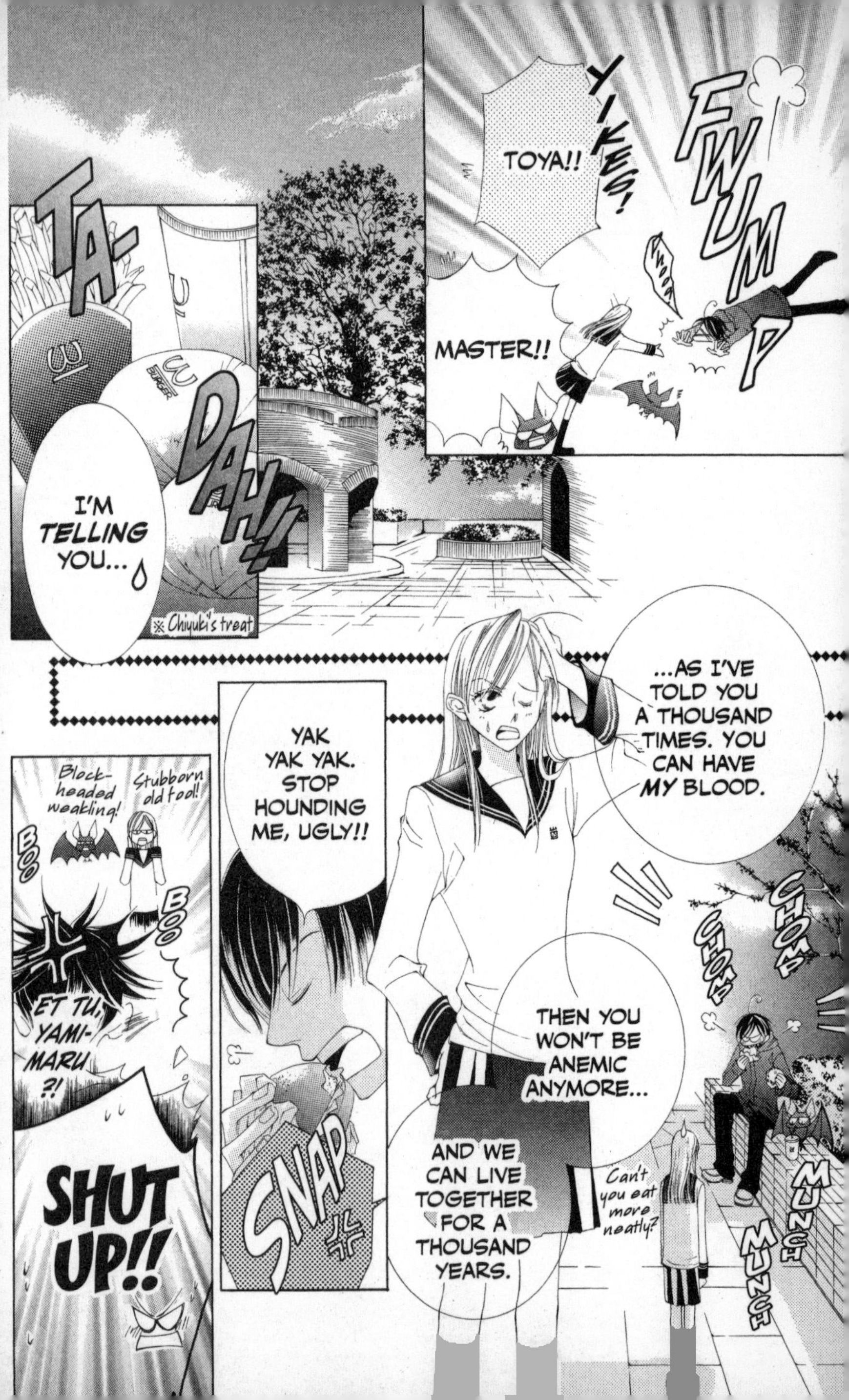
FWUMP
YIKES!
TOYA!!
MASTER!!
TA-DAH!!
I'M TELLING YOU...
※Chiyuki's treat
...AS I'VE TOLD YOU A THOUSAND TIMES. YOU CAN HAVE MY BLOOD.
CHOMP CHOMP
THEN YOU WON'T BE ANEMIC ANYMORE...
AND WE CAN LIVE TOGETHER FOR A THOUSAND YEARS.
Can't you eat more neatly?
MUNCH MUNCH
YAK YAK YAK. STOP HOUNDING ME, UGLY!!
SNAP
Stubborn old fool!
Block-headed weakling!
BOO BOO
ET TU, YAMI-MARU ?!
SHUT UP!!

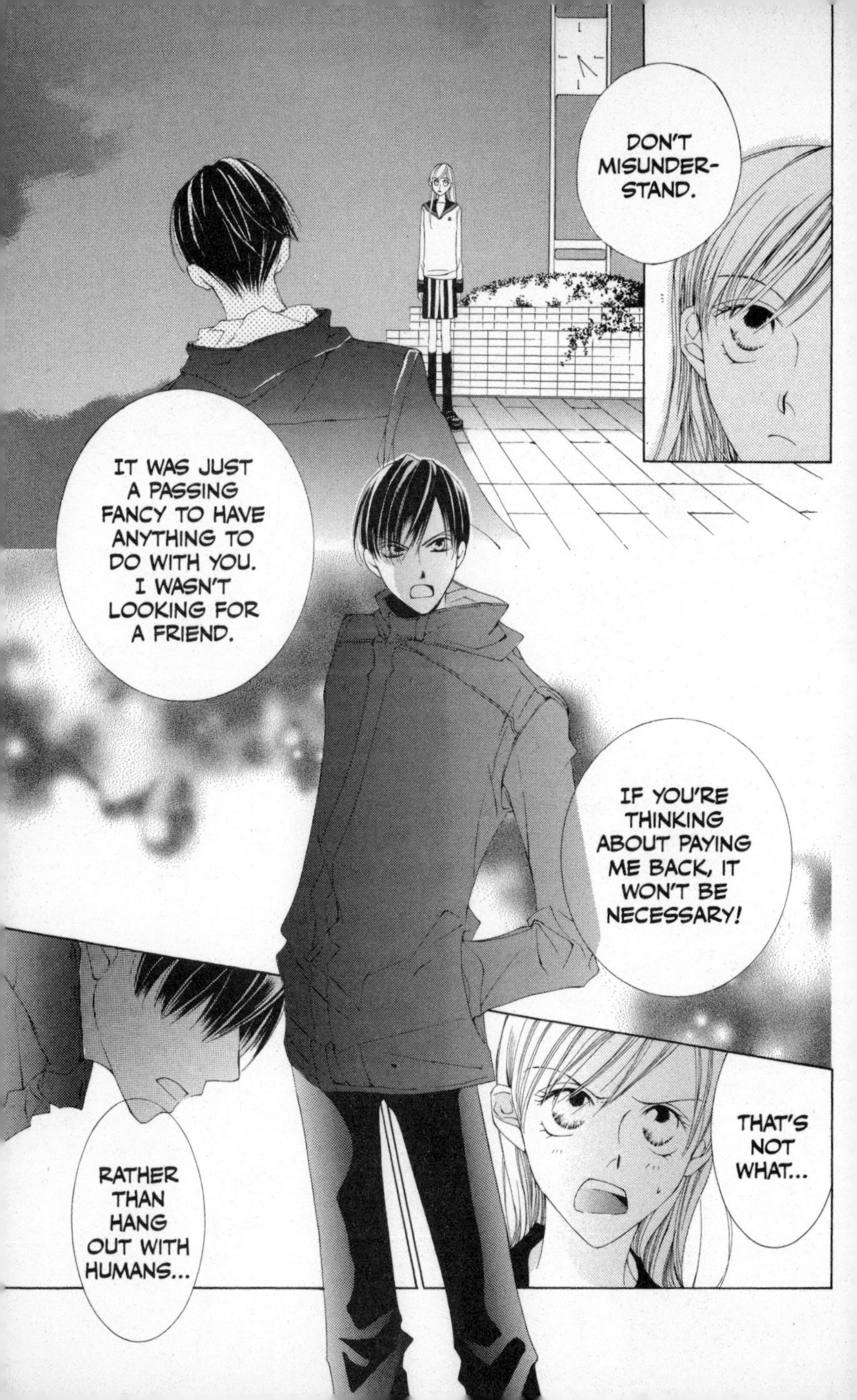
DON'T MISUNDERSTAND.
IT WAS JUST A PASSING FANCY TO HAVE ANYTHING TO DO WITH YOU. I WASN'T LOOKING FOR A FRIEND.
IF YOU'RE THINKING ABOUT PAYING ME BACK, IT WON'T BE NECESSARY!
THAT'S NOT WHAT...
RATHER THAN HANG OUT WITH HUMANS...

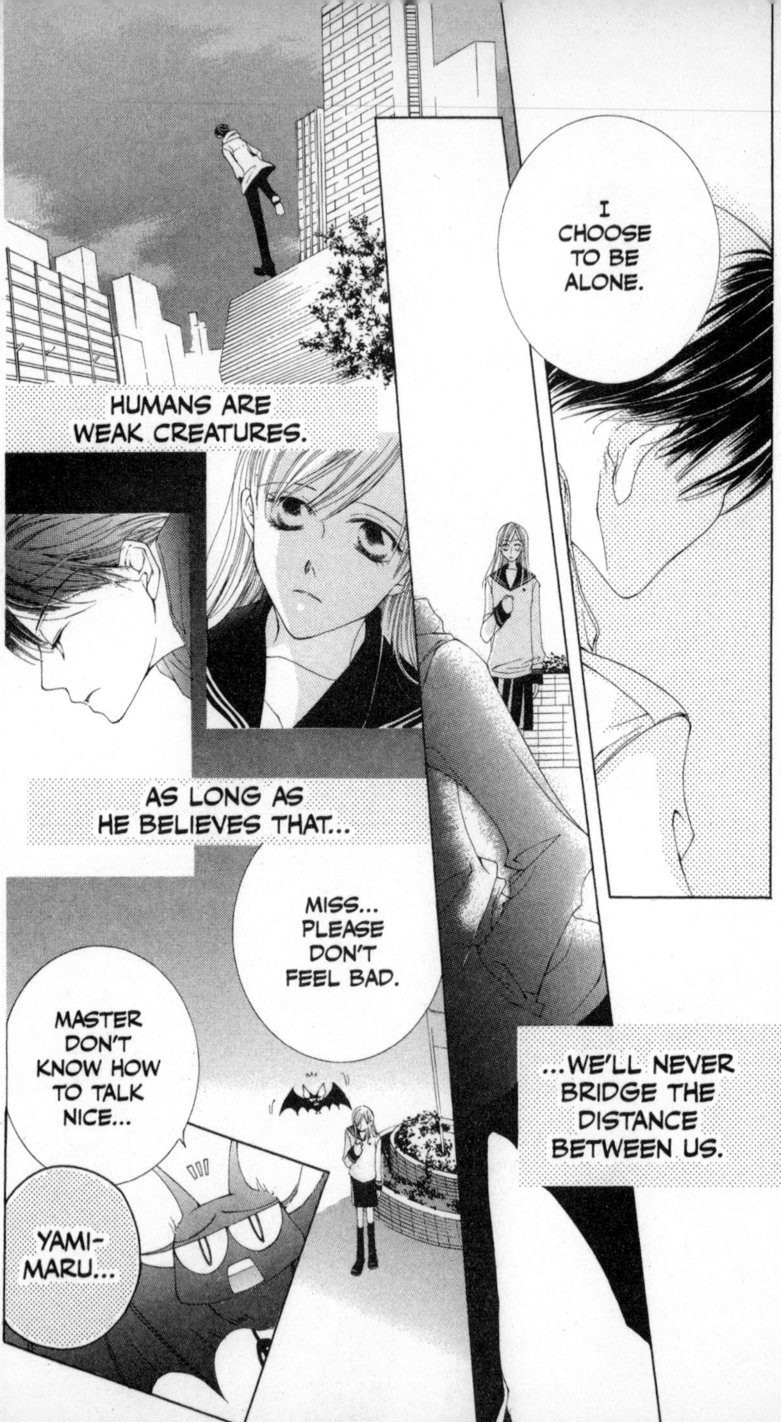
I CHOOSE TO BE ALONE.
HUMANS ARE WEAK CREATURES.
AS LONG AS HE BELIEVES THAT...
...WE'LL NEVER BRIDGE THE DISTANCE BETWEEN US.
MISS... PLEASE DON'T FEEL BAD.
MASTER DON'T KNOW HOW TO TALK NICE...
YAMI-MARU...

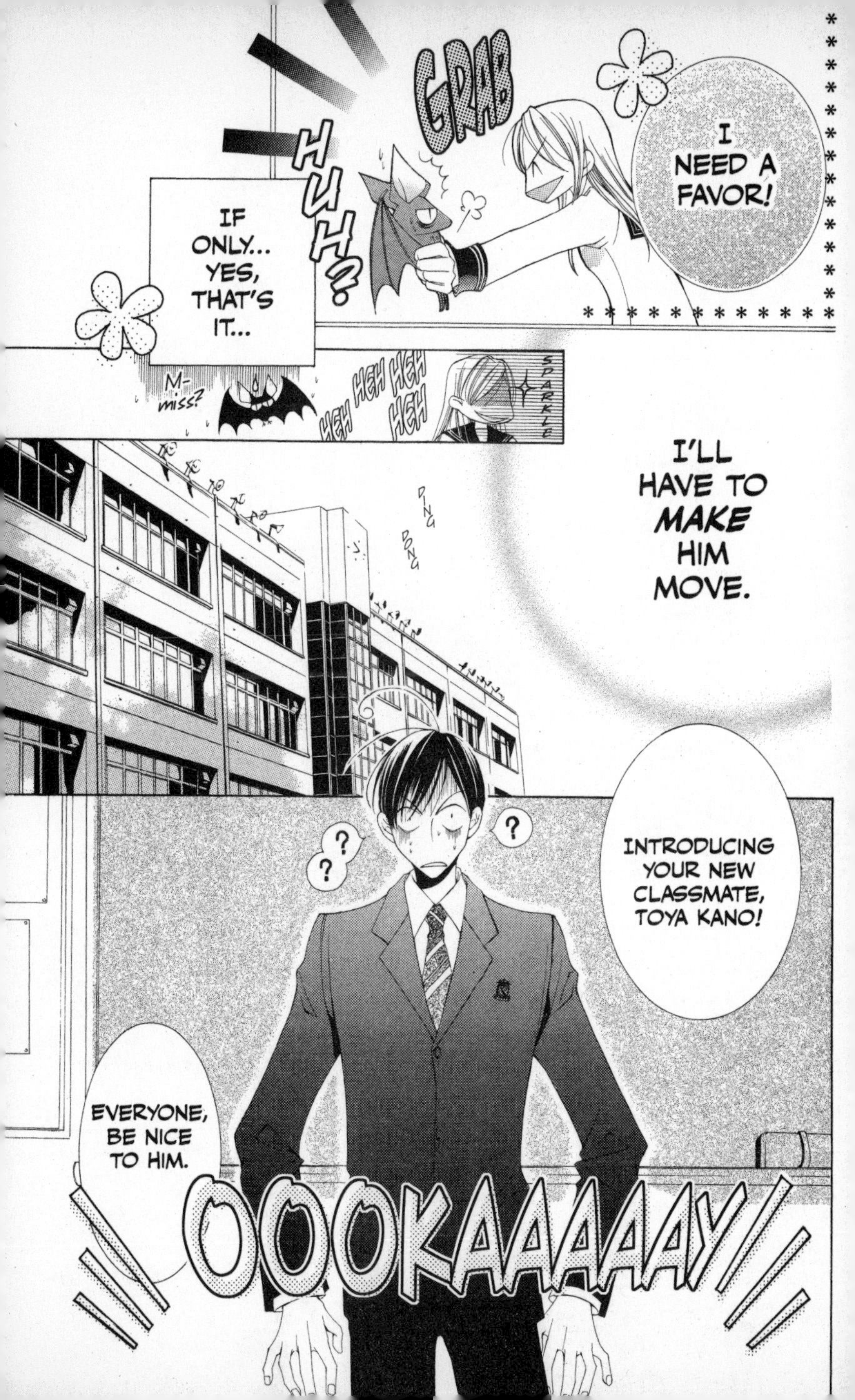
I NEED A FAVOR!
GRAB
HUH?
IF ONLY... YES, THAT'S IT...
SPARKLE
HEH HEH HEH HEH HEH
M-miss?
I'LL HAVE TO MAKE HIM MOVE.
DING DONG
INTRODUCING YOUR NEW CLASSMATE, TOYA KANO!
EVERYONE, BE NICE TO HIM.
OOOKAAAAAY!

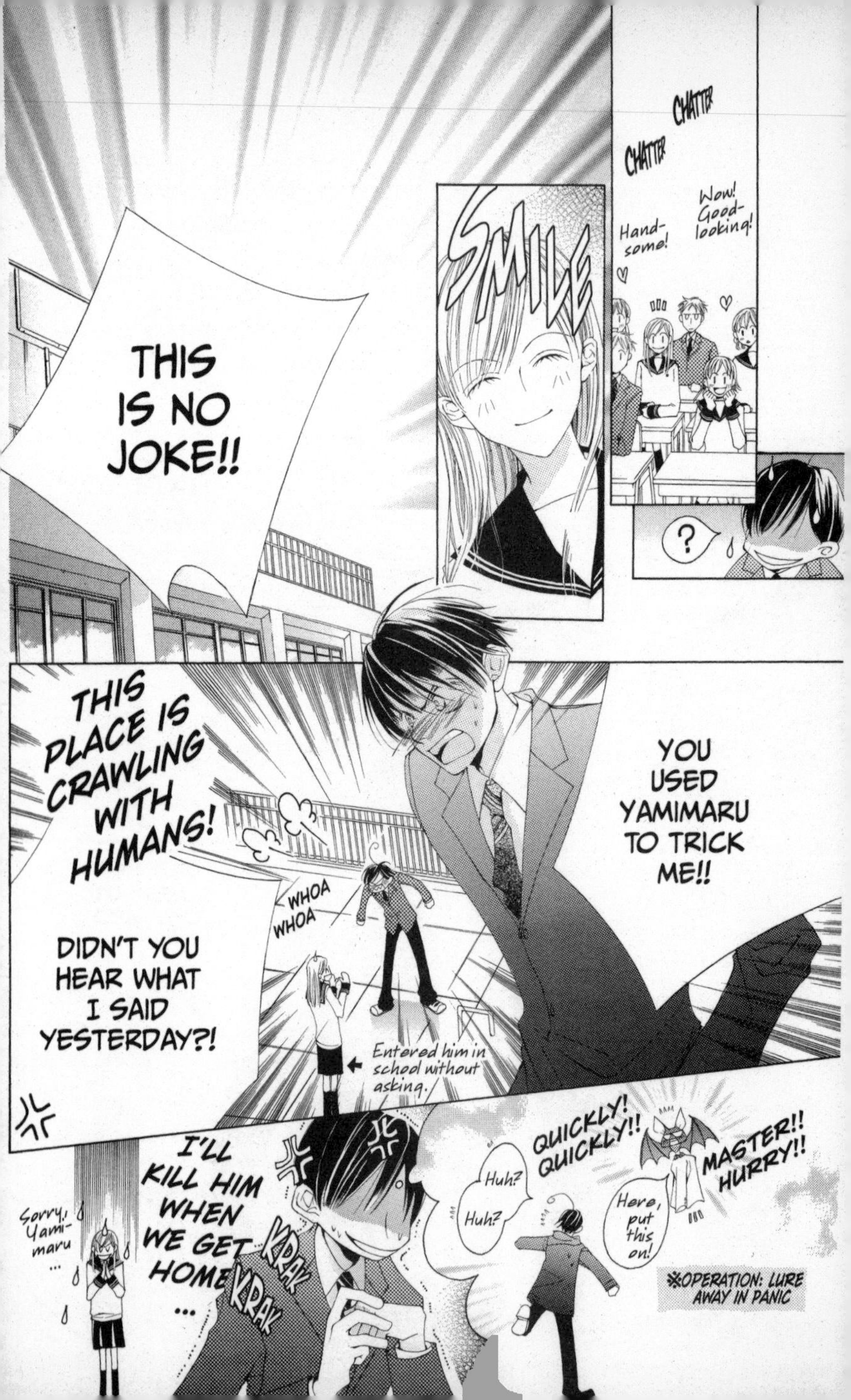
CHATTER
CHATTER
Wow! Good-looking!
Hand-some!
?
SMILE
THIS IS NO JOKE!!
YOU USED YAMIMARU TO TRICK ME!!
THIS PLACE IS CRAWLING WITH HUMANS!
WHOA WHOA
DIDN'T YOU HEAR WHAT I SAID YESTERDAY?!
Entered him in school without asking.
MASTER!! HURRY!!
Here, put this on!
QUICKLY! QUICKLY!!
Huh?
Huh?
※OPERATION: LURE AWAY IN PANIC
KRAK
KRAK
I'LL KILL HIM WHEN WE GET HOME...
Sorry, Yami-maru...

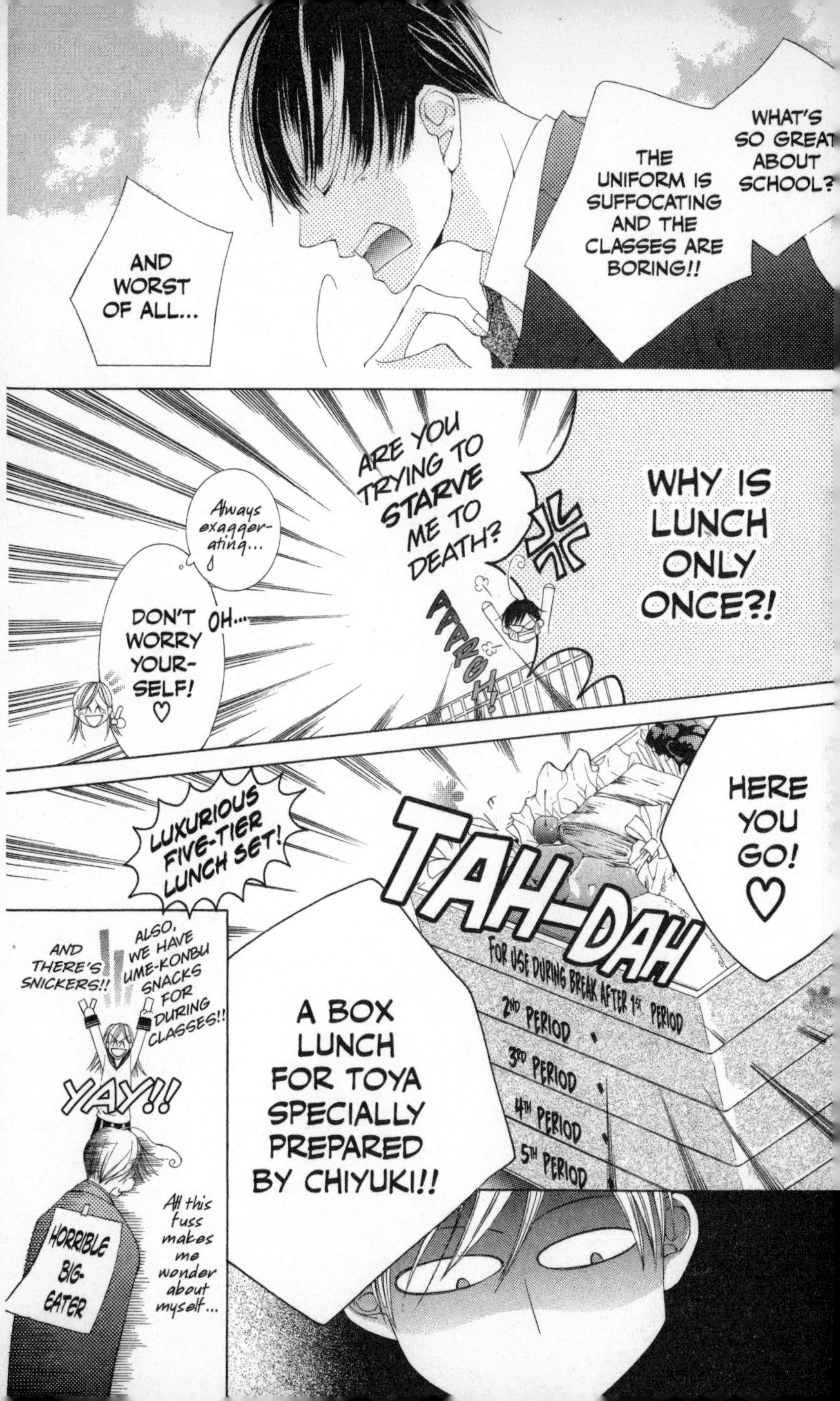
WHAT'S SO GREAT ABOUT SCHOOL?
THE UNIFORM IS SUFFOCATING AND THE CLASSES ARE BORING!!
AND WORST OF ALL...
WHY IS LUNCH ONLY ONCE?!
ARE YOU TRYING TO STARVE ME TO DEATH?
Always exaggerating...
OH...
DON'T WORRY YOURSELF! ♡
HERE YOU GO! ♡
TAH-DAH
LUXURIOUS FIVE-TIER LUNCH SET!
FOR USE DURING BREAK AFTER 1ST PERIOD
2ND PERIOD
3RD PERIOD
4TH PERIOD
5TH PERIOD
A BOX LUNCH FOR TOYA SPECIALLY PREPARED BY CHIYUKI!!
ALSO, WE HAVE UME-KONBU SNACKS FOR DURING CLASSES!!
AND THERE'S SNICKERS!!
YAY!!
HORRIBLE BIG-EATER
All this fuss makes me wonder about myself...

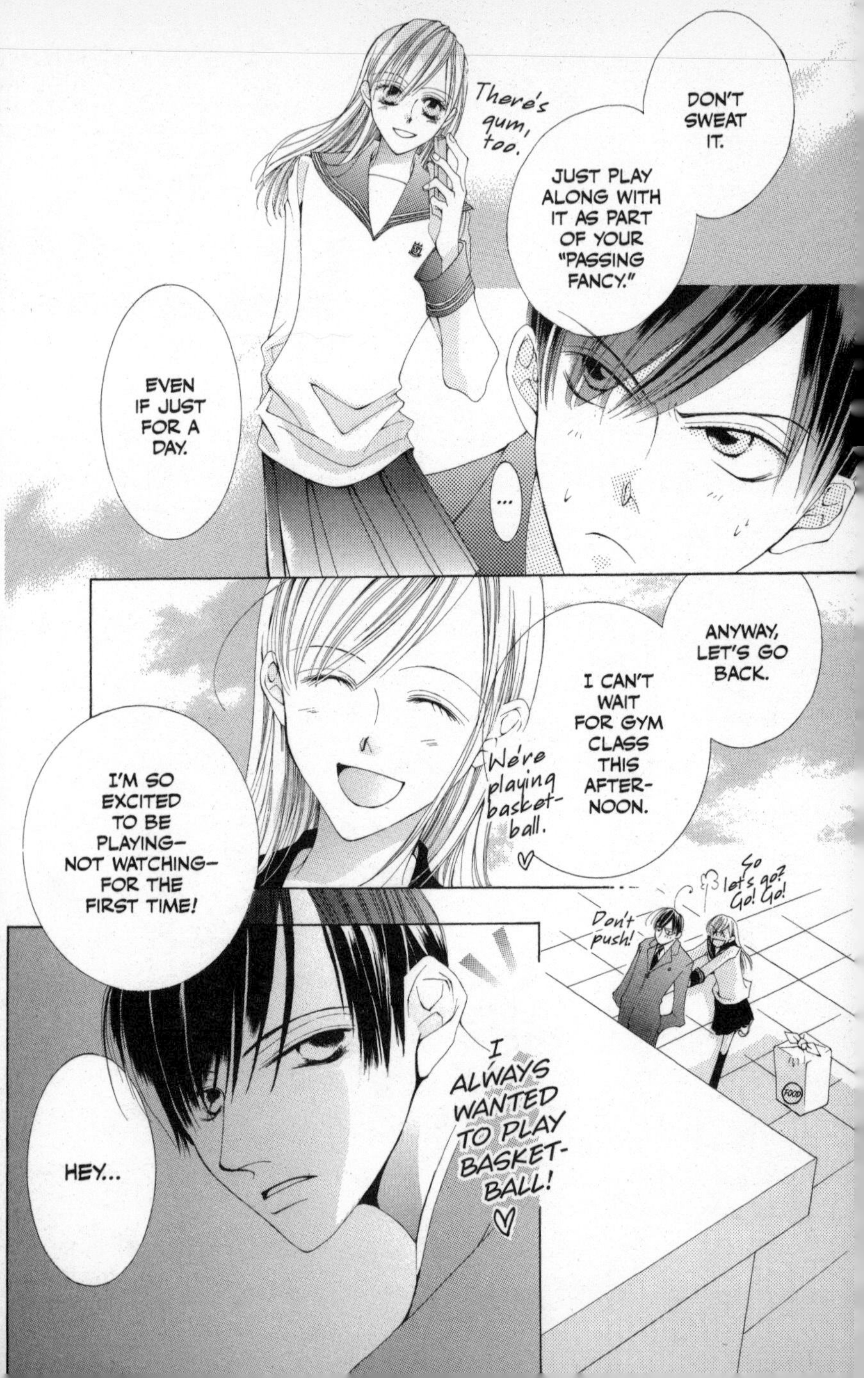
DON'T SWEAT IT.
JUST PLAY ALONG WITH IT AS PART OF YOUR "PASSING FANCY."
There's gum, too.
...
EVEN IF JUST FOR A DAY.
ANYWAY, LET'S GO BACK.
I CAN'T WAIT FOR GYM CLASS THIS AFTER-NOON.
We're playing basket-ball. ♥
I'M SO EXCITED TO BE PLAYING— NOT WATCHING— FOR THE FIRST TIME!
So let's go? Go! Go!
Don't push!
I ALWAYS WANTED TO PLAY BASKET-BALL! ♥
HEY...

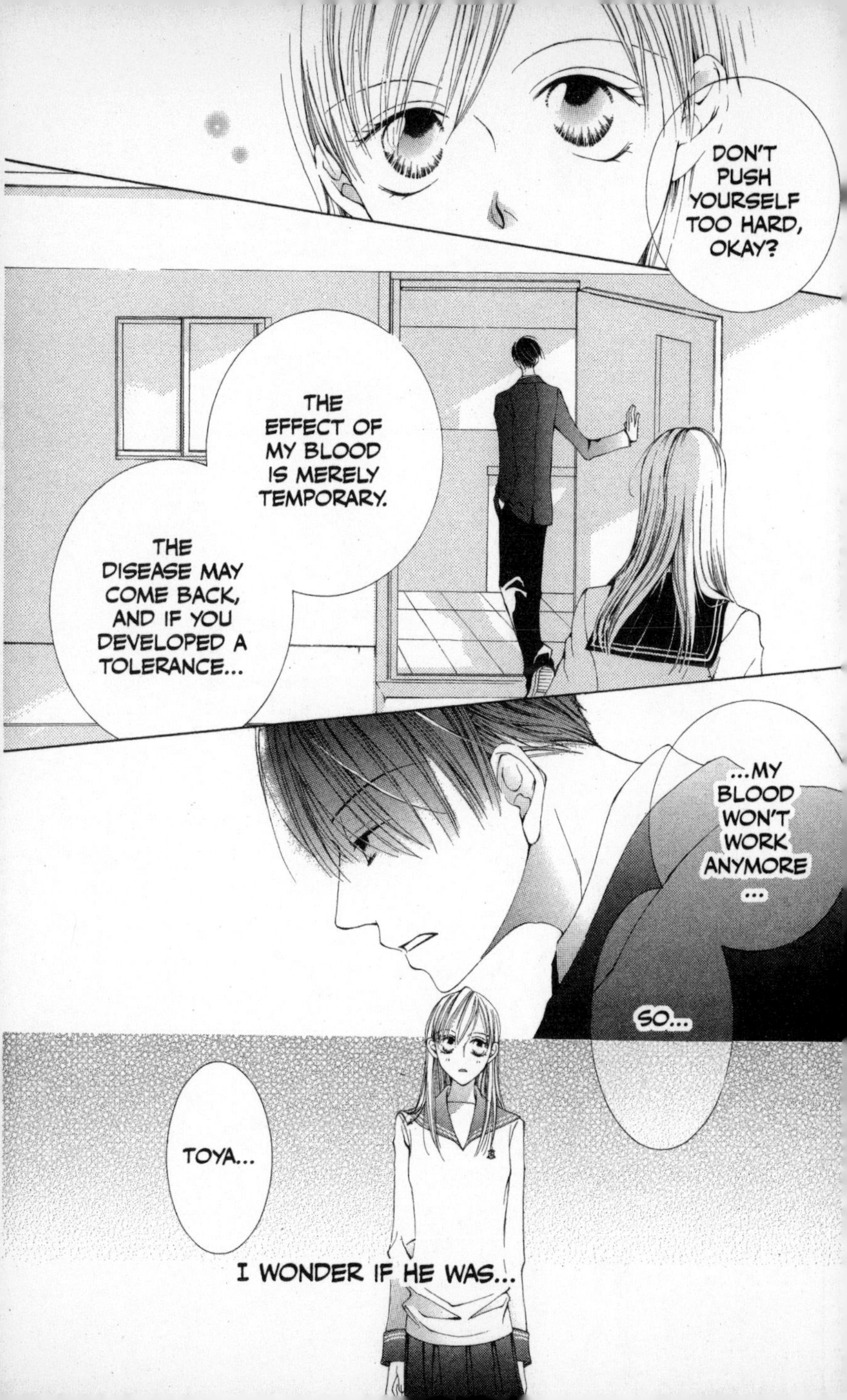
DON'T PUSH YOURSELF TOO HARD, OKAY?
THE EFFECT OF MY BLOOD IS MERELY TEMPORARY.
THE DISEASE MAY COME BACK, AND IF YOU DEVELOPED A TOLERANCE...
...MY BLOOD WON'T WORK ANYMORE...
SO...
TOYA...
I WONDER IF HE WAS...

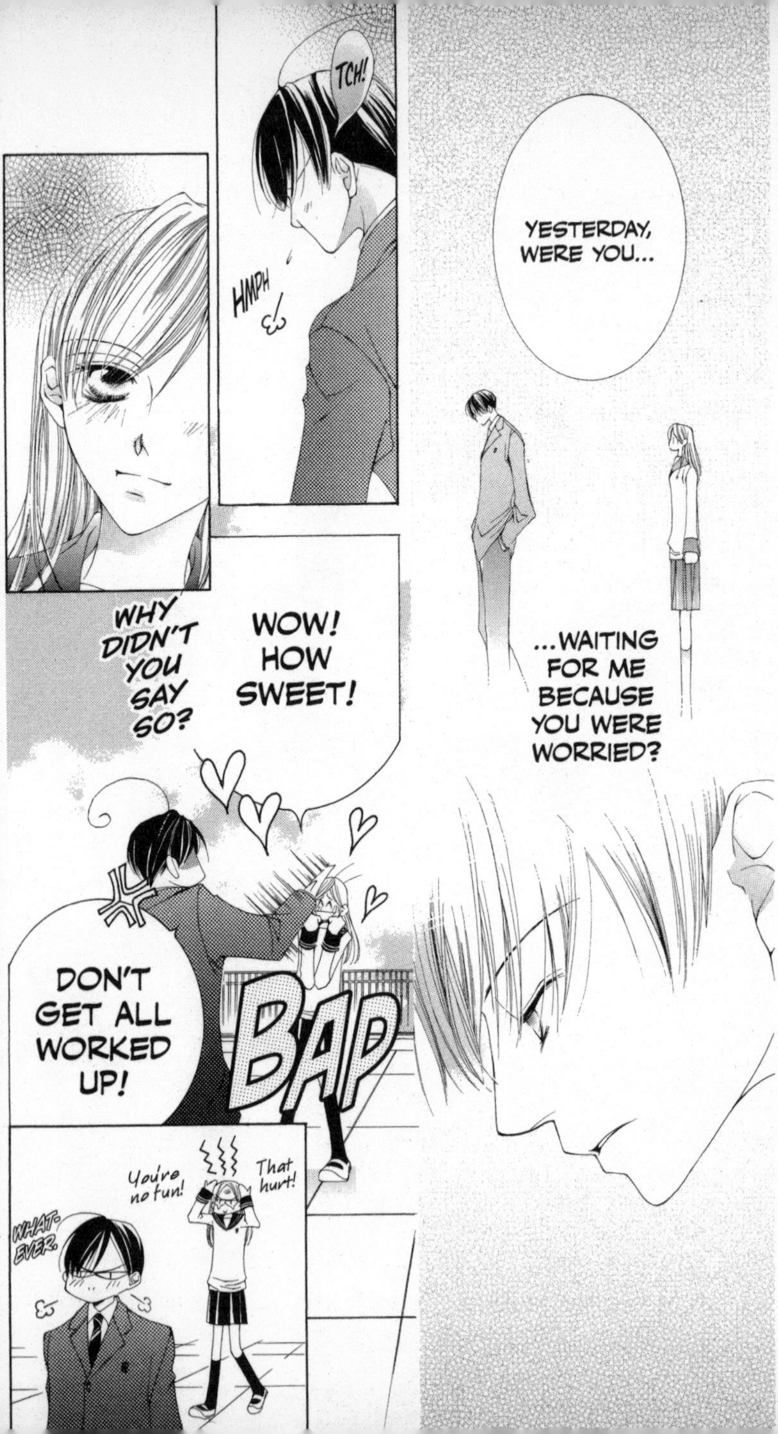
YESTERDAY, WERE YOU...
...WAITING FOR ME BECAUSE YOU WERE WORRIED?
TCH!
HMPH
WOW! HOW SWEET!
WHY DIDN'T YOU SAY SO?
DON'T GET ALL WORKED UP!
BAP
That hurt!
You're no fun!
WHAT-EVER.

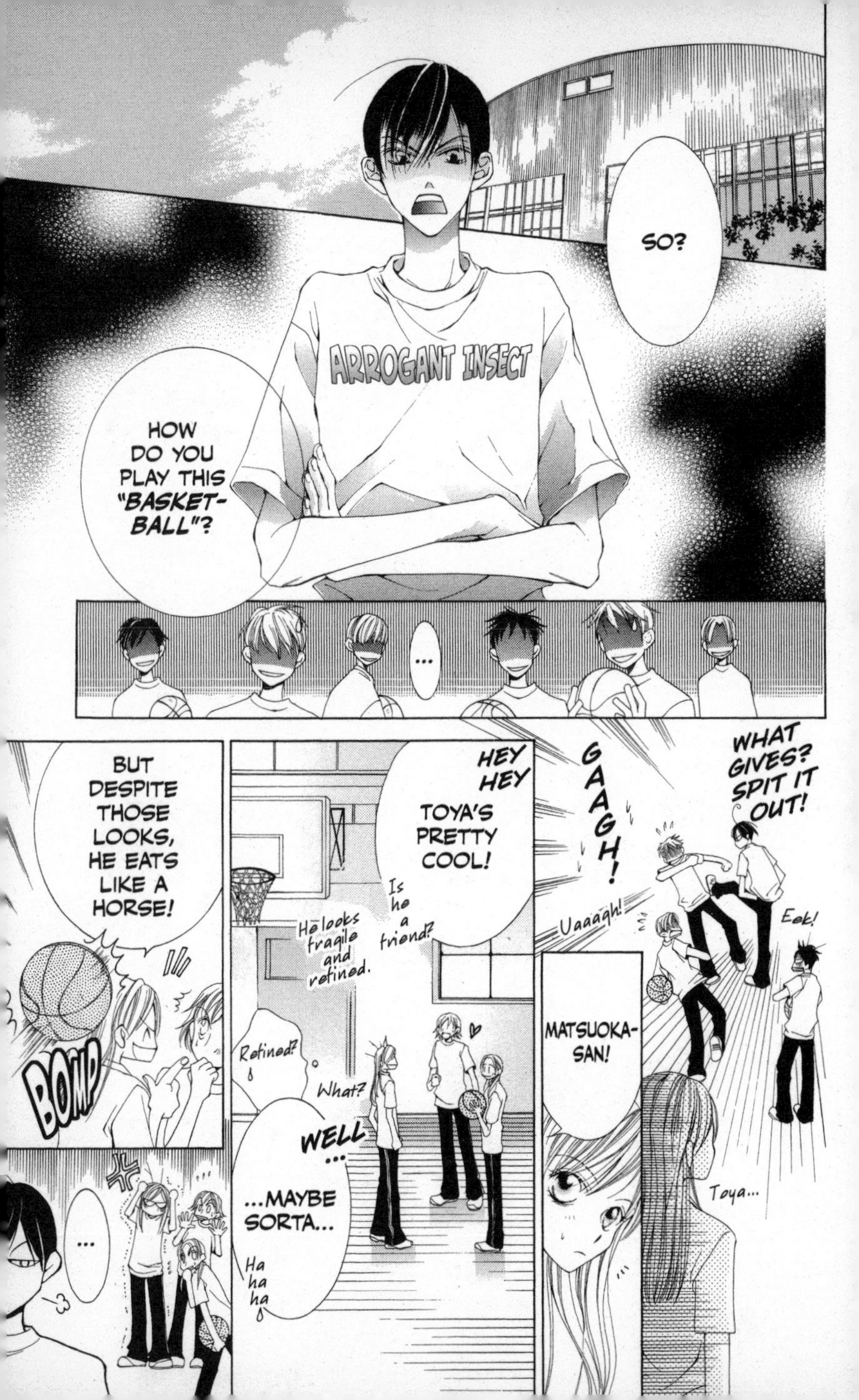
SO?
HOW DO YOU PLAY THIS "BASKET-BALL"?
ARROGANT INSECT
...
WHAT GIVES? SPIT IT OUT!
GAAGH!
Uaaagh!
Eek!
MATSUOKA-SAN!
Toya...
HEY HEY
TOYA'S PRETTY COOL!
Is he a friend?
He looks fragile and refined.
Refined?
What?
WELL...
...MAYBE SORTA...
Ha ha ha
BUT DESPITE THOSE LOOKS, HE EATS LIKE A HORSE!
BOMP
...

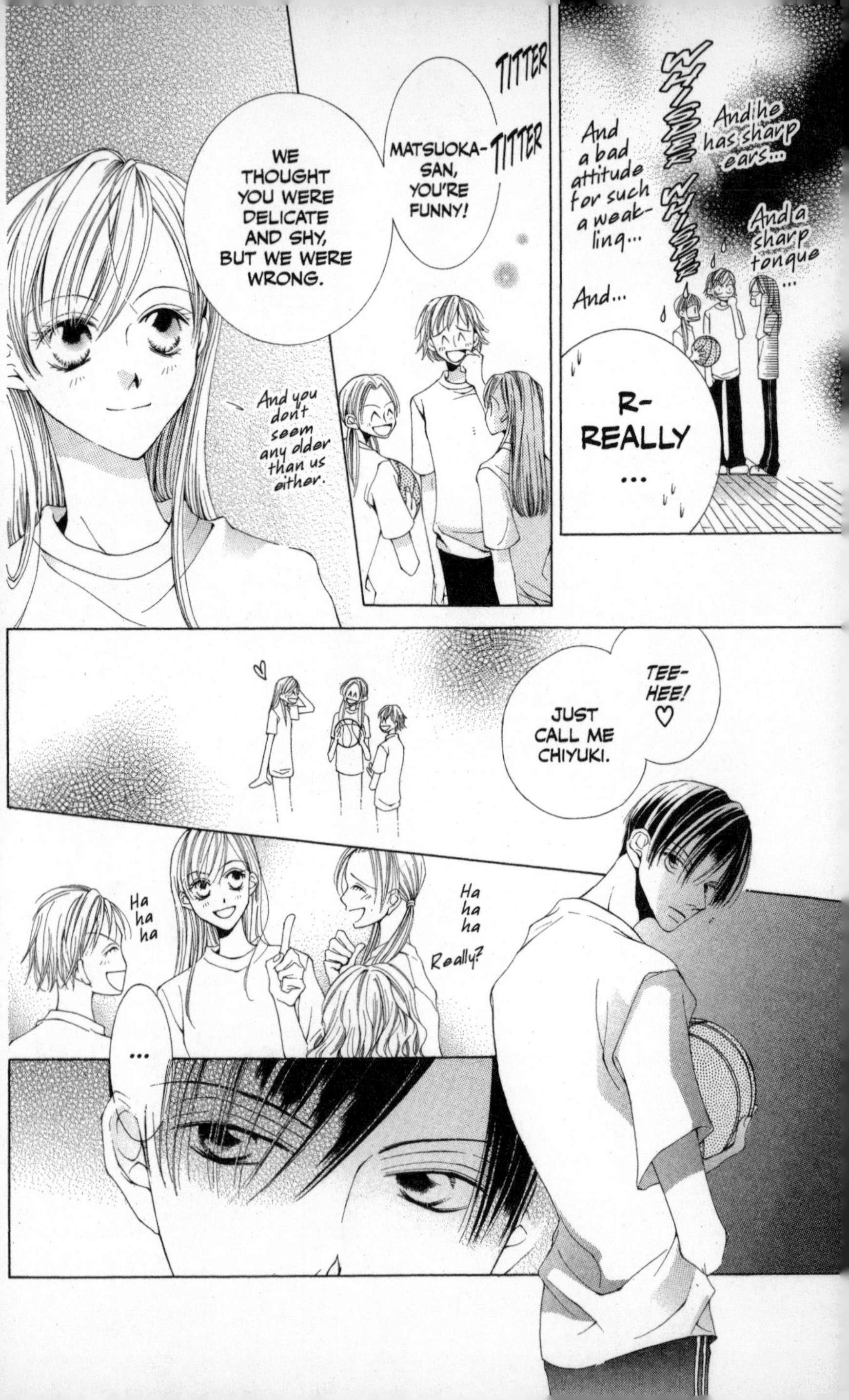
And he has sharp ears...
And a sharp tongue...
And a bad attitude for such a weakling...
And...
R-REALLY...
TITTER
TITTER
MATSUOKA-SAN, YOU'RE FUNNY!
WE THOUGHT YOU WERE DELICATE AND SHY, BUT WE WERE WRONG.
And you don't seem any older than us either.
TEE-HEE! ♡
JUST CALL ME CHIYUKI.
Ha ha ha
Really?
Ha ha ha
...

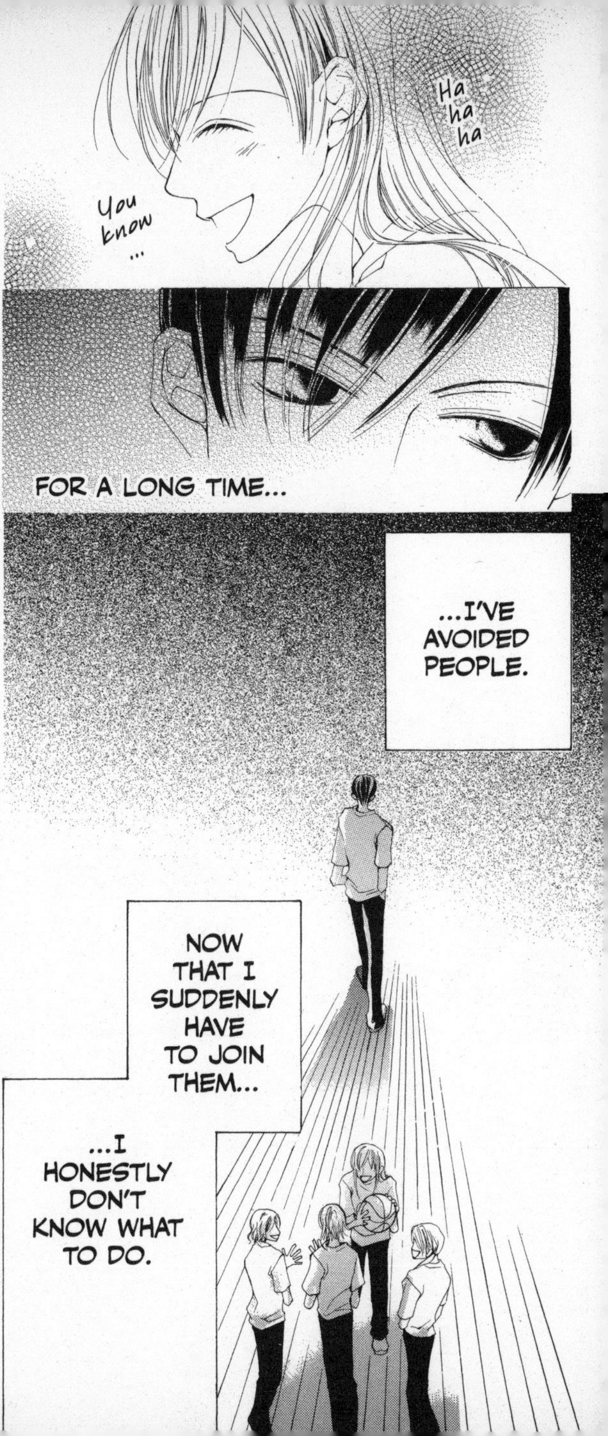
Ha ha ha
You know ...
FOR A LONG TIME...
...I'VE AVOIDED PEOPLE.
NOW THAT I SUDDENLY HAVE TO JOIN THEM...
...I HONESTLY DON'T KNOW WHAT TO DO.

02

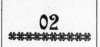

MANY PEOPLE ASK ME ABOUT MY PEN NAME, SO HERE I GO...

WITH "HATORI," I WANTED TO USE A JAPANESE CHARACTER FROM MY REAL NAME AND AT THE SAME TIME INCLUDE THE SOUND "HATO."

THE "BIS" OF "BISCO" SIGNIFIES A SCREW. I HAVE A WEAK SPOT FOR ITEMS REPRESENTATIVE OF THE PAST, LIKE SPRING-WOUND DEVICES.

AT FIRST I THOUGHT ABOUT "NEJIKO," BUT "BISCO" SOUNDS LIKE "BISQUE DOLL" (OR DOES IT?) AND THE VOWEL SOUNDS ARE SIMILAR TO THOSE IN MY REAL NAME. MANY PEOPLE HAVE TOLD ME THAT IT'S AN EASY NAME TO REMEMBER, SO I'M PRETTY HAPPY WITH IT.

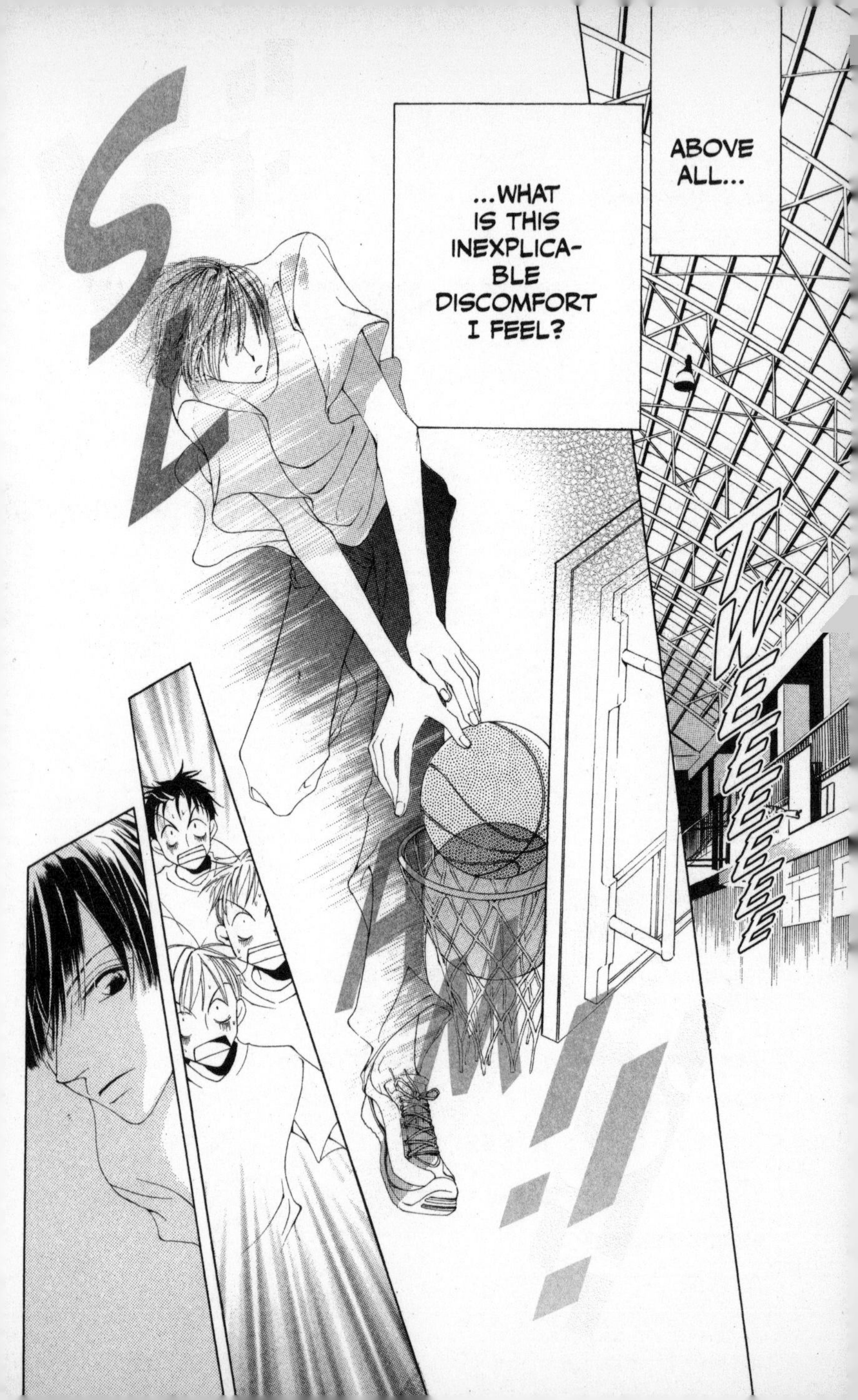
ABOVE ALL...
...WHAT IS THIS INEXPLICA-BLE DISCOMFORT I FEEL?
TWEEEEEE
SLAM!!

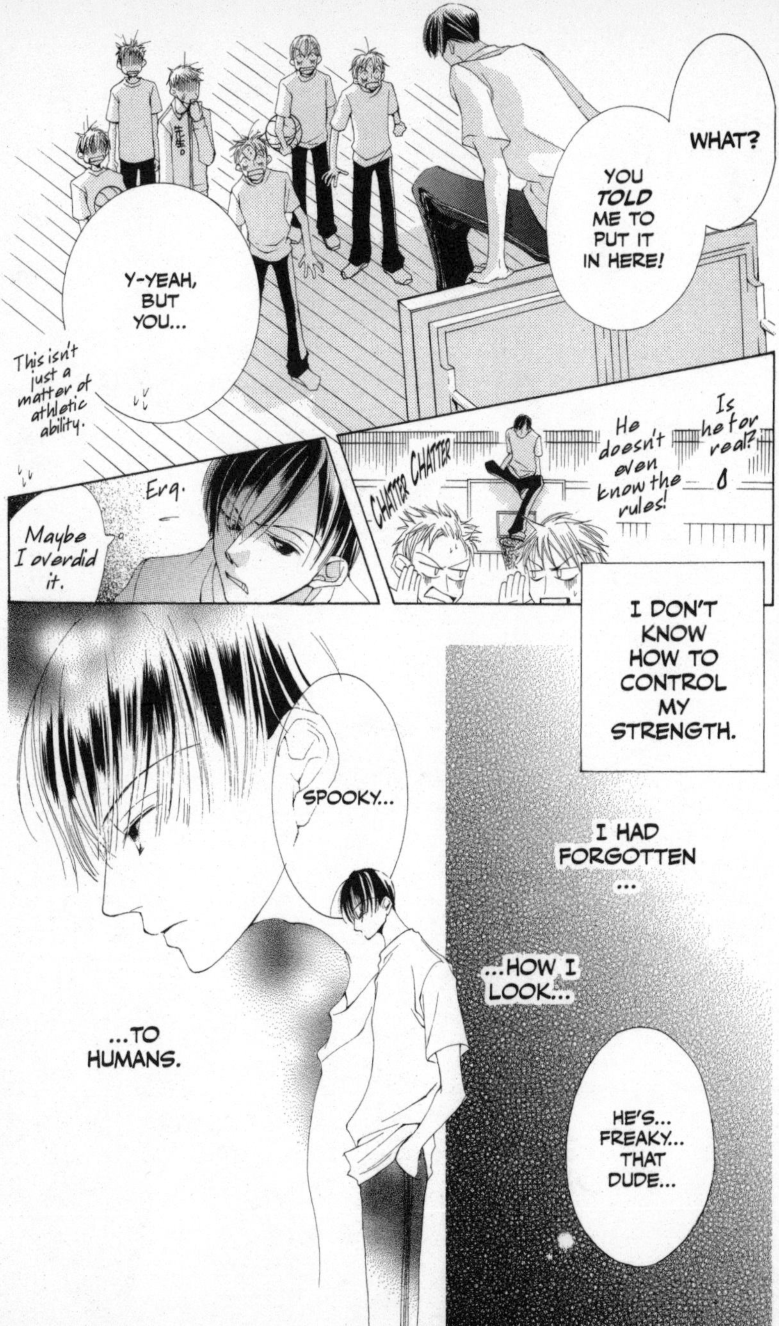
WHAT?
YOU TOLD ME TO PUT IT IN HERE!
Y-YEAH, BUT YOU...
This isn't just a matter of athletic ability.
Is he for real?
He doesn't even know the rules!
CHATTER CHATTER
Erg.
Maybe I overdid it.
I DON'T KNOW HOW TO CONTROL MY STRENGTH.
I HAD FORGOTTEN ...
SPOOKY...
...HOW I LOOK...
HE'S... FREAKY... THAT DUDE...
...TO HUMANS.

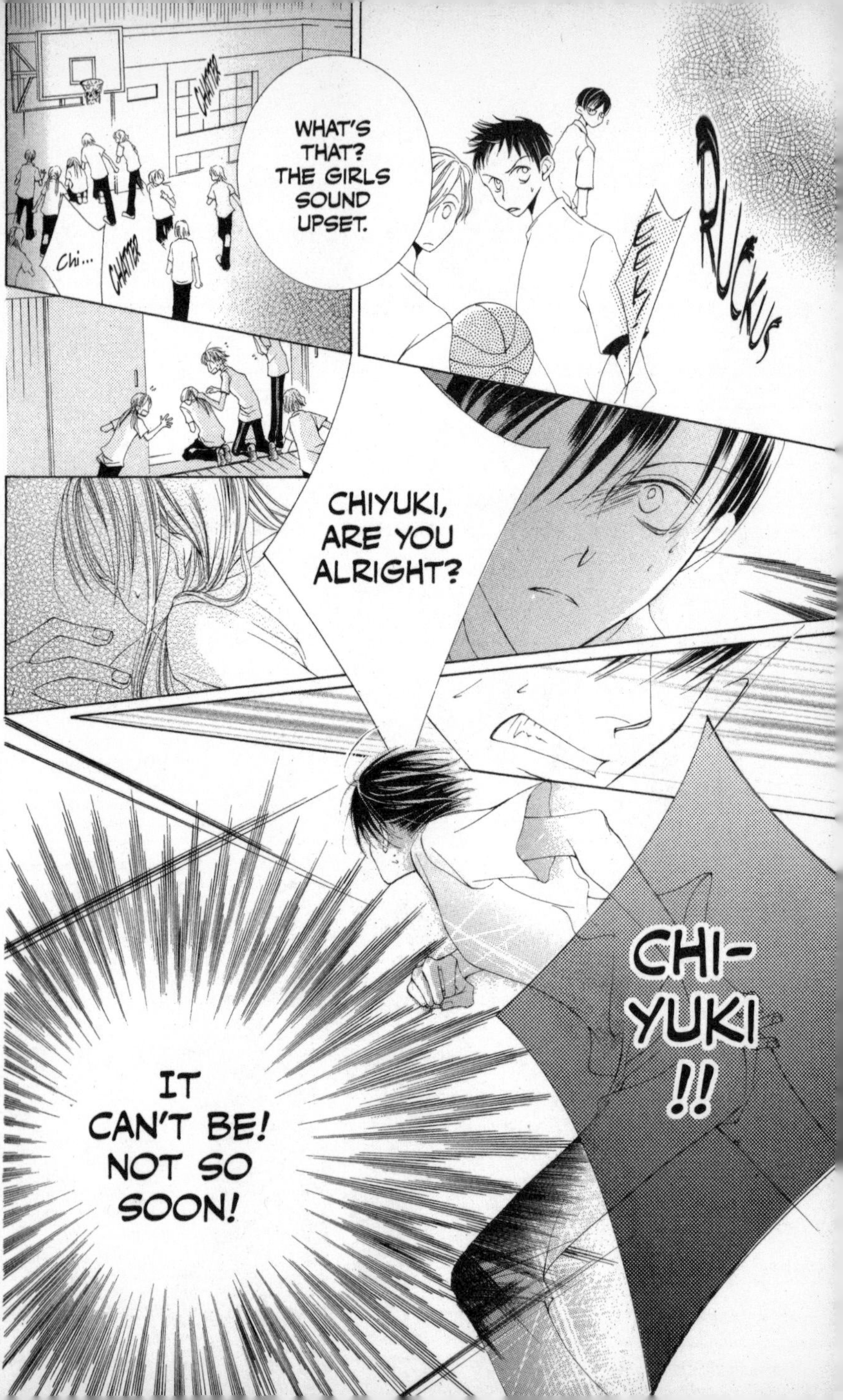
RUCKUS
EEK!
WHAT'S THAT? THE GIRLS SOUND UPSET.
CHATTER
Chi...
CHATTER
CHIYUKI, ARE YOU ALRIGHT?
CHI-YUKI!!
IT CAN'T BE! NOT SO SOON!

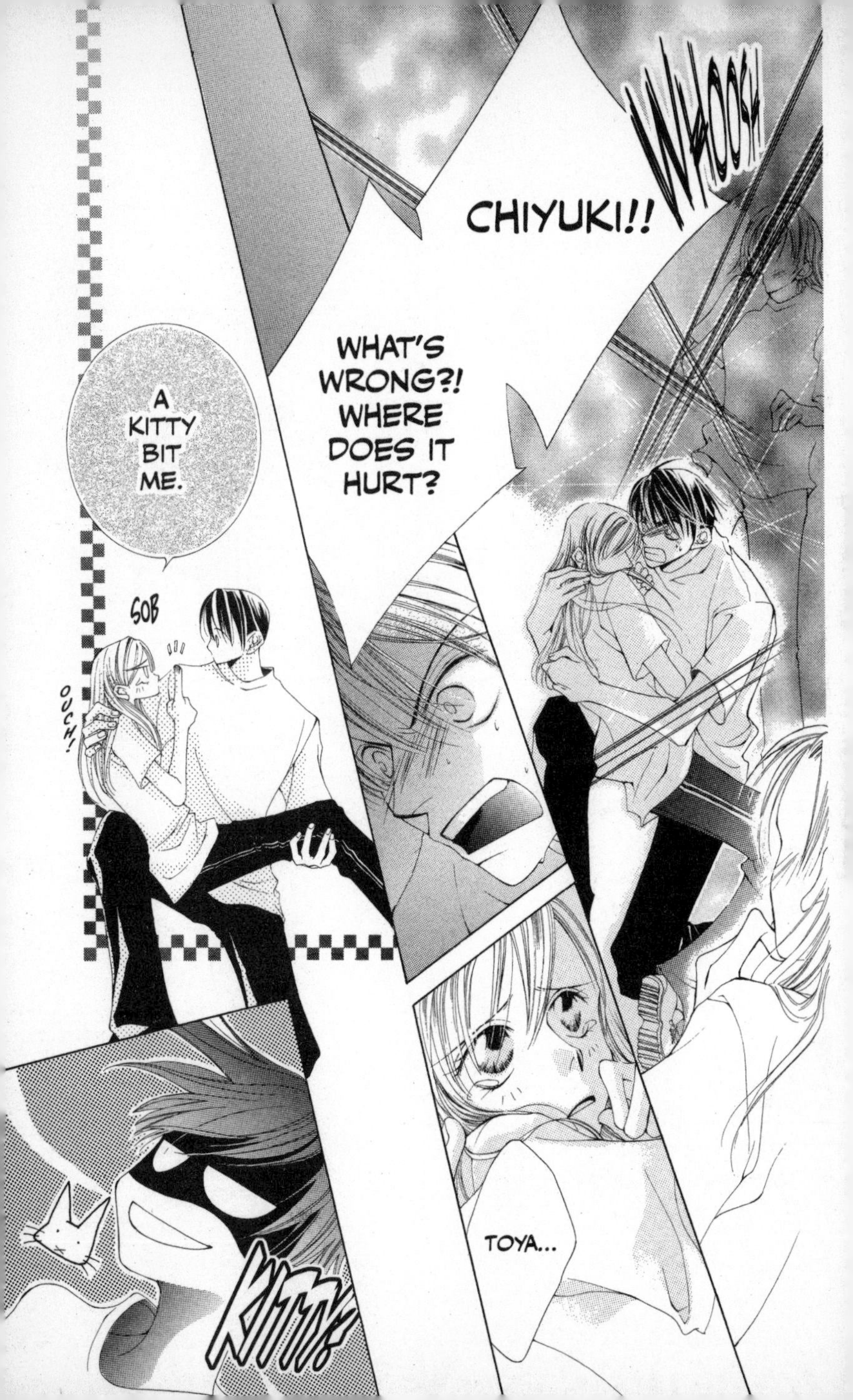
WHOOSH
CHIYUKI!!
WHAT'S WRONG?! WHERE DOES IT HURT?
A KITTY BIT ME.
SOB
OUCH!
TOYA...

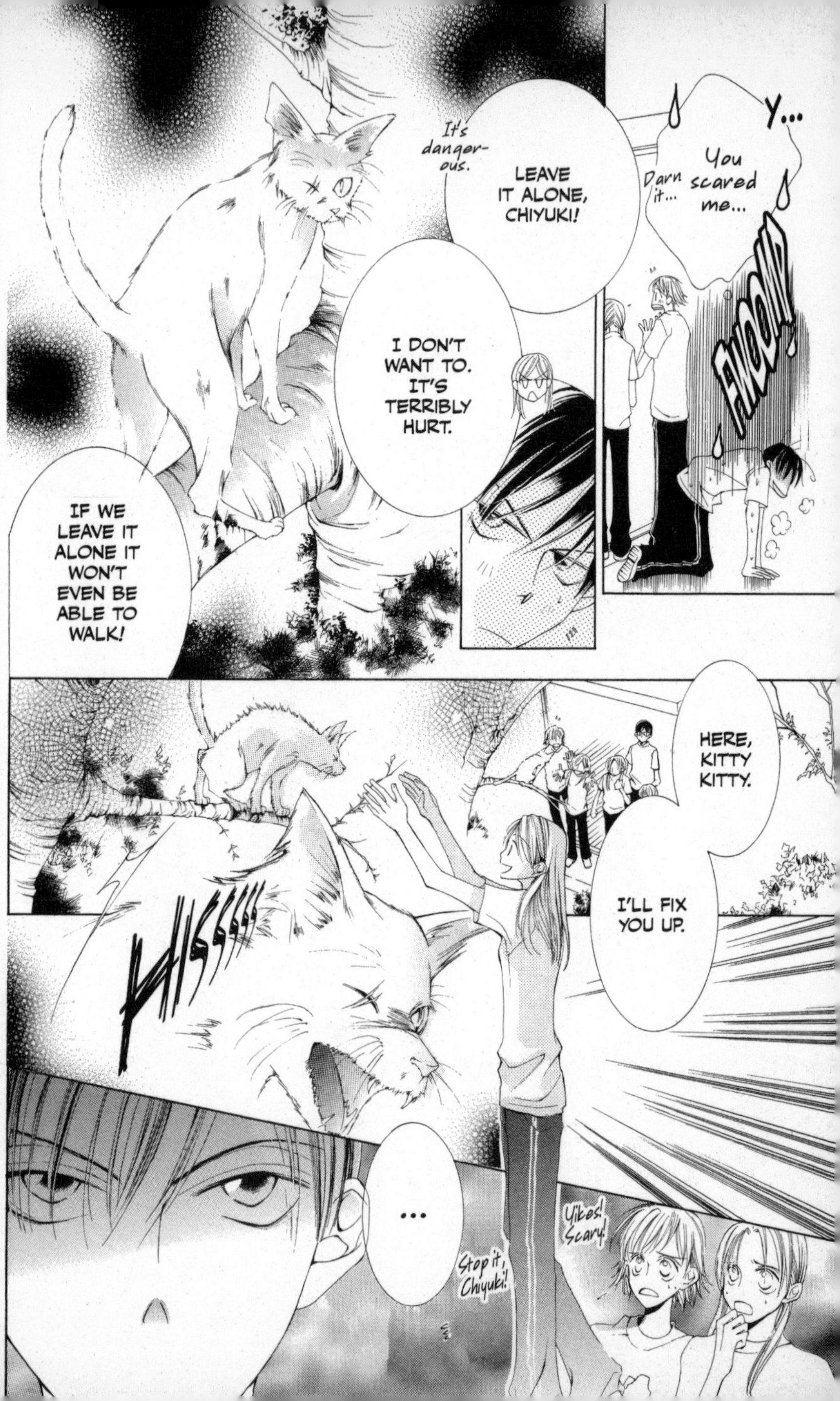
Y...
You scared me...
Darn it...
FWOOM!!
LEAVE IT ALONE, CHIYUKI!
It's danger-ous.
I DON'T WANT TO. IT'S TERRIBLY HURT.
IF WE LEAVE IT ALONE IT WON'T EVEN BE ABLE TO WALK!
HERE, KITTY KITTY.
I'LL FIX YOU UP.
HISSSSS
...
Stop it, Chiyuki!
Yikes! Scary!

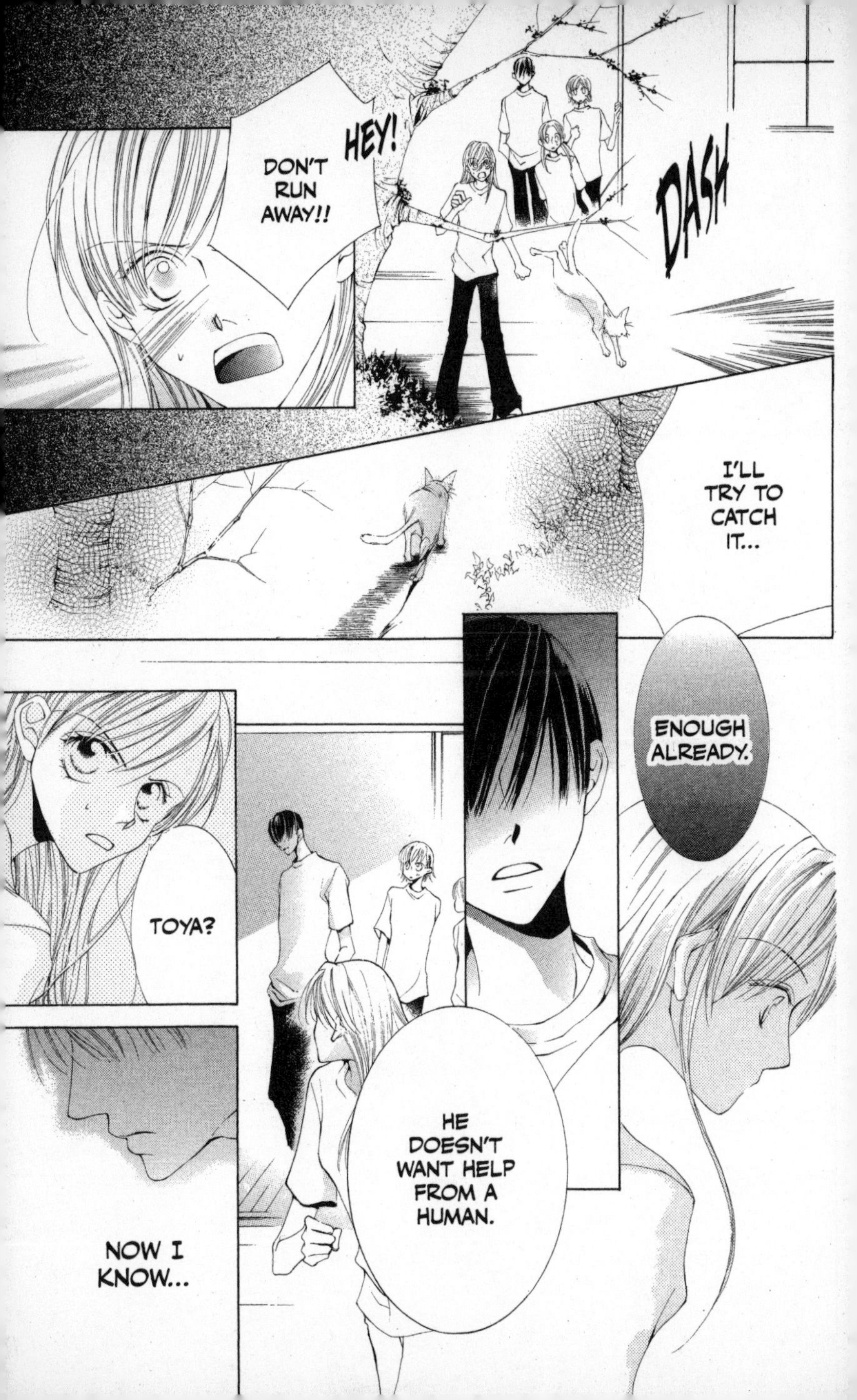
DASH
HEY!
DON'T RUN AWAY!!
I'LL TRY TO CATCH IT...
ENOUGH ALREADY.
HE DOESN'T WANT HELP FROM A HUMAN.
TOYA?
NOW I KNOW...

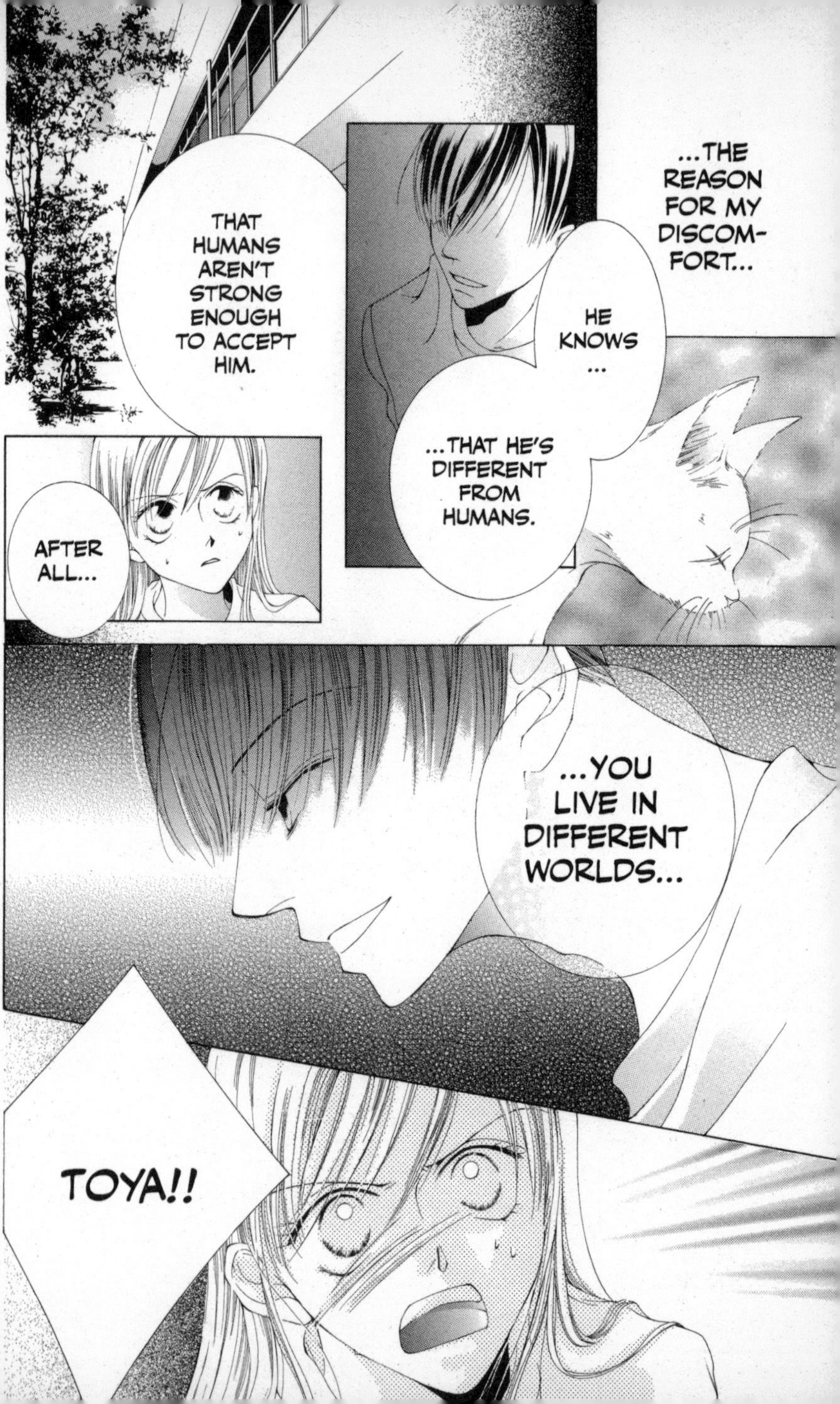
...THE REASON FOR MY DISCOMFORT...
HE KNOWS...
...THAT HE'S DIFFERENT FROM HUMANS.
THAT HUMANS AREN'T STRONG ENOUGH TO ACCEPT HIM.
AFTER ALL...
...YOU LIVE IN DIFFERENT WORLDS...
TOYA!!

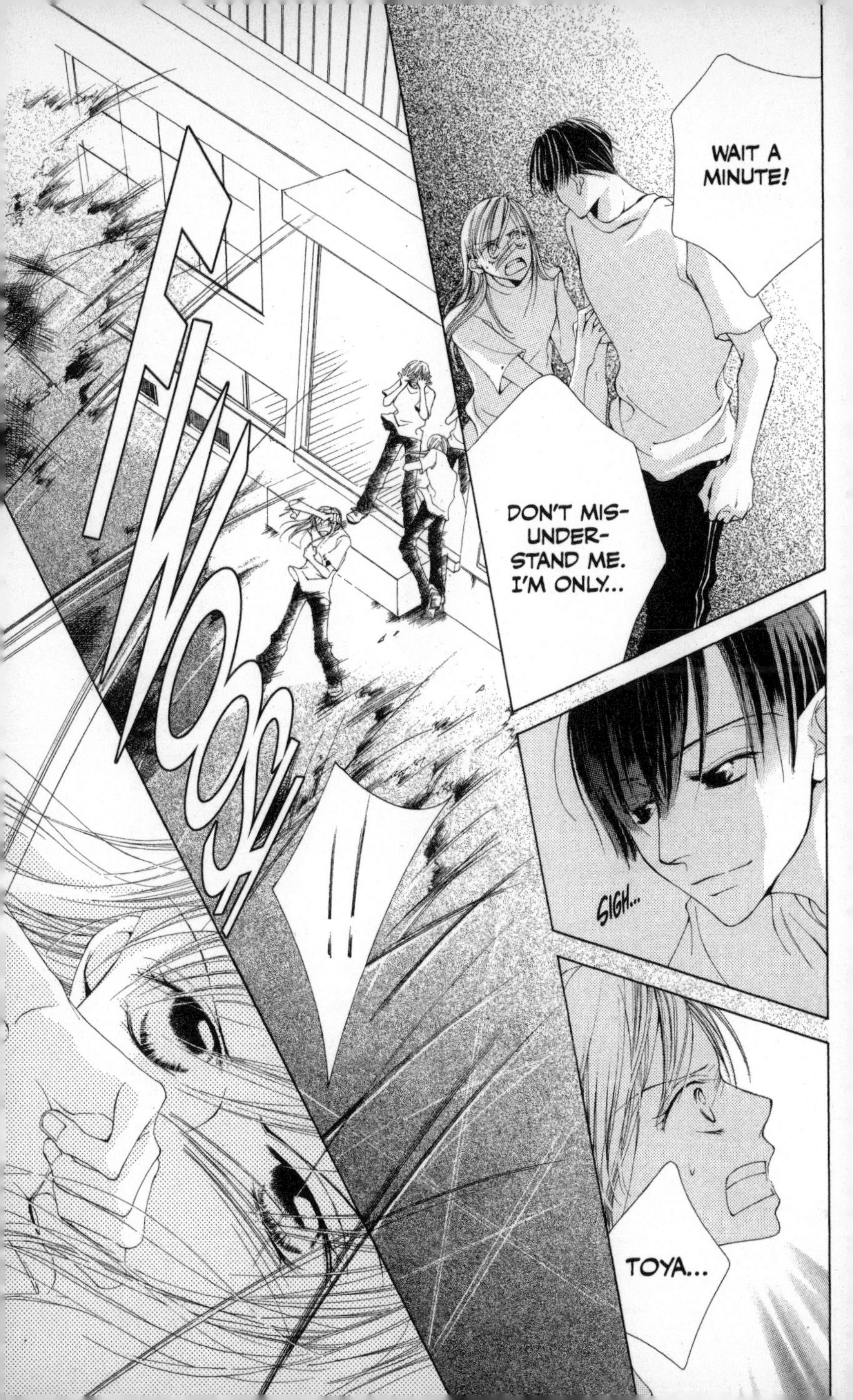
WAIT A MINUTE!
DON'T MIS-UNDER-STAND ME. I'M ONLY...
FWOOSH!
!!
SIGH...
TOYA...

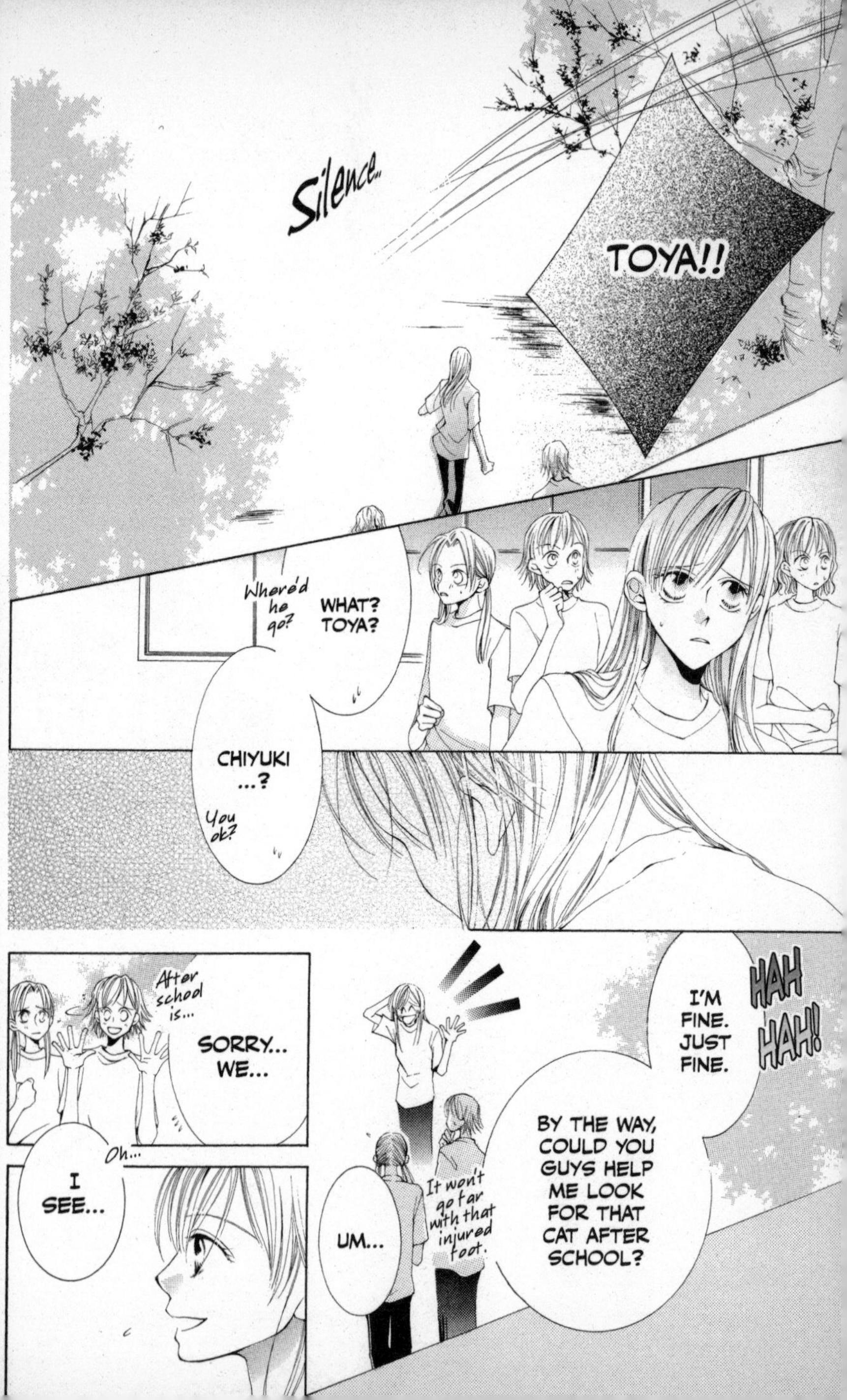
TOYA!!
Silence...
WHAT? TOYA?
Where'd he go?
CHIYUKI ...?
You ok?
HAH HAH!
I'M FINE. JUST FINE.
BY THE WAY, COULD YOU GUYS HELP ME LOOK FOR THAT CAT AFTER SCHOOL?
It won't go far with that injured foot.
UM...
SORRY... WE...
After school is...
Oh...
I SEE...

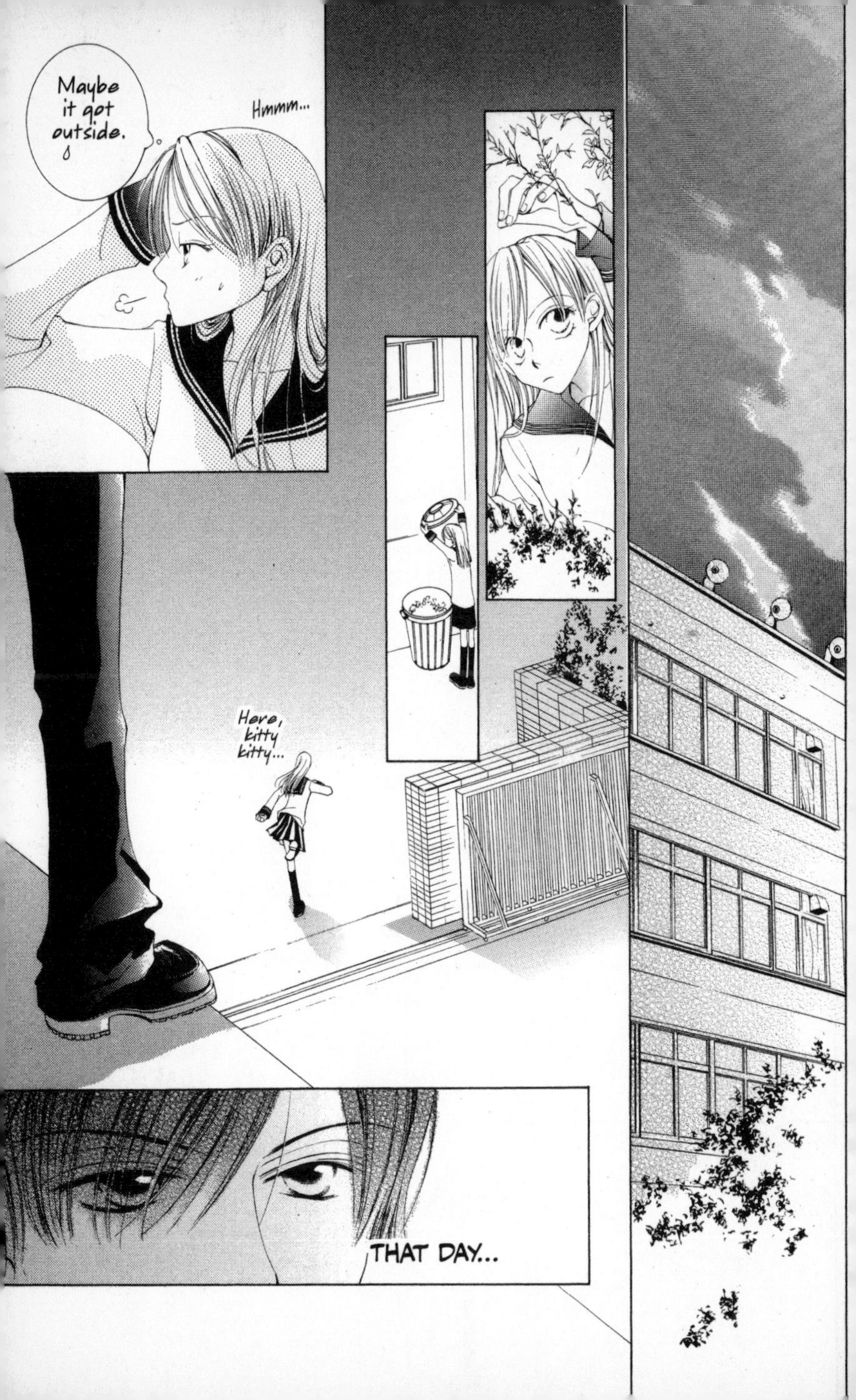
Hmmm...
Maybe it got outside.
Here, kitty kitty...
THAT DAY...

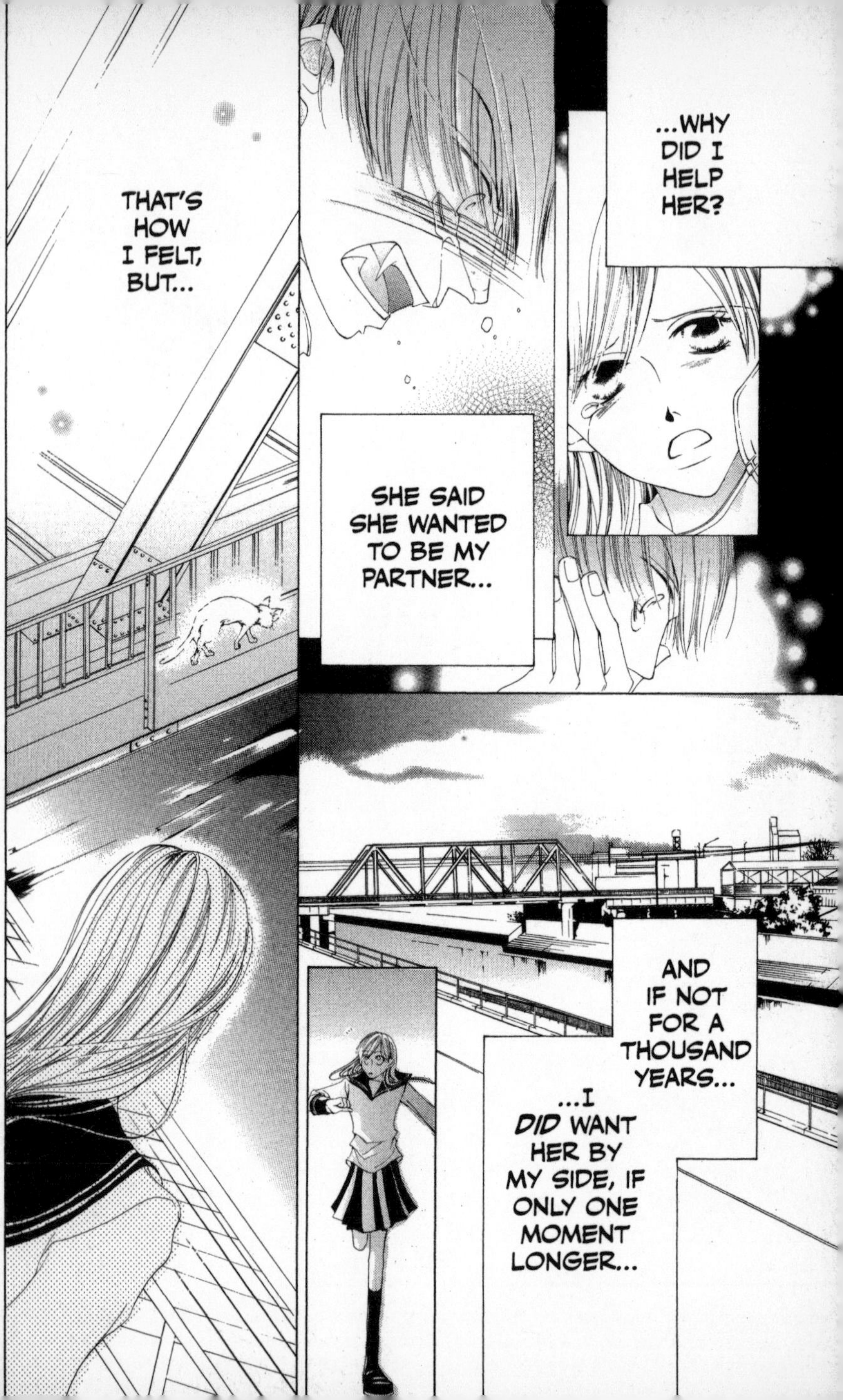
...WHY DID I HELP HER?
SHE SAID SHE WANTED TO BE MY PARTNER...
AND IF NOT FOR A THOUSAND YEARS...
...I *DID* WANT HER BY MY SIDE, IF ONLY ONE MOMENT LONGER...
THAT'S HOW I FELT, BUT...

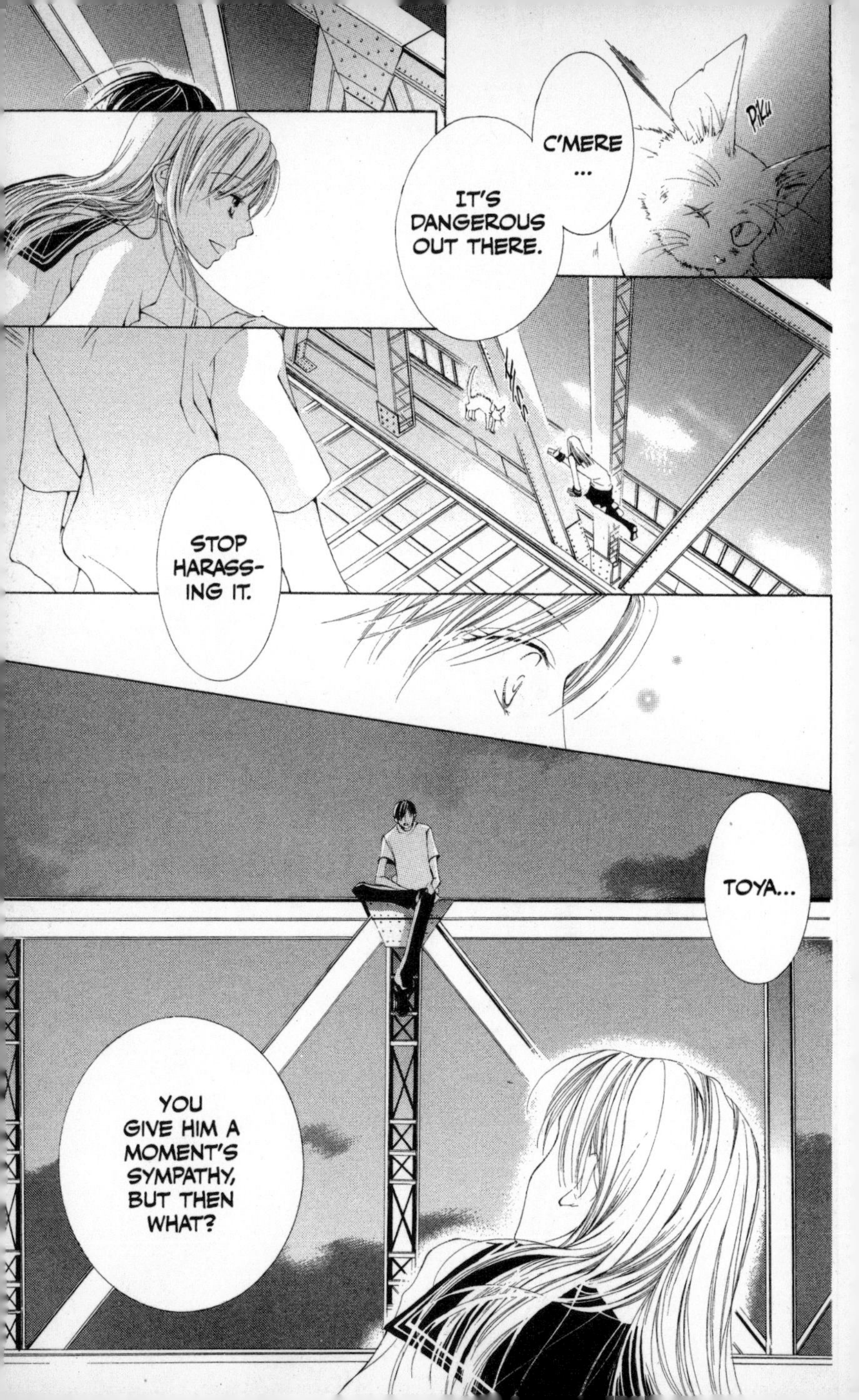
PIKU
C'MERE ...
IT'S DANGEROUS OUT THERE.
HISS
STOP HARASS-ING IT.
TOYA...
YOU GIVE HIM A MOMENT'S SYMPATHY, BUT THEN WHAT?

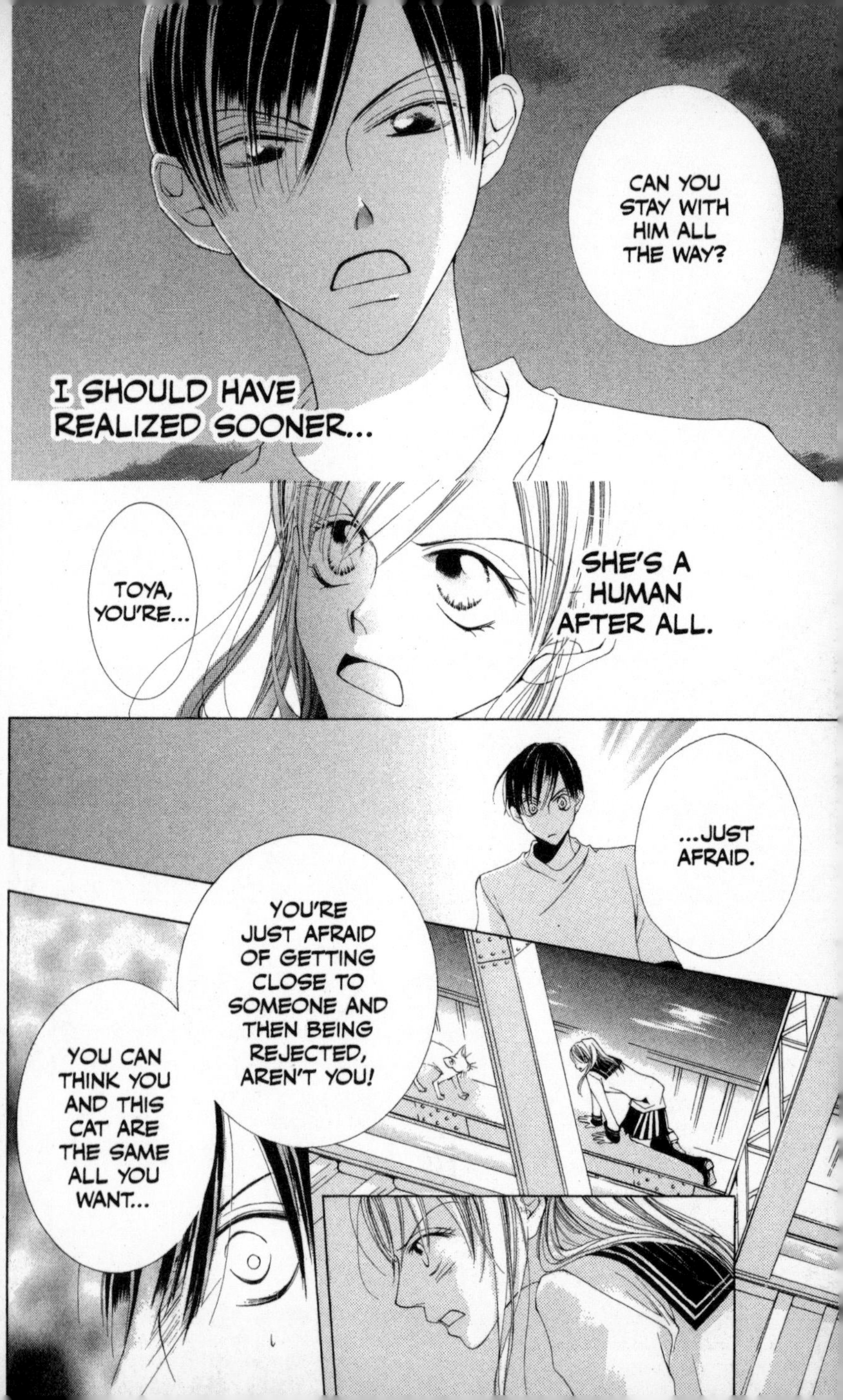
CAN YOU STAY WITH HIM ALL THE WAY?
I SHOULD HAVE REALIZED SOONER...
SHE'S A HUMAN AFTER ALL.
TOYA, YOU'RE...
...JUST AFRAID.
YOU'RE JUST AFRAID OF GETTING CLOSE TO SOMEONE AND THEN BEING REJECTED, AREN'T YOU!
YOU CAN THINK YOU AND THIS CAT ARE THE SAME ALL YOU WANT...

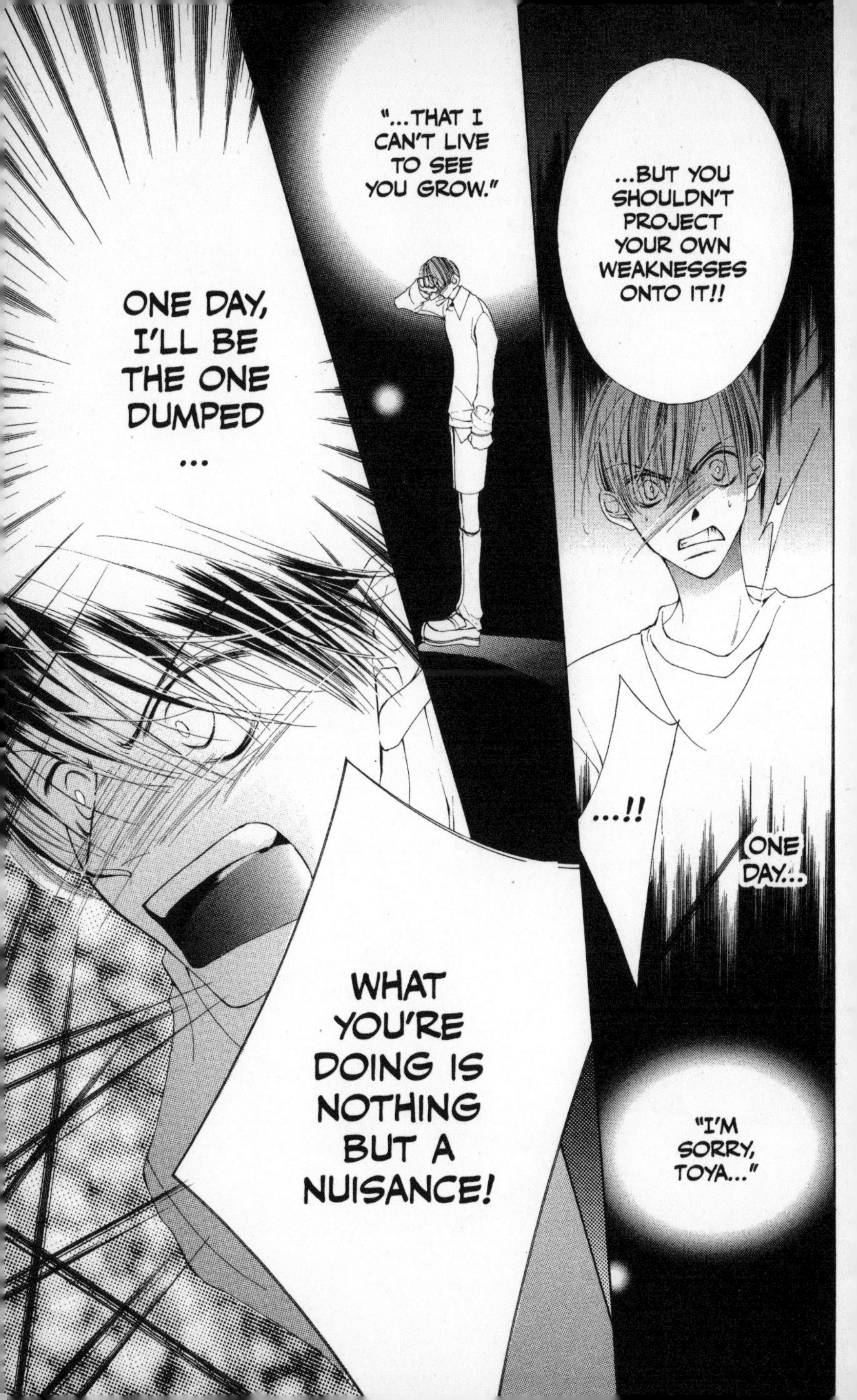
...BUT YOU SHOULDN'T PROJECT YOUR OWN WEAKNESSES ONTO IT!!
"...THAT I CAN'T LIVE TO SEE YOU GROW."
ONE DAY, I'LL BE THE ONE DUMPED ...
...!!
ONE DAY...
WHAT YOU'RE DOING IS NOTHING BUT A NUISANCE!
"I'M SORRY, TOYA..."

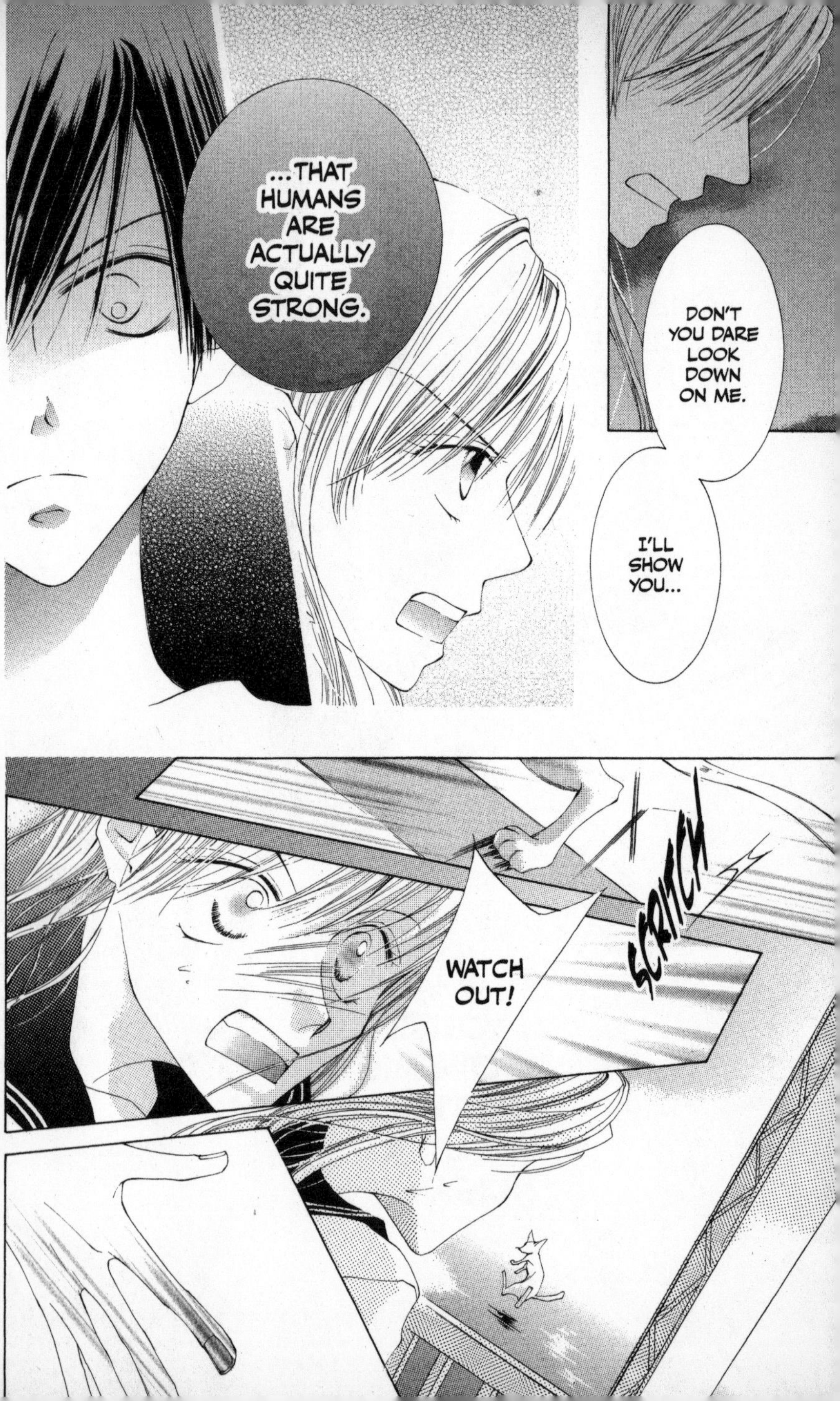
DON'T YOU DARE LOOK DOWN ON ME.
I'LL SHOW YOU...
...THAT HUMANS ARE ACTUALLY QUITE STRONG.
SCRITCH
WATCH OUT!

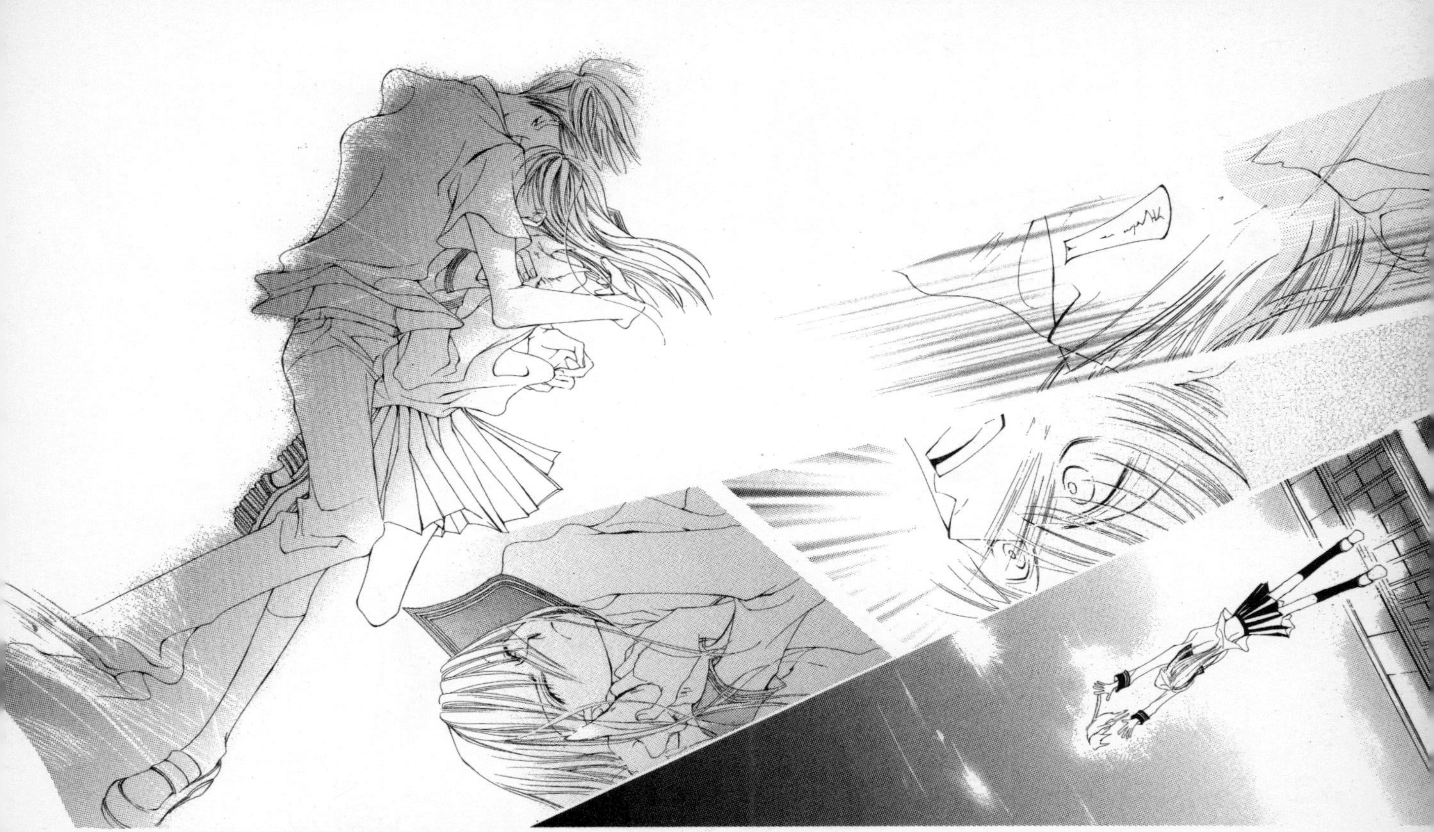

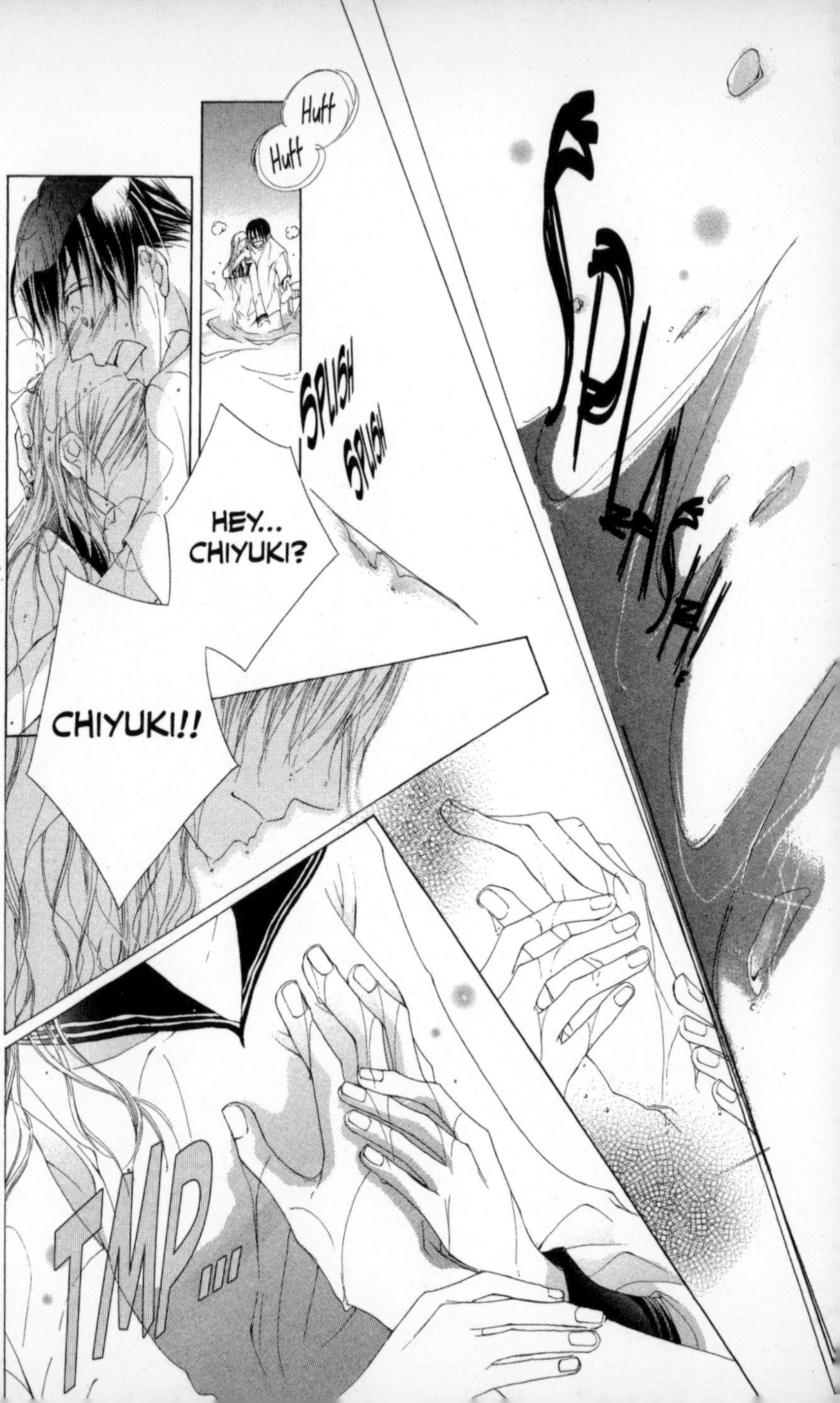
SPLASH!!
Huff
Huff
SPLISH
SPLISH
HEY... CHIYUKI?
CHIYUKI!!
TMP...

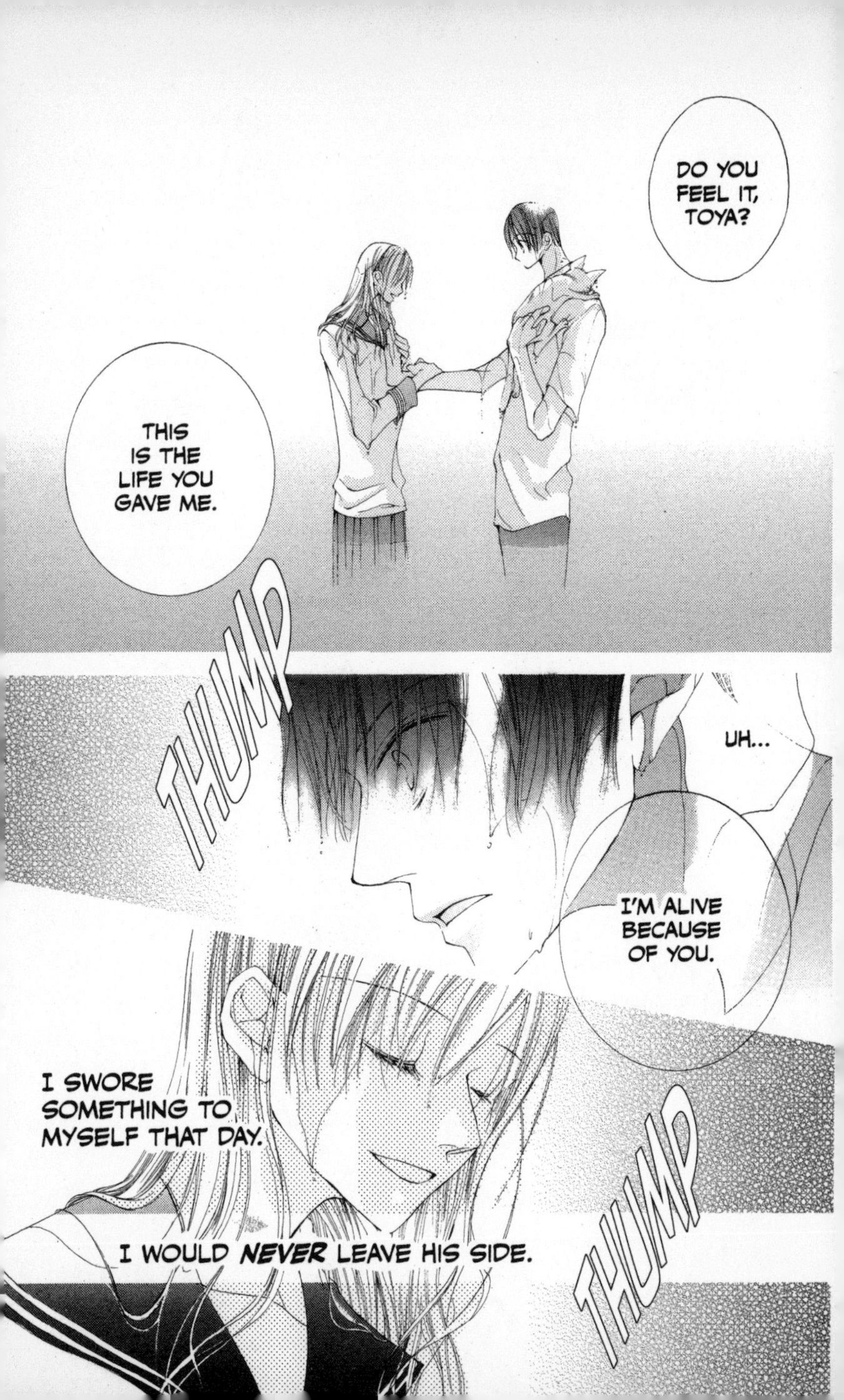
DO YOU FEEL IT, TOYA?
THIS IS THE LIFE YOU GAVE ME.
THUMP
UH...
I'M ALIVE BECAUSE OF YOU.
THUMP
I SWORE SOMETHING TO MYSELF THAT DAY.
I WOULD NEVER LEAVE HIS SIDE.

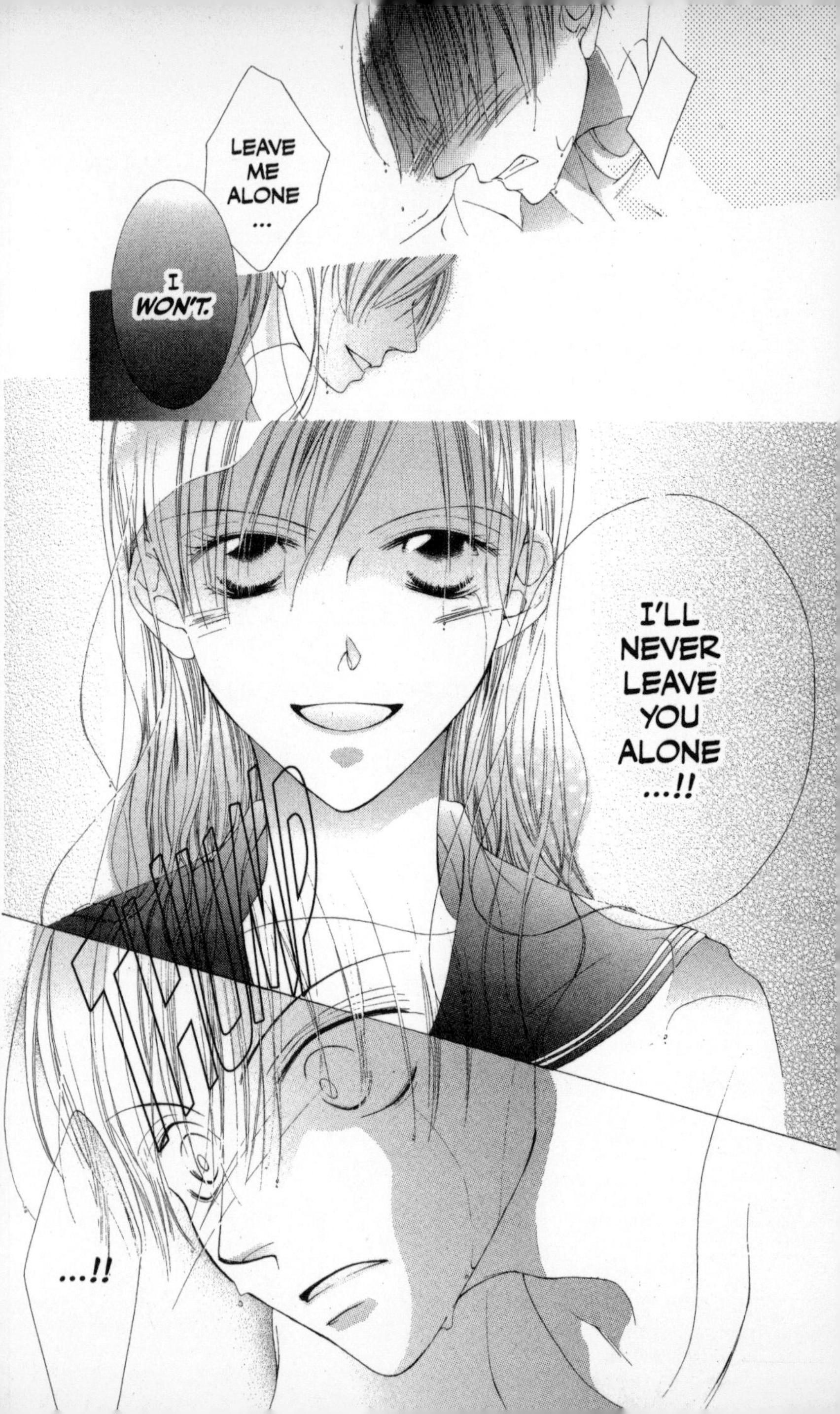
LEAVE ME ALONE ...
I WON'T.
I'LL NEVER LEAVE YOU ALONE ...!!
THUMP
...!!

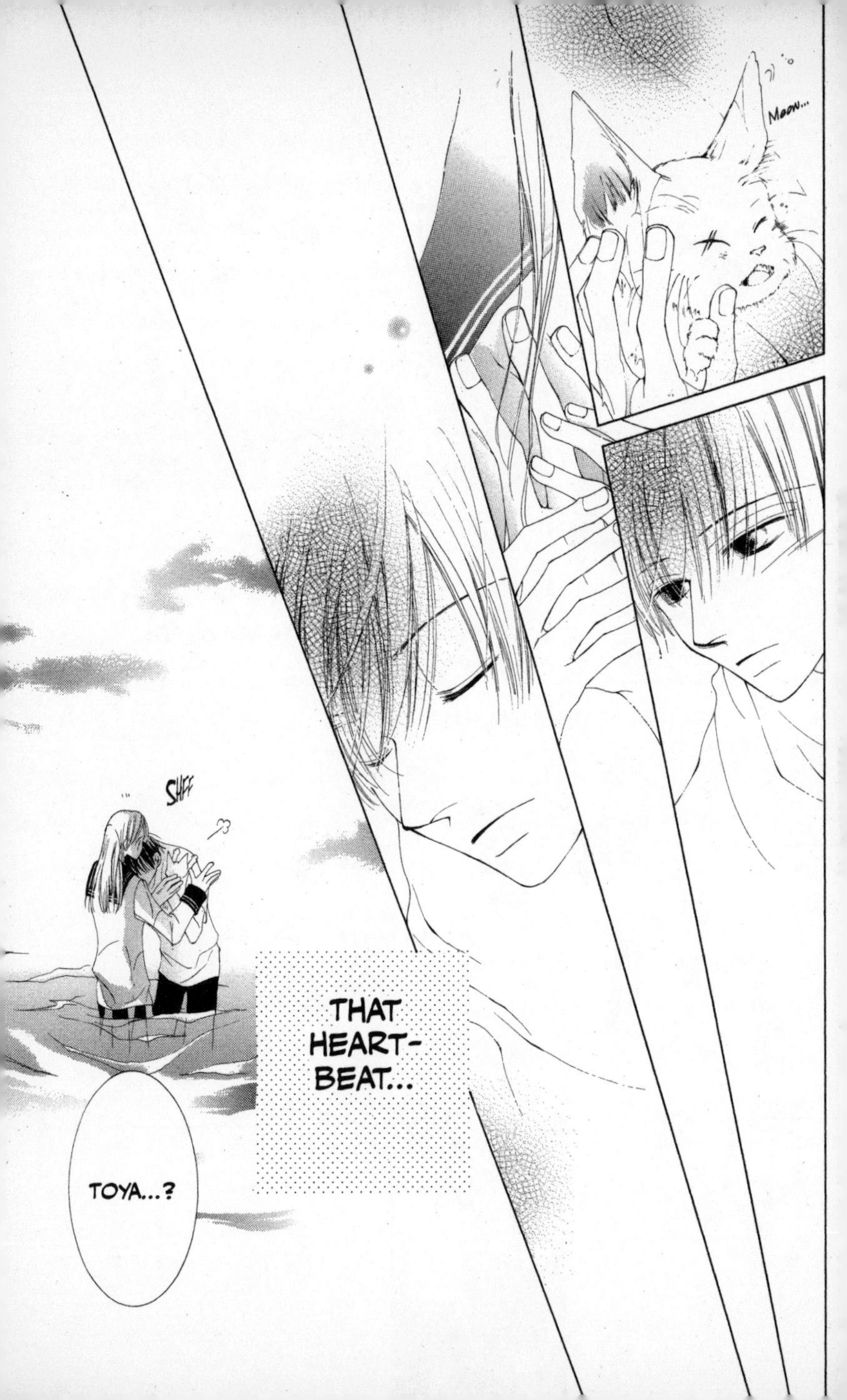
Meow...
THAT HEART-BEAT...
SHFF
TOYA...?

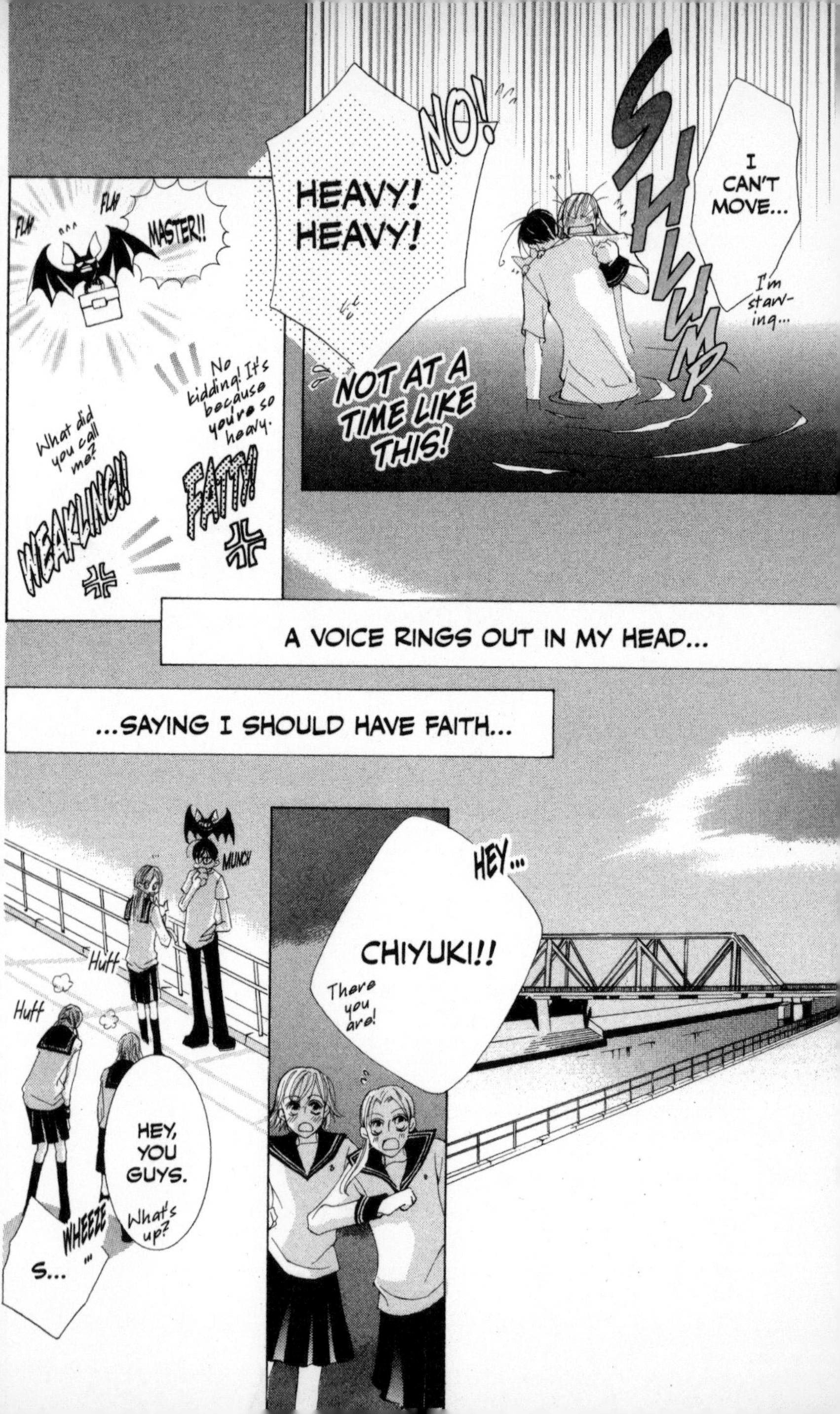
I CAN'T MOVE...
I'm starving...
SHLUMP
NO!
HEAVY! HEAVY!
NOT AT A TIME LIKE THIS!
FLAP
FLAP
MASTER!!
No kidding! It's because you're so heavy.
FAITH!
What did you call me?
WEAKLING!!
A VOICE RINGS OUT IN MY HEAD...
...SAYING I SHOULD HAVE FAITH...
HEY...
CHIYUKI!!
There you are!
MUNCH
Huff
Huff
HEY, YOU GUYS.
What's up?
WHEEZE
S...

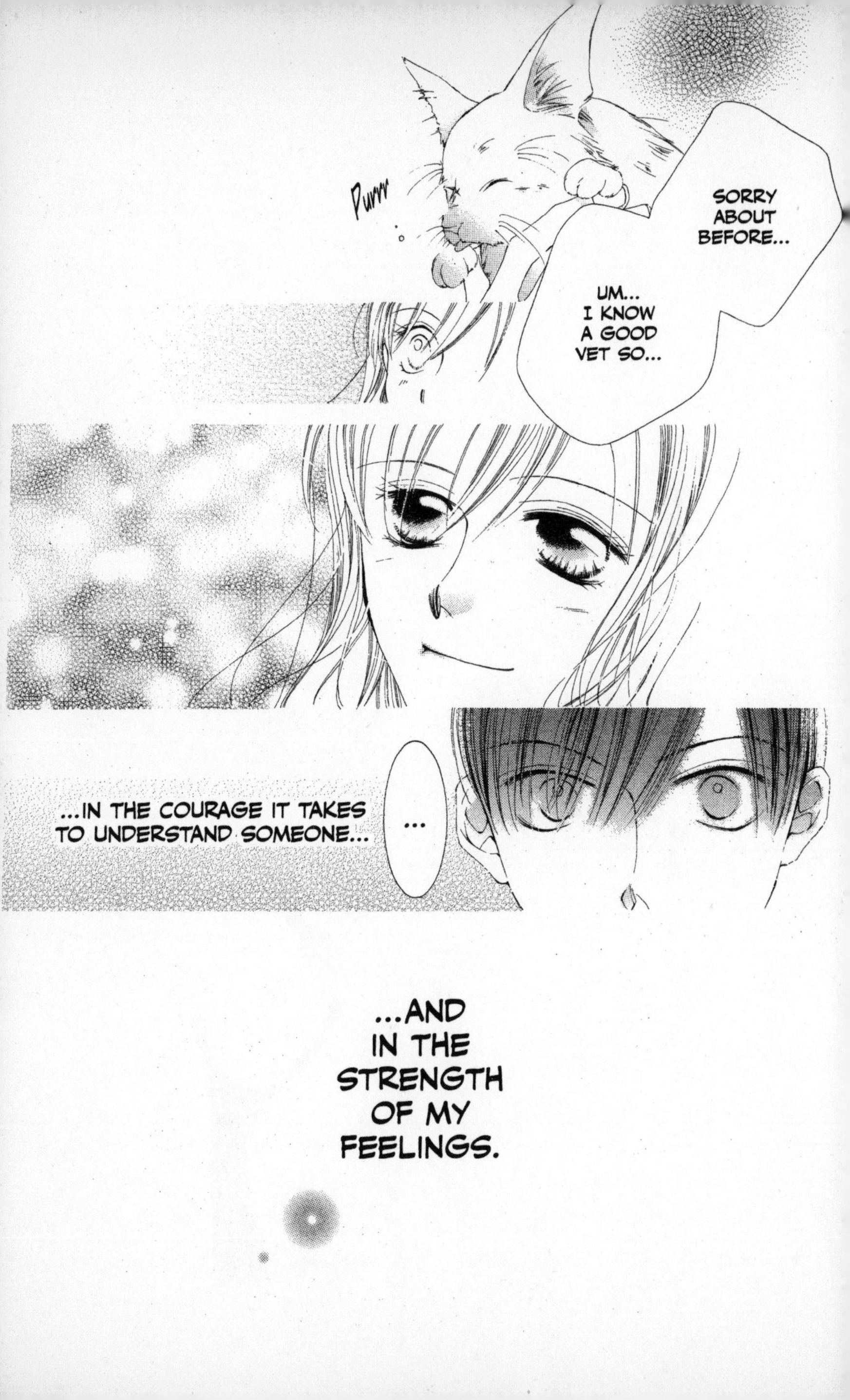
SORRY ABOUT BEFORE...
Purrr
UM... I KNOW A GOOD VET SO...
...
...IN THE COURAGE IT TAKES TO UNDERSTAND SOMEONE...
...AND IN THE STRENGTH OF MY FEELINGS.

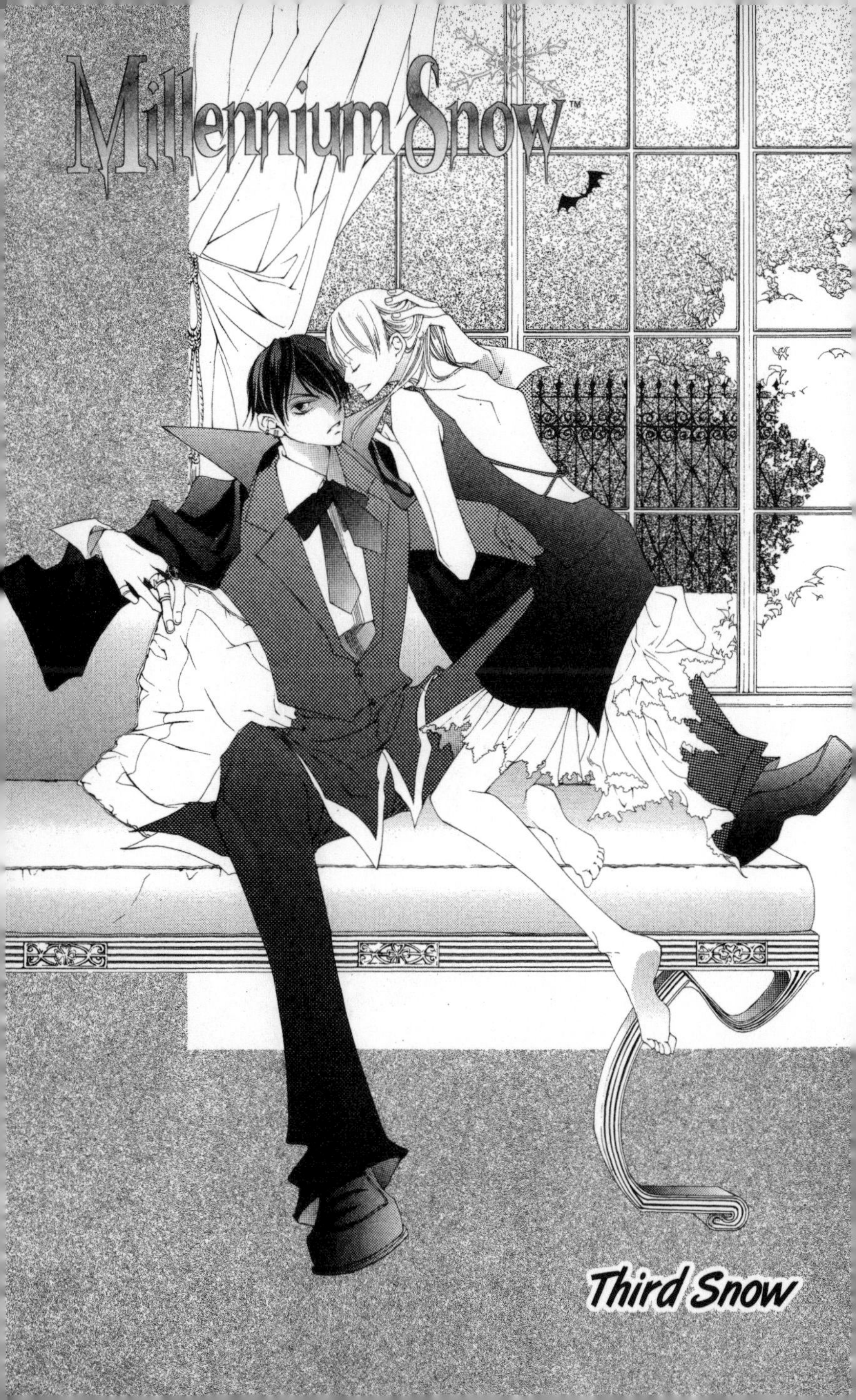
Millennium Snow™
Third Snow

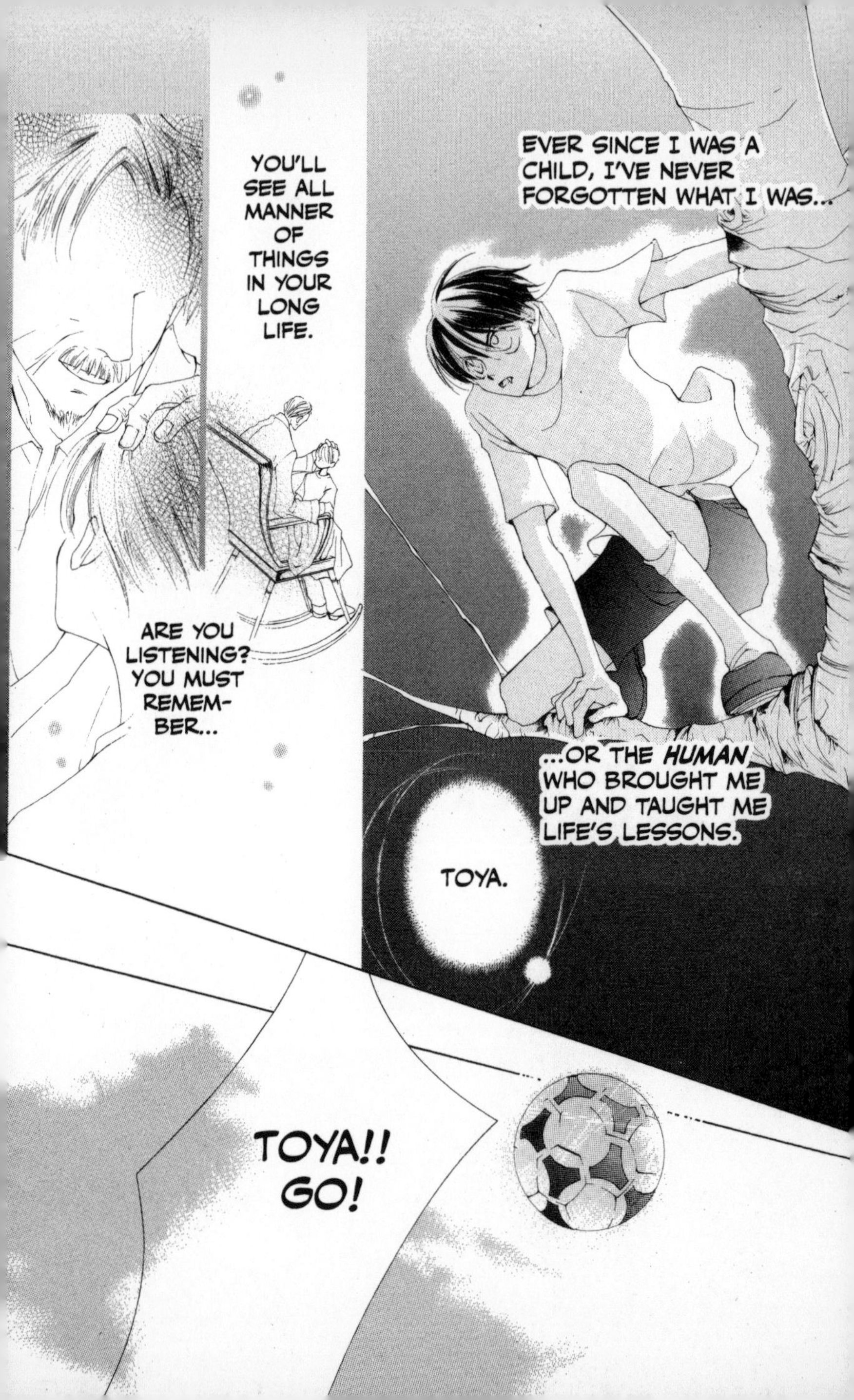
EVER SINCE I WAS A CHILD, I'VE NEVER FORGOTTEN WHAT I WAS...
...OR THE *HUMAN* WHO BROUGHT ME UP AND TAUGHT ME LIFE'S LESSONS.
TOYA.
YOU'LL SEE ALL MANNER OF THINGS IN YOUR LONG LIFE.
ARE YOU LISTENING? YOU MUST REMEMBER...
TOYA!! GO!

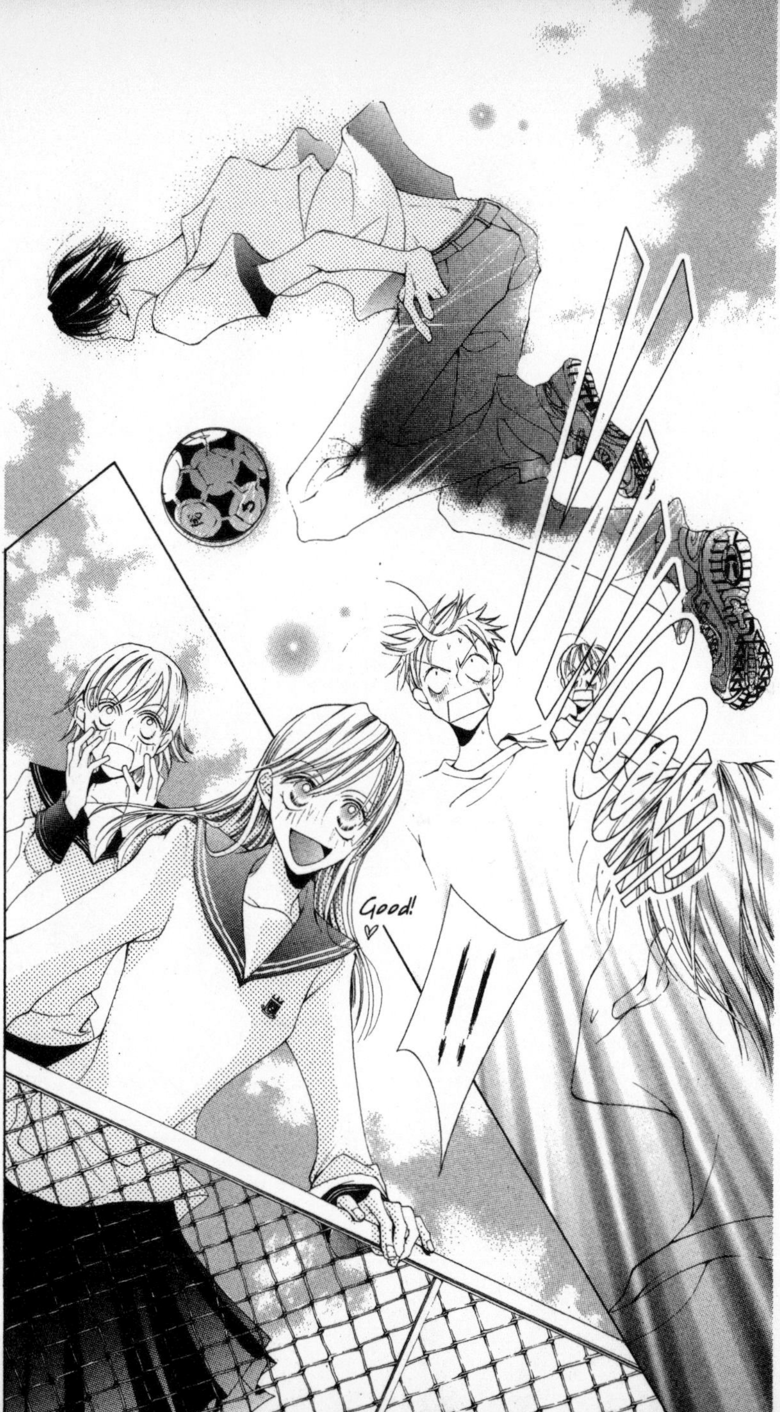
WHOOOMP!
Good! ♥
!!

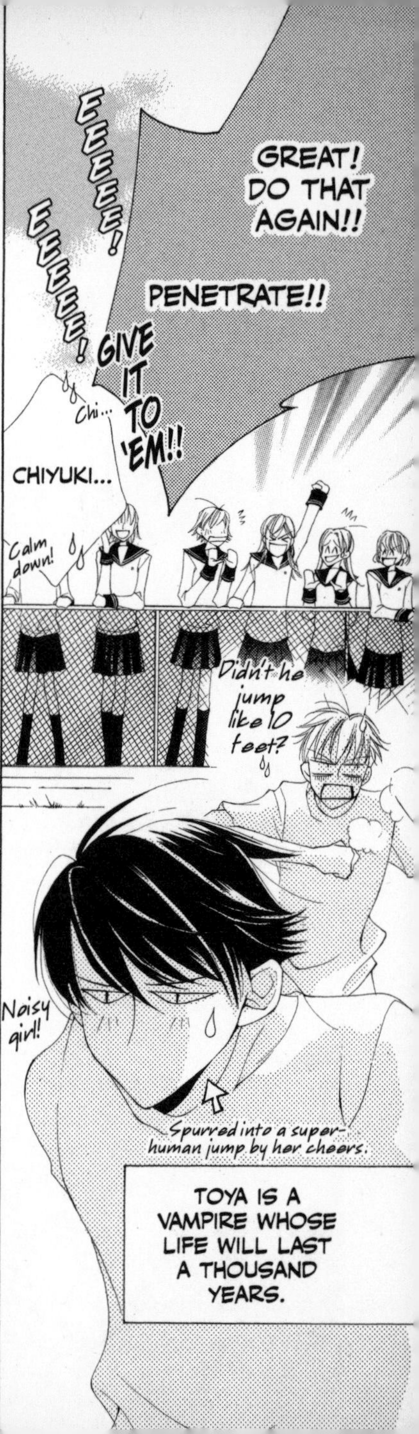
GREAT! DO THAT AGAIN!!
PENETRATE!!
EEEEE!
EEEEE!
GIVE IT TO 'EM!!
Chi...
CHIYUKI...
Calm down!
Didn't he jump like 10 feet?
Spurred into a super-human jump by her cheers.
Noisy girl!
TOYA IS A VAMPIRE WHOSE LIFE WILL LAST A THOUSAND YEARS.

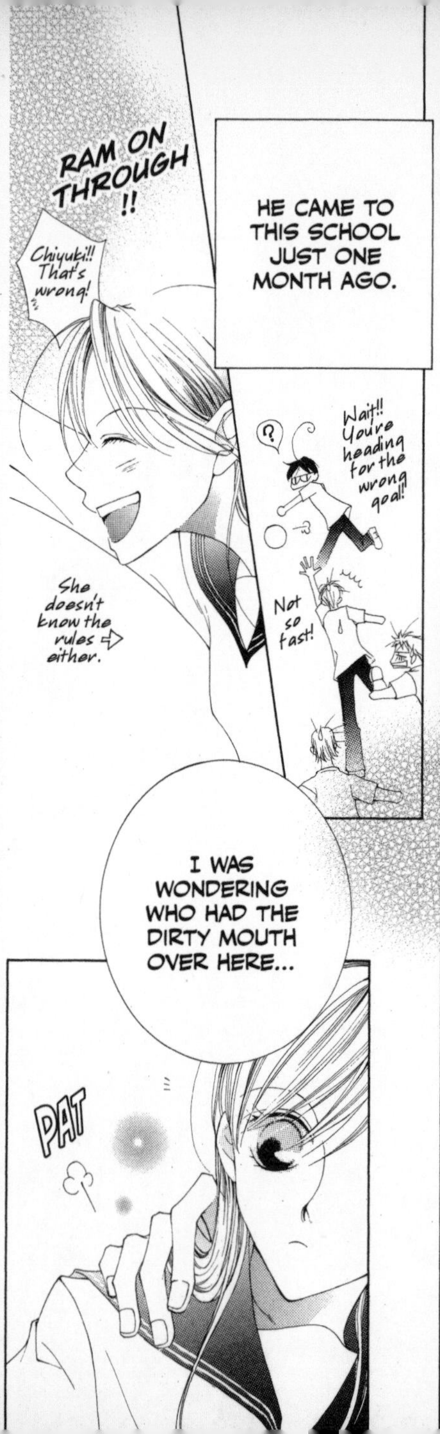
HE CAME TO THIS SCHOOL JUST ONE MONTH AGO.
Wait!! You're heading for the wrong goal!!
Not so fast!
RAM ON THROUGH!!
Chiyuki!! That's wrong!
She doesn't know the rules either.
I WAS WONDERING WHO HAD THE DIRTY MOUTH OVER HERE...
PAT

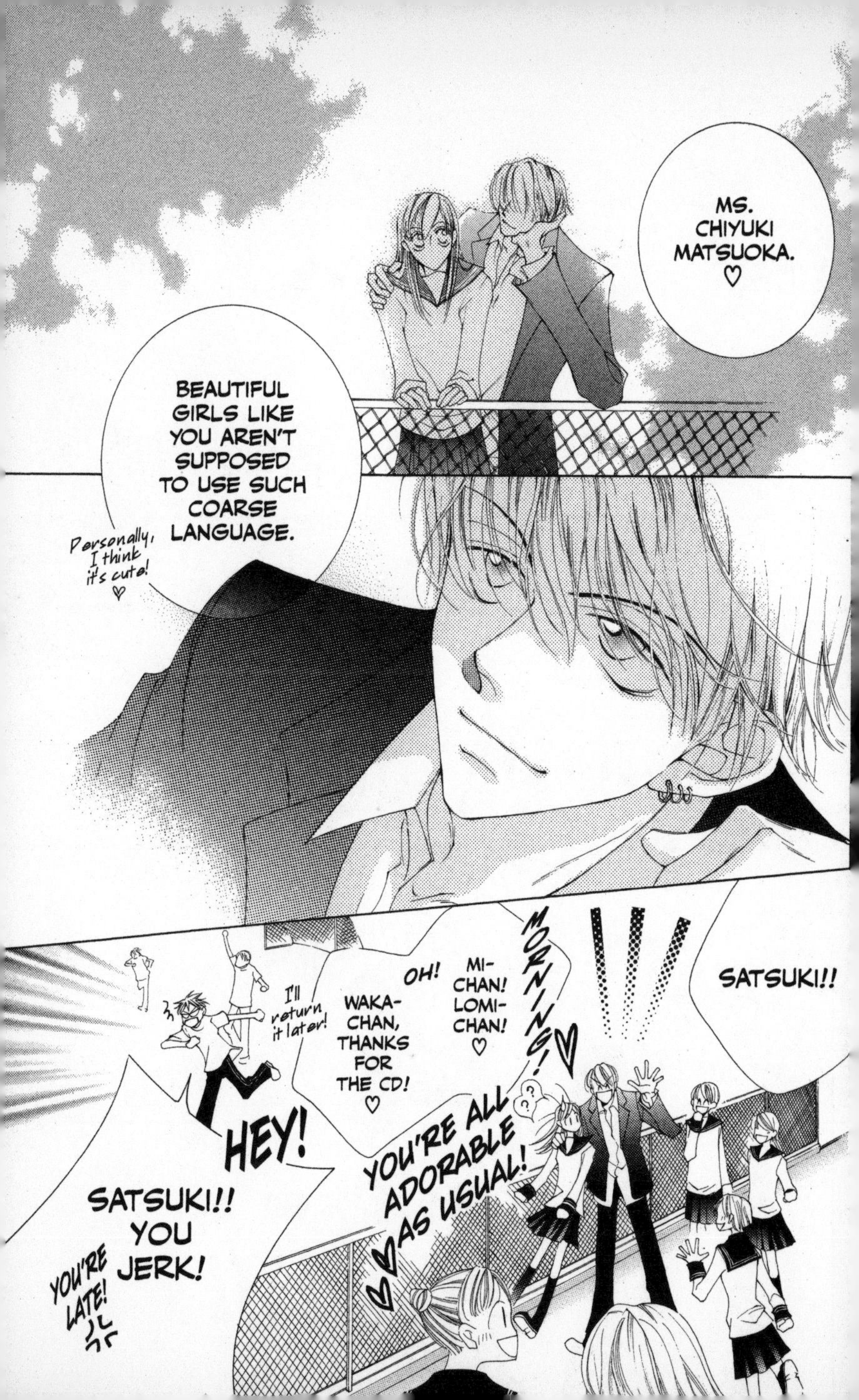
MS. CHIYUKI MATSUOKA. ♡
BEAUTIFUL GIRLS LIKE YOU AREN'T SUPPOSED TO USE SUCH COARSE LANGUAGE.
Personally, I think it's cute! ♡
SATSUKI!!
MORNING! ♡
MI-CHAN! LOMI-CHAN! ♡
OH!
WAKA-CHAN, THANKS FOR THE CD! ♡
I'll return it later!
YOU'RE ALL ADORABLE AS USUAL! ♡♡
HEY!
SATSUKI!! YOU JERK!
YOU'RE LATE!

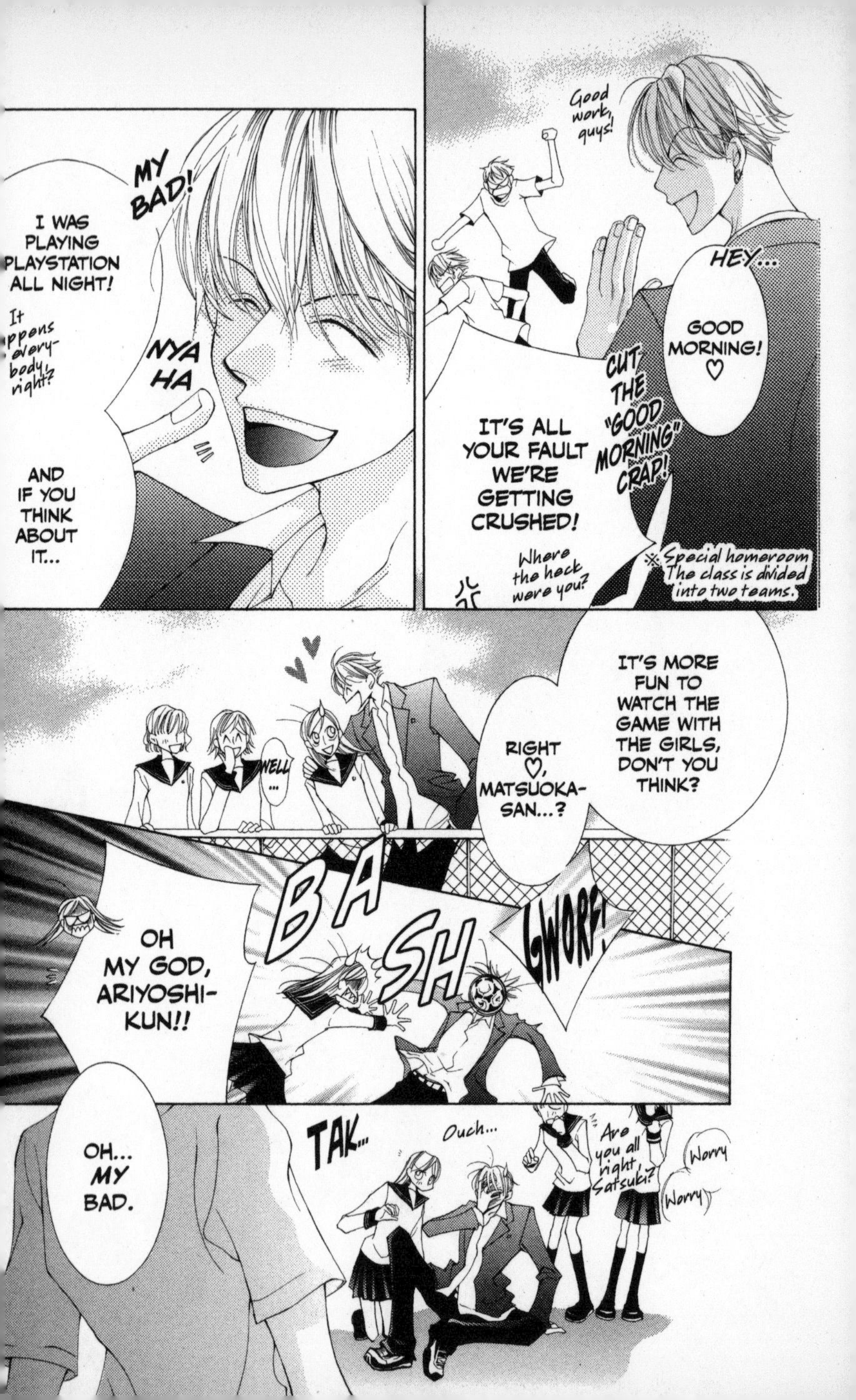
Good work, guys!
HEY...
GOOD MORNING! ♡
CUT THE "GOOD MORNING" CRAP!
IT'S ALL YOUR FAULT WE'RE GETTING CRUSHED!
Where the heck were you?
※Special homeroom The class is divided into two teams.
MY BAD!
I WAS PLAYING PLAYSTATION ALL NIGHT!
It ppens every-body, right?
NYA HA
AND IF YOU THINK ABOUT IT...
IT'S MORE FUN TO WATCH THE GAME WITH THE GIRLS, DON'T YOU THINK?
RIGHT ♡, MATSUOKA-SAN...?
WELL...
BASH
GWORF!
OH MY GOD, ARIYOSHI-KUN!!
Worry
Worry
Are you all right, Satsuki?
Ouch...
TAK...
OH... MY BAD.

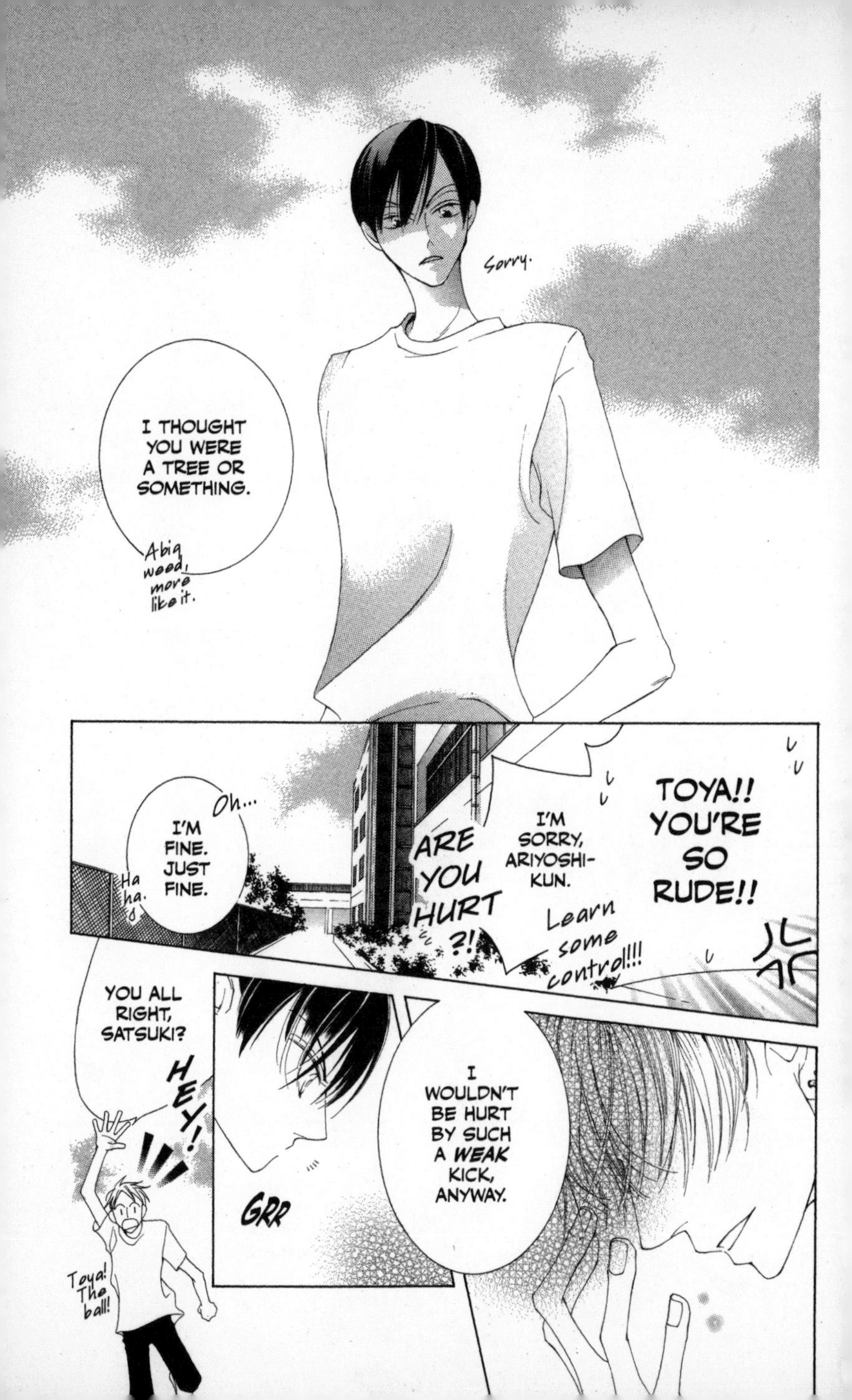
Sorry.
I THOUGHT YOU WERE A TREE OR SOMETHING.
A big weed, more like it.
TOYA!! YOU'RE SO RUDE!!
I'M SORRY, ARIYOSHI-KUN.
Learn some control!!!!
ARE YOU HURT?!
Oh...
I'M FINE. JUST FINE.
Ha ha.
I WOULDN'T BE HURT BY SUCH A WEAK KICK, ANYWAY.
GRR
YOU ALL RIGHT, SATSUKI?
HEY!
Toya! The ball!

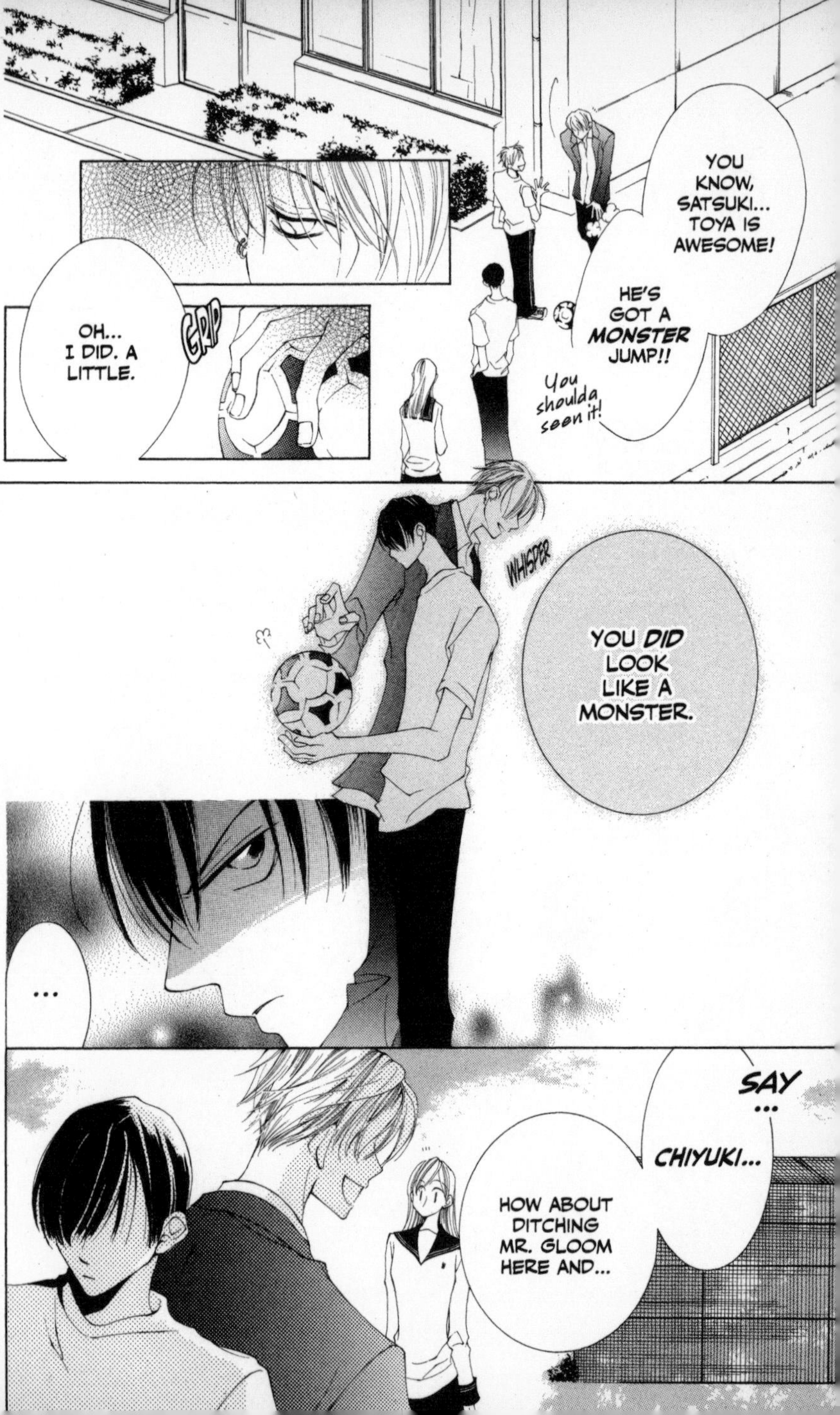
YOU KNOW, SATSUKI... TOYA IS AWESOME!
HE'S GOT A MONSTER JUMP!!
You shoulda seen it!
GRIP
OH... I DID. A LITTLE.
WHISPER
YOU DID LOOK LIKE A MONSTER.
...
SAY... CHIYUKI...
HOW ABOUT DITCHING MR. GLOOM HERE AND...

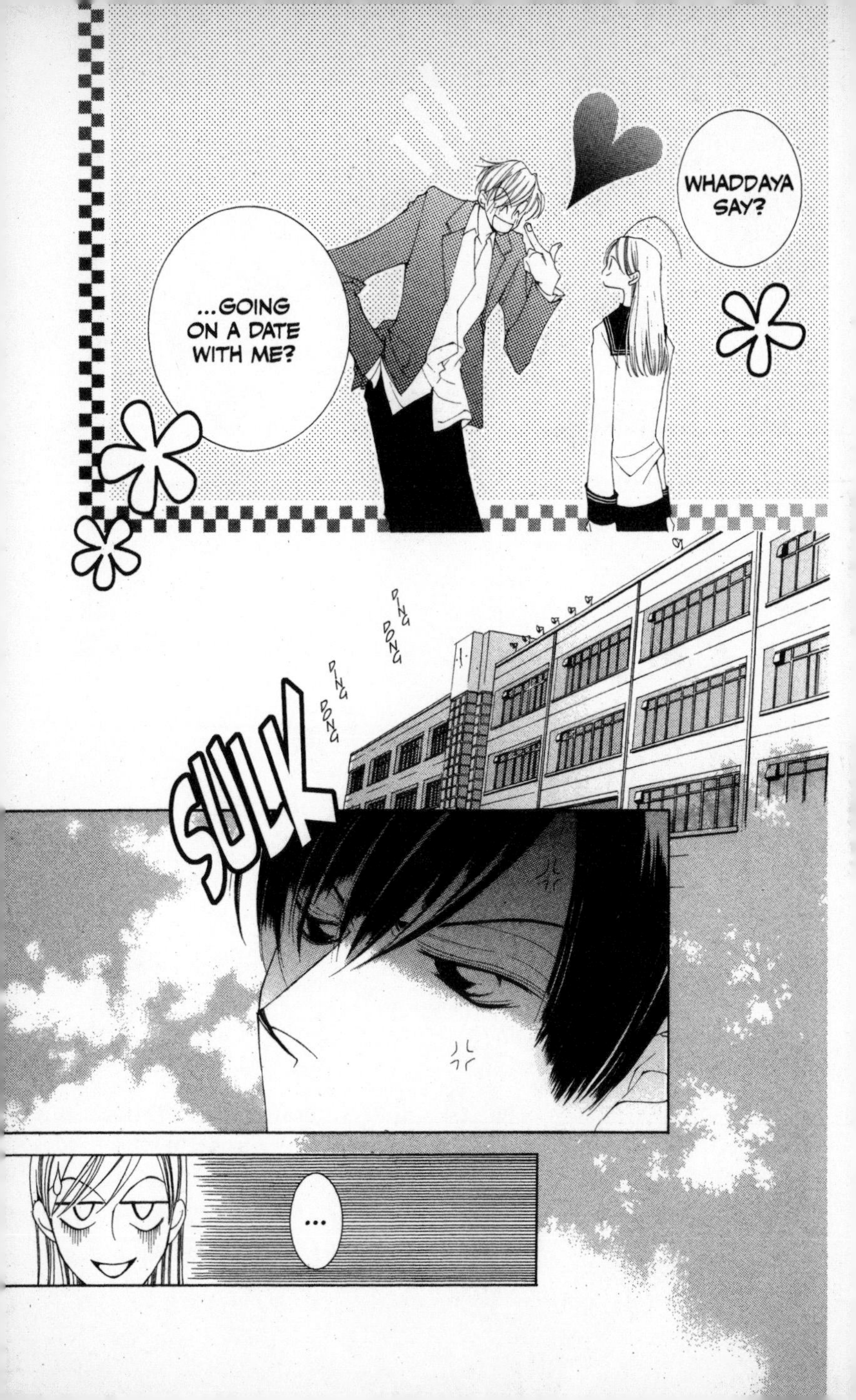
WHADDAYA SAY?
...GOING ON A DATE WITH ME?
DING DONG
DING DONG
SULK
...

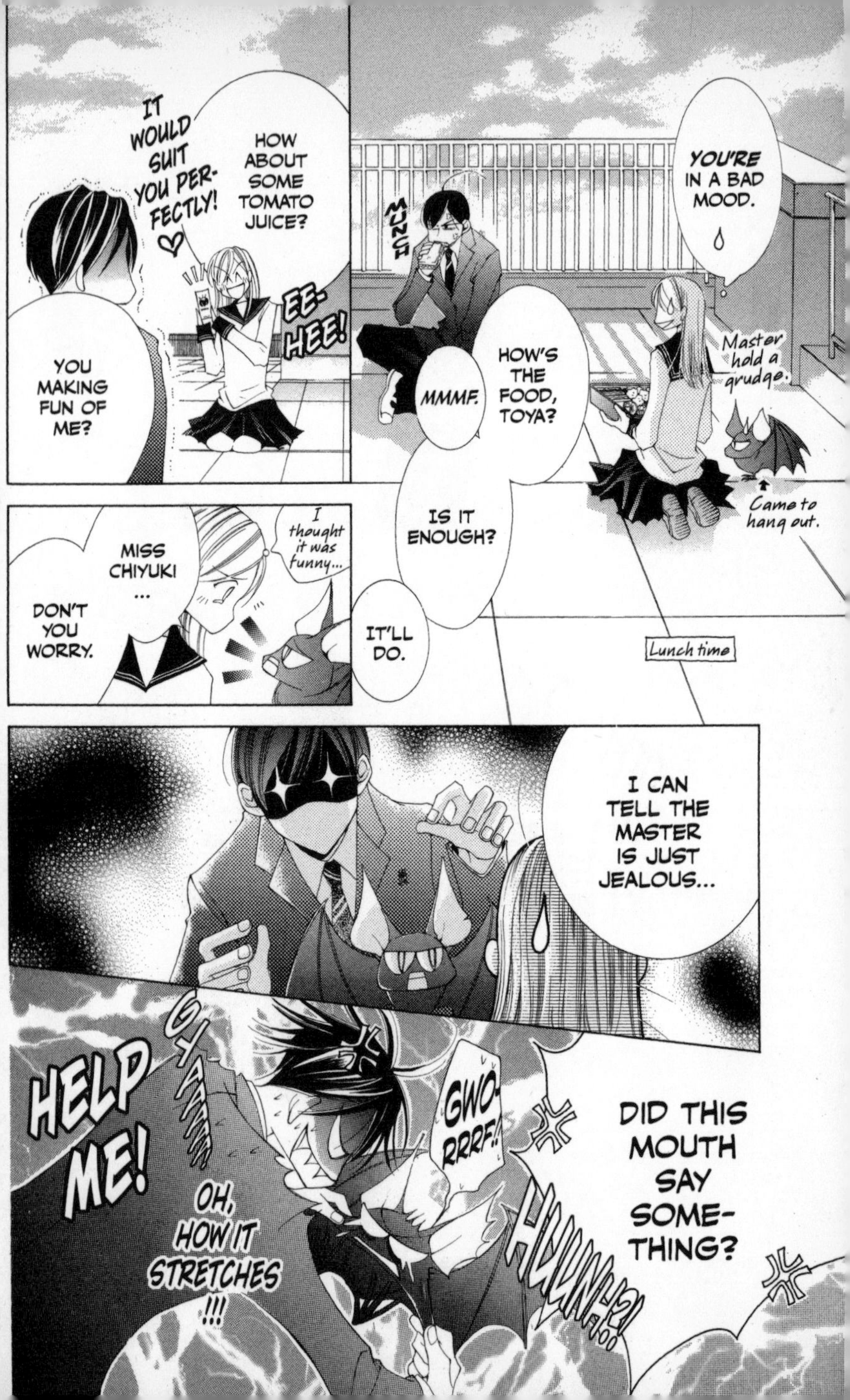
YOU'RE IN A BAD MOOD.
Master hold a grudge.
MUNCH
HOW'S THE FOOD, TOYA?
MMMF.
IS IT ENOUGH?
IT'LL DO.
Came to hang out.
Lunch time
HOW ABOUT SOME TOMATO JUICE?
IT WOULD SUIT YOU PERFECTLY! ♡
EE-HEE!
YOU MAKING FUN OF ME?
I thought it was funny...
MISS CHIYUKI ... DON'T YOU WORRY.
I CAN TELL THE MASTER IS JUST JEALOUS...
DID THIS MOUTH SAY SOMETHING?
HUUUN?!
GWO-RRRF!!
HELP ME!
OH, HOW IT STRETCHES!!!

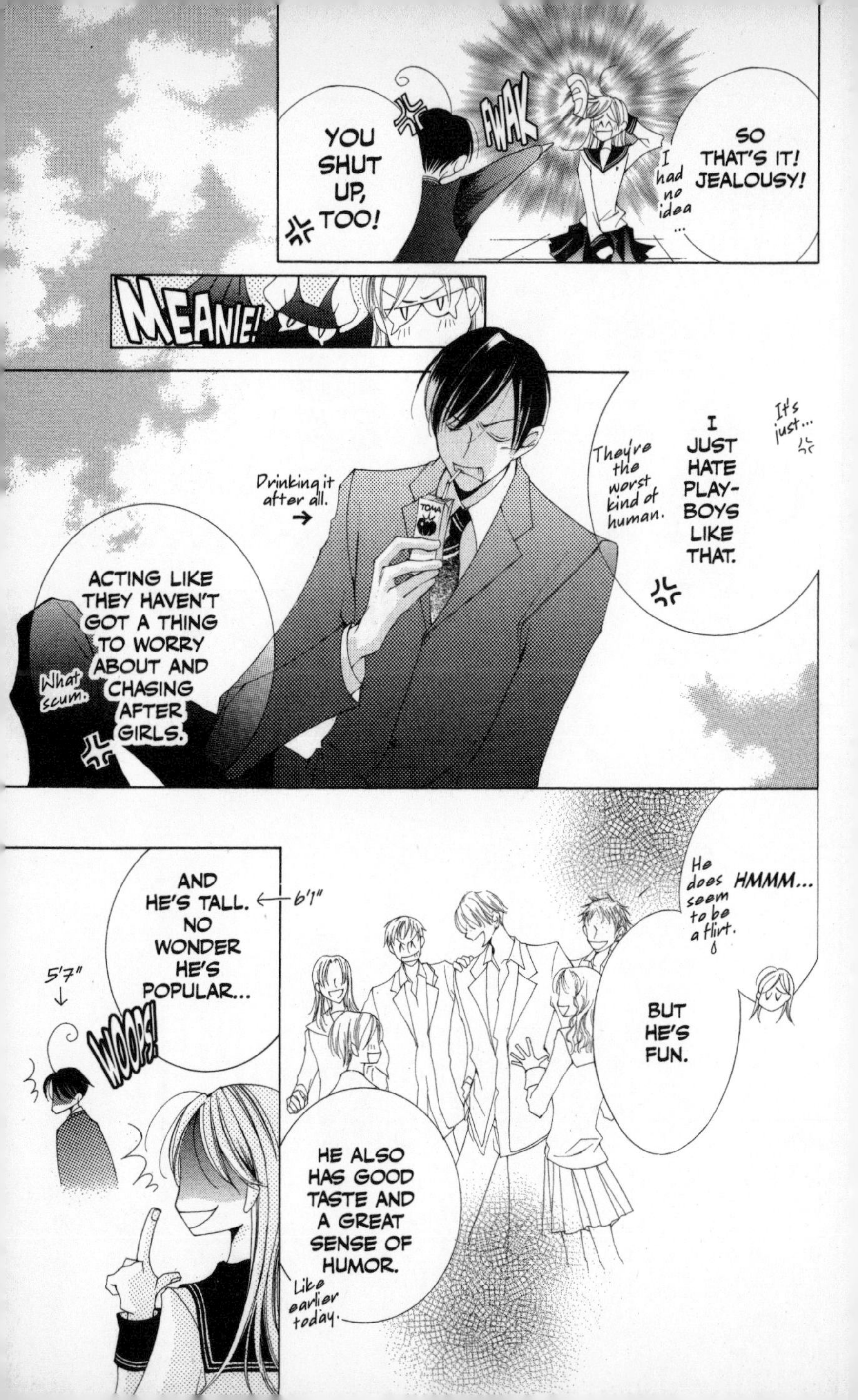
SO THAT'S IT! JEALOUSY!
I had no idea ...
FWAK
YOU SHUT UP, TOO!
MEANIE!
It's just...
I JUST HATE PLAYBOYS LIKE THAT.
They're the worst kind of human.
Drinking it after all.
ACTING LIKE THEY HAVEN'T GOT A THING TO WORRY ABOUT AND CHASING AFTER GIRLS.
What scum.
HMMM...
He does seem to be a flirt.
BUT HE'S FUN.
AND HE'S TALL. NO WONDER HE'S POPULAR...
6'1"
5'7"
WOOPS!
HE ALSO HAS GOOD TASTE AND A GREAT SENSE OF HUMOR.
Like earlier today.

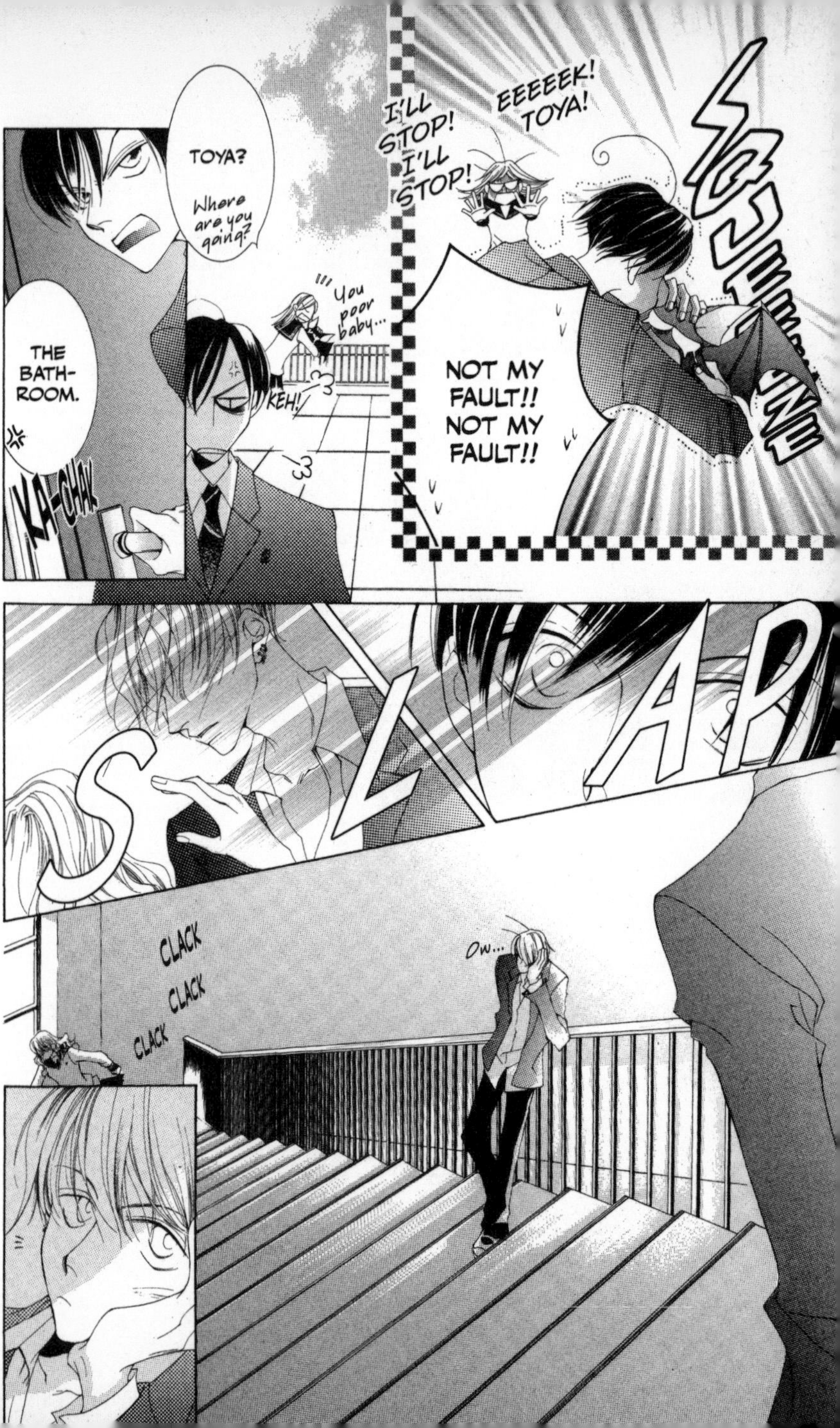
EEEEEK! TOYA!
I'LL STOP! I'LL STOP!
NOT MY FAULT!! NOT MY FAULT!!
You poor baby...
KEH!
TOYA?
Where are you going?
THE BATHROOM.
KA-CHAK
SLAP
Ow...
CLACK
CLACK
CLACK

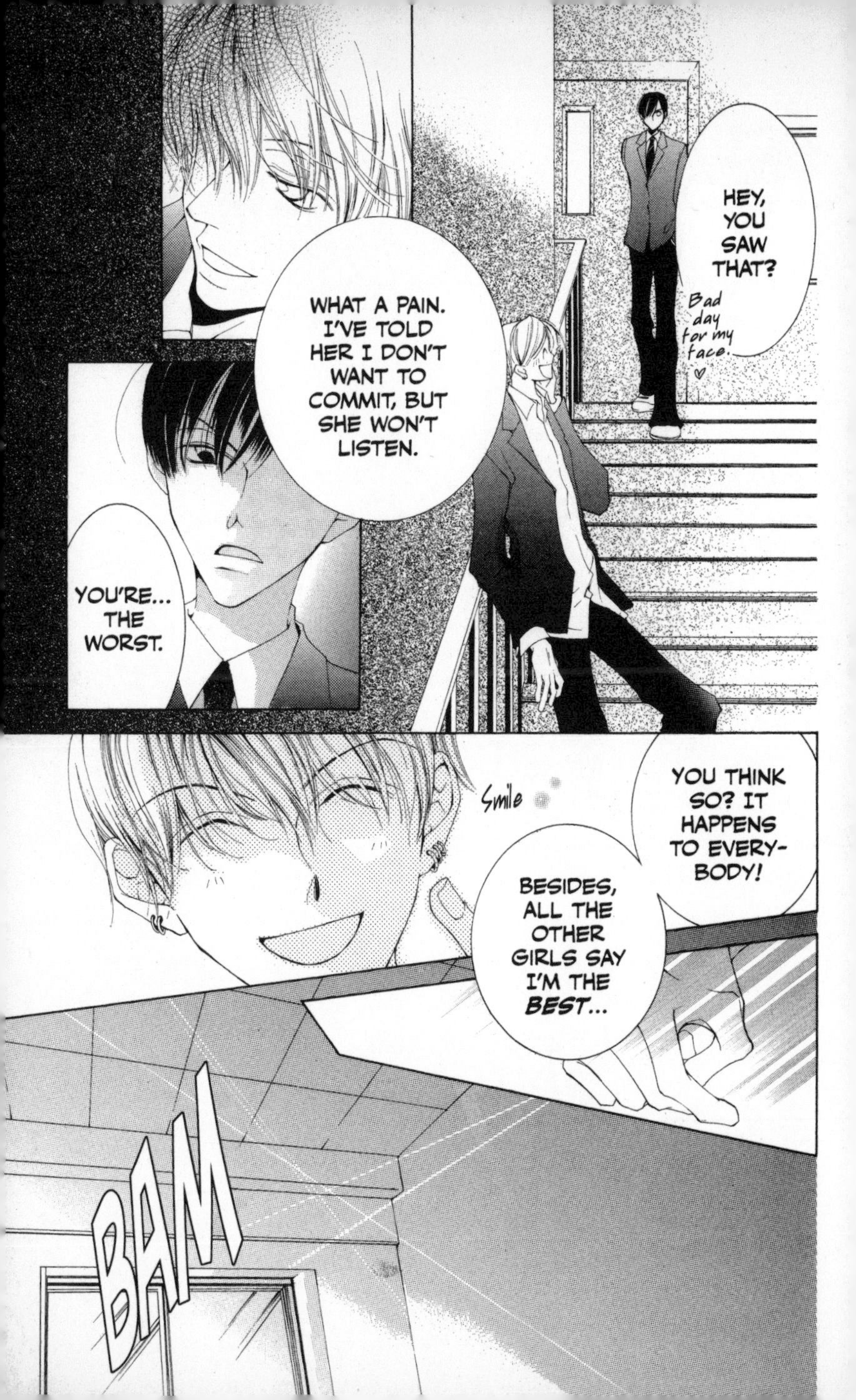
HEY, YOU SAW THAT?
Bad day for my face. ♥
WHAT A PAIN. I'VE TOLD HER I DON'T WANT TO COMMIT, BUT SHE WON'T LISTEN.
YOU'RE... THE WORST.
Smile
YOU THINK SO? IT HAPPENS TO EVERY-BODY!
BESIDES, ALL THE OTHER GIRLS SAY I'M THE *BEST*...
BAM

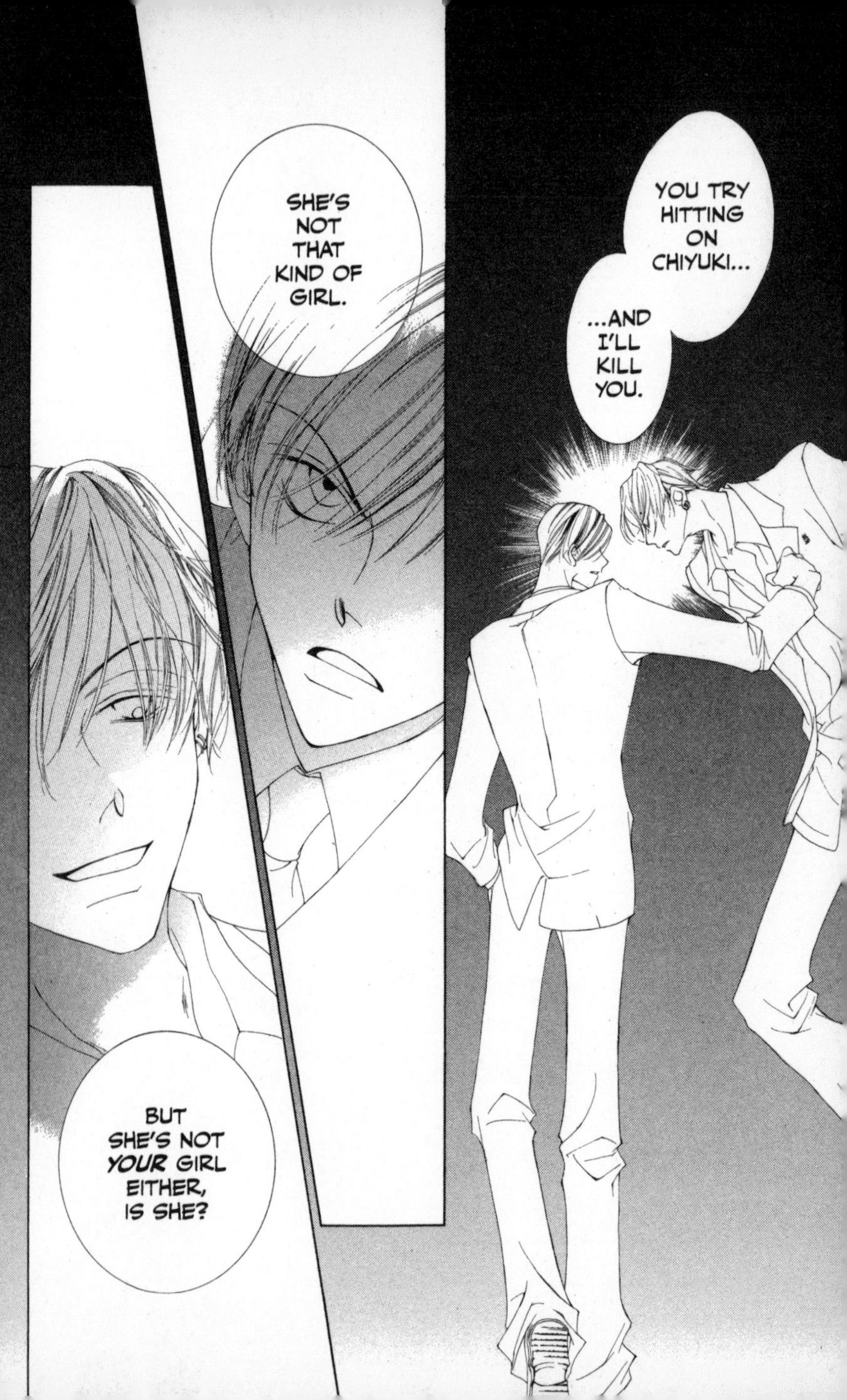
YOU TRY HITTING ON CHIYUKI...
...AND I'LL KILL YOU.
SHE'S NOT THAT KIND OF GIRL.
BUT SHE'S NOT *YOUR* GIRL EITHER, IS SHE?

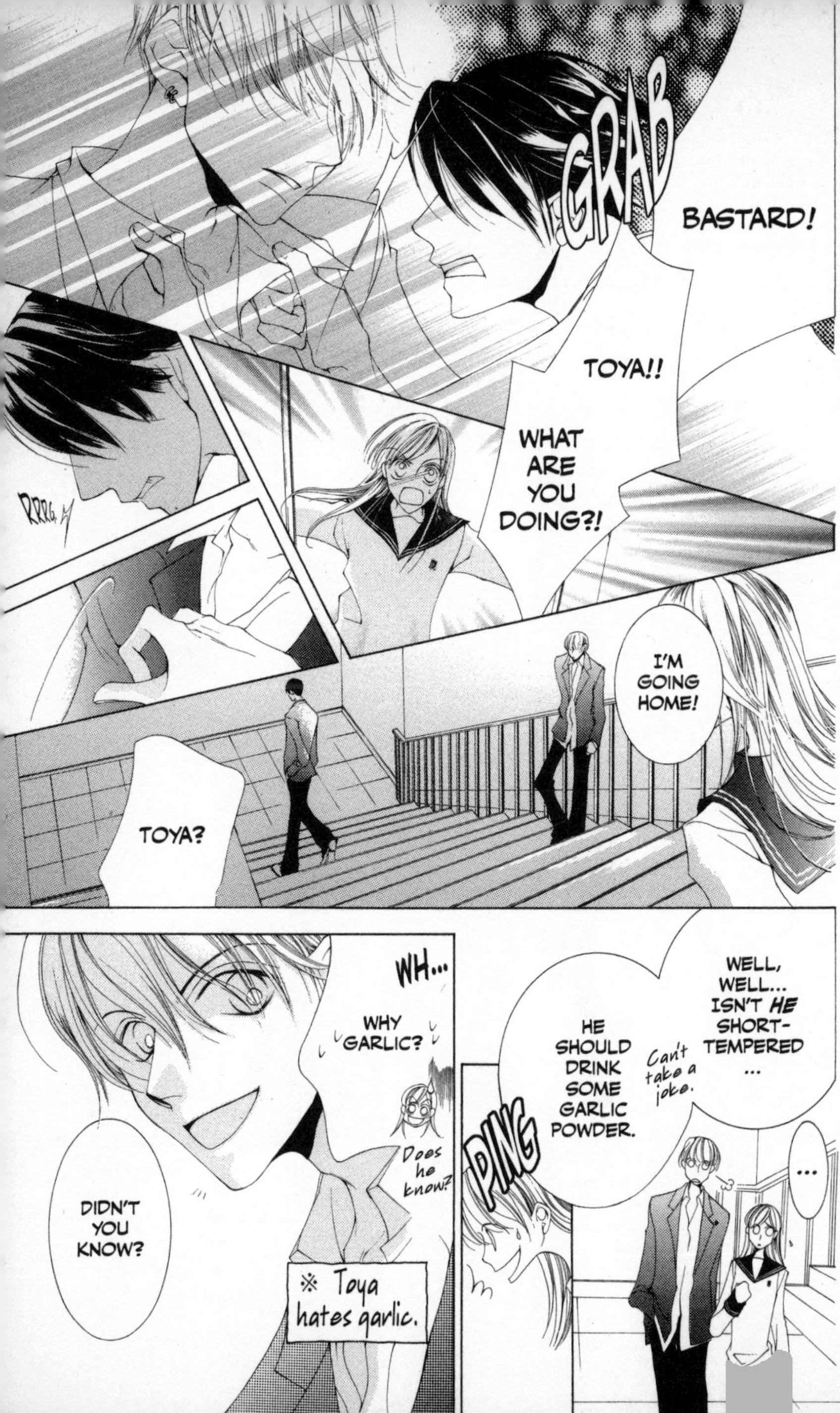
GRAB
BASTARD!
TOYA!!
WHAT ARE YOU DOING?!
RRRG
I'M GOING HOME!
TOYA?
WELL, WELL... ISN'T HE SHORT-TEMPERED ...
Can't take a joke.
HE SHOULD DRINK SOME GARLIC POWDER.
PING
...
WH...
WHY GARLIC?
Does he know?
DIDN'T YOU KNOW?
※ Toya hates garlic.

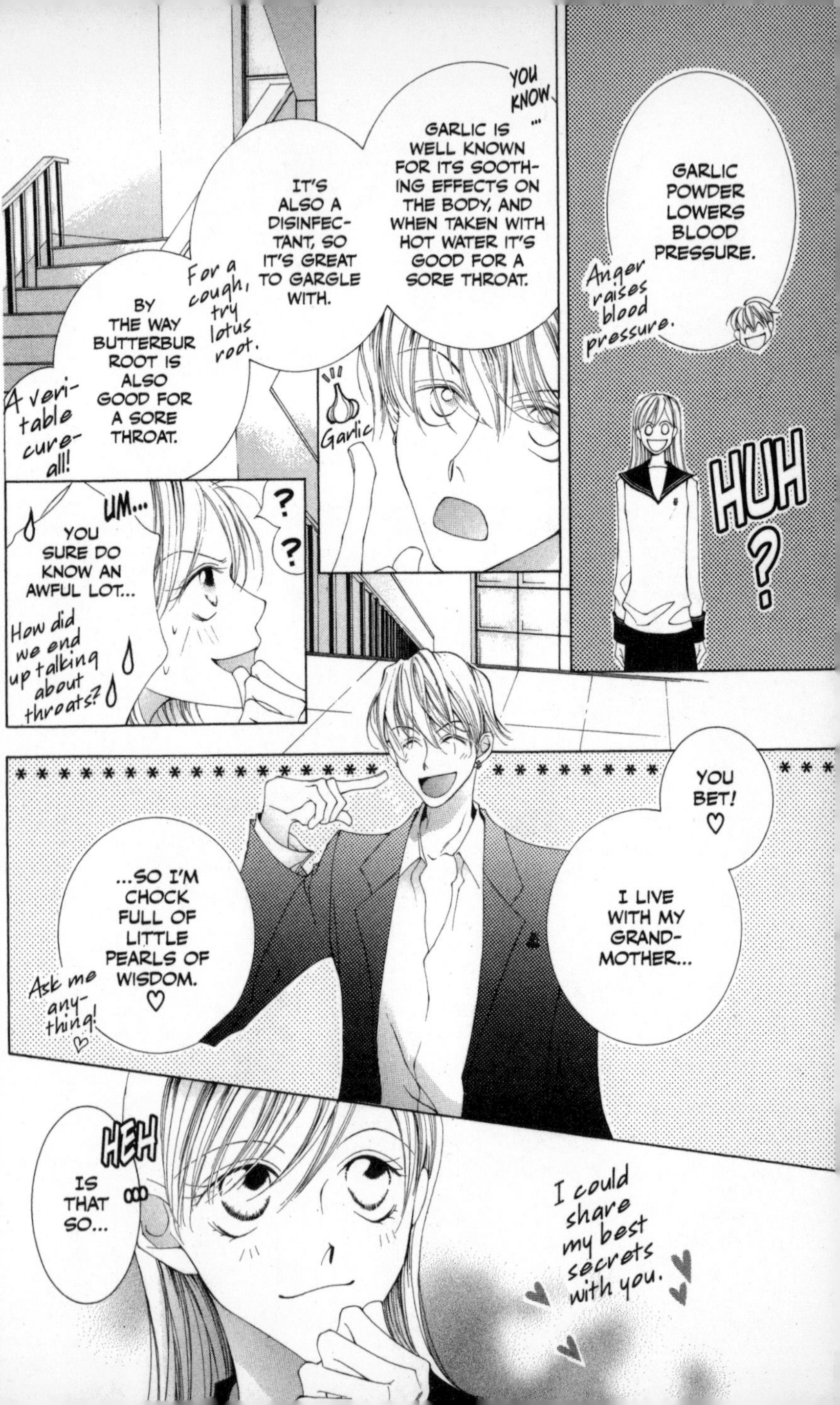
GARLIC POWDER LOWERS BLOOD PRESSURE.
Anger raises blood pressure.
HUH ?
YOU KNOW...
GARLIC IS WELL KNOWN FOR ITS SOOTHING EFFECTS ON THE BODY, AND WHEN TAKEN WITH HOT WATER IT'S GOOD FOR A SORE THROAT.
IT'S ALSO A DISINFECTANT, SO IT'S GREAT TO GARGLE WITH.
For a cough, try lotus root.
BY THE WAY BUTTERBUR ROOT IS ALSO GOOD FOR A SORE THROAT.
A veritable cure-all!
Garlic
? ?
UM...
YOU SURE DO KNOW AN AWFUL LOT...
How did we end up talking about throats?
YOU BET! ♡
I LIVE WITH MY GRANDMOTHER...
...SO I'M CHOCK FULL OF LITTLE PEARLS OF WISDOM. ♡
Ask me anything! ♡
I could share my best secrets with you.
HEH
IS THAT SO...

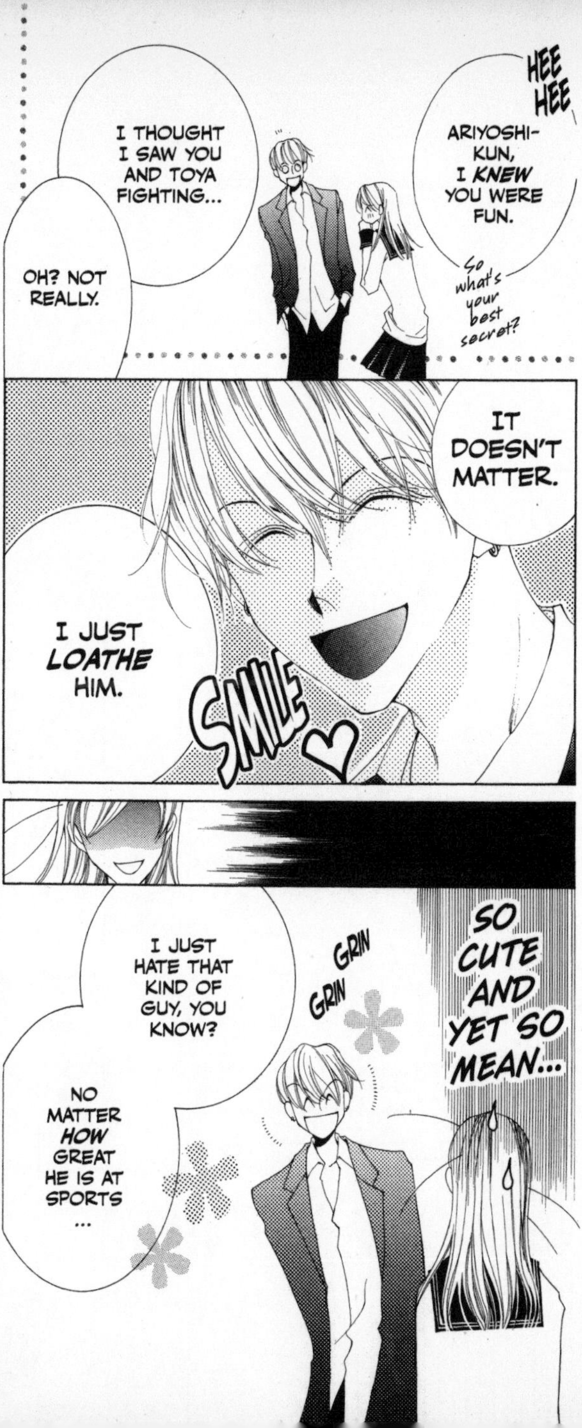
HEE HEE
ARIYOSHI-KUN, I *KNEW* YOU WERE FUN.
So what's your best secret?
I THOUGHT I SAW YOU AND TOYA FIGHTING...
OH? NOT REALLY.
IT DOESN'T MATTER.
I JUST *LOATHE* HIM.
SMILE
SO CUTE AND YET SO MEAN...
GRIN GRIN
I JUST HATE THAT KIND OF GUY, YOU KNOW?
NO MATTER *HOW* GREAT HE IS AT SPORTS...

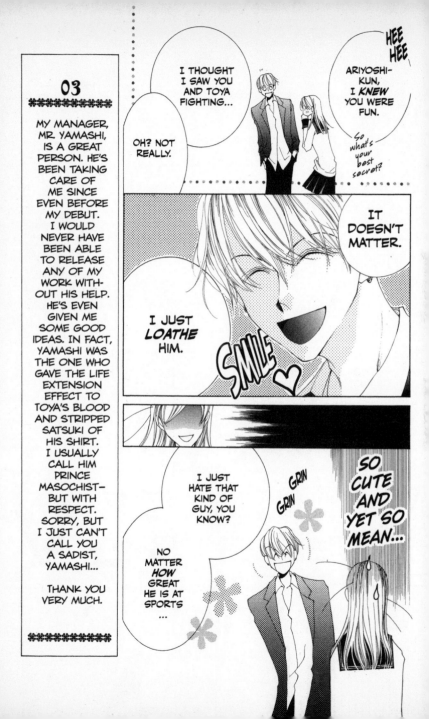

03

MY MANAGER, MR. YAMASHI, IS A GREAT PERSON. HE'S BEEN TAKING CARE OF ME SINCE EVEN BEFORE MY DEBUT. I WOULD NEVER HAVE BEEN ABLE TO RELEASE ANY OF MY WORK WITHOUT HIS HELP. HE'S EVEN GIVEN ME SOME GOOD IDEAS. IN FACT, YAMASHI WAS THE ONE WHO GAVE THE LIFE EXTENSION EFFECT TO TOYA'S BLOOD AND STRIPPED SATSUKI OF HIS SHIRT. I USUALLY CALL HIM PRINCE MASOCHIST— BUT WITH RESPECT. SORRY, BUT I JUST CAN'T CALL YOU A SADIST, YAMASHI...

THANK YOU VERY MUCH.

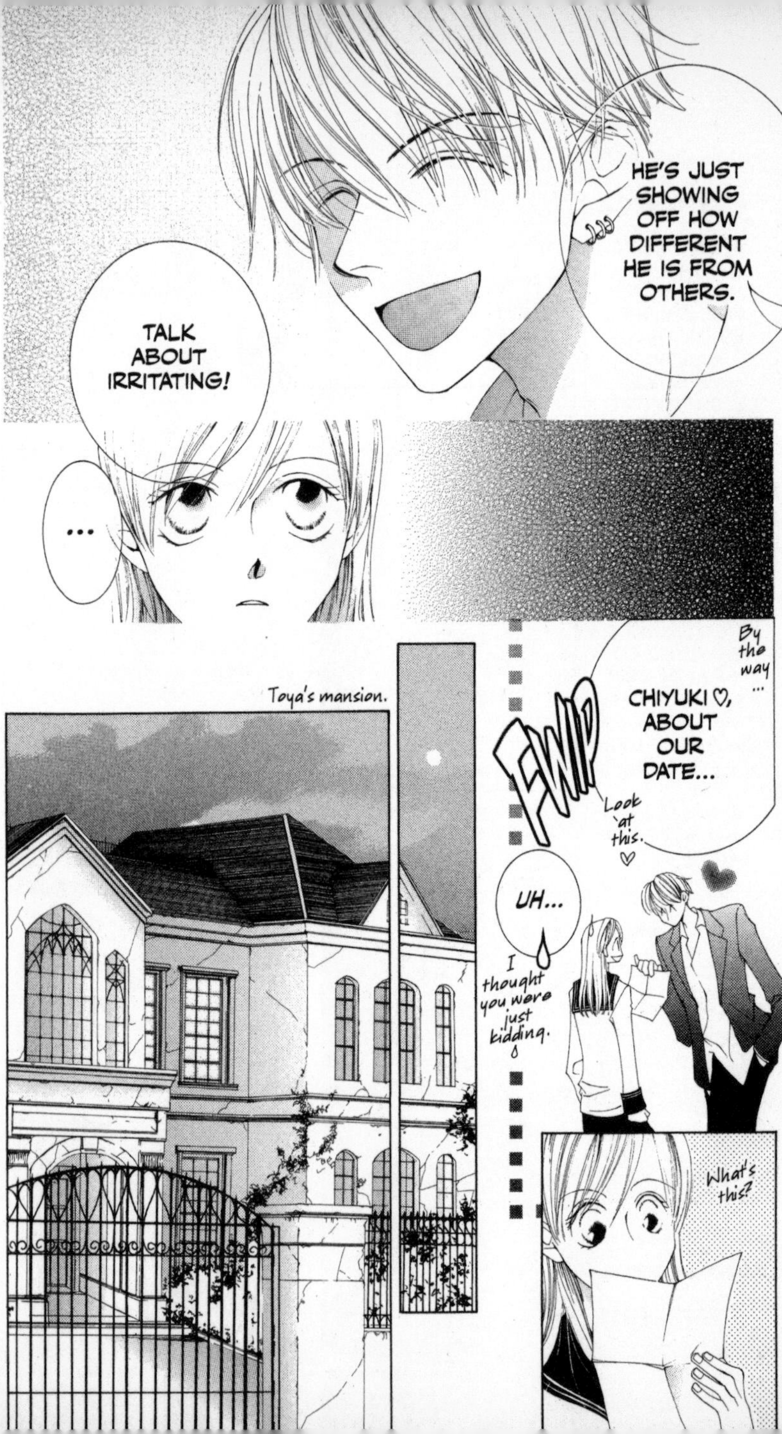
HE'S JUST SHOWING OFF HOW DIFFERENT HE IS FROM OTHERS.
TALK ABOUT IRRITATING!
...
By the way...
CHIYUKI ♡, ABOUT OUR DATE...
FWIP
Look at this. ♡
UH...
I thought you were just kidding.
What's this?
Toya's mansion.

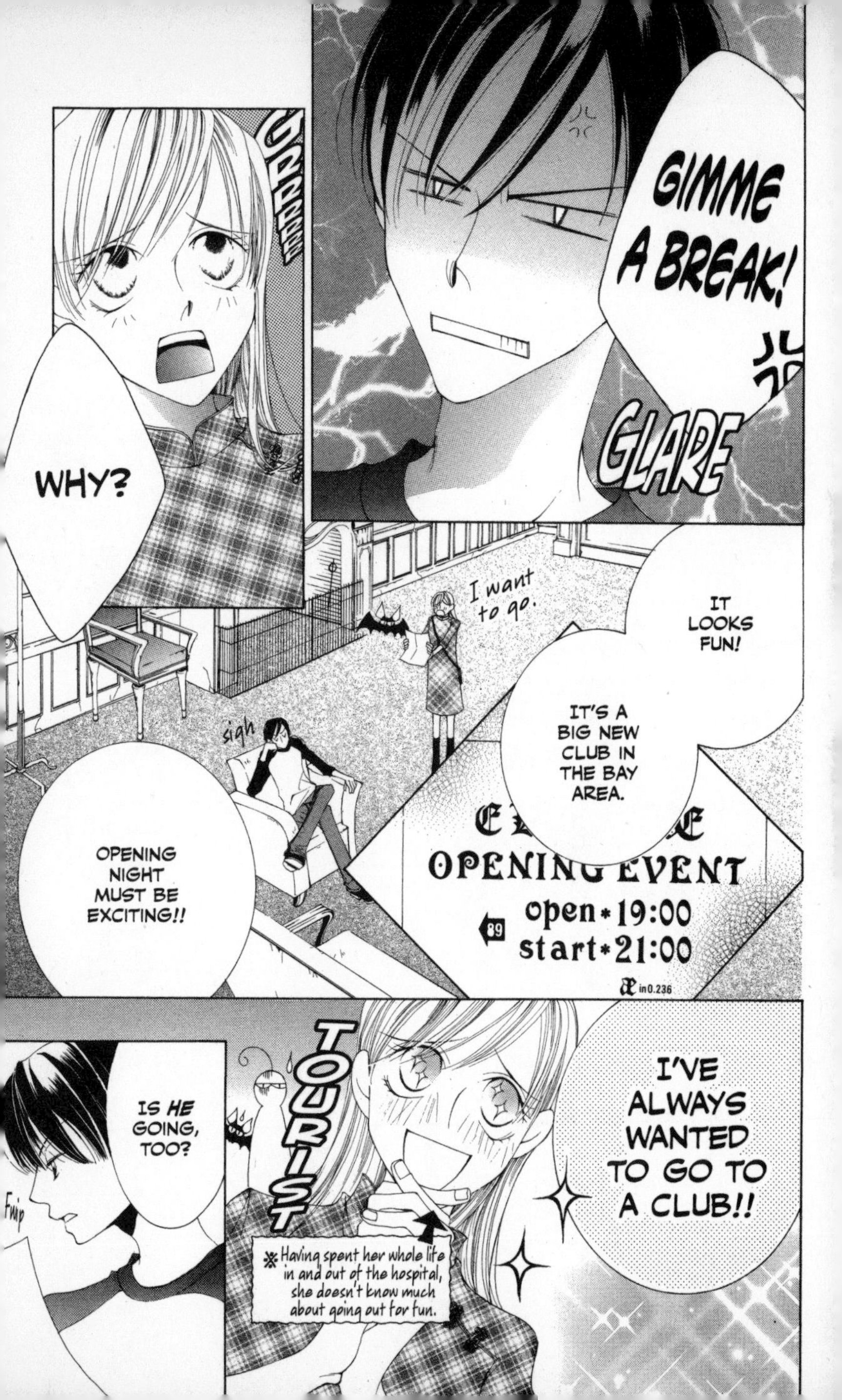
GIMME A BREAK!
GLARE
WHY?
IT LOOKS FUN!
IT'S A BIG NEW CLUB IN THE BAY AREA.
I want to go.
OPENING EVENT
open*19:00
start*21:00
sigh
OPENING NIGHT MUST BE EXCITING!!
I'VE ALWAYS WANTED TO GO TO A CLUB!!
TOURIST
※Having spent her whole life in and out of the hospital, she doesn't know much about going out for fun.
IS HE GOING, TOO?
Fwip

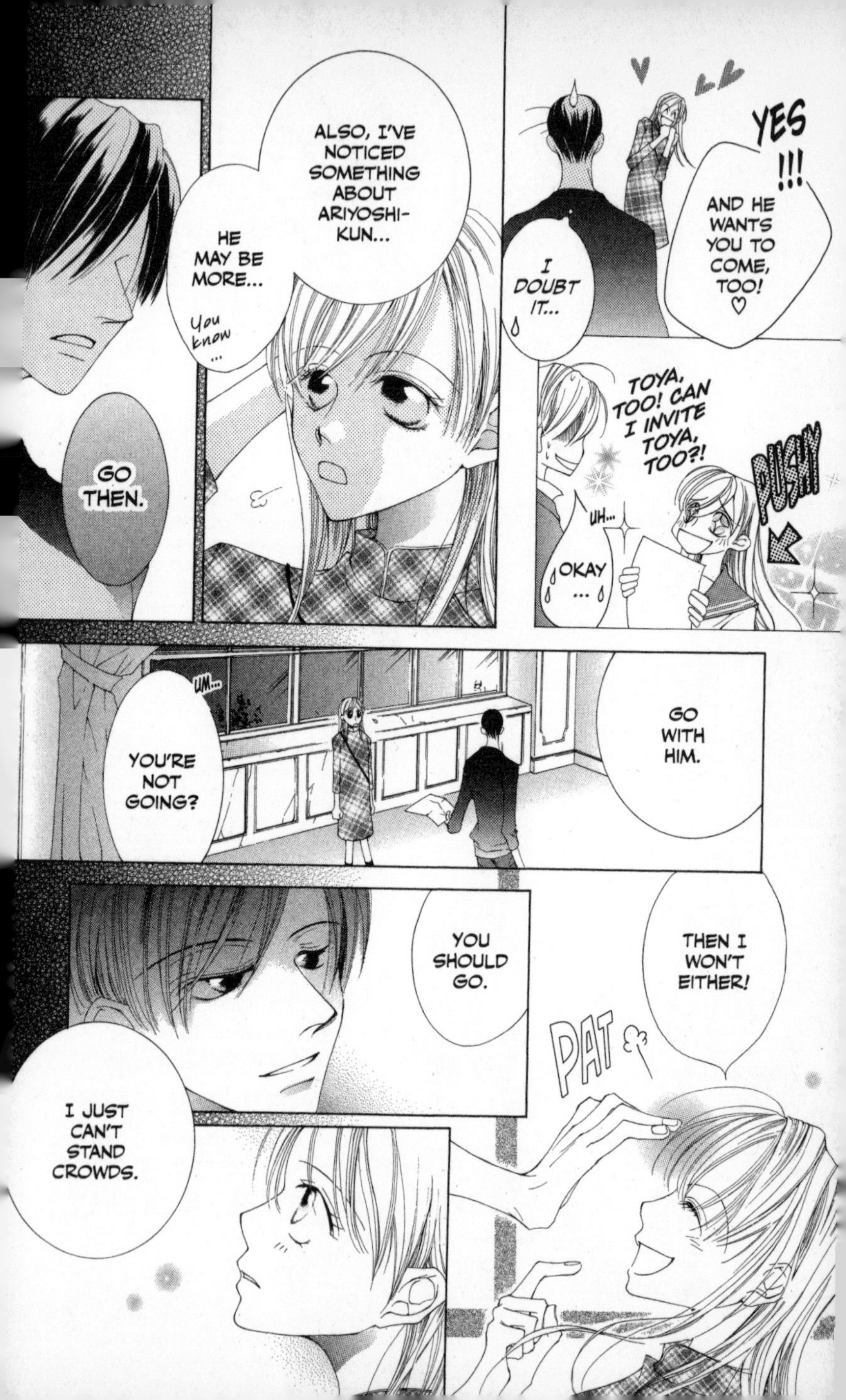
YES!!!
AND HE WANTS YOU TO COME, TOO! ♡
I DOUBT IT...
TOYA, TOO! CAN I INVITE TOYA, TOO?!
PUSHY
UH... OKAY...
ALSO, I'VE NOTICED SOMETHING ABOUT ARIYOSHI-KUN...
HE MAY BE MORE...
You know ...
GO THEN.
GO WITH HIM.
UM... YOU'RE NOT GOING?
THEN I WON'T EITHER!
PAT
YOU SHOULD GO.
I JUST CAN'T STAND CROWDS.

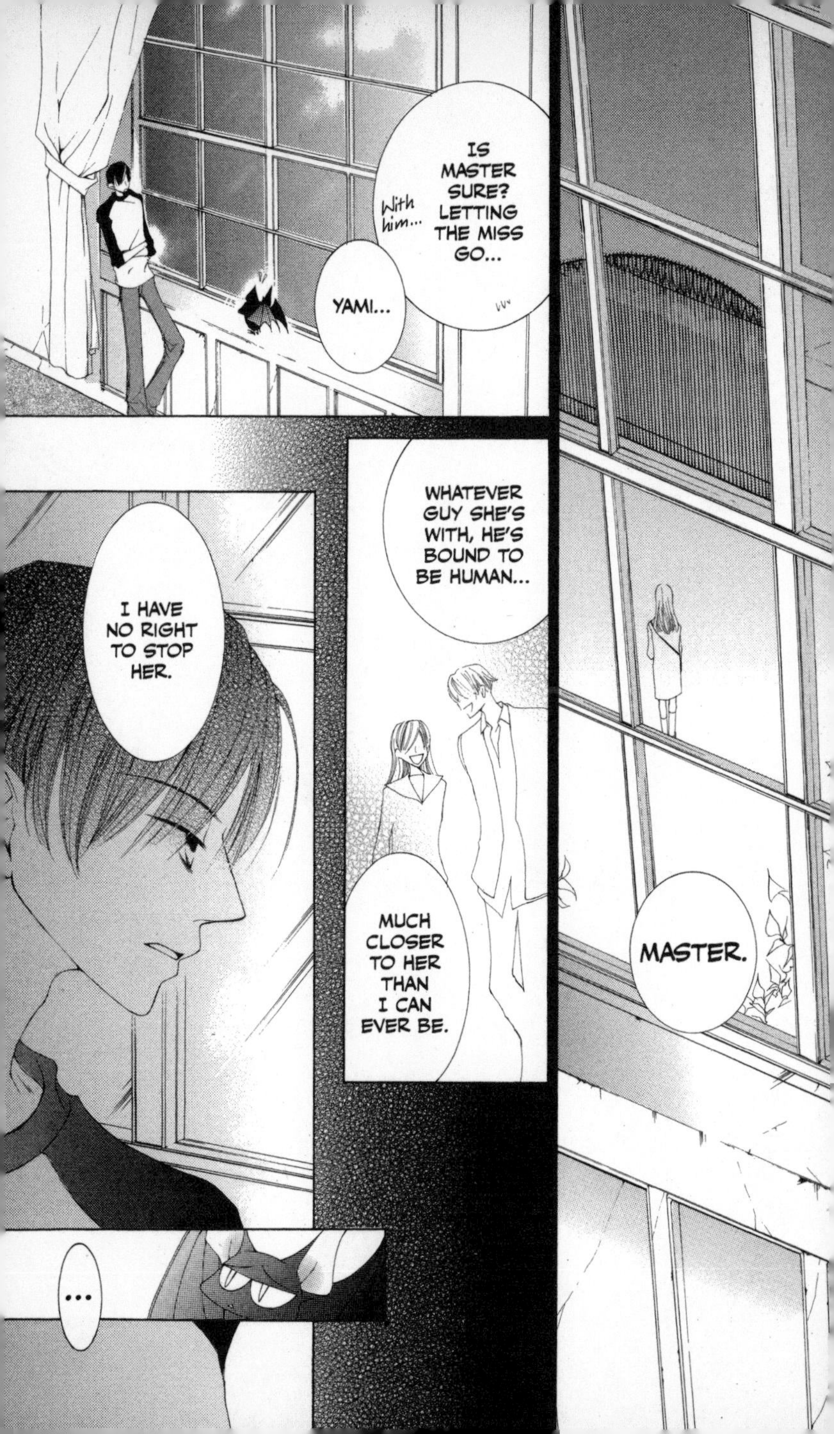
MASTER.
IS MASTER SURE? LETTING THE MISS GO...
With him...
YAMI...
WHATEVER GUY SHE'S WITH, HE'S BOUND TO BE HUMAN...
MUCH CLOSER TO HER THAN I CAN EVER BE.
I HAVE NO RIGHT TO STOP HER.
...

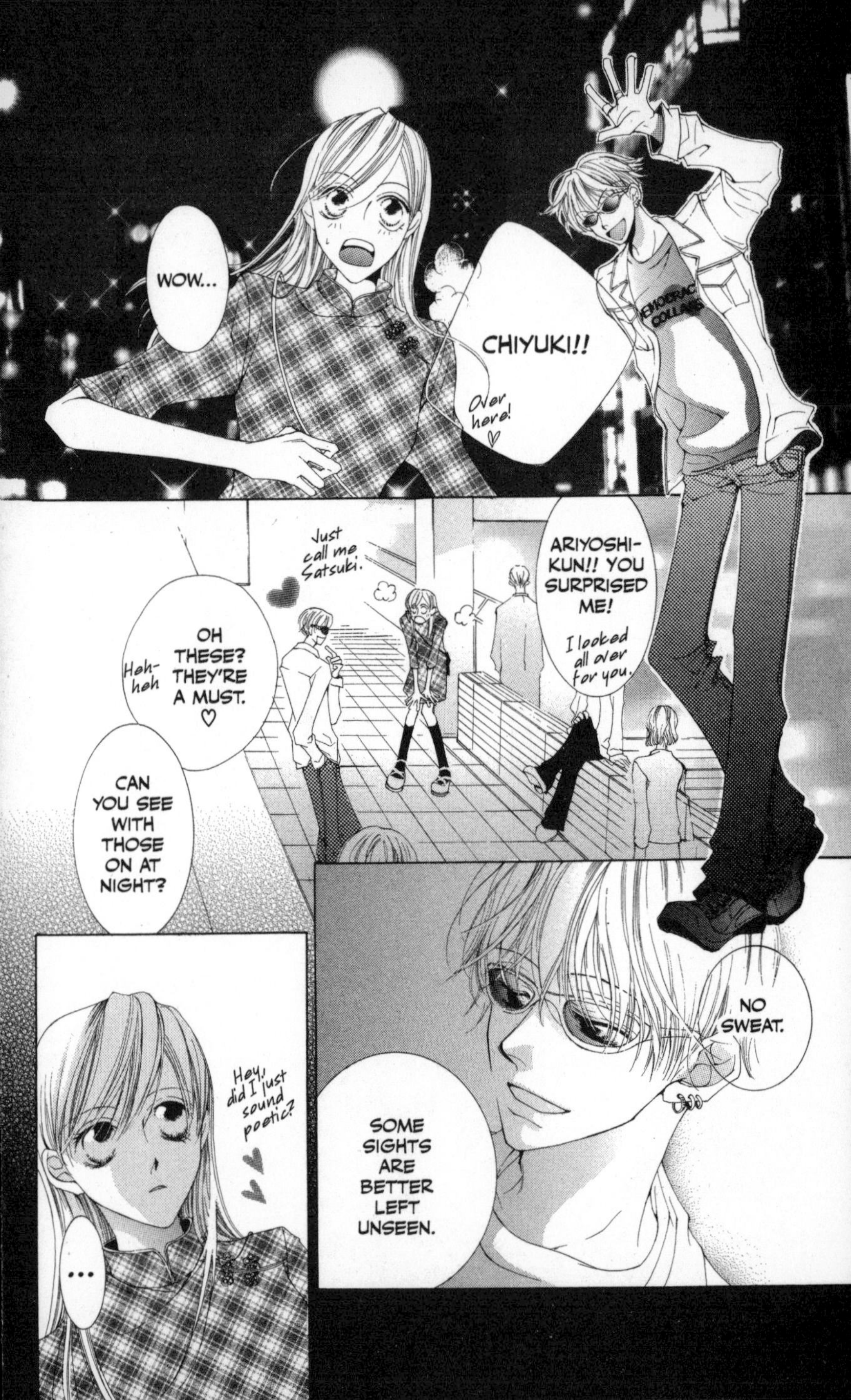
CHIYUKI!!
Over here! ♡
WOW...
ARIYOSHI-KUN!! YOU SURPRISED ME!
I looked all over for you.
Just call me Satsuki.
OH THESE? THEY'RE A MUST. ♡
Heh-heh
CAN YOU SEE WITH THOSE ON AT NIGHT?
NO SWEAT.
SOME SIGHTS ARE BETTER LEFT UNSEEN.
Hey, did I just sound poetic?
...

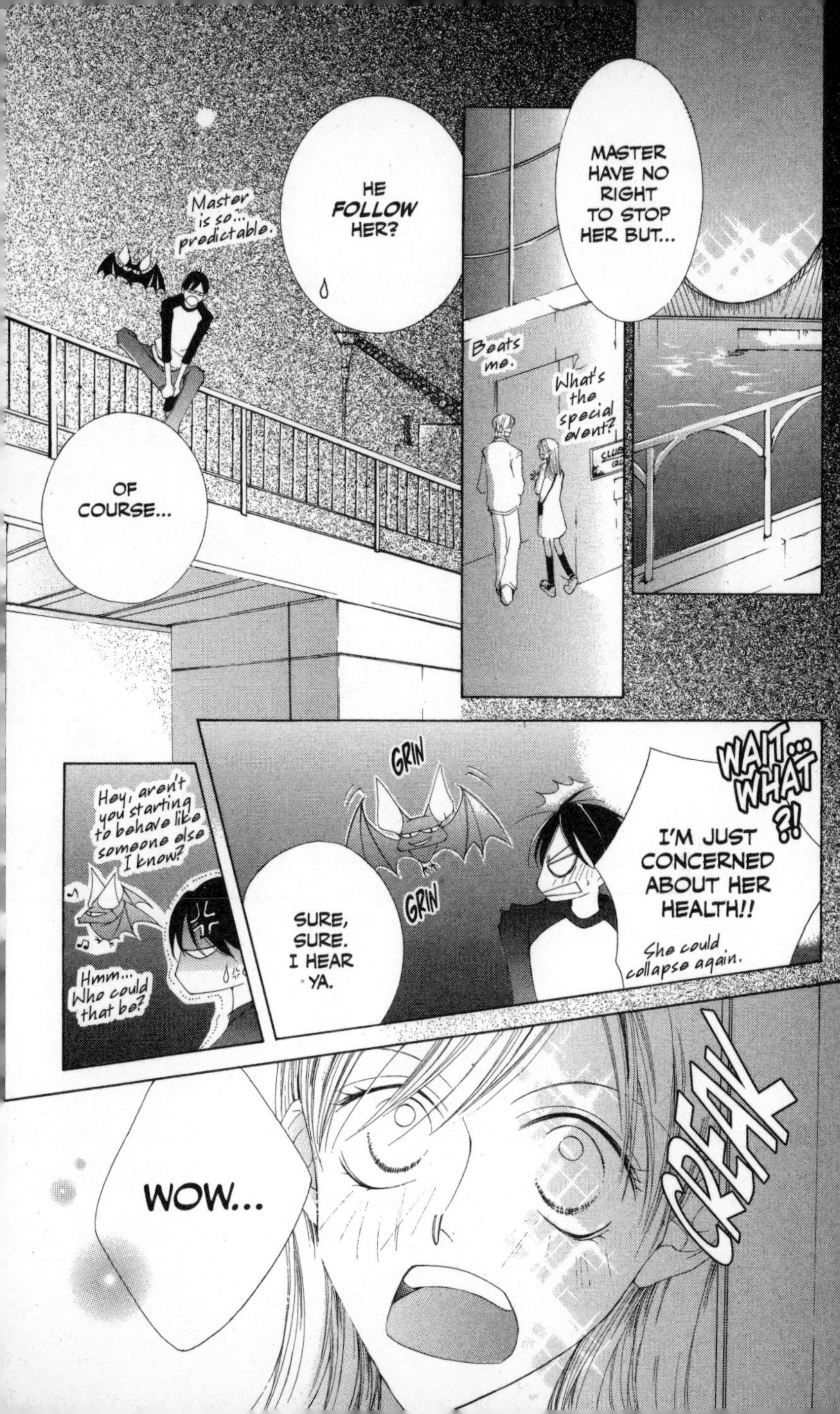
MASTER HAVE NO RIGHT TO STOP HER BUT...
What's the special event?
Beats me.
HE FOLLOW HER?
Master is so... predictable.
OF COURSE...
WAIT... WHAT?!
I'M JUST CONCERNED ABOUT HER HEALTH!!
She could collapse again.
GRIN
GRIN
SURE, SURE. I HEAR YA.
Hey, aren't you starting to behave like someone else I know?
Hmm... Who could that be?
CREAK
WOW...

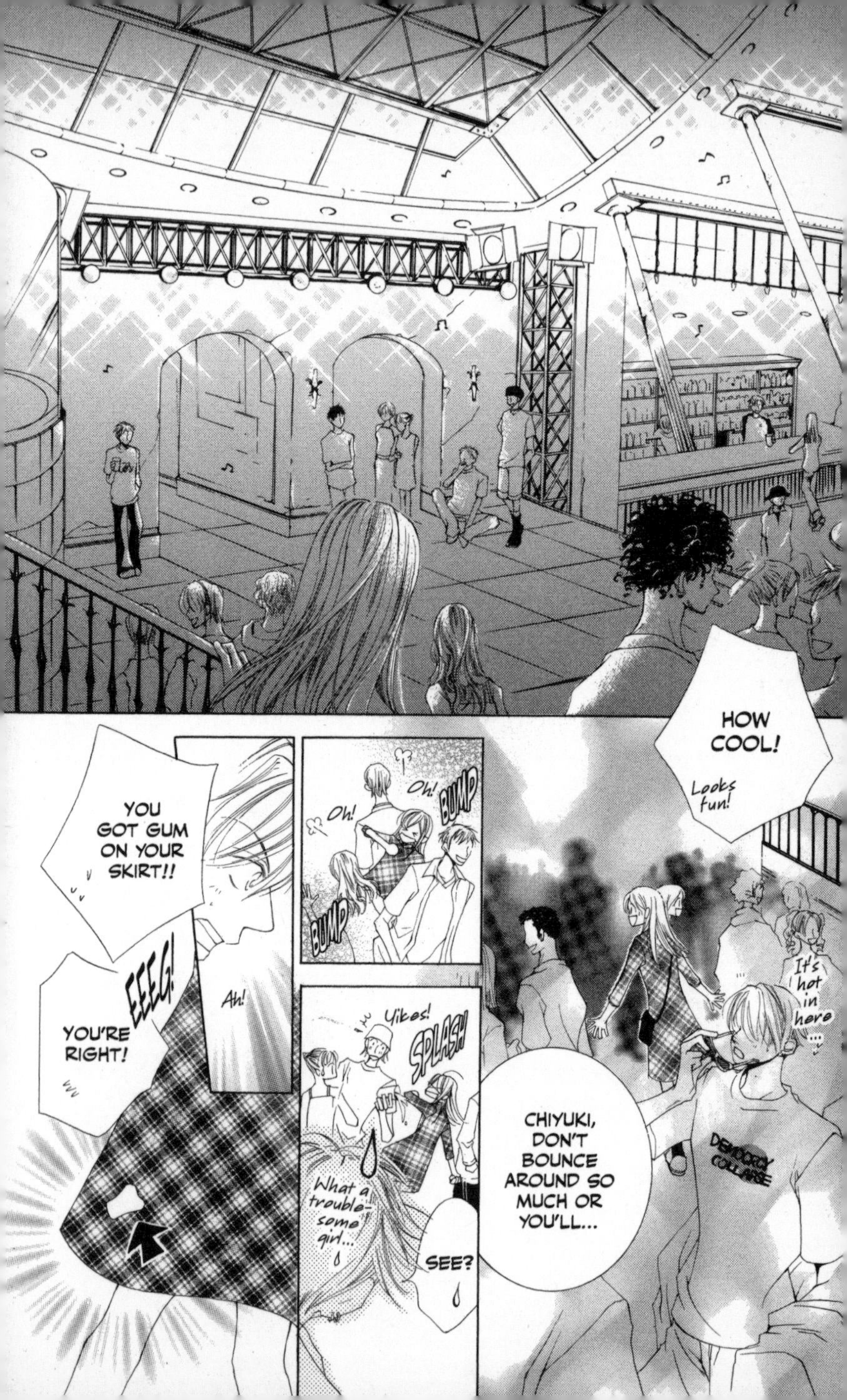
HOW COOL!
Looks fun!
It's hot in here...
CHIYUKI, DON'T BOUNCE AROUND SO MUCH OR YOU'LL...
SEE?
Oh!
BUMP
Oh!
BUMP
Yikes!
SPLASH
What a trouble-some girl...
YOU GOT GUM ON YOUR SKIRT!!
Ah!
EEEG!
YOU'RE RIGHT!

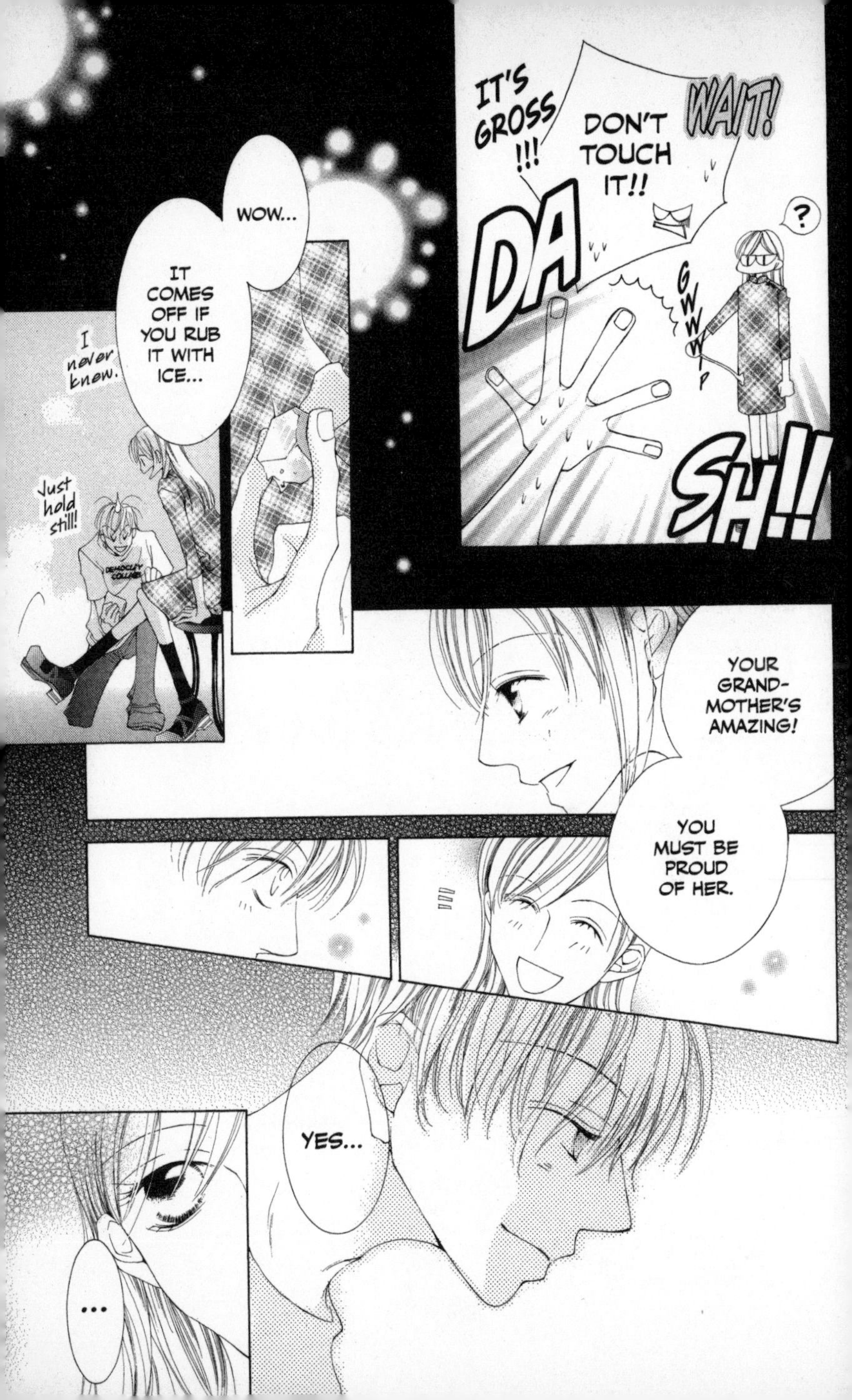
WAIT!
DON'T TOUCH IT!!
IT'S GROSS!!!
?
GWWWIP
DA
SH!!
WOW...
IT COMES OFF IF YOU RUB IT WITH ICE...
I never knew.
Just hold still!
YOUR GRAND-MOTHER'S AMAZING!
YOU MUST BE PROUD OF HER.
YES...
...

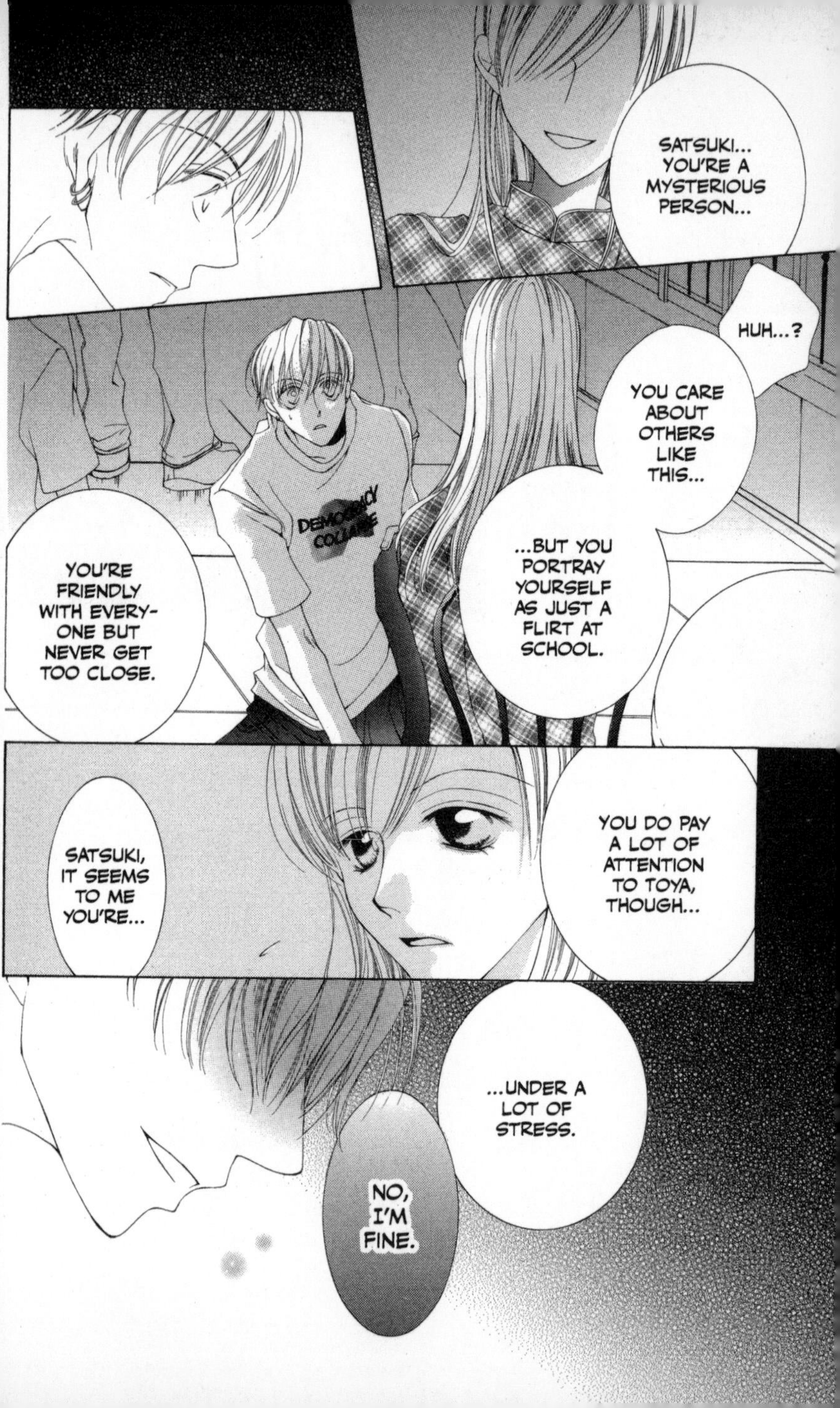
SATSUKI... YOU'RE A MYSTERIOUS PERSON...
HUH...?
YOU CARE ABOUT OTHERS LIKE THIS...
...BUT YOU PORTRAY YOURSELF AS JUST A FLIRT AT SCHOOL.
YOU'RE FRIENDLY WITH EVERY-ONE BUT NEVER GET TOO CLOSE.
YOU DO PAY A LOT OF ATTENTION TO TOYA, THOUGH...
SATSUKI, IT SEEMS TO ME YOU'RE...
...UNDER A LOT OF STRESS.
NO, I'M FINE.

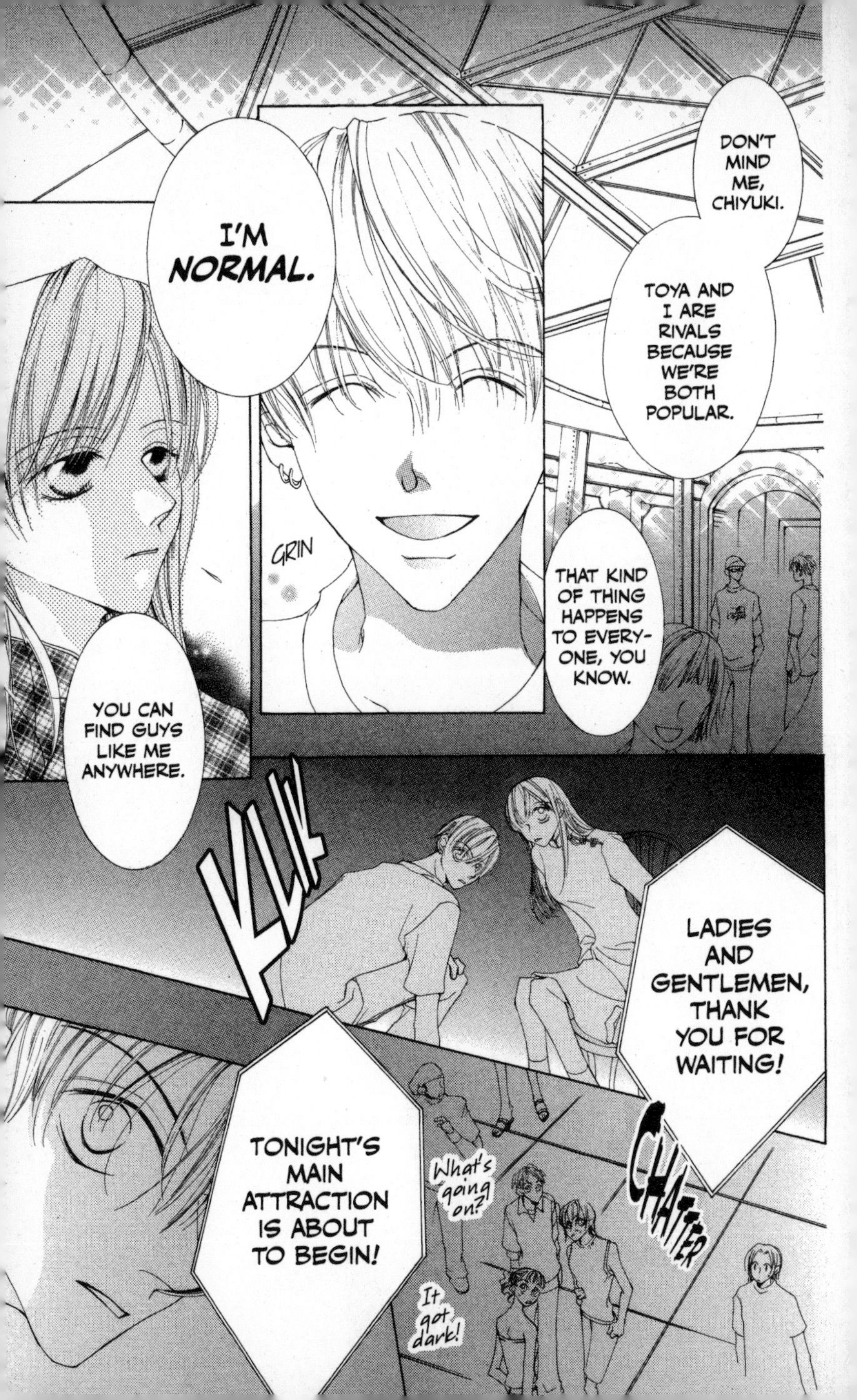
DON'T MIND ME, CHIYUKI.
TOYA AND I ARE RIVALS BECAUSE WE'RE BOTH POPULAR.
THAT KIND OF THING HAPPENS TO EVERY-ONE, YOU KNOW.
I'M NORMAL.
GRIN
YOU CAN FIND GUYS LIKE ME ANYWHERE.
LADIES AND GENTLEMEN, THANK YOU FOR WAITING!
KLIK
CHATTER
TONIGHT'S MAIN ATTRACTION IS ABOUT TO BEGIN!
What's going on?
It got dark!

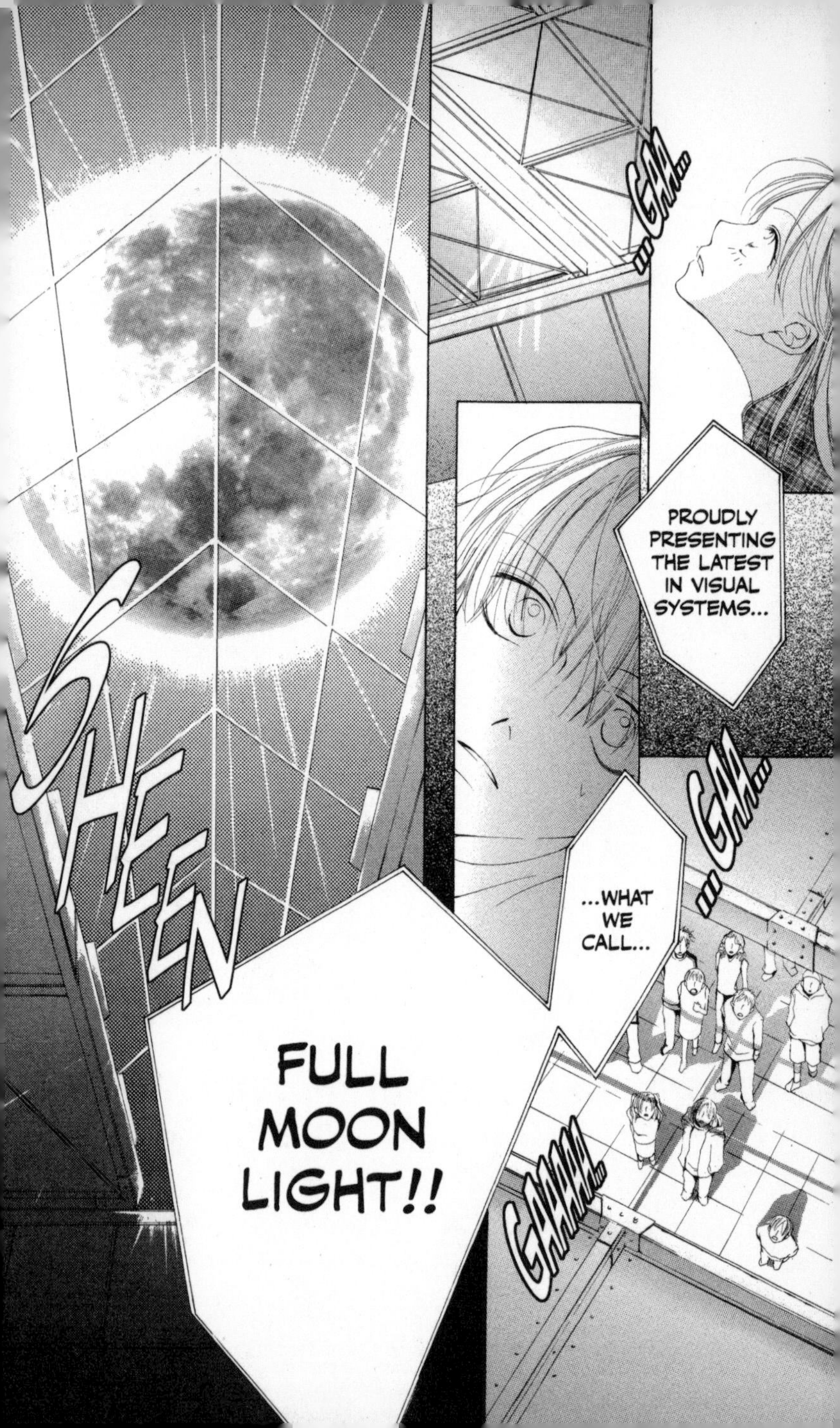
...GA...
PROUDLY PRESENTING THE LATEST IN VISUAL SYSTEMS...
...GA...
...WHAT WE CALL...
GAAAA...
SHEEN
FULL MOON LIGHT!!

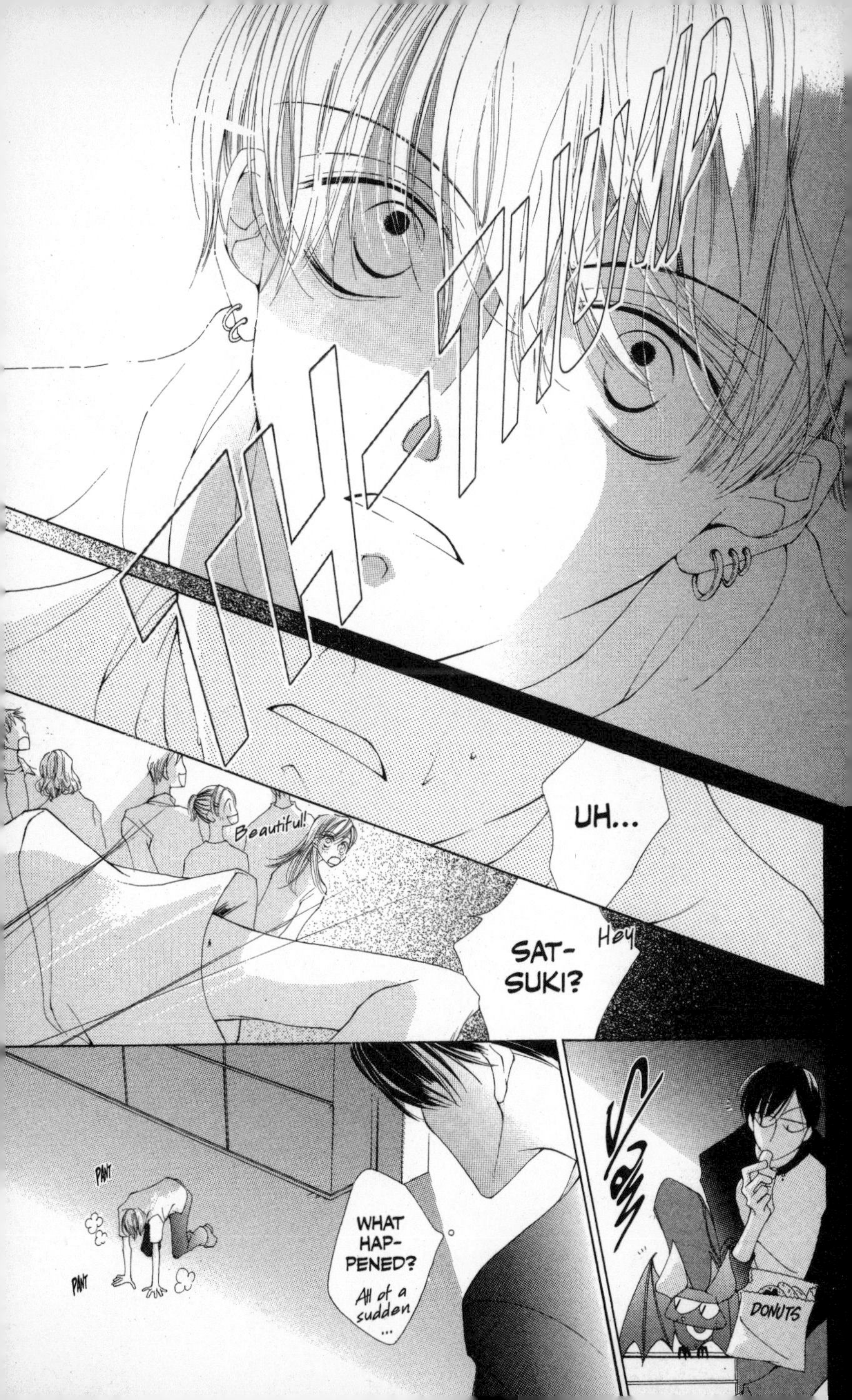

THUMP
UH...
SAT-SUKI?
Hey
Beautiful!
SLAM
WHAT HAP-PENED?
All of a sudden ...
DONUTS
PANT
PANT

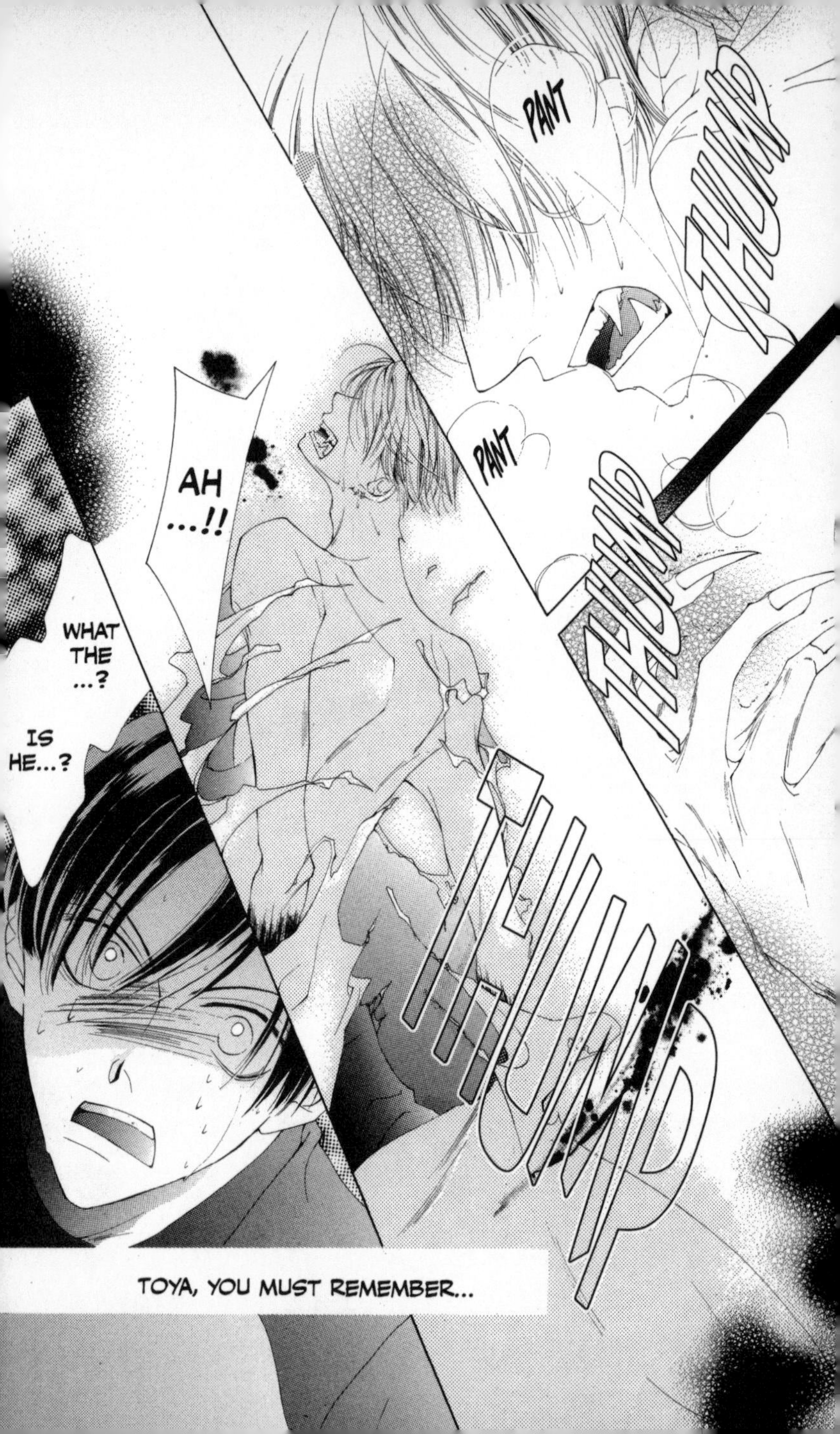
PANT
THUMP
PANT
THUMP
AH ...!!
THUMP
WHAT THE ...?
IS HE...?
TOYA, YOU MUST REMEMBER...

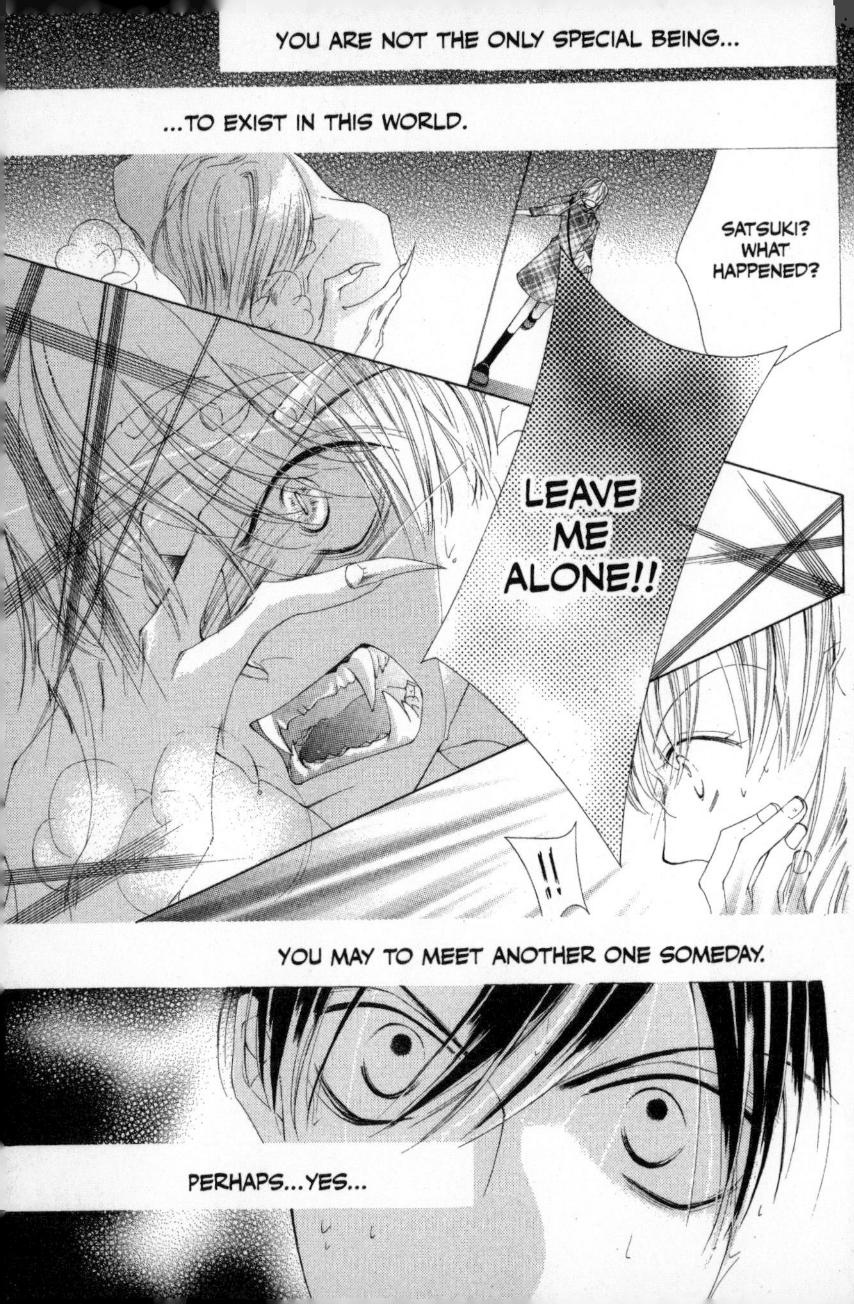
YOU ARE NOT THE ONLY SPECIAL BEING...
...TO EXIST IN THIS WORLD.
SATSUKI? WHAT HAPPENED?
LEAVE ME ALONE!!
!!
YOU MAY TO MEET ANOTHER ONE SOMEDAY.
PERHAPS...YES...

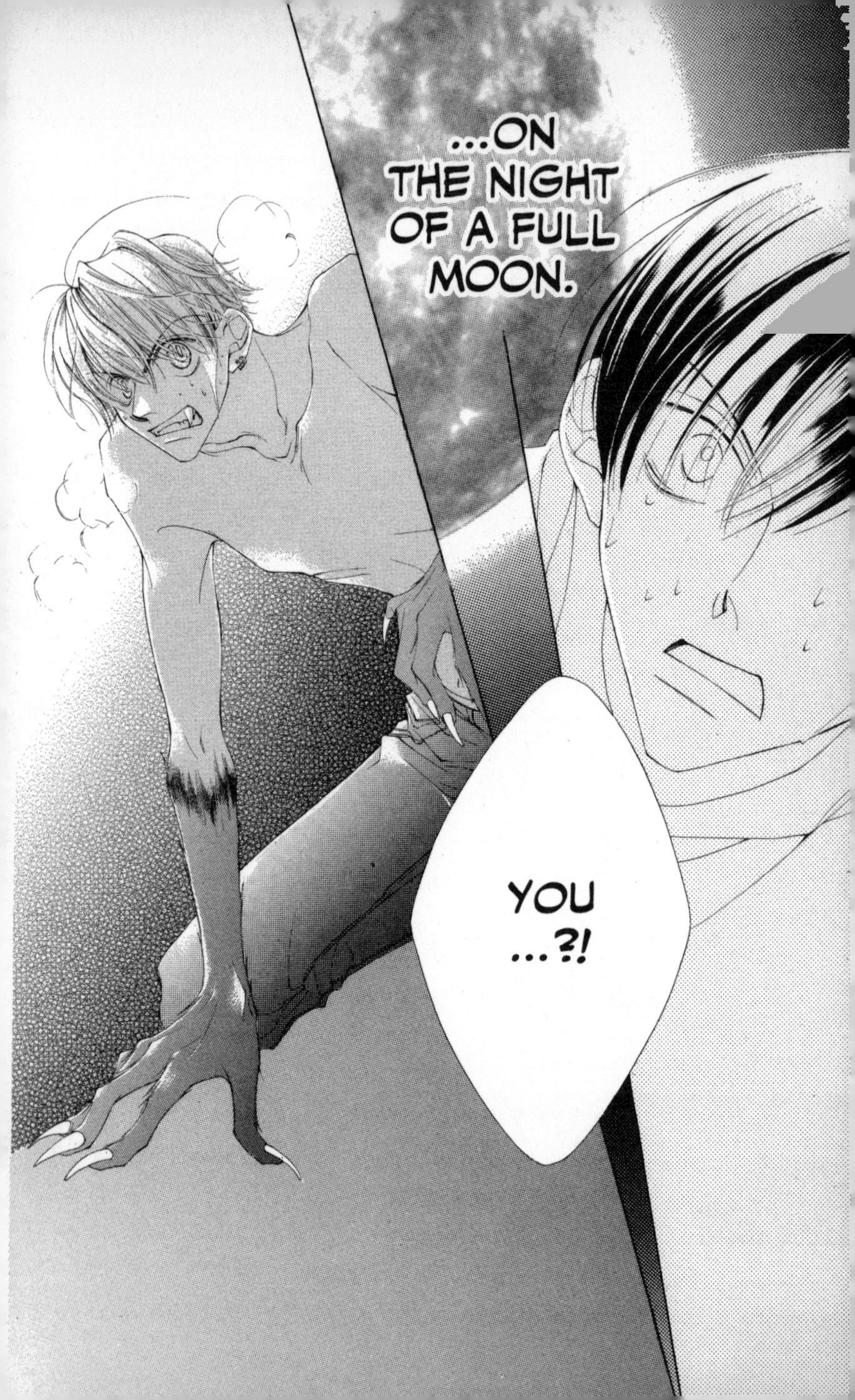
...ON THE NIGHT OF A FULL MOON.
YOU ...?!

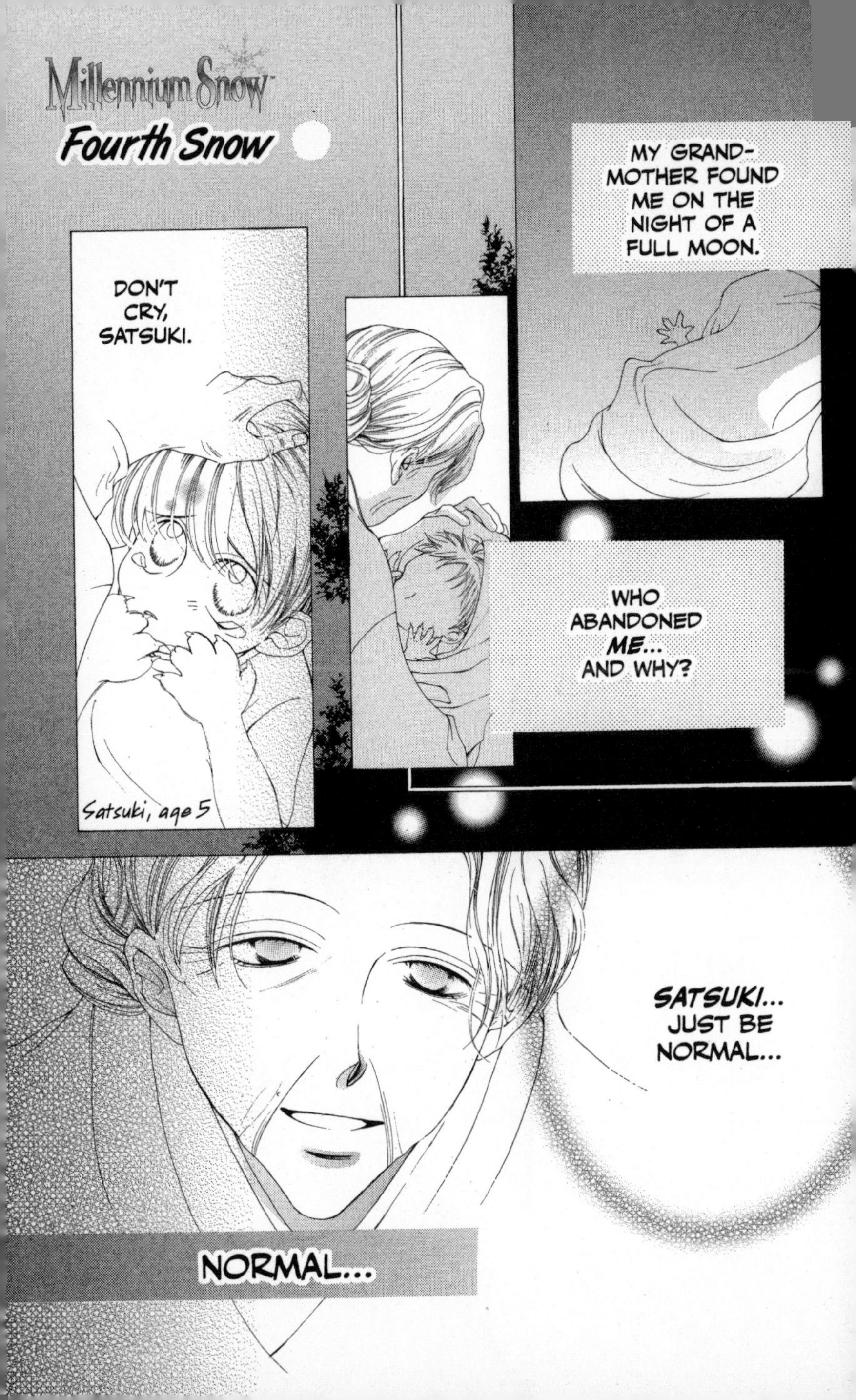
Millennium Snow
Fourth Snow
MY GRANDMOTHER FOUND ME ON THE NIGHT OF A FULL MOON.
WHO ABANDONED *ME*... AND WHY?
DON'T CRY, SATSUKI.
Satsuki, age 5
SATSUKI... JUST BE NORMAL...
NORMAL...

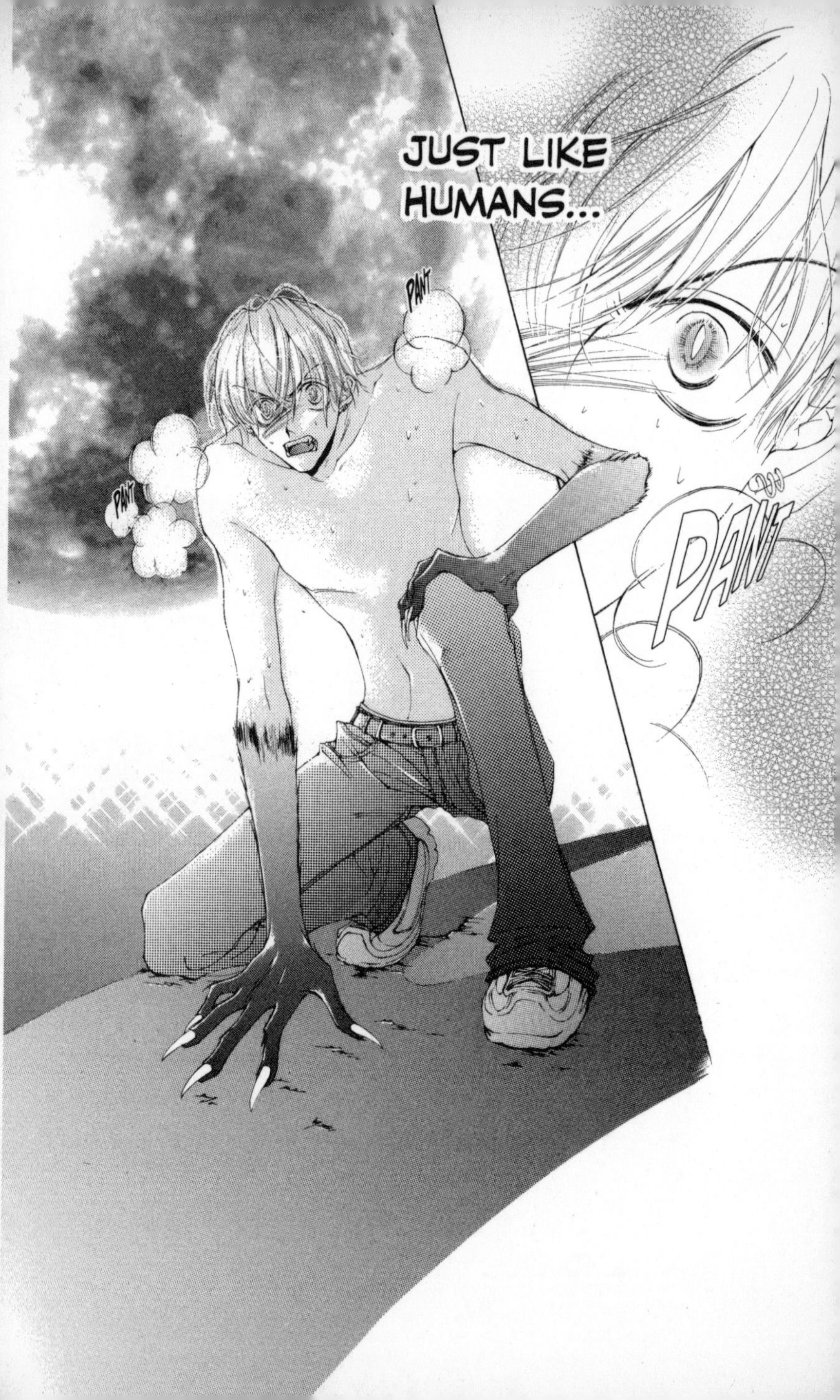
JUST LIKE HUMANS...
PANT
PANT
PANT

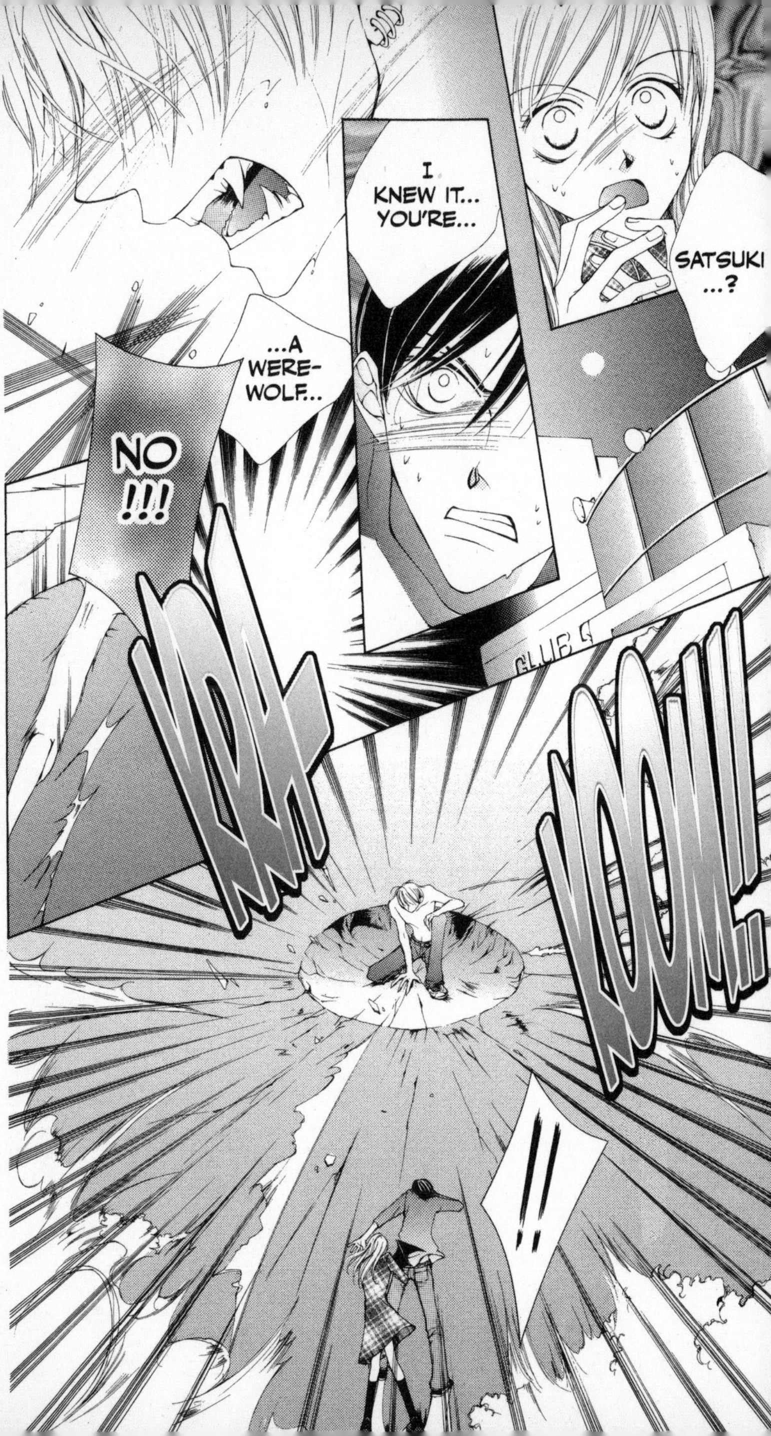
SATSUKI ...?
I KNEW IT... YOU'RE...
...A WERE-WOLF...
NO !!!
!!

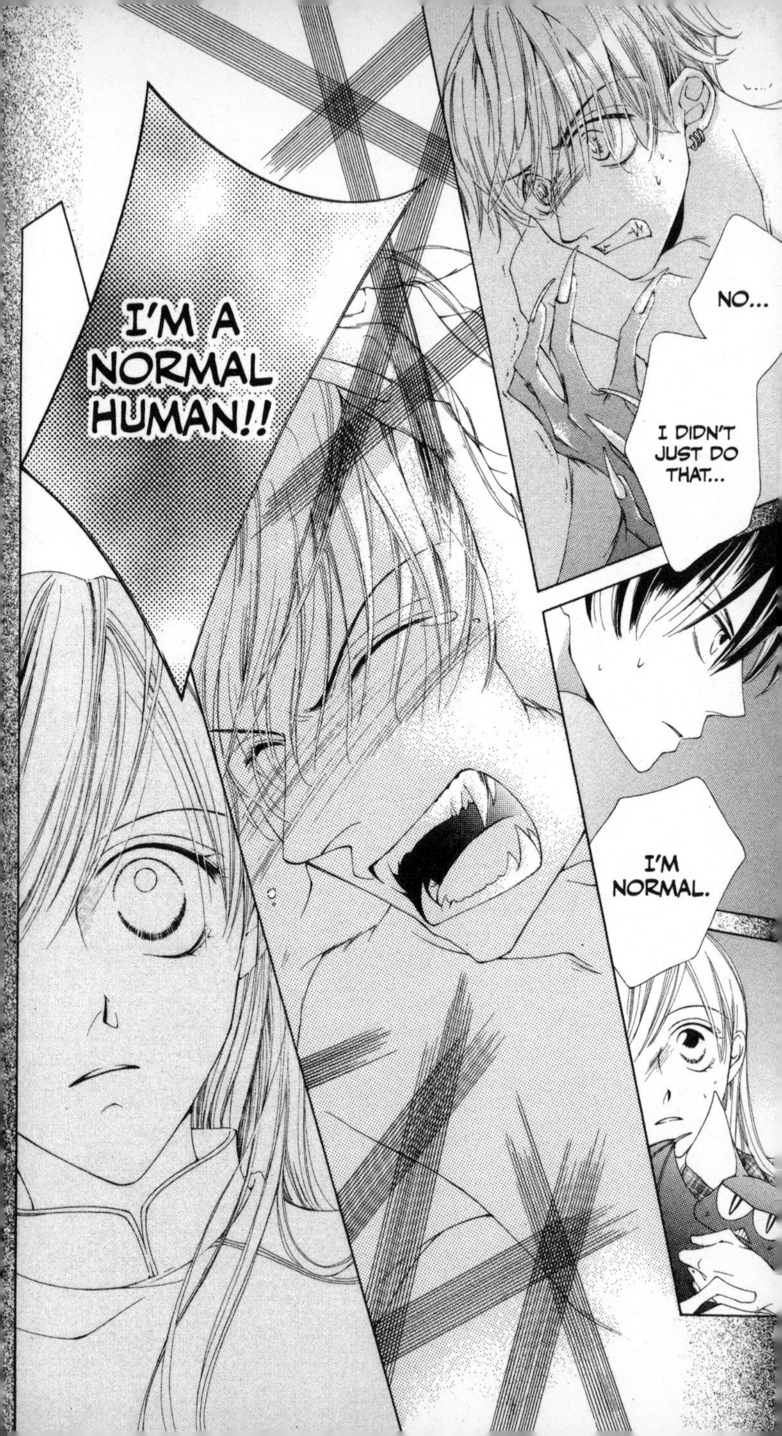
...
NO...
I DIDN'T JUST DO THAT...
I'M NORMAL.
I'M A NORMAL HUMAN!!

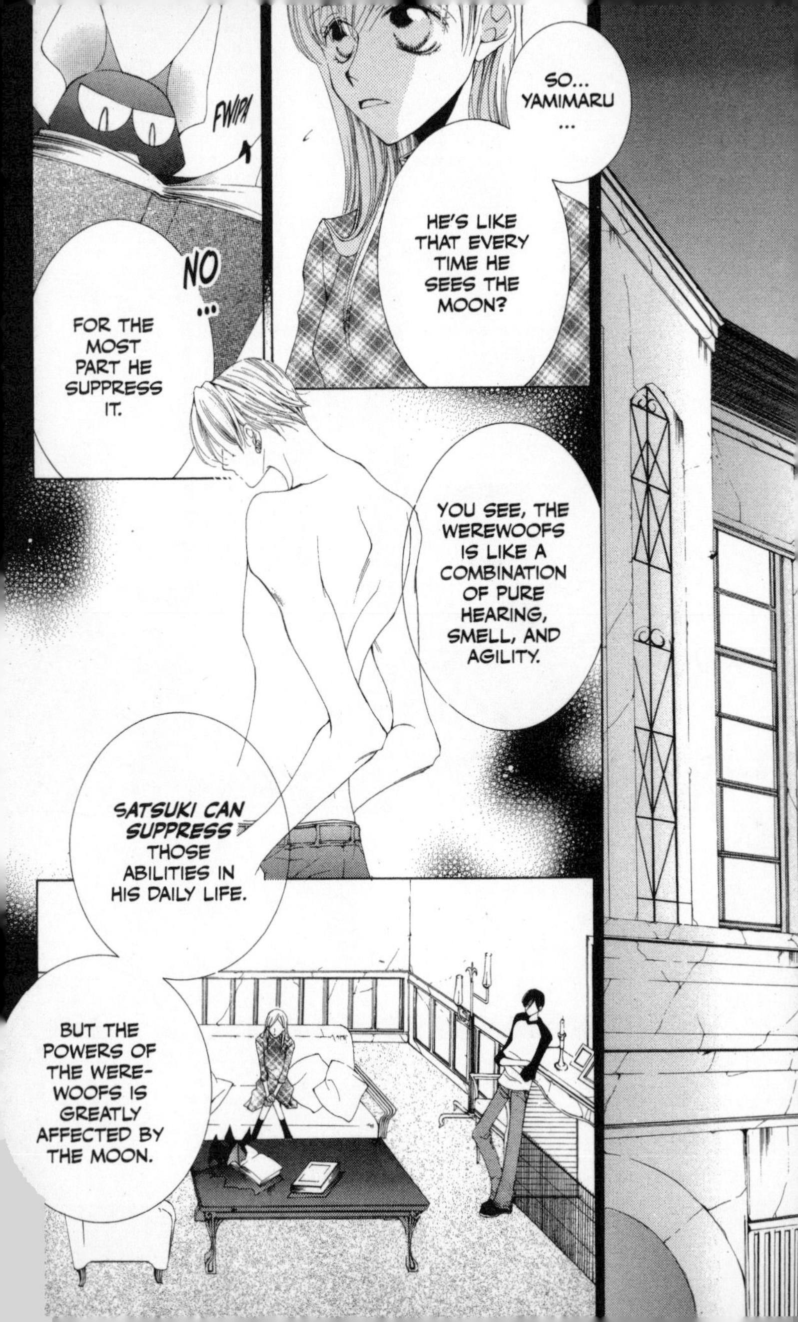
SO... YAMIMARU ...
HE'S LIKE THAT EVERY TIME HE SEES THE MOON?
FWIPA
NO ...
FOR THE MOST PART HE SUPPRESS IT.
YOU SEE, THE WEREWOOFS IS LIKE A COMBINATION OF PURE HEARING, SMELL, AND AGILITY.
SATSUKI CAN SUPPRESS THOSE ABILITIES IN HIS DAILY LIFE.
BUT THE POWERS OF THE WERE-WOOFS IS GREATLY AFFECTED BY THE MOON.

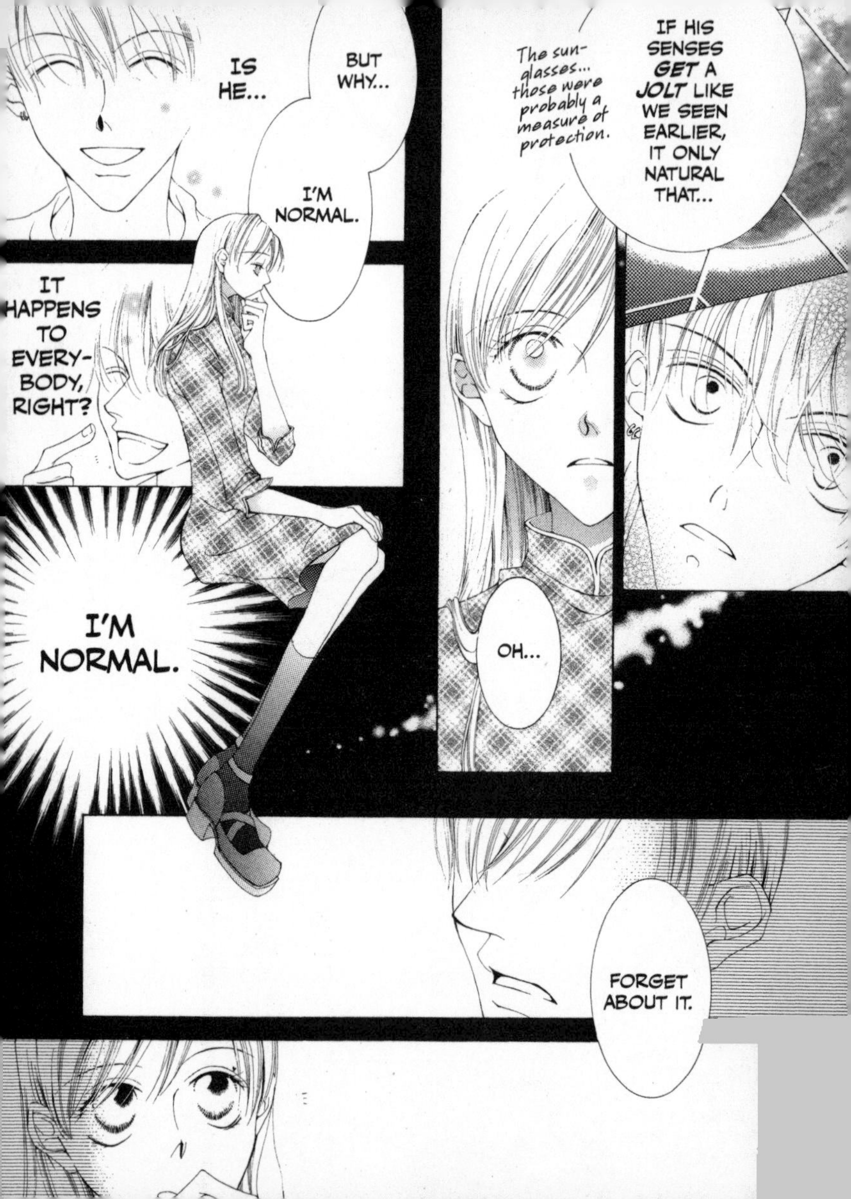
IF HIS SENSES GET A JOLT LIKE WE SEEN EARLIER, IT ONLY NATURAL THAT...
The sun-glasses... those were probably a measure of protection.
OH...
BUT WHY...
IS HE...
I'M NORMAL.
IT HAPPENS TO EVERY-BODY, RIGHT?
I'M NORMAL.
FORGET ABOUT IT.

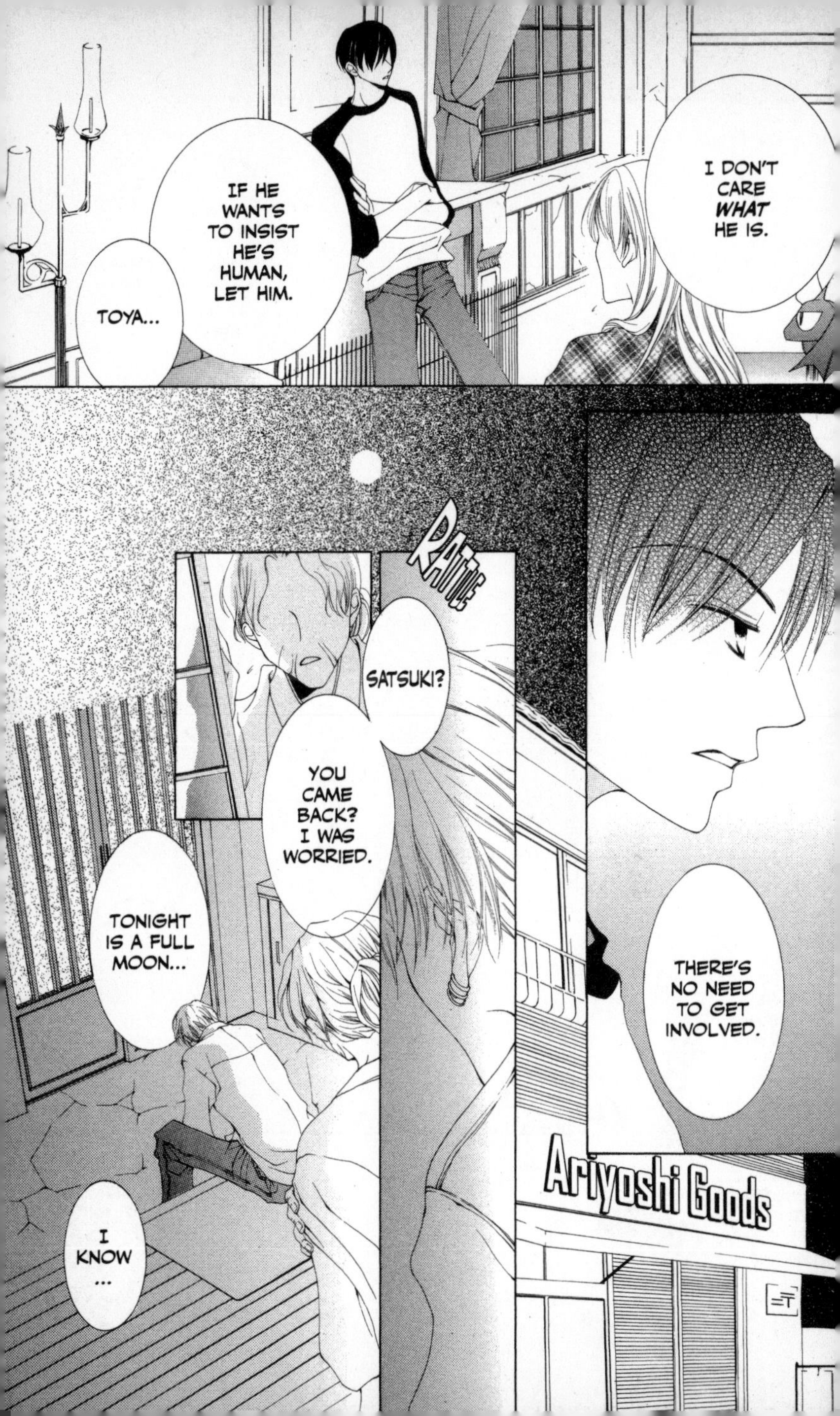
I DON'T CARE *WHAT* HE IS.
IF HE WANTS TO INSIST HE'S HUMAN, LET HIM.
TOYA...
THERE'S NO NEED TO GET INVOLVED.
Ariyoshi Goods
RATTLE
SATSUKI?
YOU CAME BACK? I WAS WORRIED.
TONIGHT IS A FULL MOON...
I KNOW ...

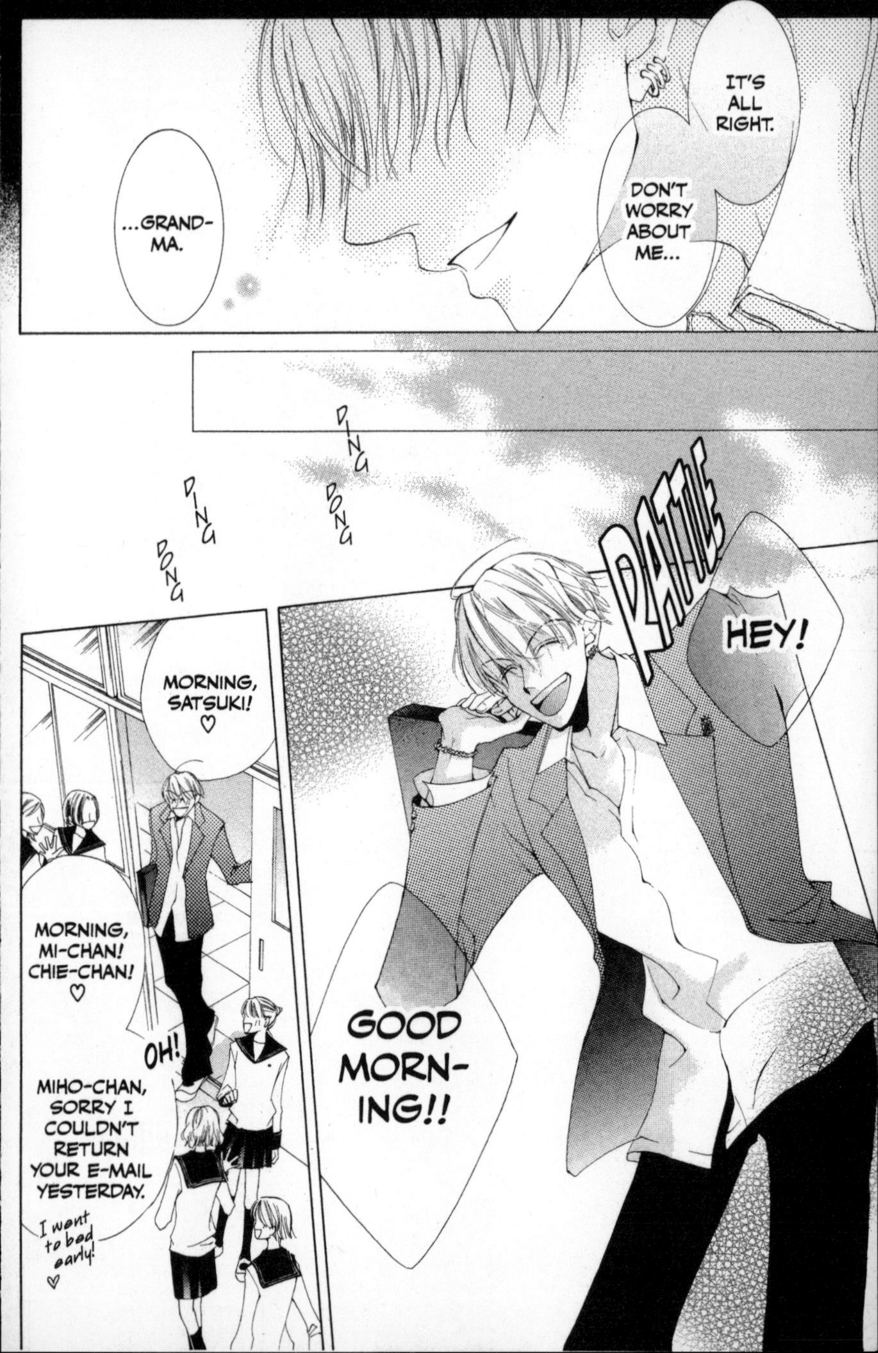
IT'S ALL RIGHT.
DON'T WORRY ABOUT ME...
...GRAND-MA.
DING DONG
DING DONG
RATTLE
HEY!
GOOD MORN-ING!!
MORNING, SATSUKI! ♡
MORNING, MI-CHAN! CHIE-CHAN! ♡
OH!
MIHO-CHAN, SORRY I COULDN'T RETURN YOUR E-MAIL YESTERDAY.
I went to bed early! ♡

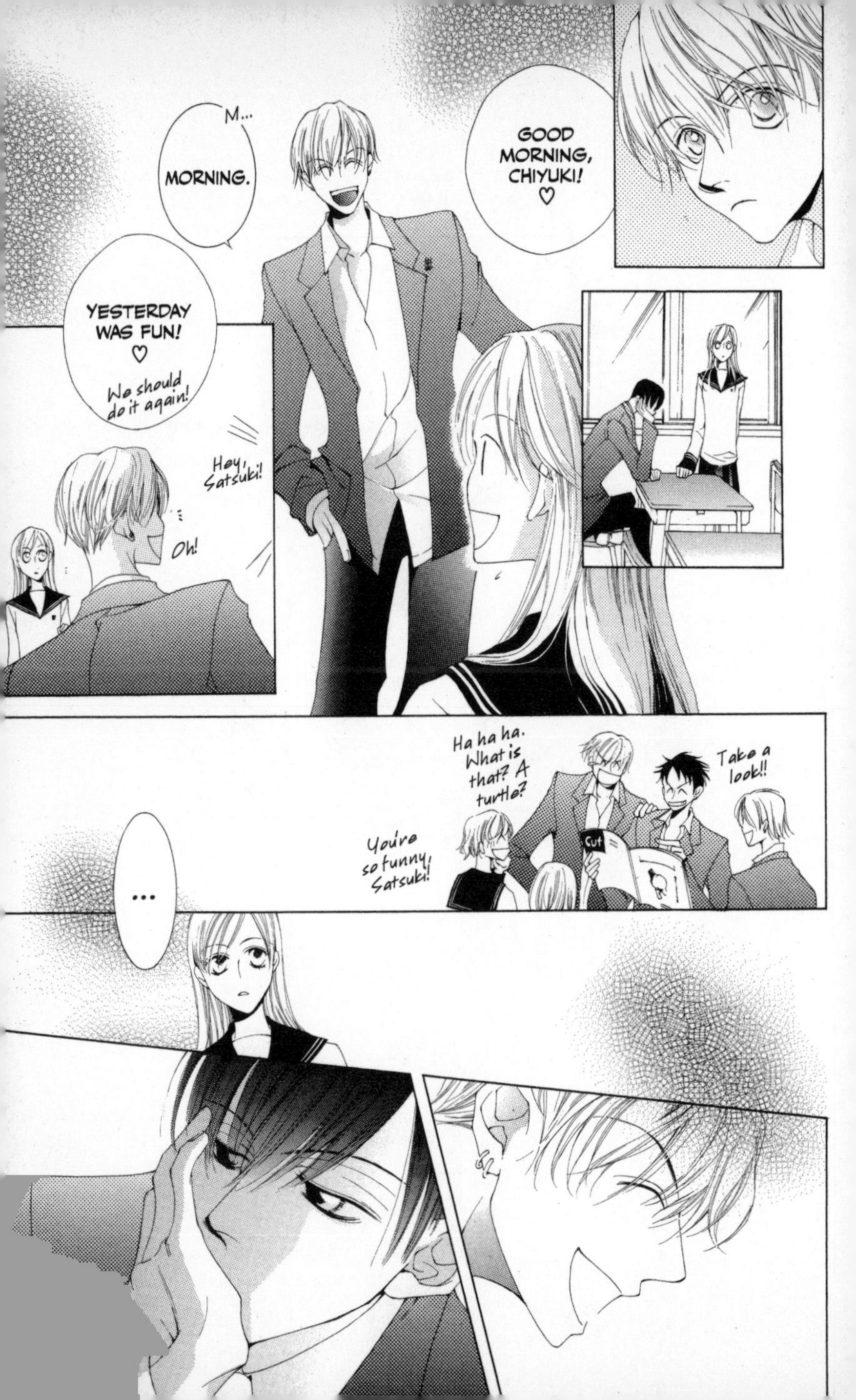
GOOD MORNING, CHIYUKI! ♡
M... MORNING.
YESTERDAY WAS FUN! ♡
We should do it again!
Hey, Satsuki!
Oh!
Take a look!!
Ha ha ha. What is that? A turtle?
Cut
You're so funny, Satsuki!
...

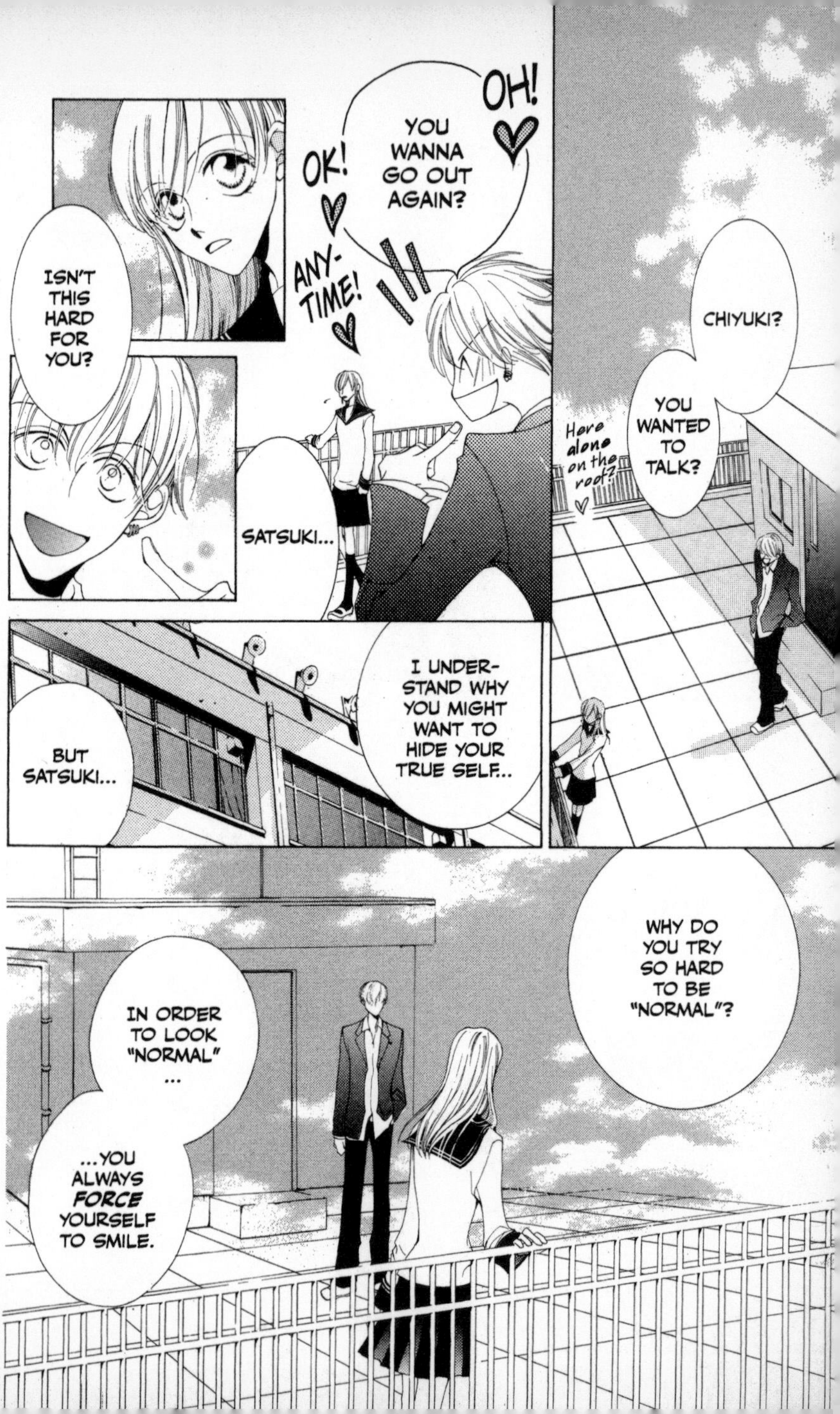
CHIYUKI?
YOU WANTED TO TALK?
Here alone on the roof?
OH!
YOU WANNA GO OUT AGAIN?
OK!
ANY-TIME!
SATSUKI...
ISN'T THIS HARD FOR YOU?
I UNDER-STAND WHY YOU MIGHT WANT TO HIDE YOUR TRUE SELF...
BUT SATSUKI...
WHY DO YOU TRY SO HARD TO BE "NORMAL"?
IN ORDER TO LOOK "NORMAL" ...
...YOU ALWAYS *FORCE* YOURSELF TO SMILE.

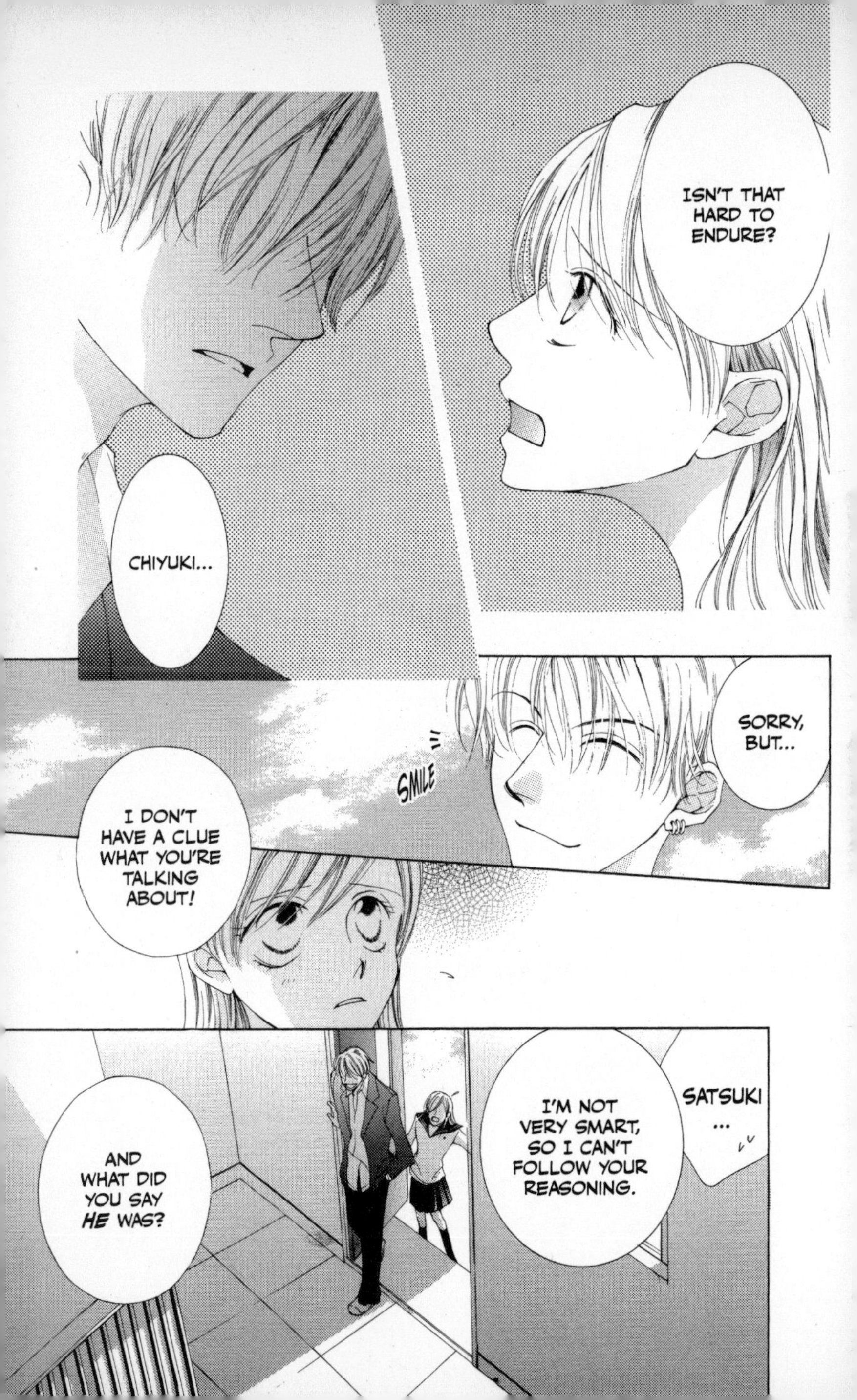
ISN'T THAT HARD TO ENDURE?
CHIYUKI...
SORRY, BUT...
SMILE
I DON'T HAVE A CLUE WHAT YOU'RE TALKING ABOUT!
SATSUKI ...
I'M NOT VERY SMART, SO I CAN'T FOLLOW YOUR REASONING.
AND WHAT DID YOU SAY HE WAS?

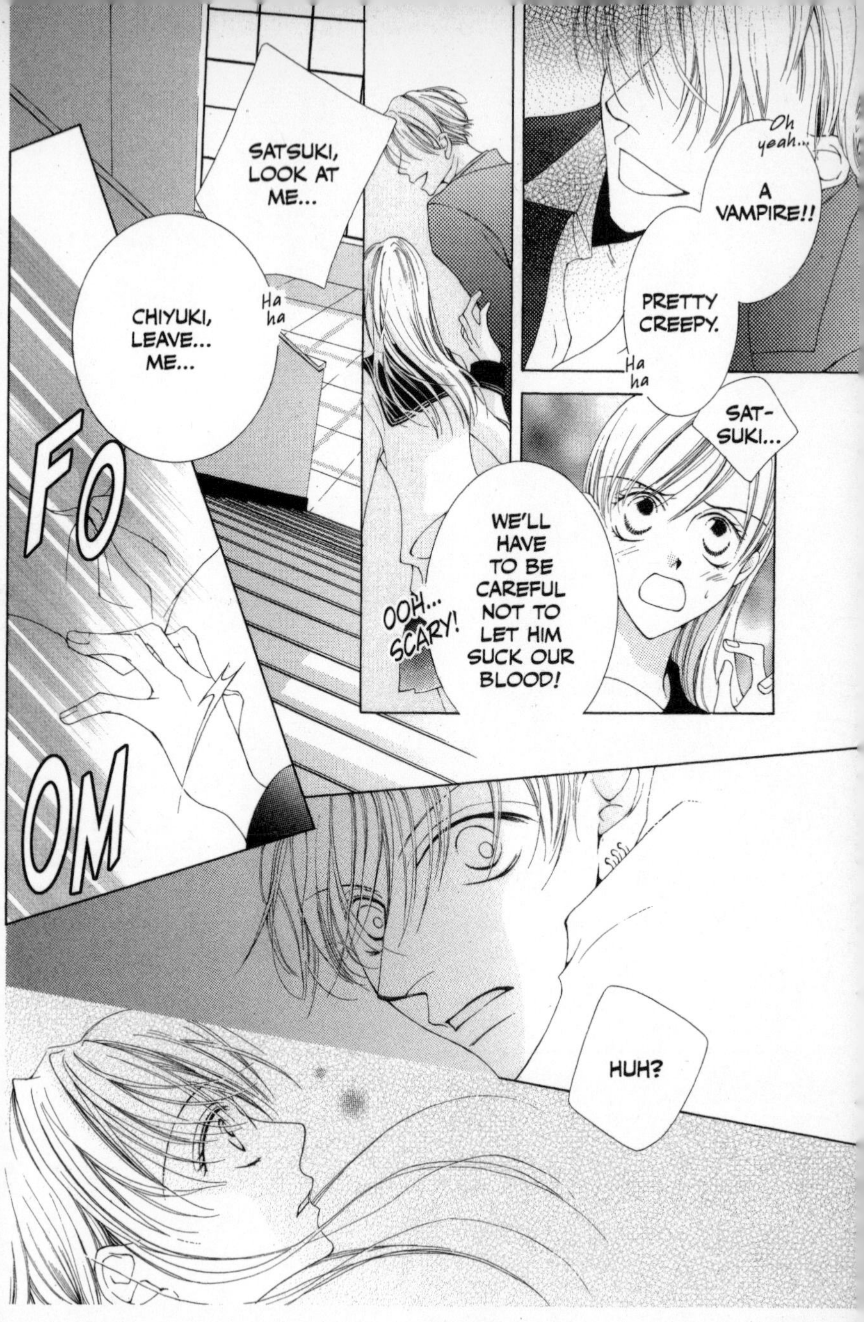
Oh yeah...
A VAMPIRE!!
PRETTY CREEPY.
Ha ha
SAT-SUKI...
WE'LL HAVE TO BE CAREFUL NOT TO LET HIM SUCK OUR BLOOD!
SATSUKI, LOOK AT ME...
OOH... SCARY!
Ha ha
CHIYUKI, LEAVE... ME...
FOOM
HUH?

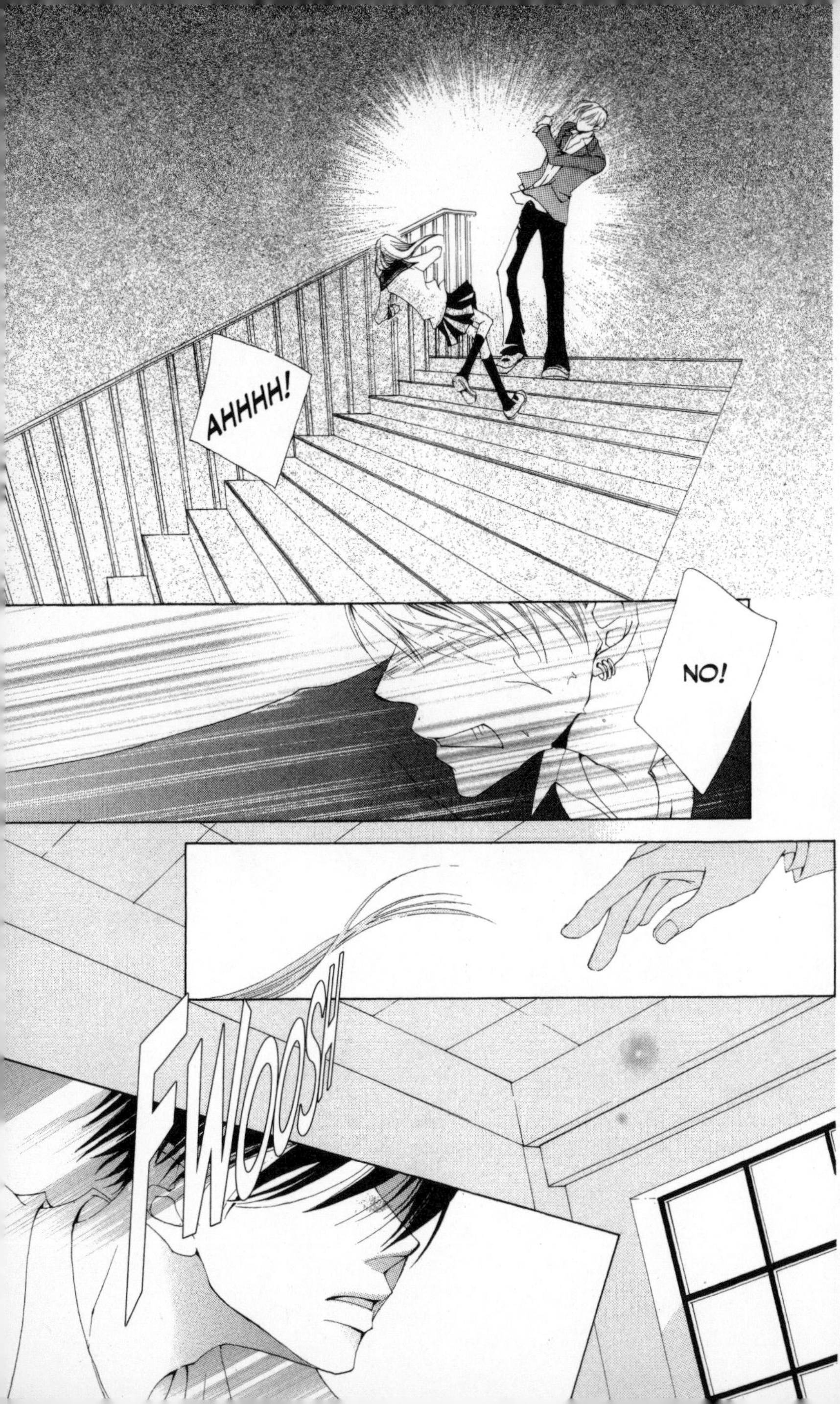
AHHHH!
NO!
FWOOSH

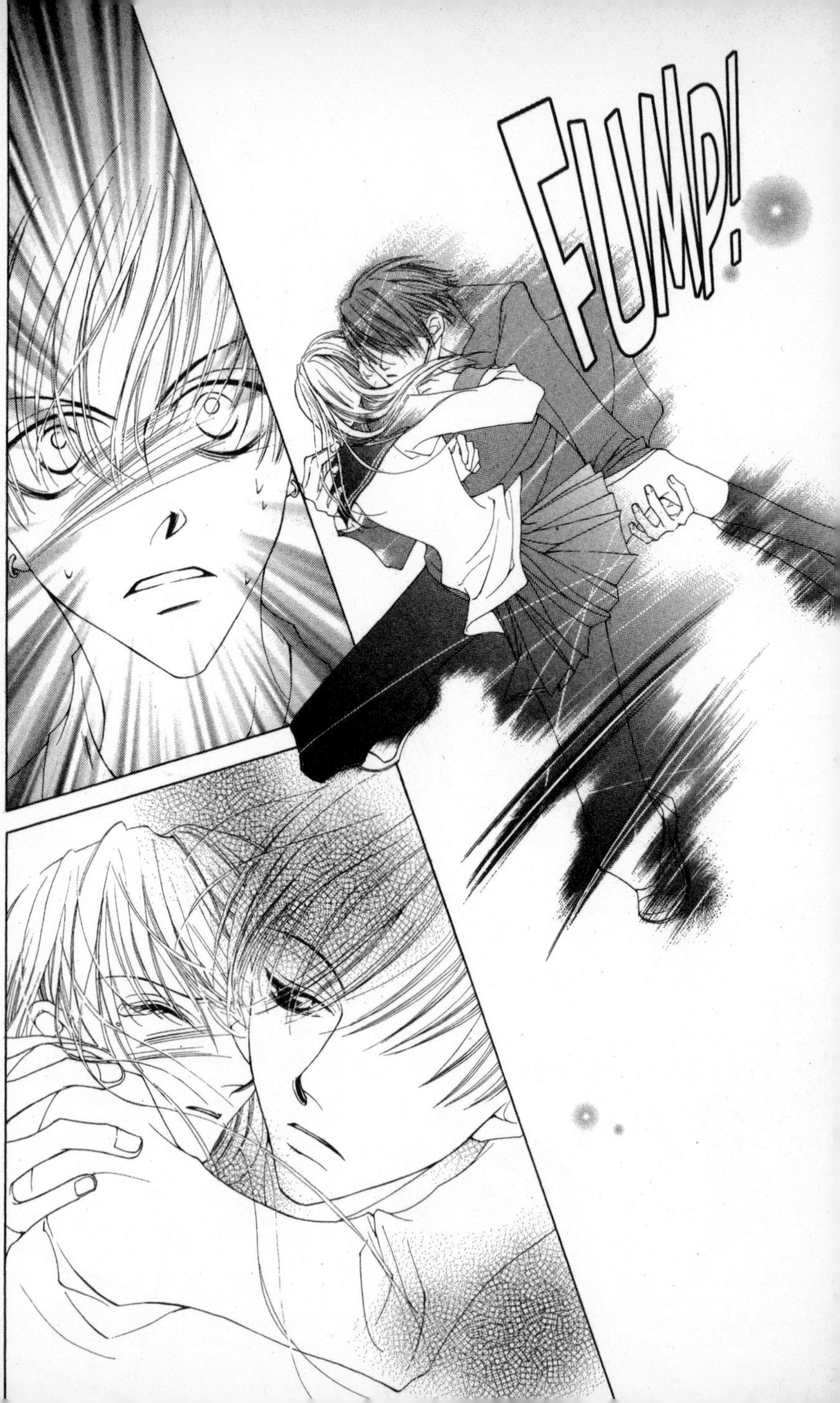
FLUMP!

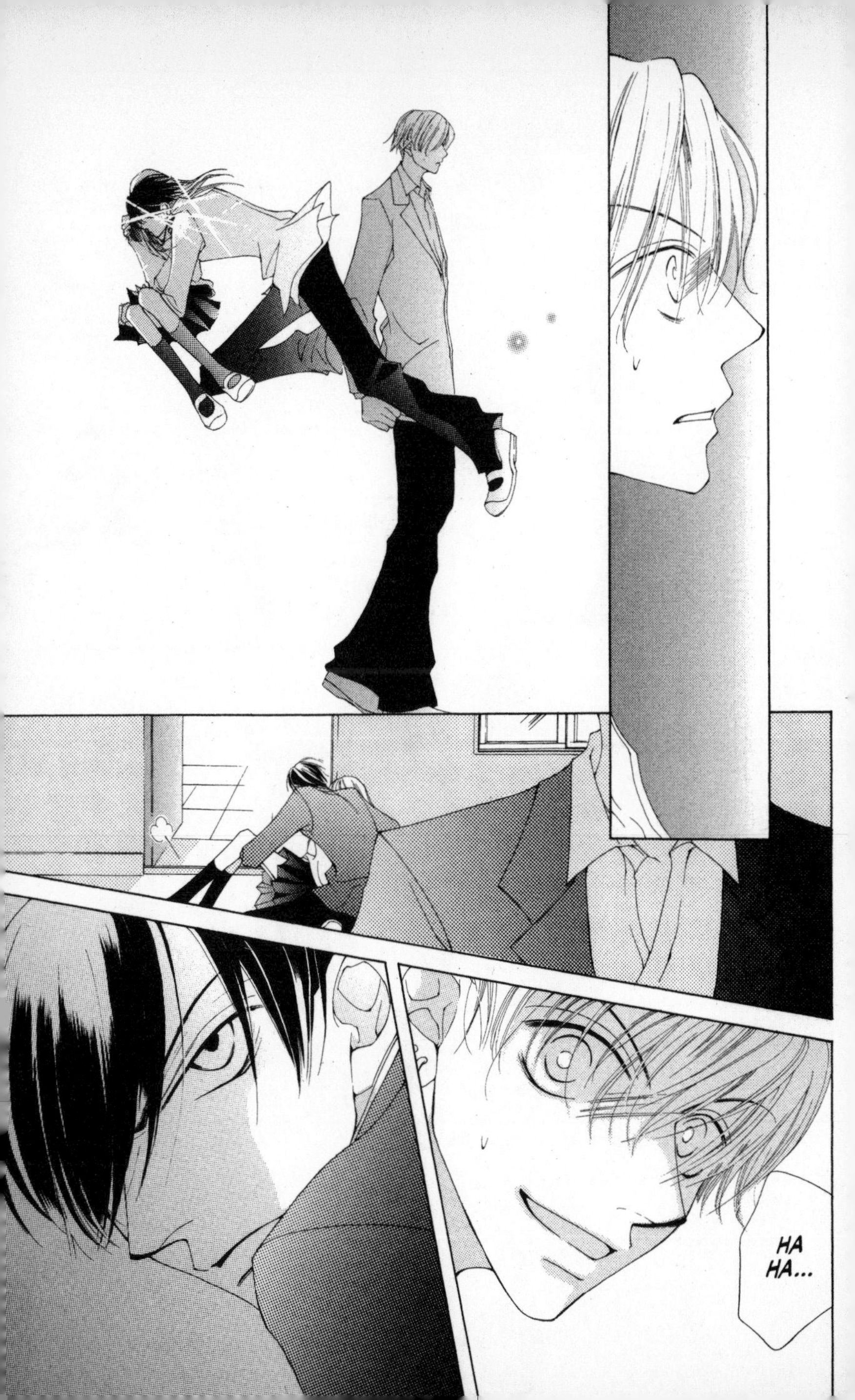
HA
HA...

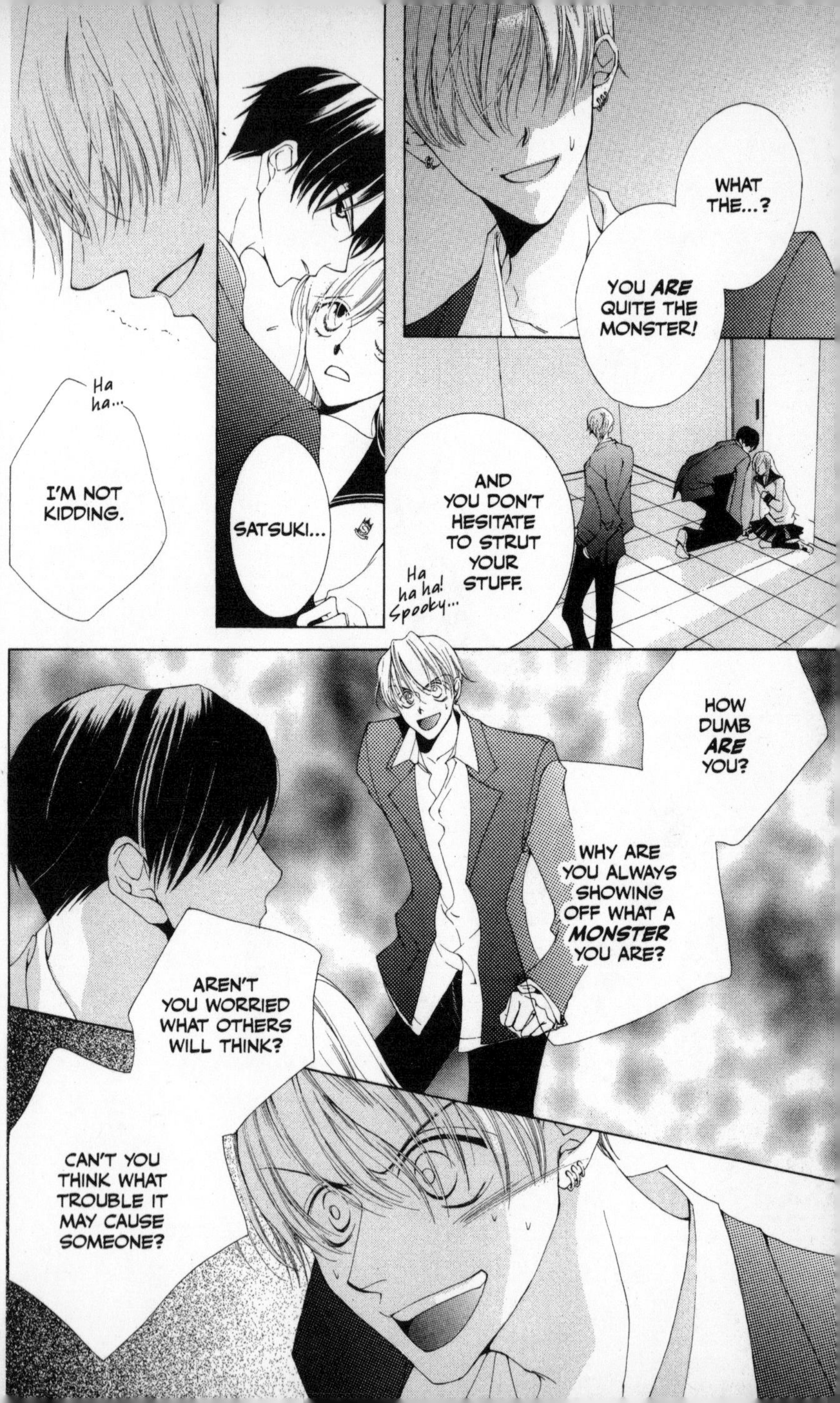
WHAT THE...?
YOU ARE QUITE THE MONSTER!
AND YOU DON'T HESITATE TO STRUT YOUR STUFF.
Ha ha ha! Spooky...
SATSUKI...
Ha ha...
I'M NOT KIDDING.
HOW DUMB ARE YOU?
WHY ARE YOU ALWAYS SHOWING OFF WHAT A MONSTER YOU ARE?
AREN'T YOU WORRIED WHAT OTHERS WILL THINK?
CAN'T YOU THINK WHAT TROUBLE IT MAY CAUSE SOMEONE?

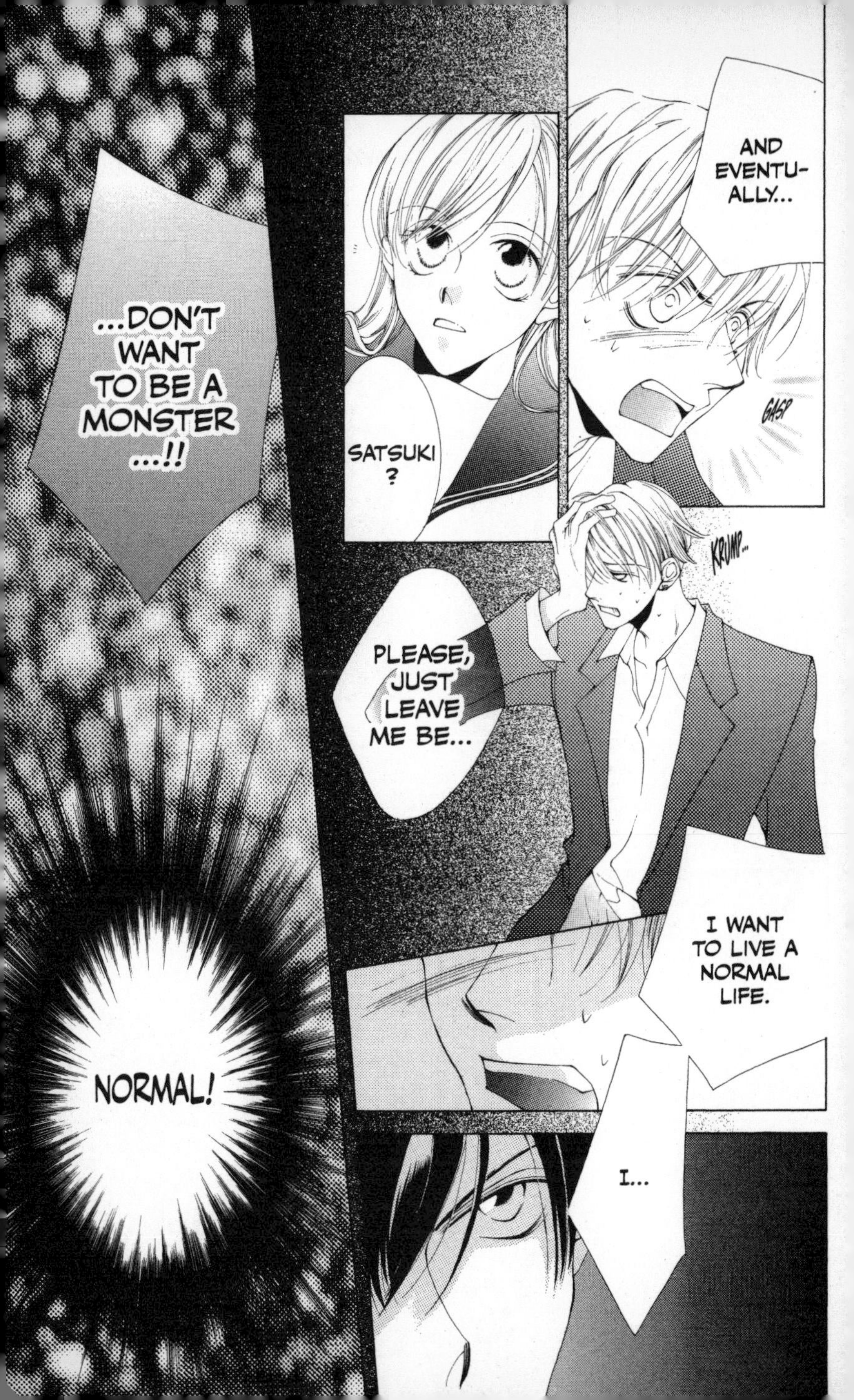
AND EVENTU-ALLY...
GASP
SATSUKI ?
KRUMP...
PLEASE, JUST LEAVE ME BE...
I WANT TO LIVE A NORMAL LIFE.
I...
...DON'T WANT TO BE A MONSTER ...!!
NORMAL!

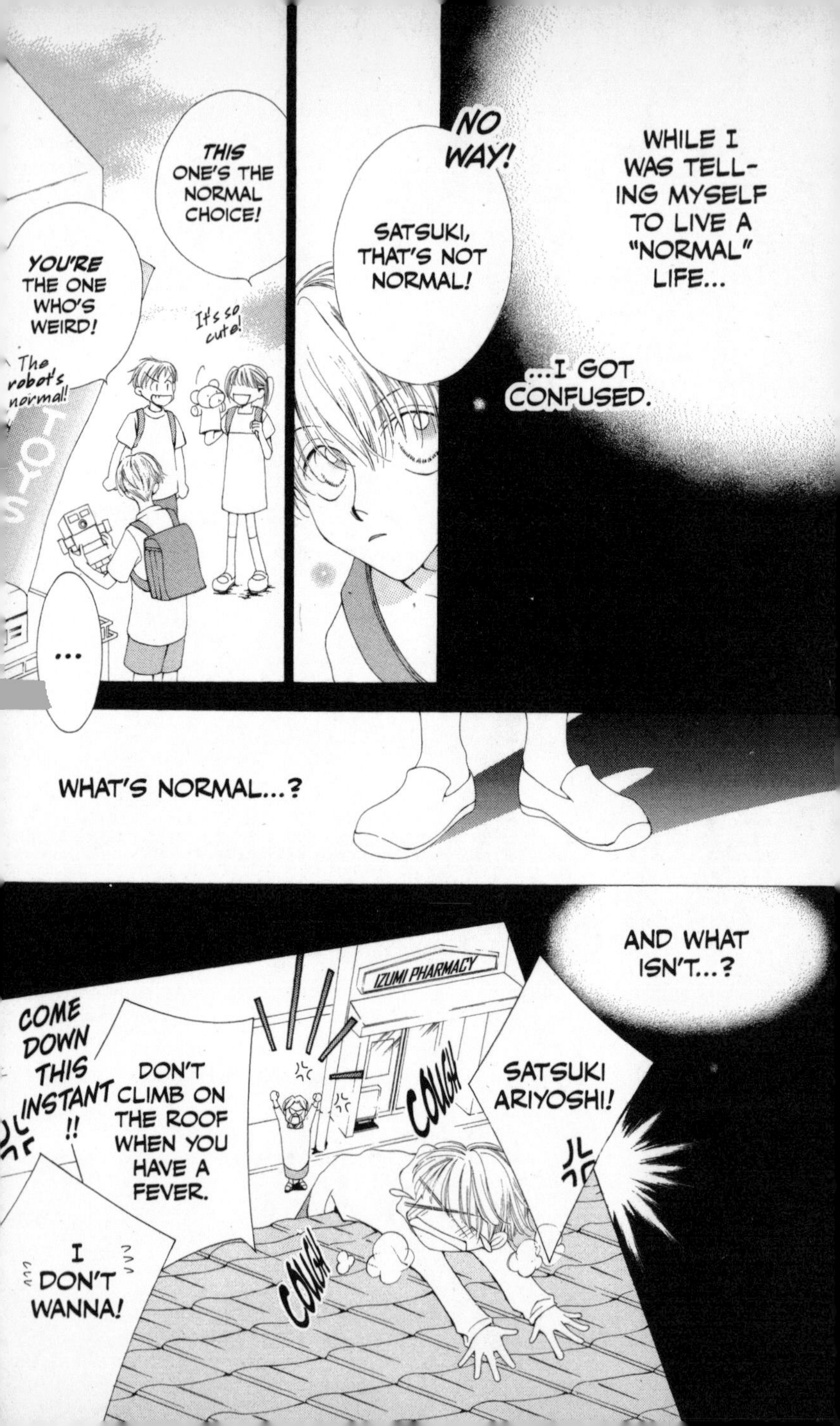

WHILE I WAS TELL-ING MYSELF TO LIVE A "NORMAL" LIFE...
NO WAY!
SATSUKI, THAT'S NOT NORMAL!
...I GOT CONFUSED.
THIS ONE'S THE NORMAL CHOICE!
It's so cute!
YOU'RE THE ONE WHO'S WEIRD!
The robot's normal!
TOYS
...
WHAT'S NORMAL...?
AND WHAT ISN'T...?
SATSUKI ARIYOSHI!
IZUMI PHARMACY
COUGH
DON'T CLIMB ON THE ROOF WHEN YOU HAVE A FEVER.
COME DOWN THIS INSTANT!!
COUGH
I DON'T WANNA!

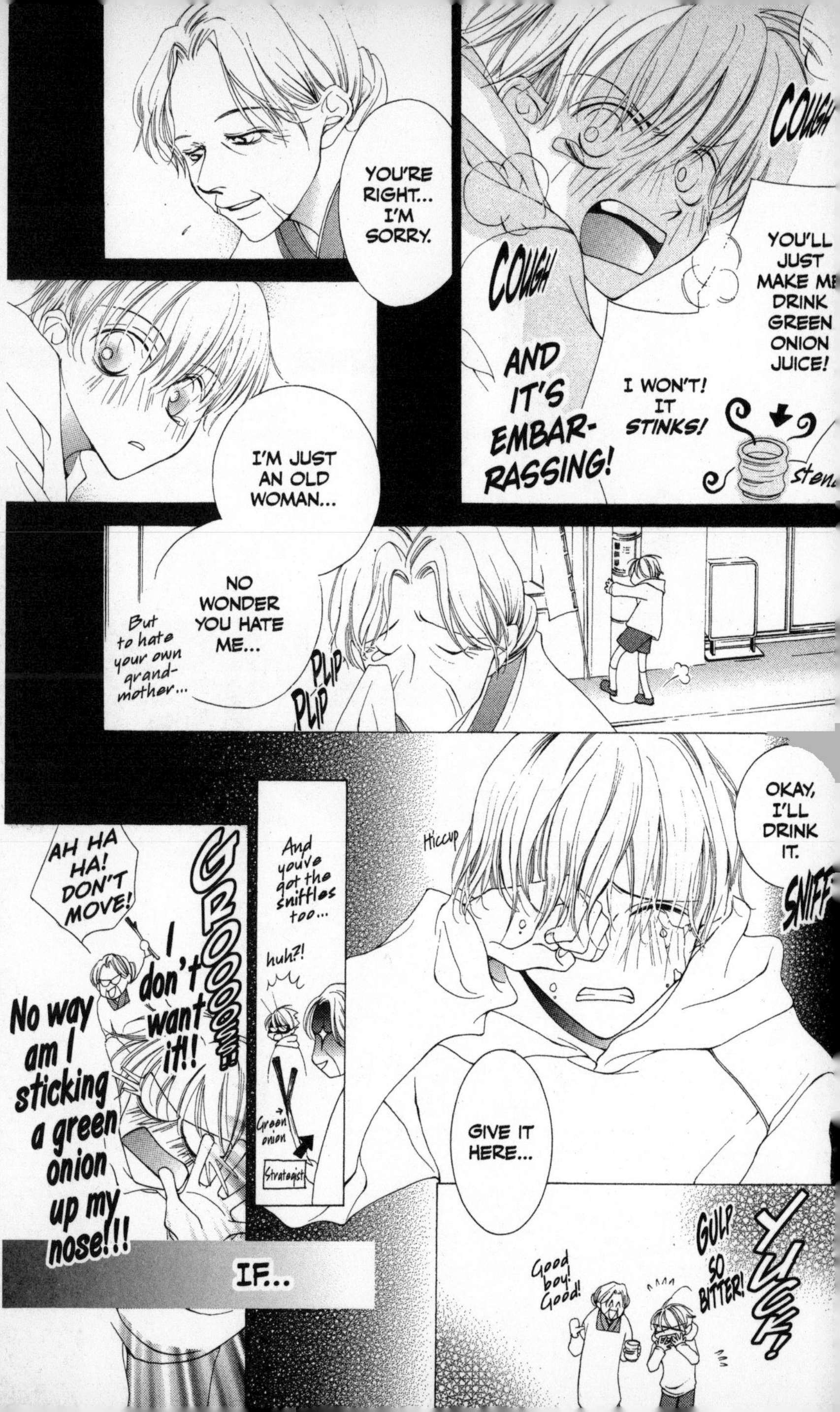
COUGH
YOU'LL JUST MAKE ME DRINK GREEN ONION JUICE!
COUGH
AND IT'S EMBARRASSING!
I WON'T! IT STINKS!
YOU'RE RIGHT... I'M SORRY.
I'M JUST AN OLD WOMAN...
NO WONDER YOU HATE ME...
But to hate your own grandmother...
PLIP PLIP
OKAY, I'LL DRINK IT.
SNIFF
Hiccup
GIVE IT HERE...
YUCK!
GULP SO BITTER!
Good boy! Good!
And you've got the sniffles too...
huh?!
Green onion
Strategist
AH HA HA! DON'T MOVE!
GROOOOOS!!
I don't want it!!
No way am I sticking a green onion up my nose!!!
IF...

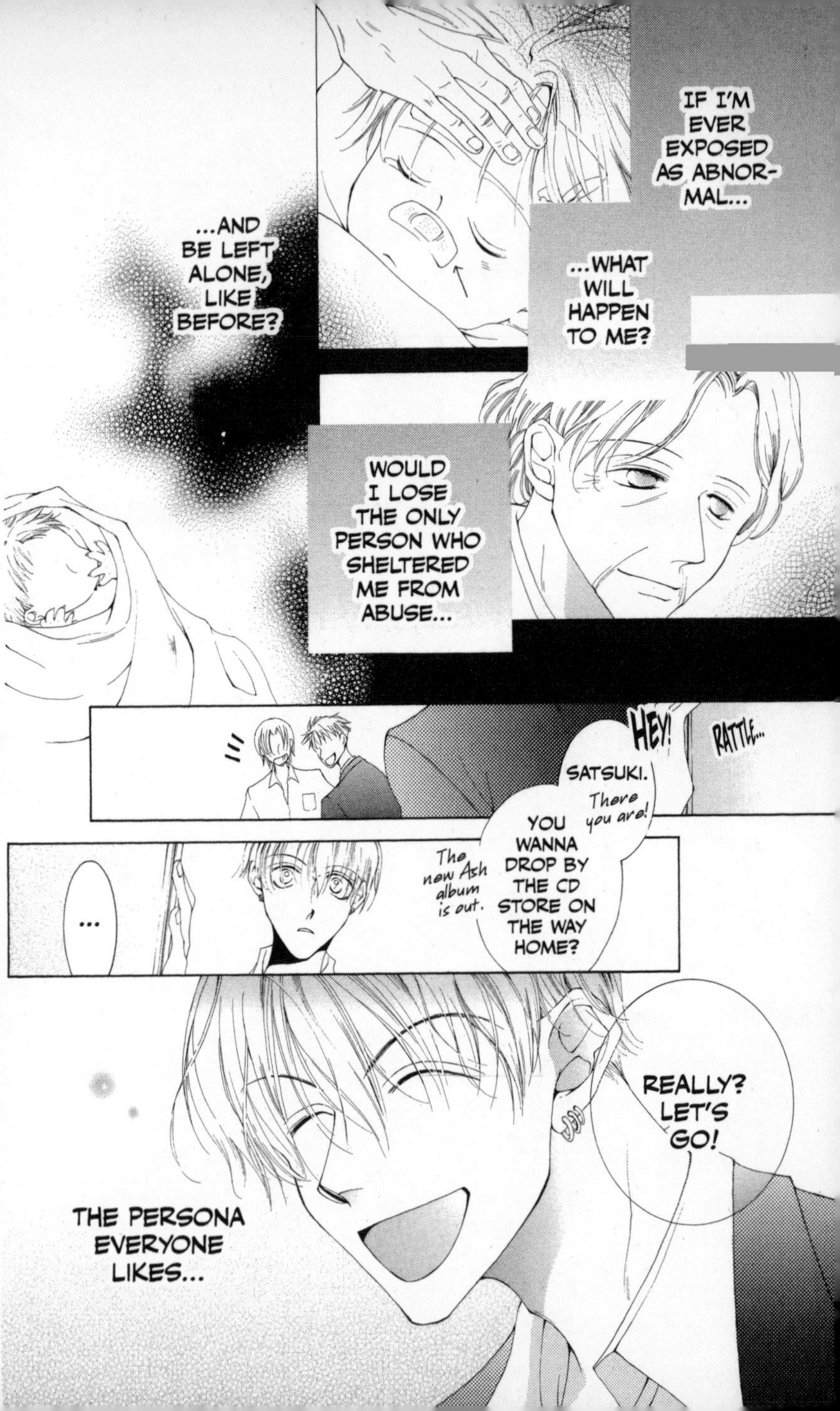

IF I'M EVER EXPOSED AS ABNORMAL...
...WHAT WILL HAPPEN TO ME?
WOULD I LOSE THE ONLY PERSON WHO SHELTERED ME FROM ABUSE...
...AND BE LEFT ALONE, LIKE BEFORE?
RATTLE...
HEY!
SATSUKI.
There you are!
YOU WANNA DROP BY THE CD STORE ON THE WAY HOME?
The new Ash album is out.
...
REALLY? LET'S GO!
THE PERSONA EVERYONE LIKES...

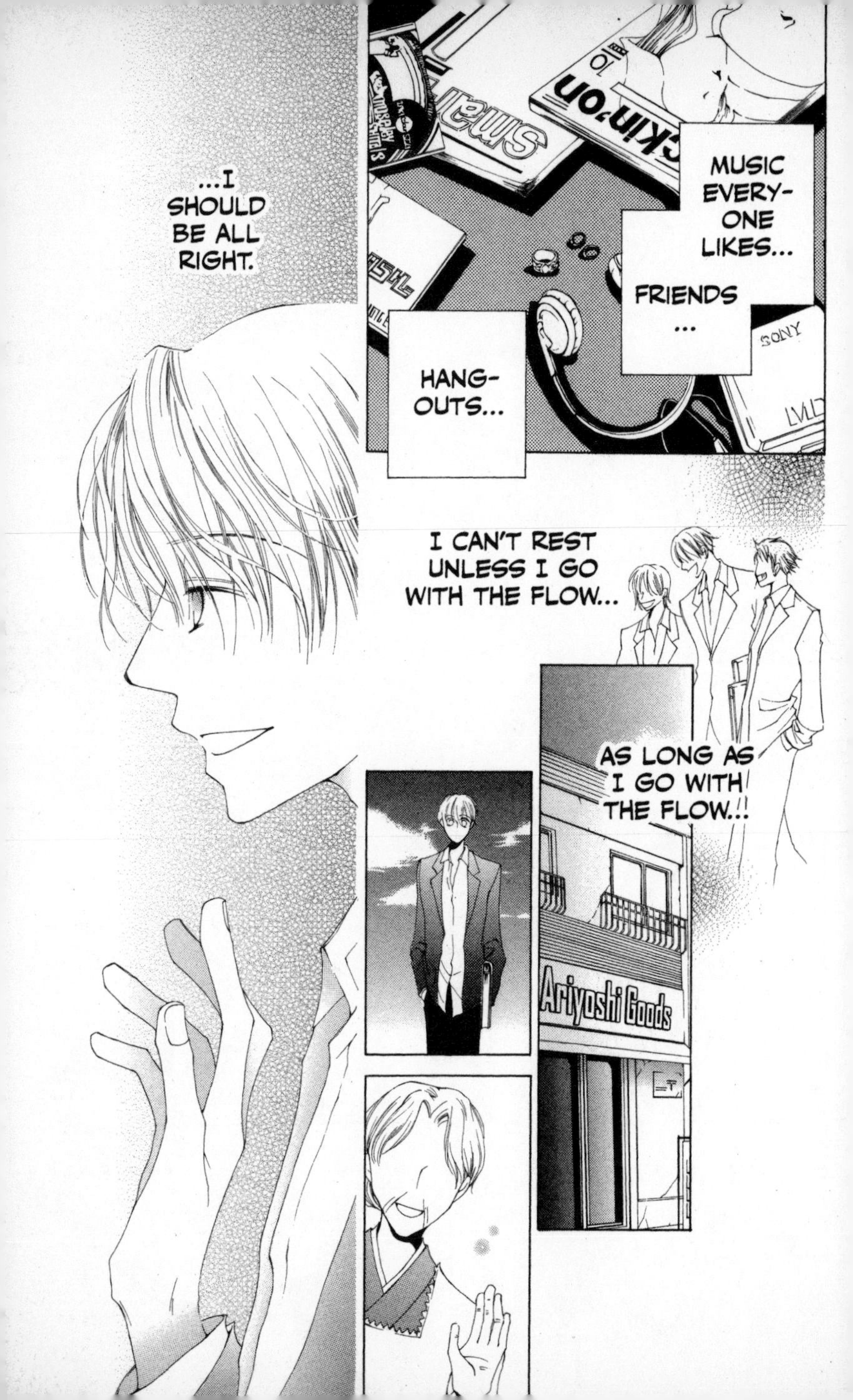
MUSIC EVERY-ONE LIKES...
FRIENDS ...
HANG-OUTS...
I CAN'T REST UNLESS I GO WITH THE FLOW...
AS LONG AS I GO WITH THE FLOW...!
Ariyoshi Goods
...I SHOULD BE ALL RIGHT.

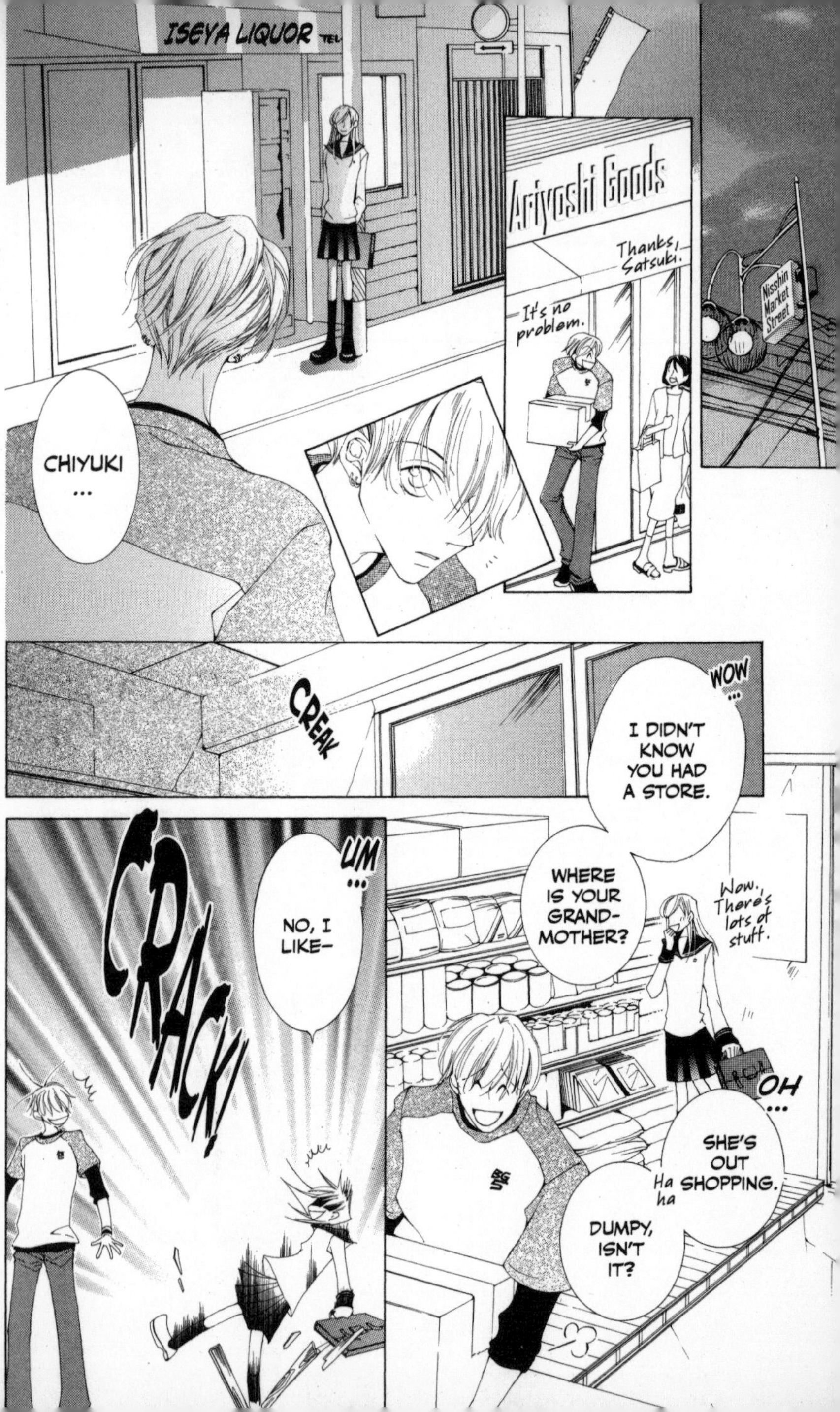
Nisshin Market Street
Ariyoshi Goods
Thanks, Satsuki.
It's no problem.
ISEYA LIQUOR TEL
CHIYUKI ...
CREAK
WOW ...
I DIDN'T KNOW YOU HAD A STORE.
Wow. There's lots of stuff.
WHERE IS YOUR GRAND-MOTHER?
OH ...
SHE'S OUT SHOPPING.
Ha ha
DUMPY, ISN'T IT?
UM ...
NO, I LIKE—
CRACK!

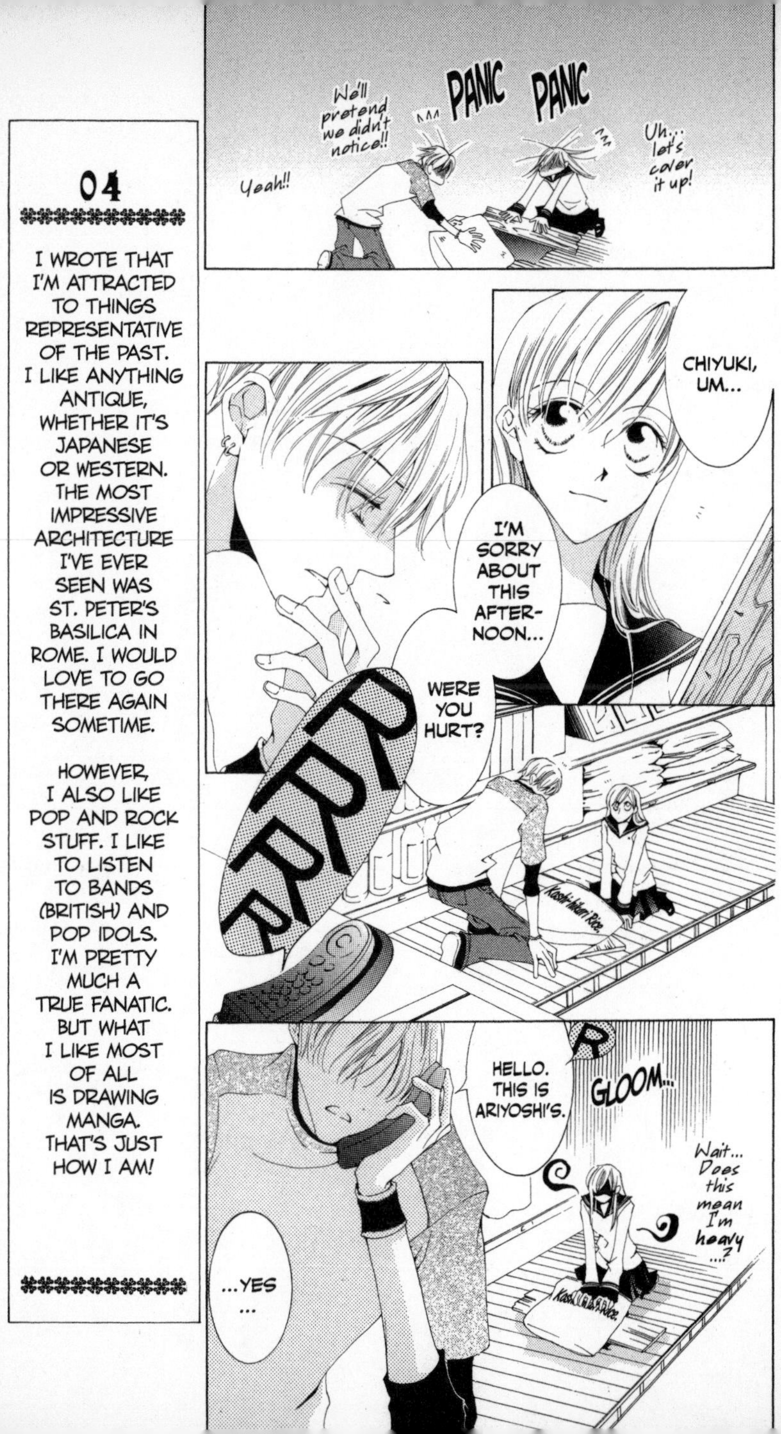
Uh... let's cover it up!
PANIC
PANIC
We'll pretend we didn't notice!!
Yeah!!
CHIYUKI, UM...
I'M SORRY ABOUT THIS AFTER-NOON...
WERE YOU HURT?
RRRR
Koshi-hikari Rice.
HELLO. THIS IS ARIYOSHI'S.
R
GLOOM...
Wait... Does this mean I'm heavy...?
...YES ...
Koshi-hikari Rice.

04

I WROTE THAT I'M ATTRACTED TO THINGS REPRESENTATIVE OF THE PAST. I LIKE ANYTHING ANTIQUE, WHETHER IT'S JAPANESE OR WESTERN. THE MOST IMPRESSIVE ARCHITECTURE I'VE EVER SEEN WAS ST. PETER'S BASILICA IN ROME. I WOULD LOVE TO GO THERE AGAIN SOMETIME.

HOWEVER, I ALSO LIKE POP AND ROCK STUFF. I LIKE TO LISTEN TO BANDS (BRITISH) AND POP IDOLS. I'M PRETTY MUCH A TRUE FANATIC. BUT WHAT I LIKE MOST OF ALL IS DRAWING MANGA. THAT'S JUST HOW I AM!

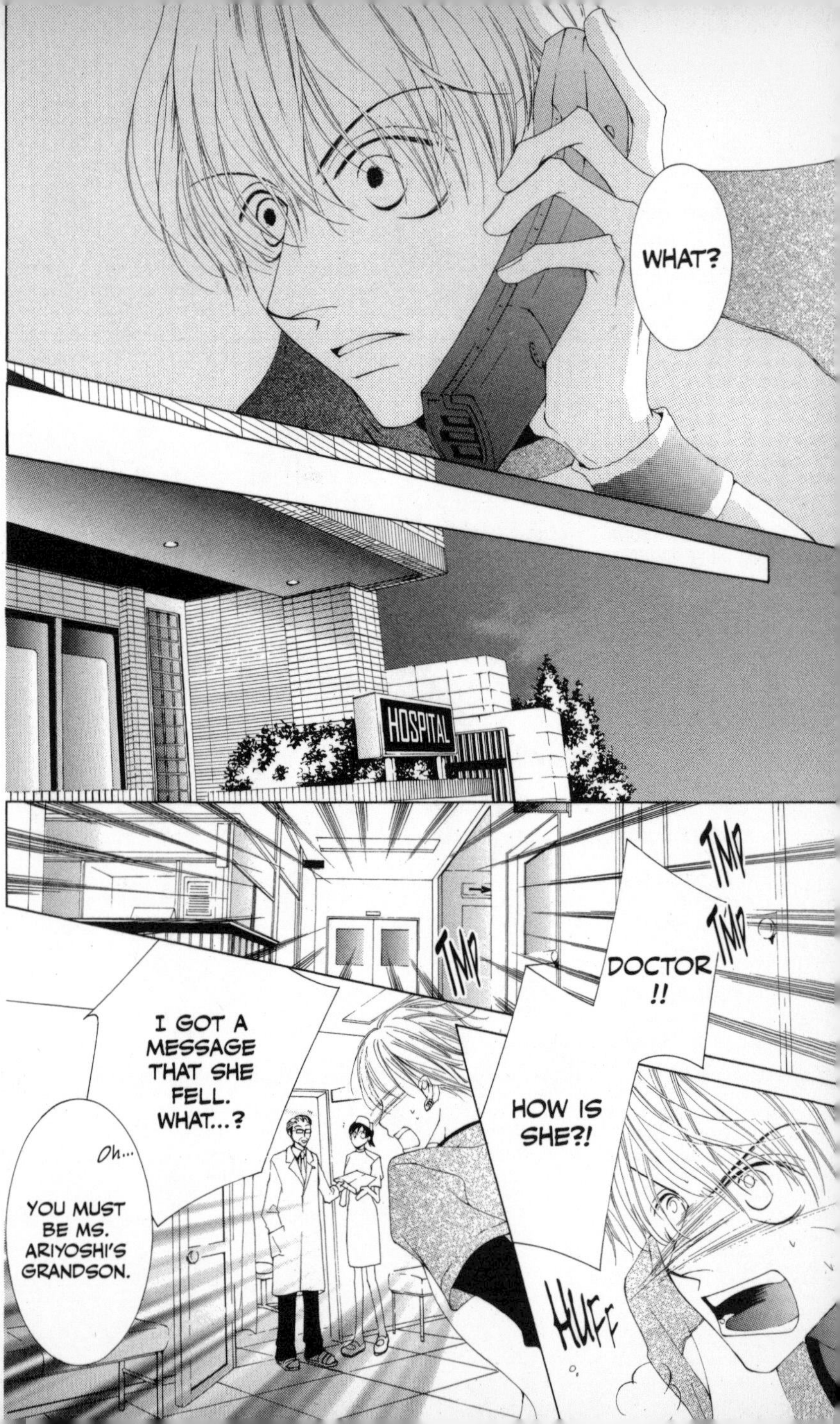
WHAT?
HOSPITAL
TMP
TMP
DOCTOR !!
HOW IS SHE?!
HUFF
TMP
I GOT A MESSAGE THAT SHE FELL. WHAT...?
Oh...
YOU MUST BE MS. ARIYOSHI'S GRANDSON.

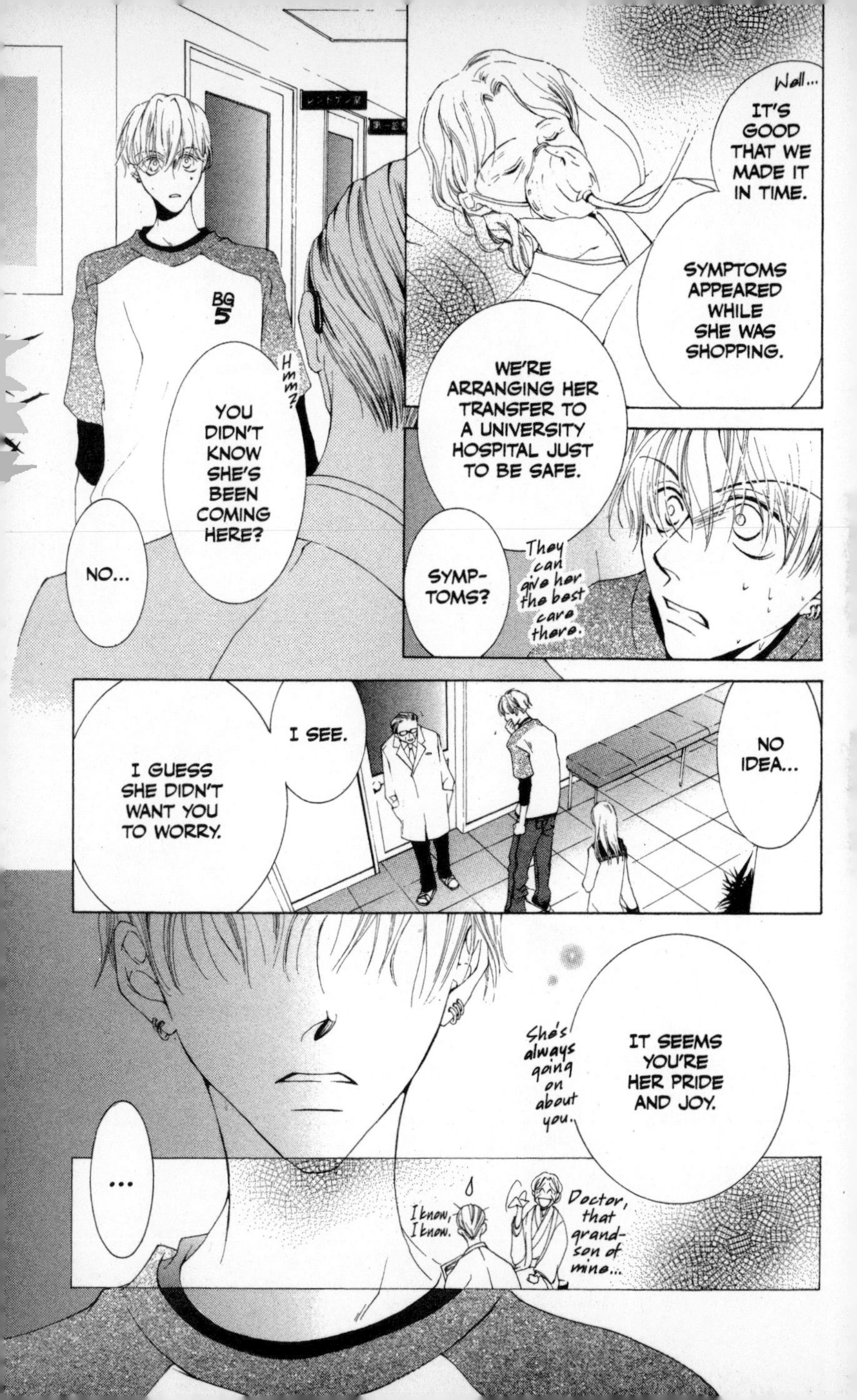
Well...
IT'S GOOD THAT WE MADE IT IN TIME.
SYMPTOMS APPEARED WHILE SHE WAS SHOPPING.
WE'RE ARRANGING HER TRANSFER TO A UNIVERSITY HOSPITAL JUST TO BE SAFE.
They can give her the best care there.
SYMP-TOMS?
Hmm?
YOU DIDN'T KNOW SHE'S BEEN COMING HERE?
NO...
NO IDEA...
I SEE.
I GUESS SHE DIDN'T WANT YOU TO WORRY.
IT SEEMS YOU'RE HER PRIDE AND JOY.
She's always going on about you..
Doctor, that grand-son of mine...
I know, I know.
...

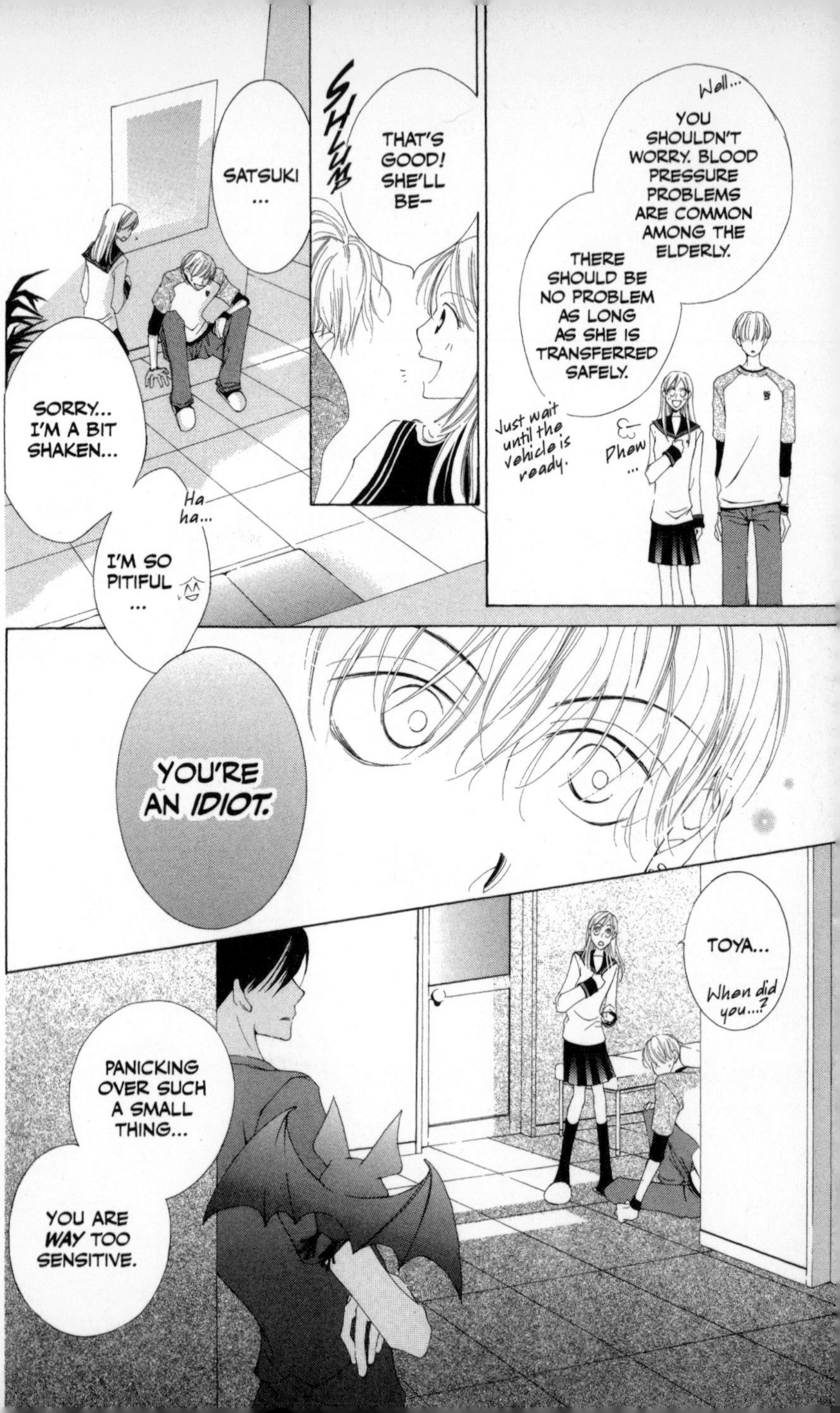

Well...
YOU SHOULDN'T WORRY. BLOOD PRESSURE PROBLEMS ARE COMMON AMONG THE ELDERLY.
THERE SHOULD BE NO PROBLEM AS LONG AS SHE IS TRANSFERRED SAFELY.
Phew...
Just wait until the vehicle is ready.
SHUMP
THAT'S GOOD! SHE'LL BE–
SATSUKI...
SORRY... I'M A BIT SHAKEN...
Ha ha...
I'M SO PITIFUL...
YOU'RE AN IDIOT.
TOYA...
When did you...?
PANICKING OVER SUCH A SMALL THING...
YOU ARE WAY TOO SENSITIVE.

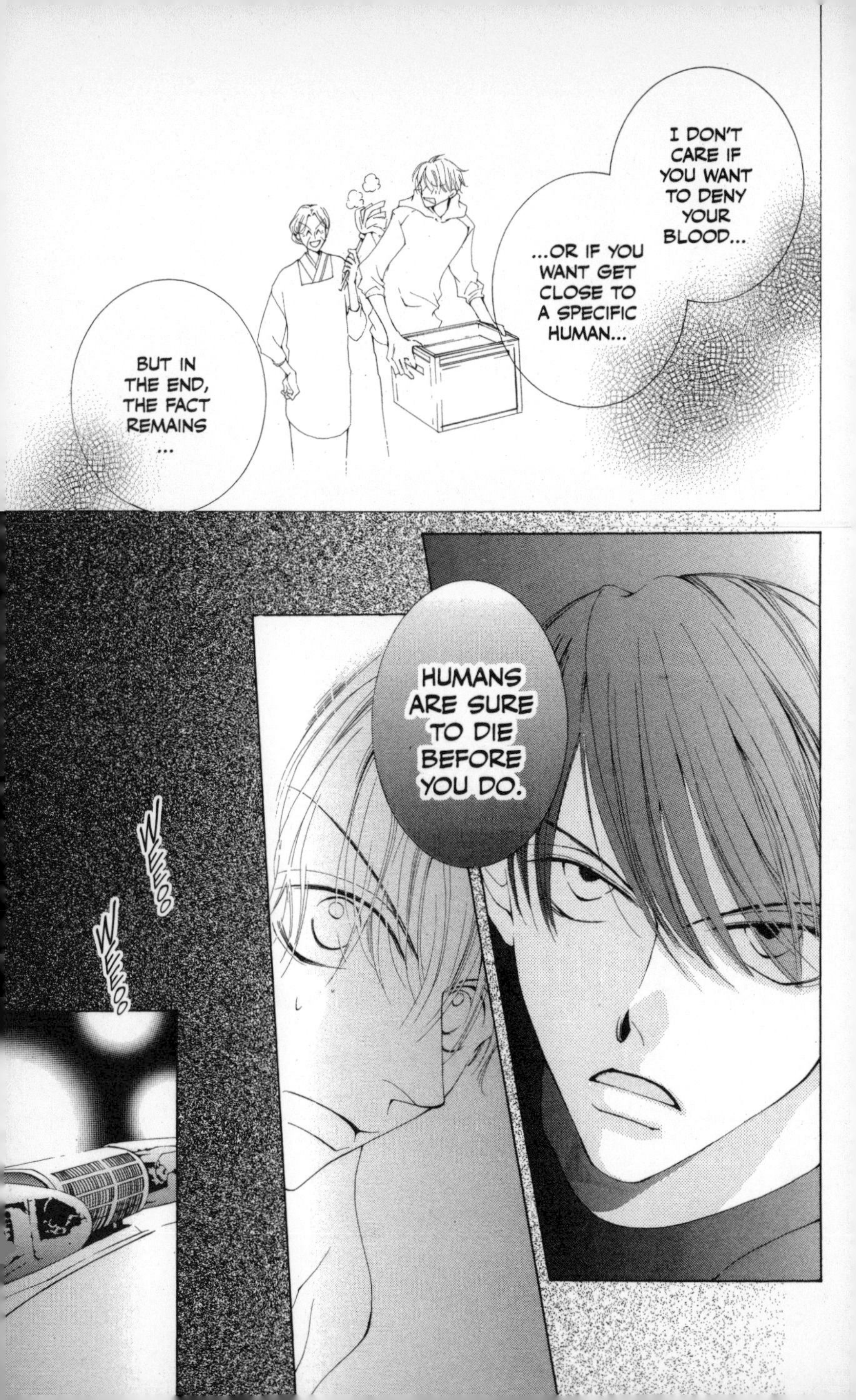
I DON'T CARE IF YOU WANT TO DENY YOUR BLOOD...
...OR IF YOU WANT GET CLOSE TO A SPECIFIC HUMAN...
BUT IN THE END, THE FACT REMAINS ...
HUMANS ARE SURE TO DIE BEFORE YOU DO.
WHOOO
WHOOO

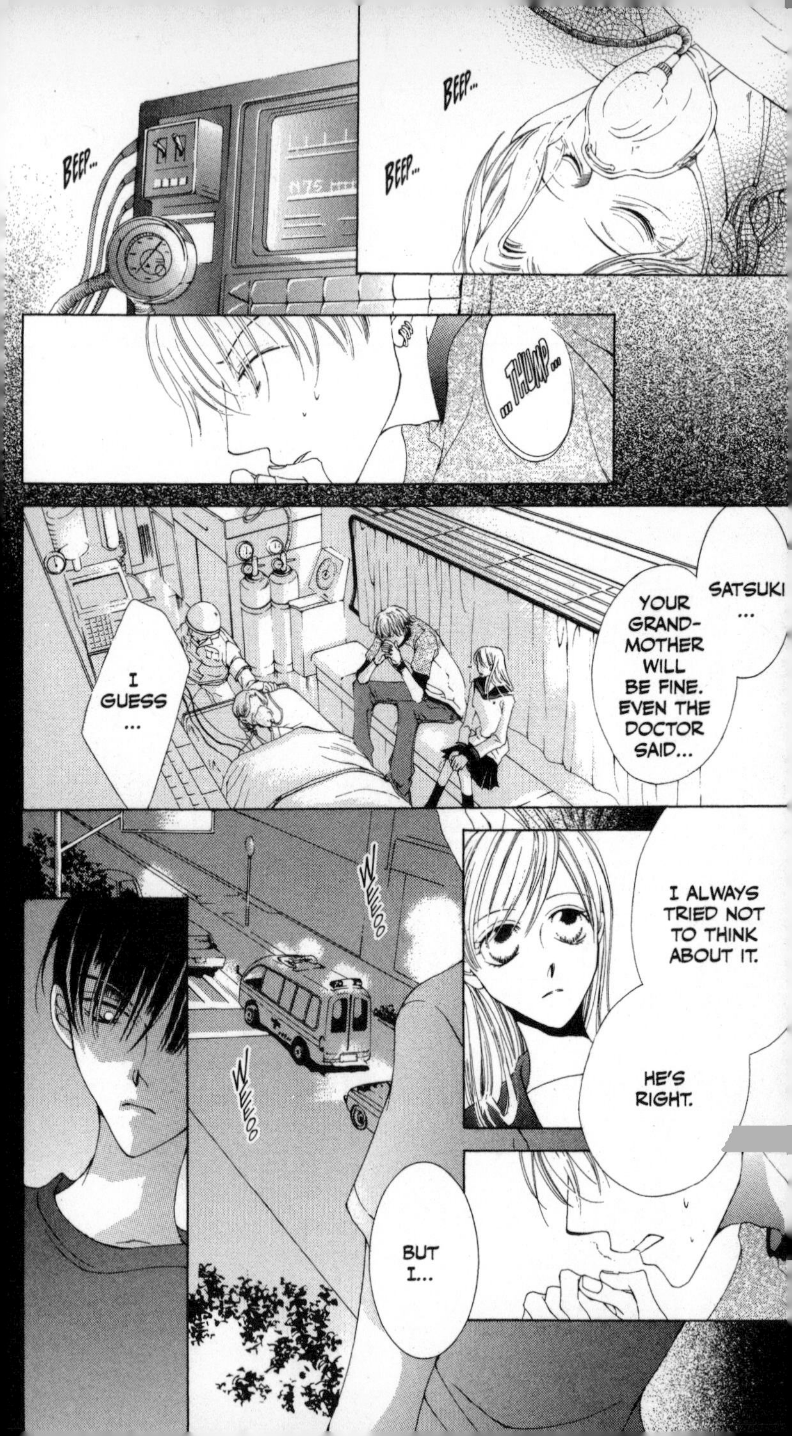
BEEP...
BEEP...
BEEP...
...THUMP...
SATSUKI...
YOUR GRANDMOTHER WILL BE FINE. EVEN THE DOCTOR SAID...
I GUESS...
I ALWAYS TRIED NOT TO THINK ABOUT IT.
HE'S RIGHT.
BUT I...
WEEOO
WEEOO

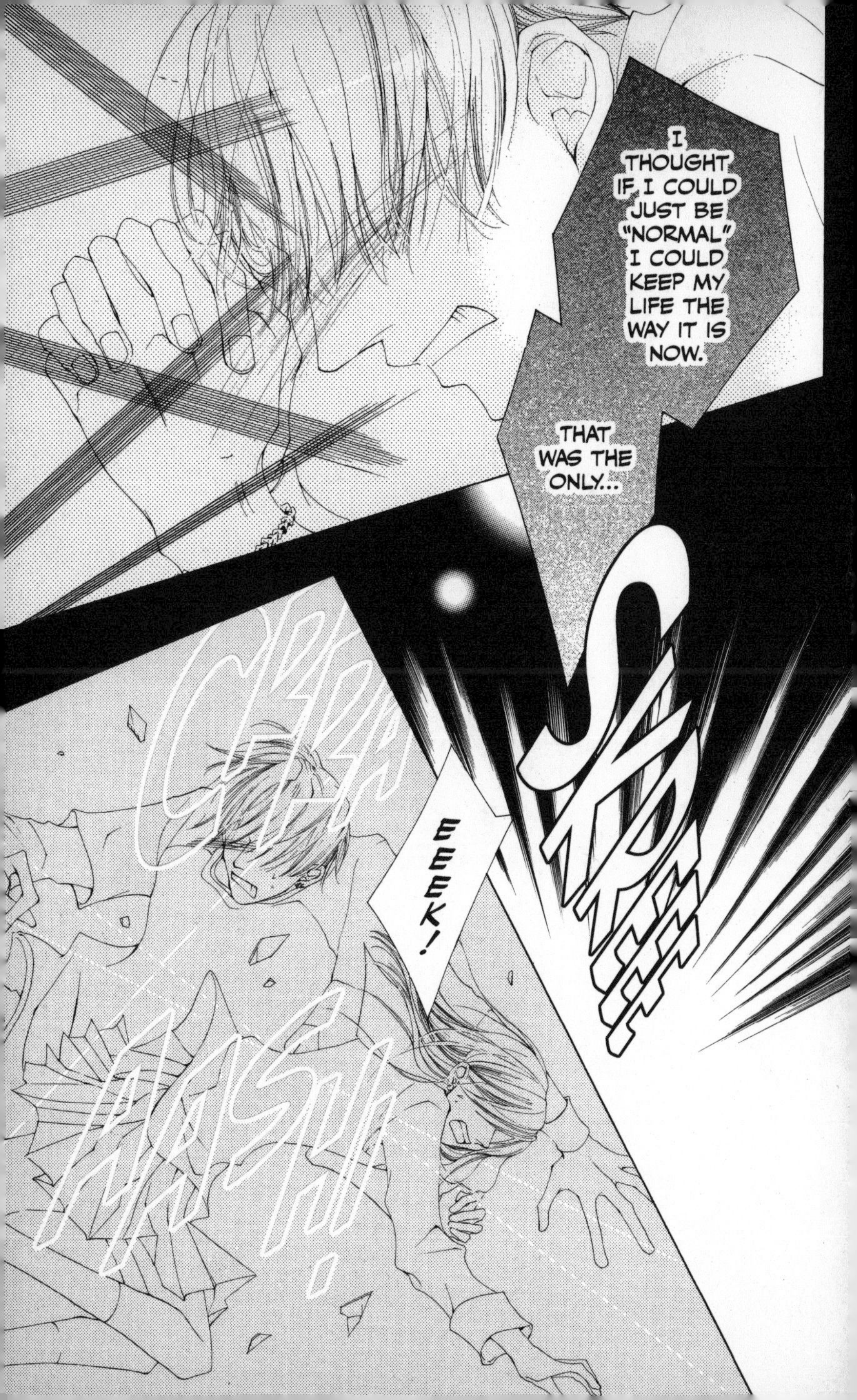
I THOUGHT IF I COULD JUST BE "NORMAL" I COULD KEEP MY LIFE THE WAY IT IS NOW.
THAT WAS THE ONLY...
EEEEK!

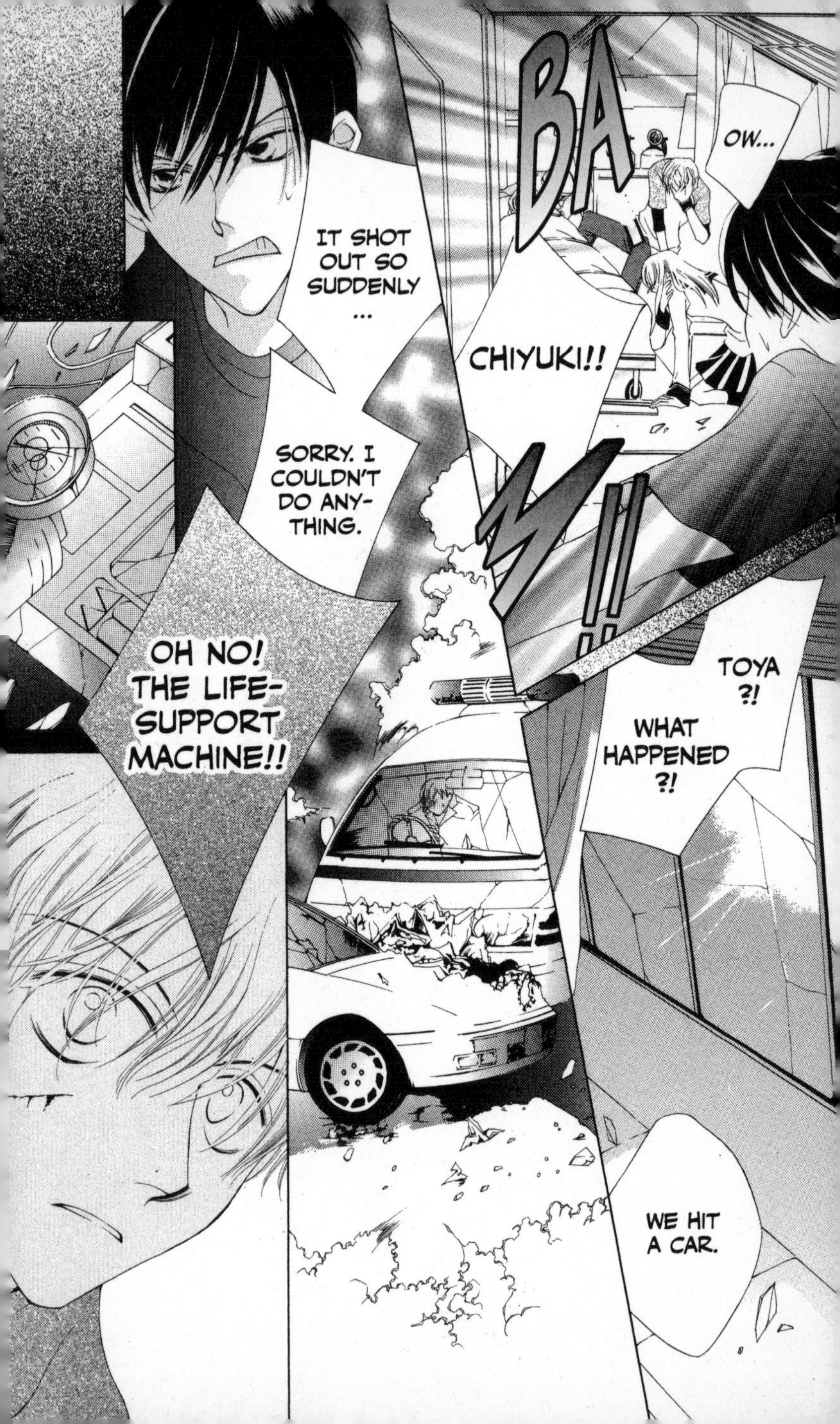
BAM!!
OW...
CHIYUKI!!
TOYA?!
WHAT HAPPENED?!
WE HIT A CAR.
IT SHOT OUT SO SUDDENLY...
SORRY. I COULDN'T DO ANYTHING.
OH NO! THE LIFE-SUPPORT MACHINE!!

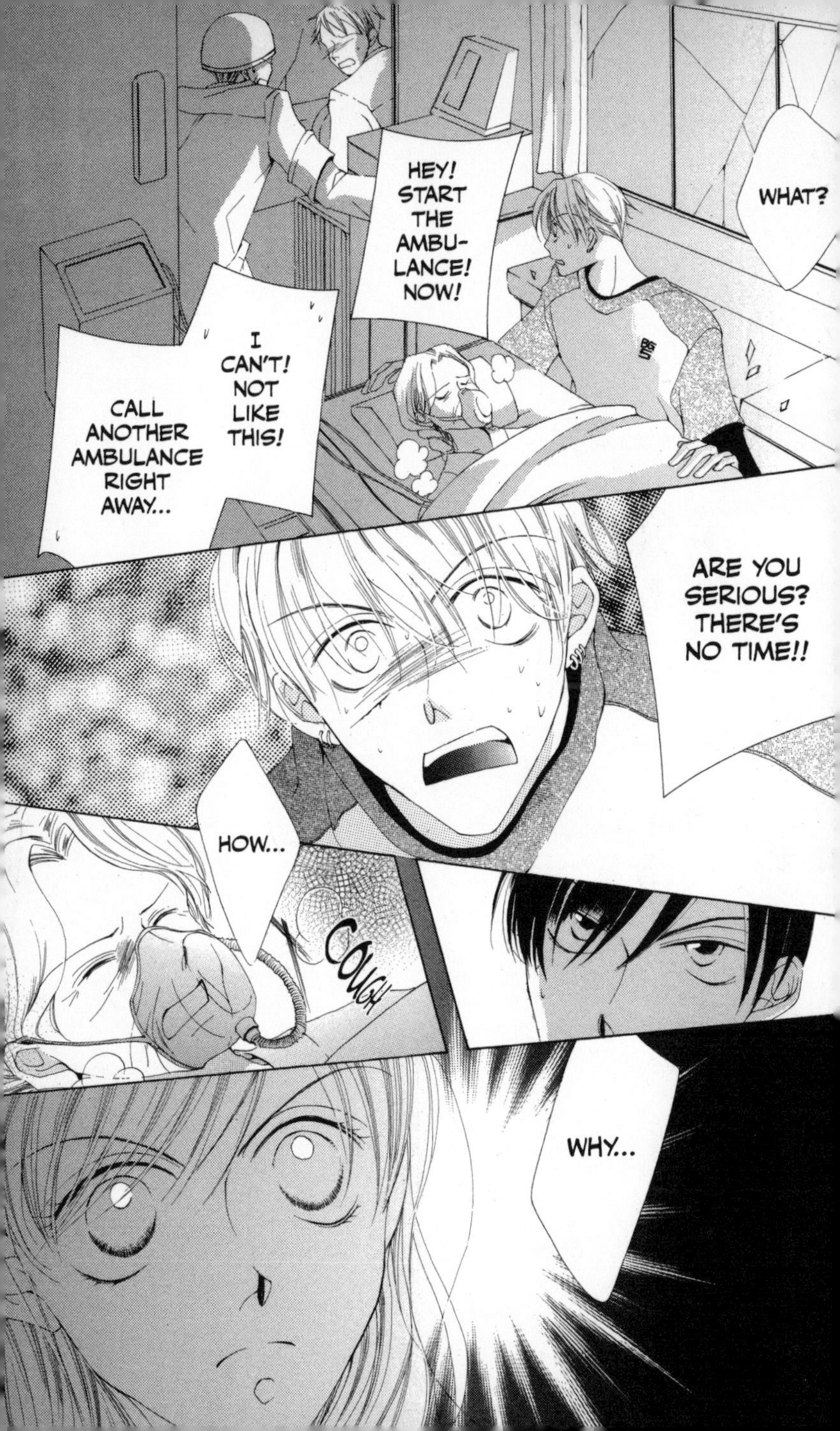
WHAT?
HEY! START THE AMBULANCE! NOW!
I CAN'T! NOT LIKE THIS!
CALL ANOTHER AMBULANCE RIGHT AWAY...
ARE YOU SERIOUS? THERE'S NO TIME!!
HOW...
COUGH
WHY...

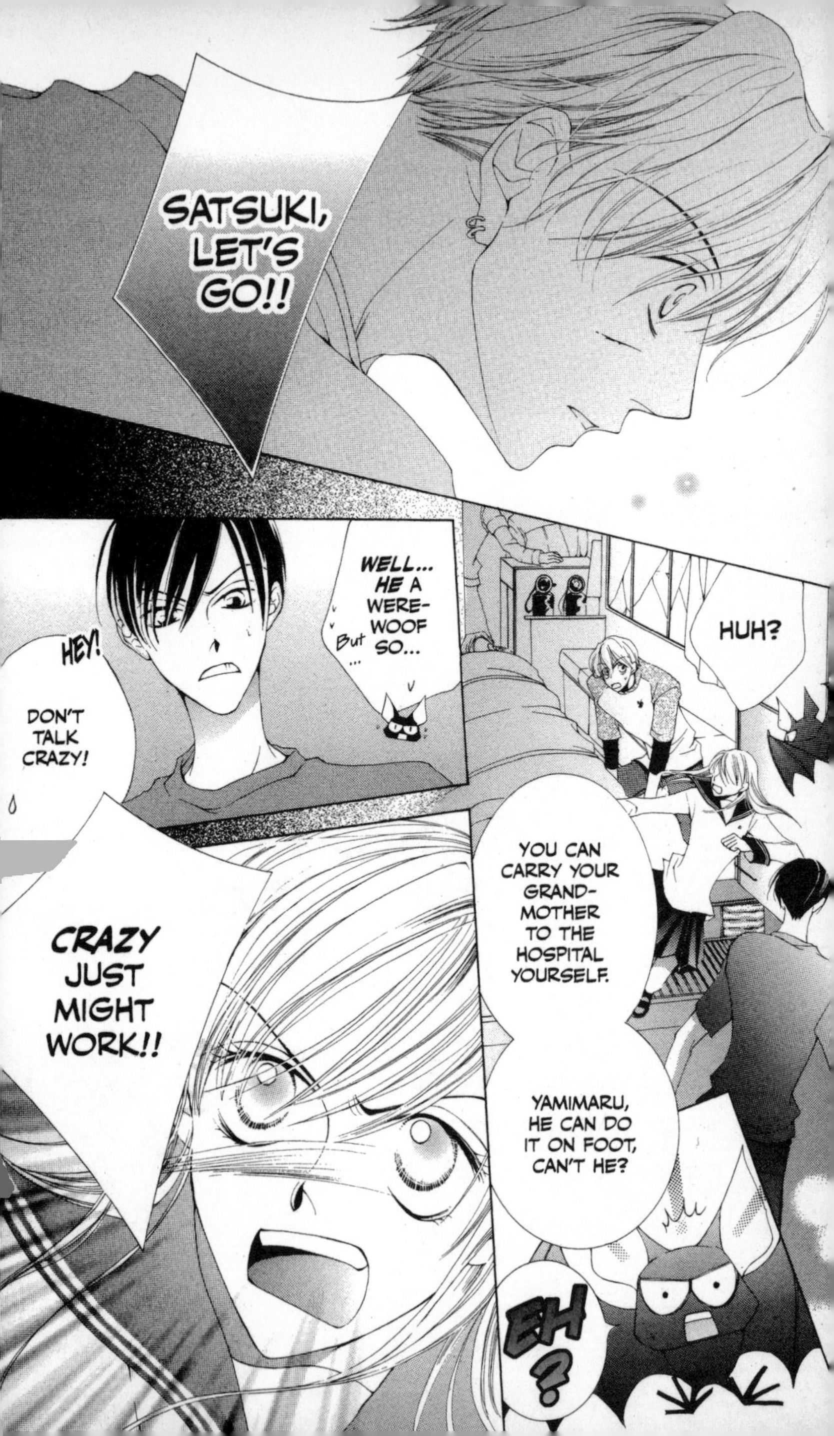

SATSUKI, LET'S GO!!
HUH?
YOU CAN CARRY YOUR GRANDMOTHER TO THE HOSPITAL YOURSELF.
YAMIMARU, HE CAN DO IT ON FOOT, CAN'T HE?
EH?
WELL... HE A WERE-WOOF SO...
But...
HEY!
DON'T TALK CRAZY!
CRAZY JUST MIGHT WORK!!

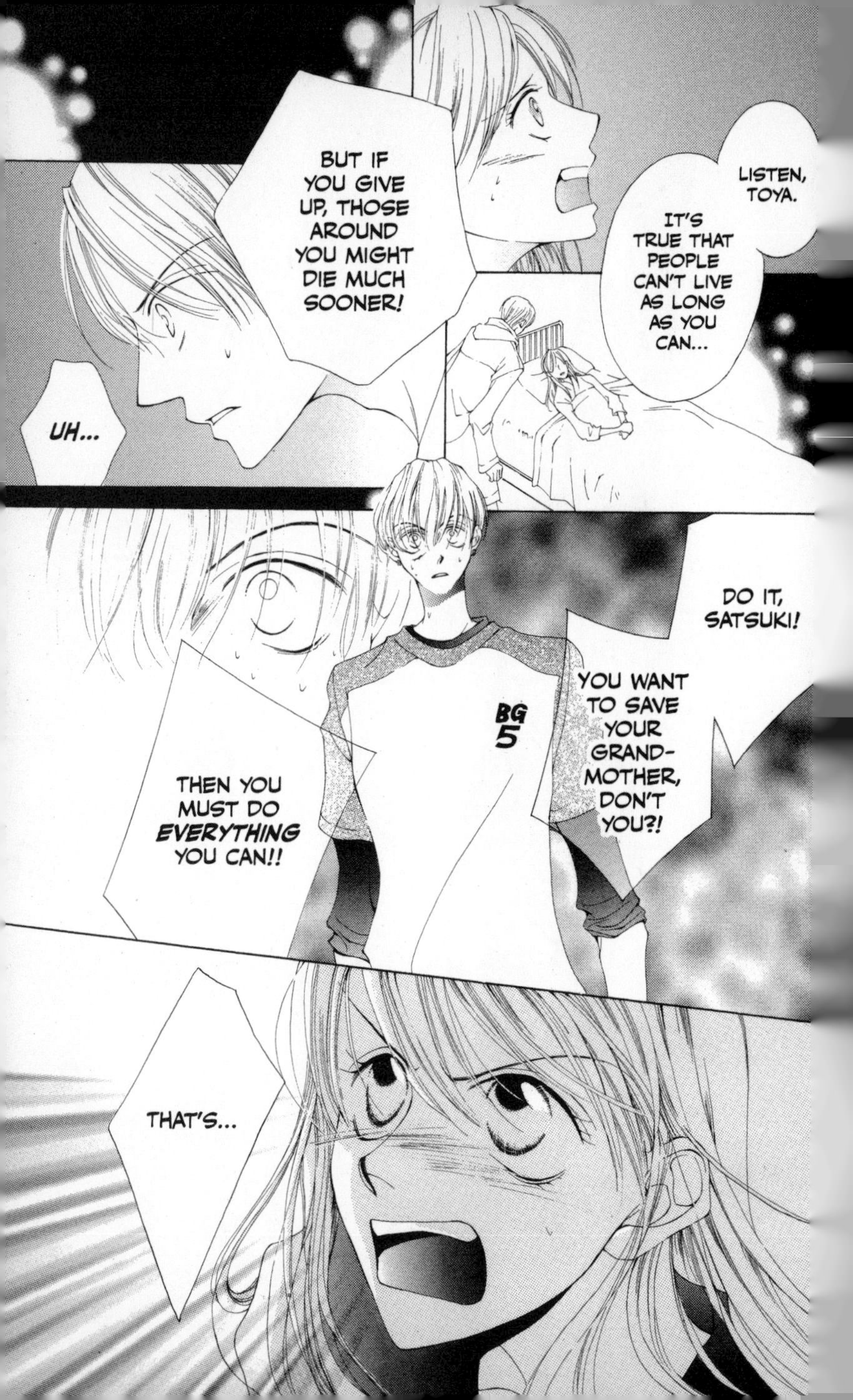
LISTEN, TOYA.
IT'S TRUE THAT PEOPLE CAN'T LIVE AS LONG AS YOU CAN...
BUT IF YOU GIVE UP, THOSE AROUND YOU MIGHT DIE MUCH SOONER!
UH...
DO IT, SATSUKI!
YOU WANT TO SAVE YOUR GRANDMOTHER, DON'T YOU?!
BG 5
THEN YOU MUST DO *EVERYTHING* YOU CAN!!
THAT'S...

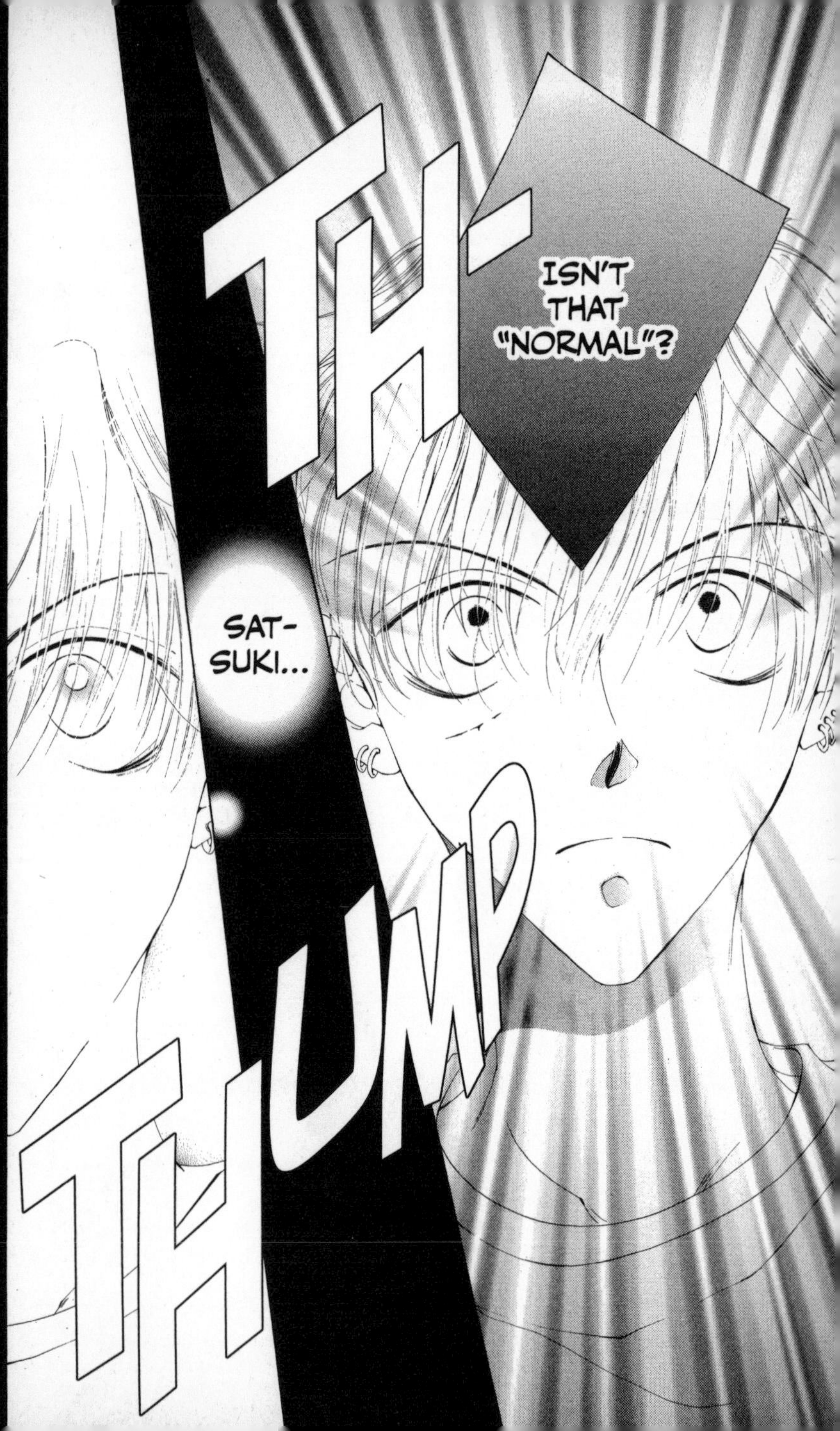
ISN'T THAT "NORMAL"?
TH-
SAT-SUKI...
THUMP

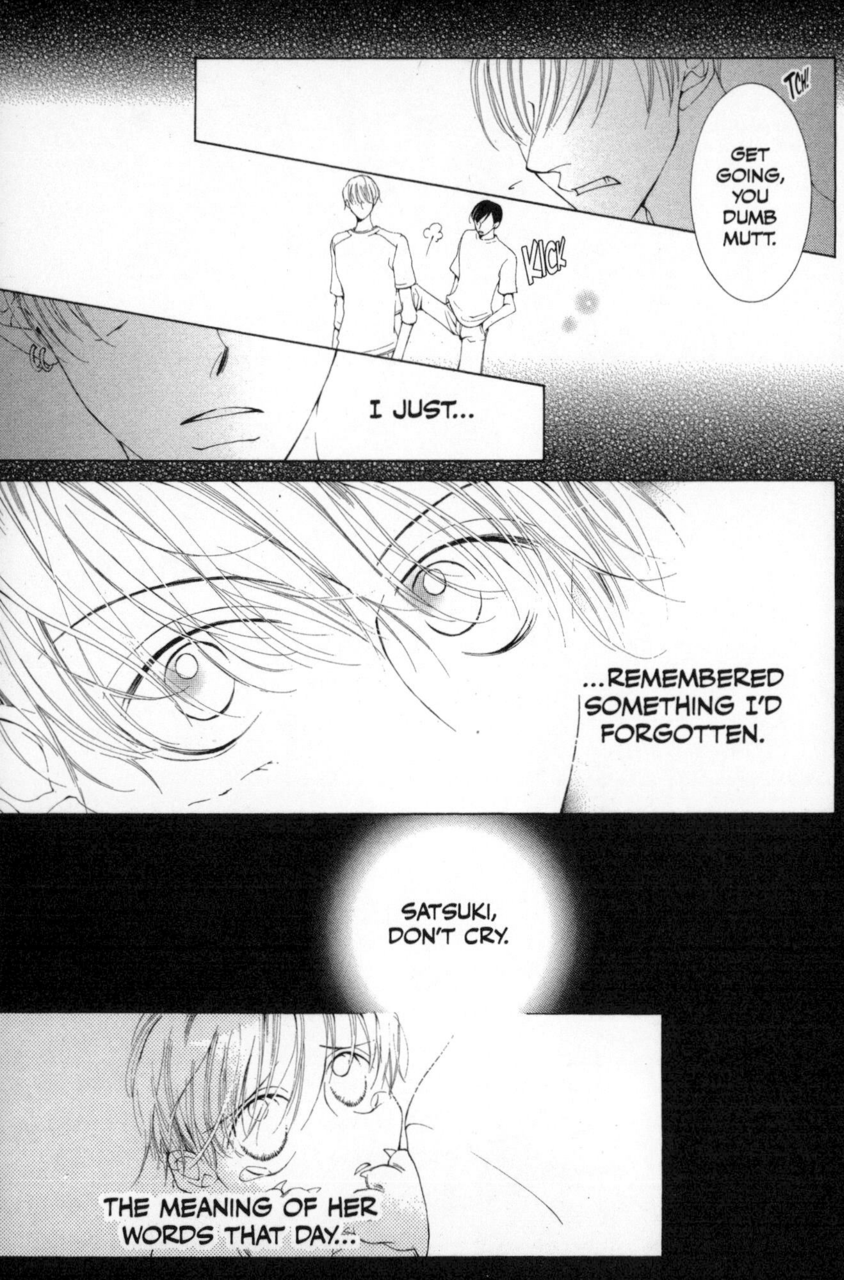
TCH!
GET GOING, YOU DUMB MUTT.
KICK
I JUST...
...REMEMBERED SOMETHING I'D FORGOTTEN.
SATSUKI, DON'T CRY.
THE MEANING OF HER WORDS THAT DAY...

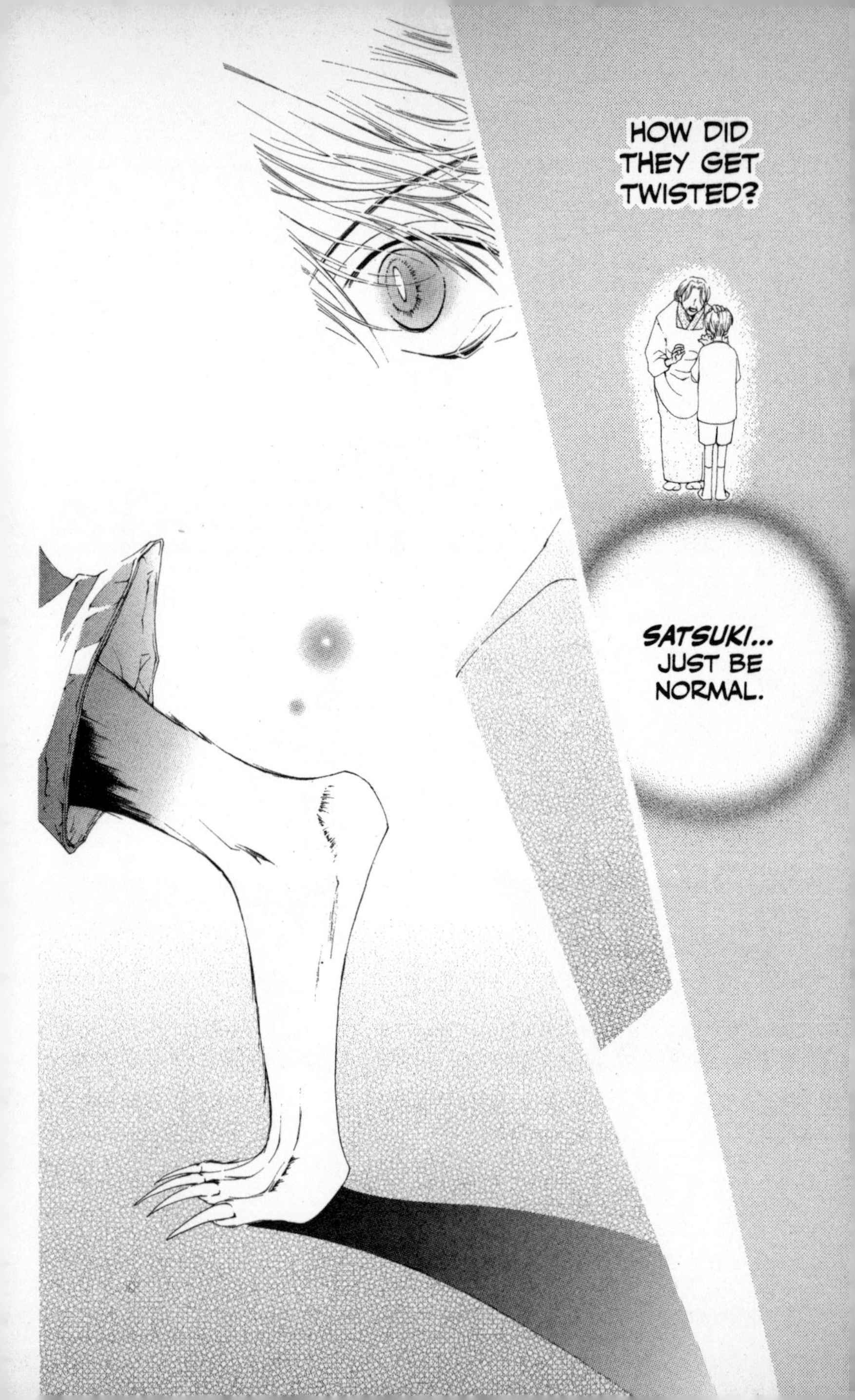
HOW DID THEY GET TWISTED?
SATSUKI... JUST BE NORMAL.

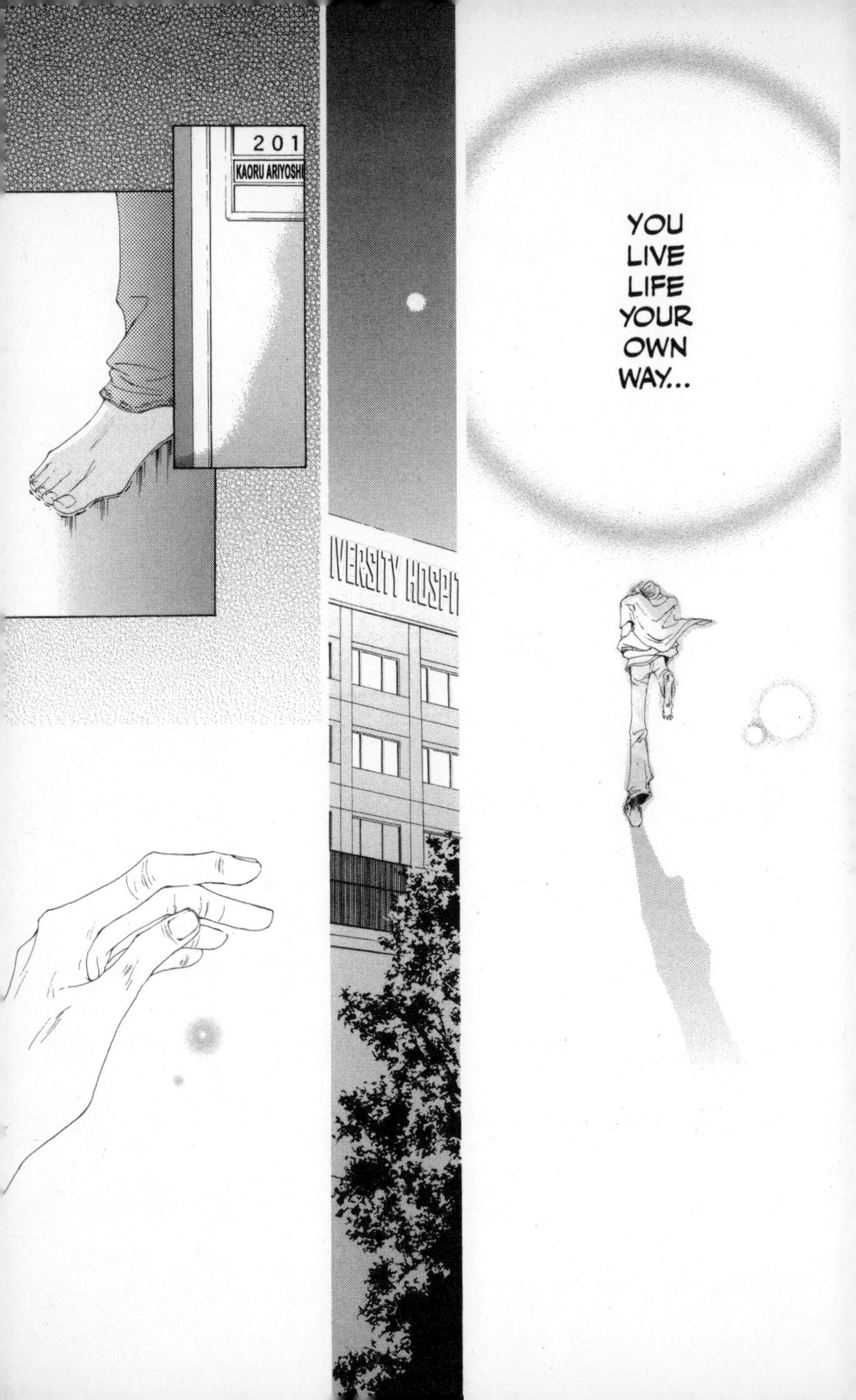
YOU LIVE LIFE YOUR OWN WAY...
IVERSITY HOSPIT
201
KAORU ARIYOSHI

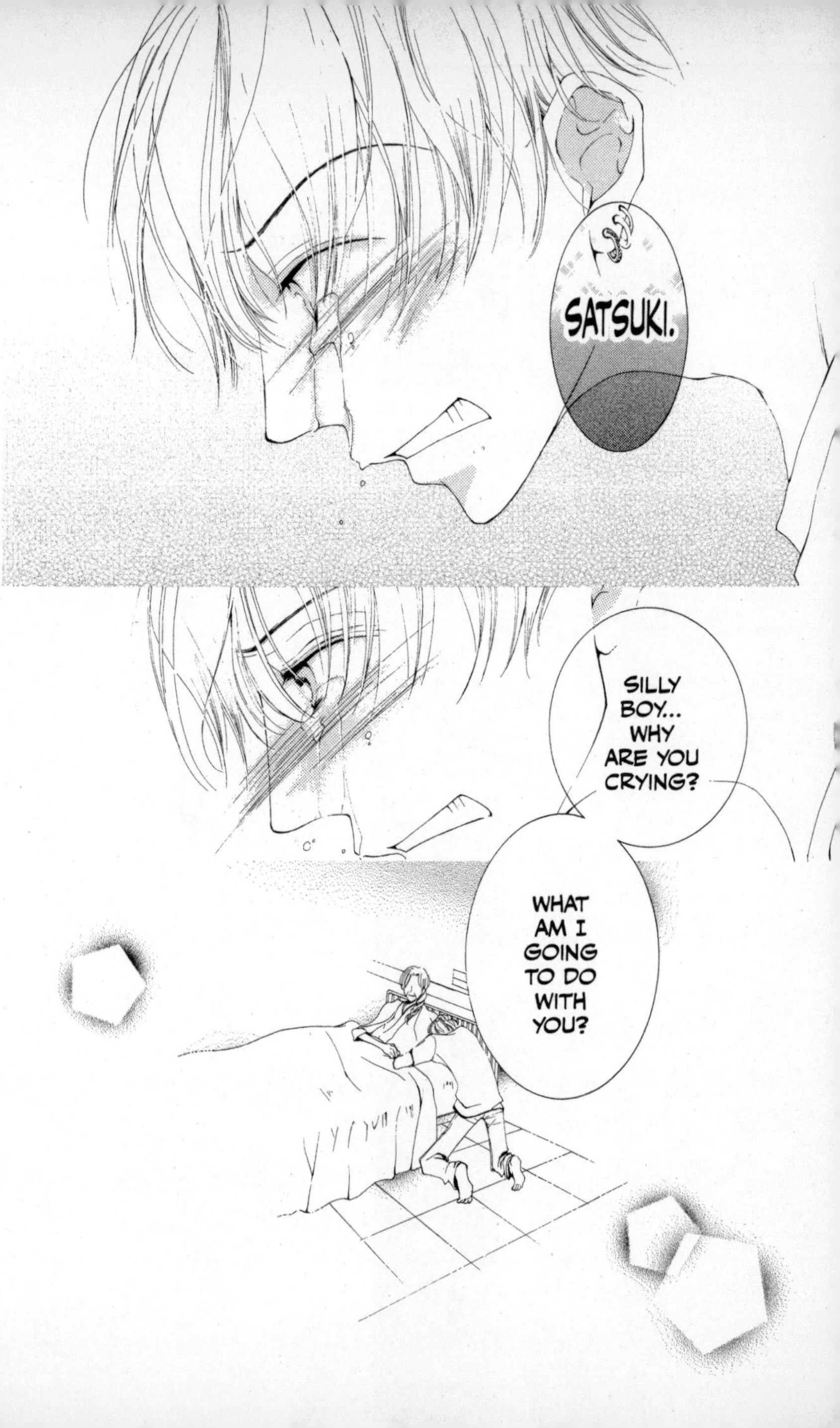
SATSUKI.
SILLY BOY... WHY ARE YOU CRYING?
WHAT AM I GOING TO DO WITH YOU?

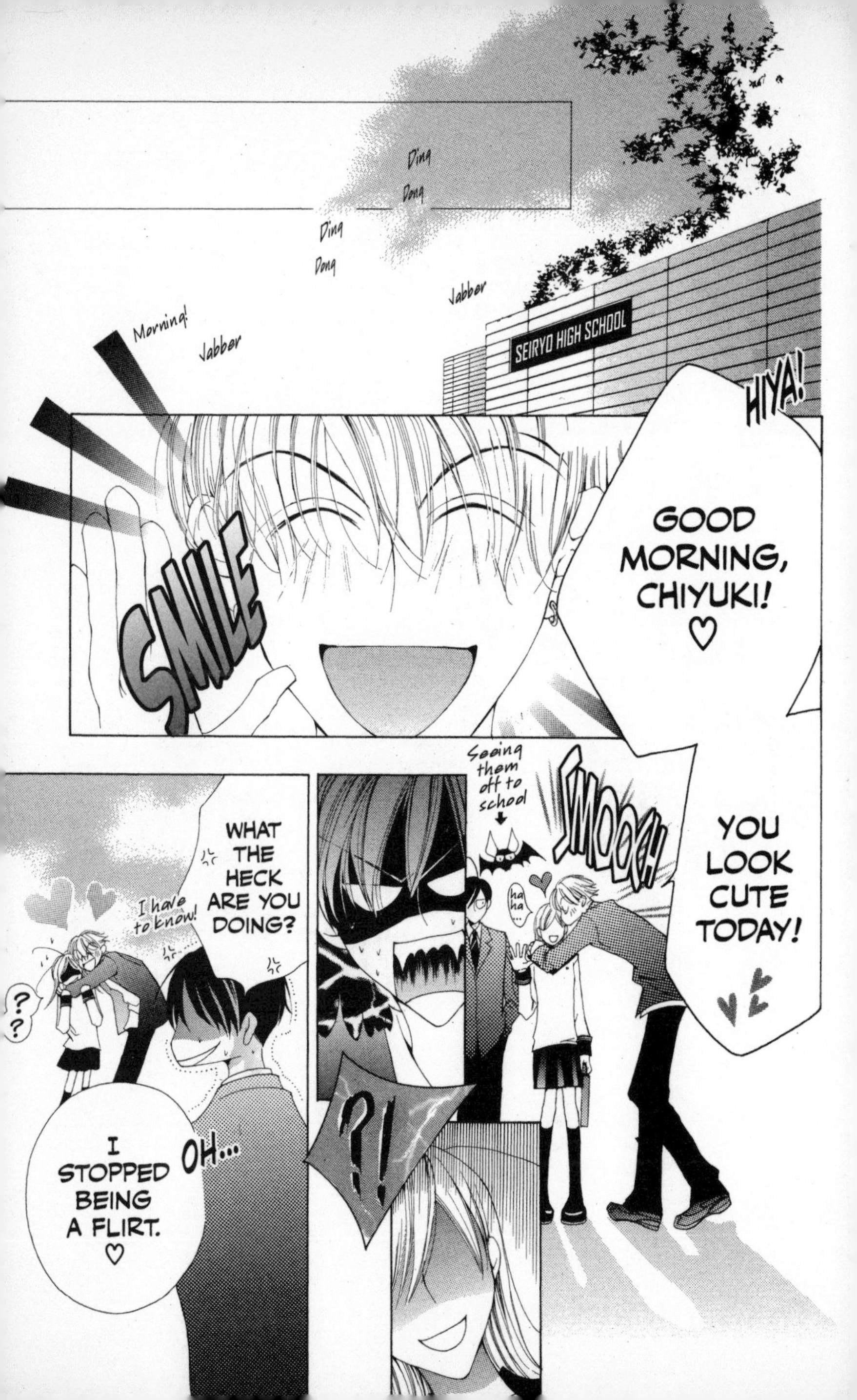
Ding
Dong
Ding
Dong
Jabber
Morning!
Jabber
SEIRYO HIGH SCHOOL
HIYA!
GOOD MORNING, CHIYUKI! ♡
SMILE
SMOOCH!
YOU LOOK CUTE TODAY!
Seeing them off to school
ha ha...
?!
WHAT THE HECK ARE YOU DOING?
I have to know!
??
OH...
I STOPPED BEING A FLIRT. ♡

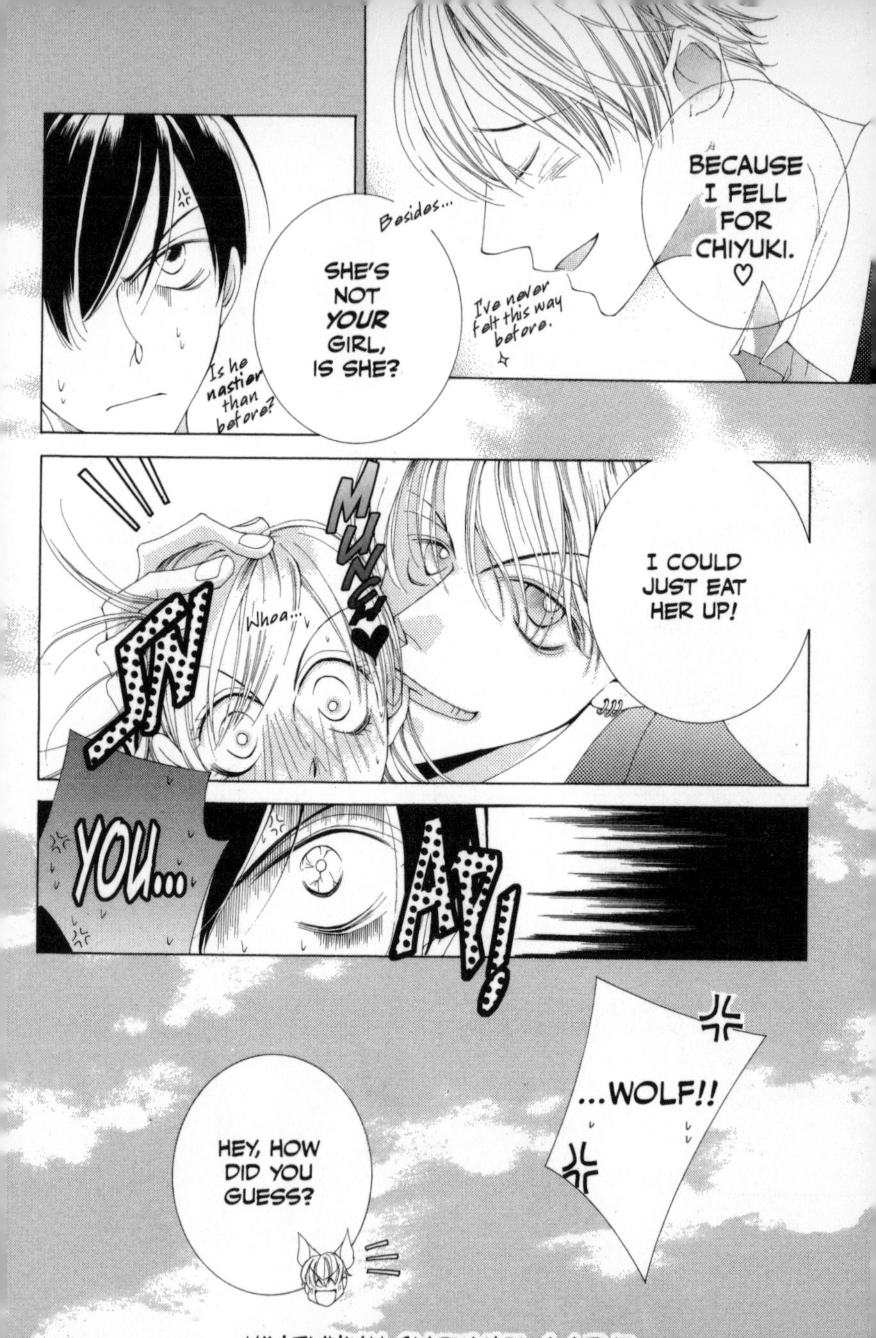
BECAUSE I FELL FOR CHIYUKI. ♡
I've never felt this way before.
Besides...
SHE'S NOT YOUR GIRL, IS SHE?
Is he nastier than before?
I COULD JUST EAT HER UP!
MUNCH! ♥
Whoa...
YOU...
...WOLF!!
HEY, HOW DID YOU GUESS?

MILLENNIUM SNOW VOL 1 / END

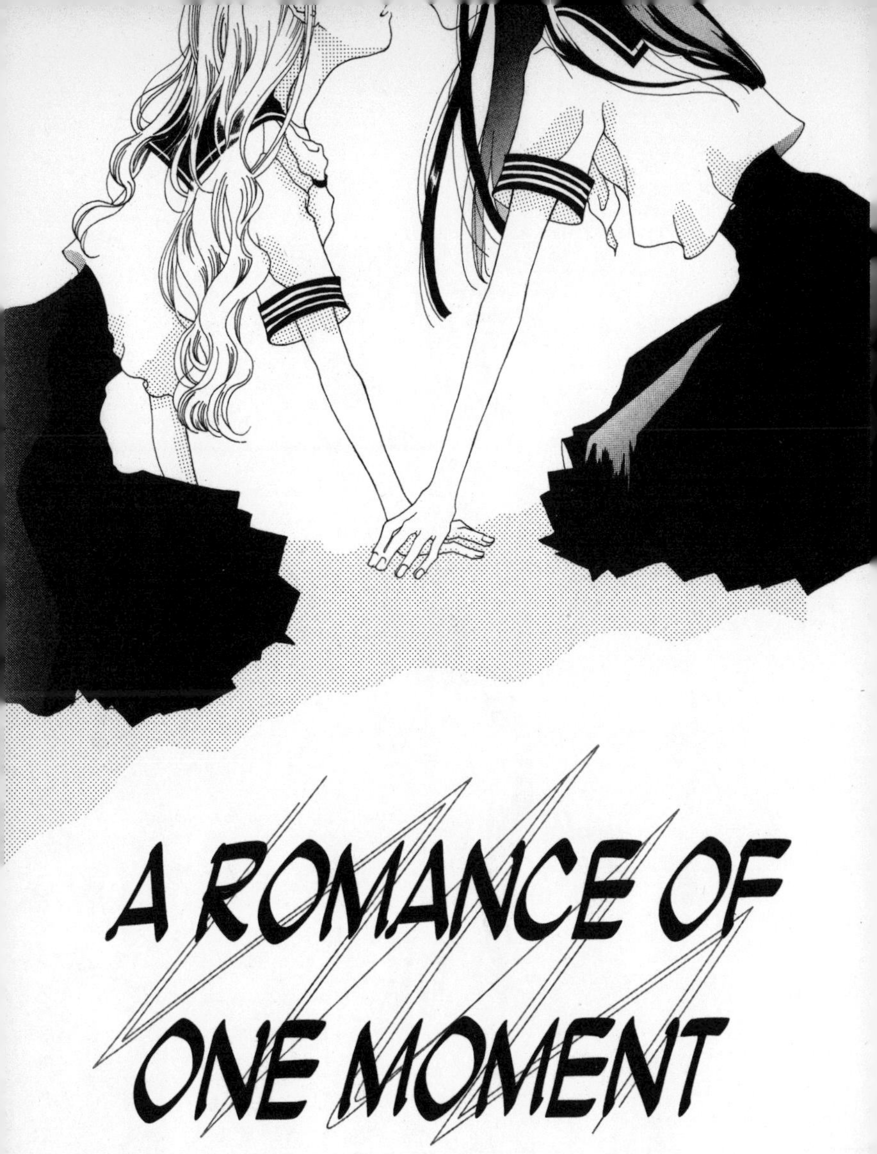

A ROMANCE OF ONE MOMENT

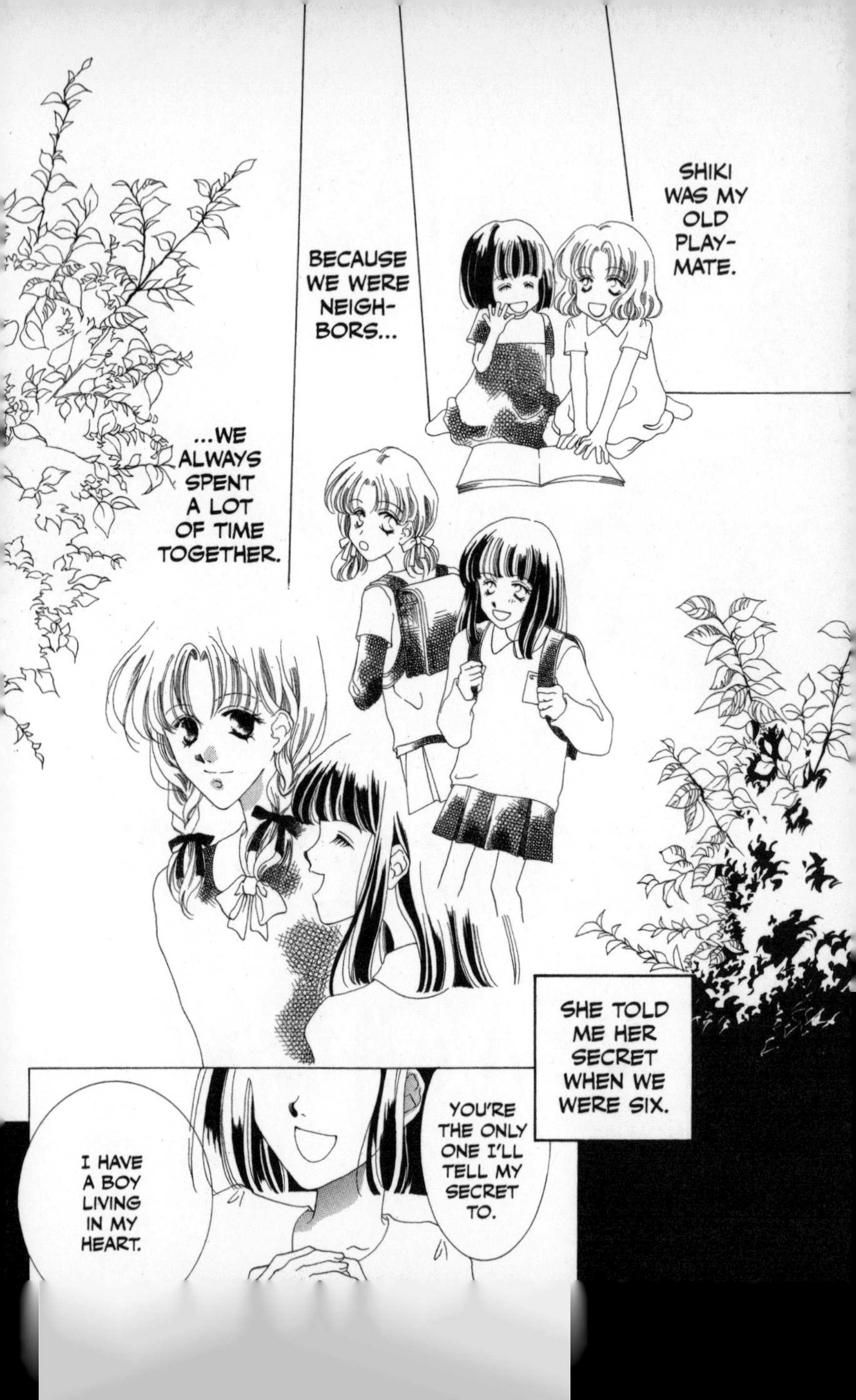
SHIKI WAS MY OLD PLAY-MATE.
BECAUSE WE WERE NEIGH-BORS...
...WE ALWAYS SPENT A LOT OF TIME TOGETHER.
SHE TOLD ME HER SECRET WHEN WE WERE SIX.
YOU'RE THE ONLY ONE I'LL TELL MY SECRET TO.
I HAVE A BOY LIVING IN MY HEART.

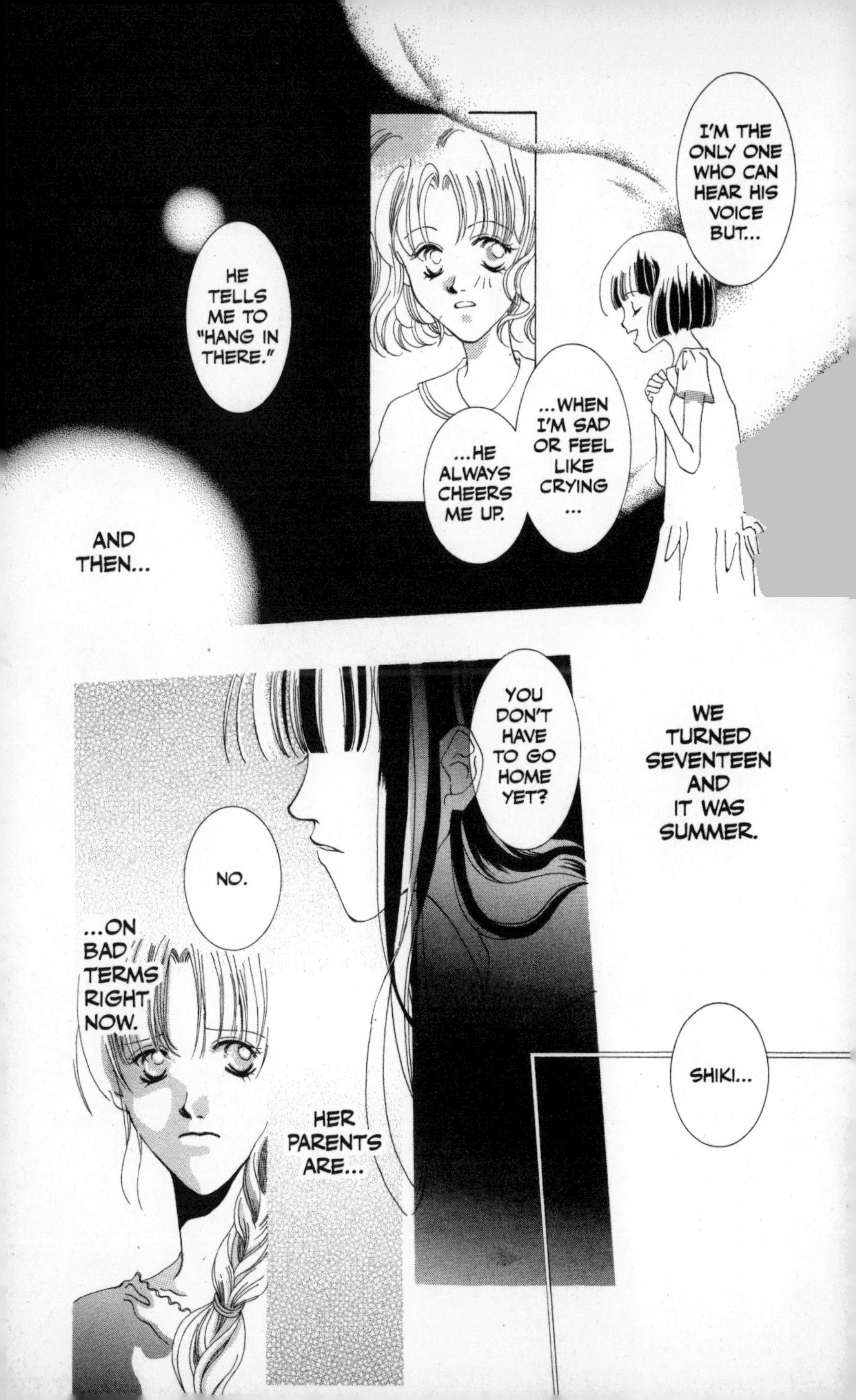
I'M THE ONLY ONE WHO CAN HEAR HIS VOICE BUT...
...WHEN I'M SAD OR FEEL LIKE CRYING...
...HE ALWAYS CHEERS ME UP.
HE TELLS ME TO "HANG IN THERE."
AND THEN...
WE TURNED SEVENTEEN AND IT WAS SUMMER.
YOU DON'T HAVE TO GO HOME YET?
NO.
HER PARENTS ARE...
...ON BAD TERMS RIGHT NOW.
SHIKI...

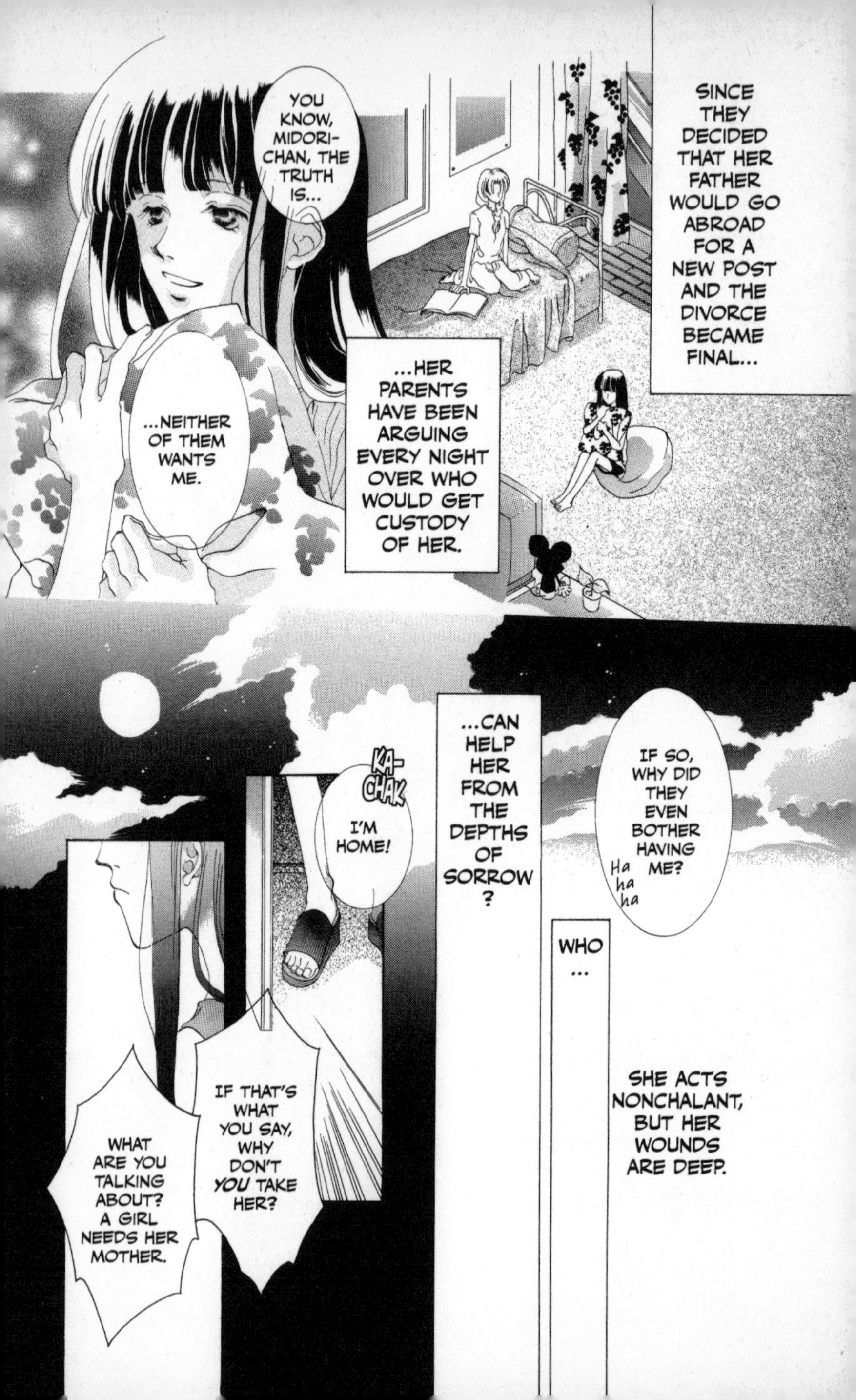
SINCE THEY DECIDED THAT HER FATHER WOULD GO ABROAD FOR A NEW POST AND THE DIVORCE BECAME FINAL...
...HER PARENTS HAVE BEEN ARGUING EVERY NIGHT OVER WHO WOULD GET CUSTODY OF HER.
YOU KNOW, MIDORI-CHAN, THE TRUTH IS...
...NEITHER OF THEM WANTS ME.
IF SO, WHY DID THEY EVEN BOTHER HAVING ME?
Ha ha ha
WHO...
SHE ACTS NONCHALANT, BUT HER WOUNDS ARE DEEP.
...CAN HELP HER FROM THE DEPTHS OF SORROW?
KA-CHAK
I'M HOME!
IF THAT'S WHAT YOU SAY, WHY DON'T *YOU* TAKE HER?
WHAT ARE YOU TALKING ABOUT? A GIRL NEEDS HER MOTHER.

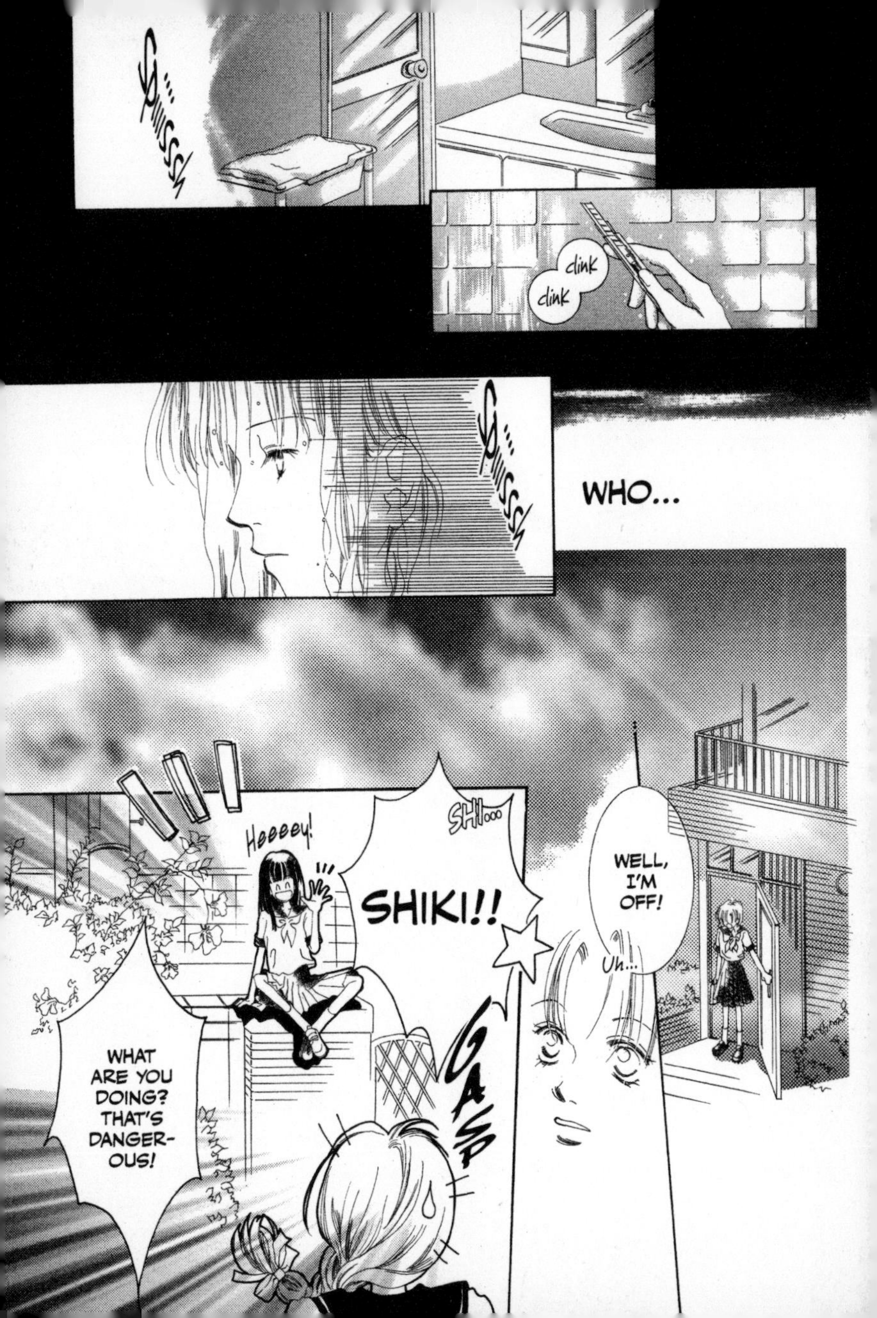

Spiiisssh
clink
clink
WHO...
Spiiisssh
WELL, I'M OFF!
Uh...
SHI...
SHIKI!!
GASP
Heeeey!
WHAT ARE YOU DOING? THAT'S DANGER-OUS!

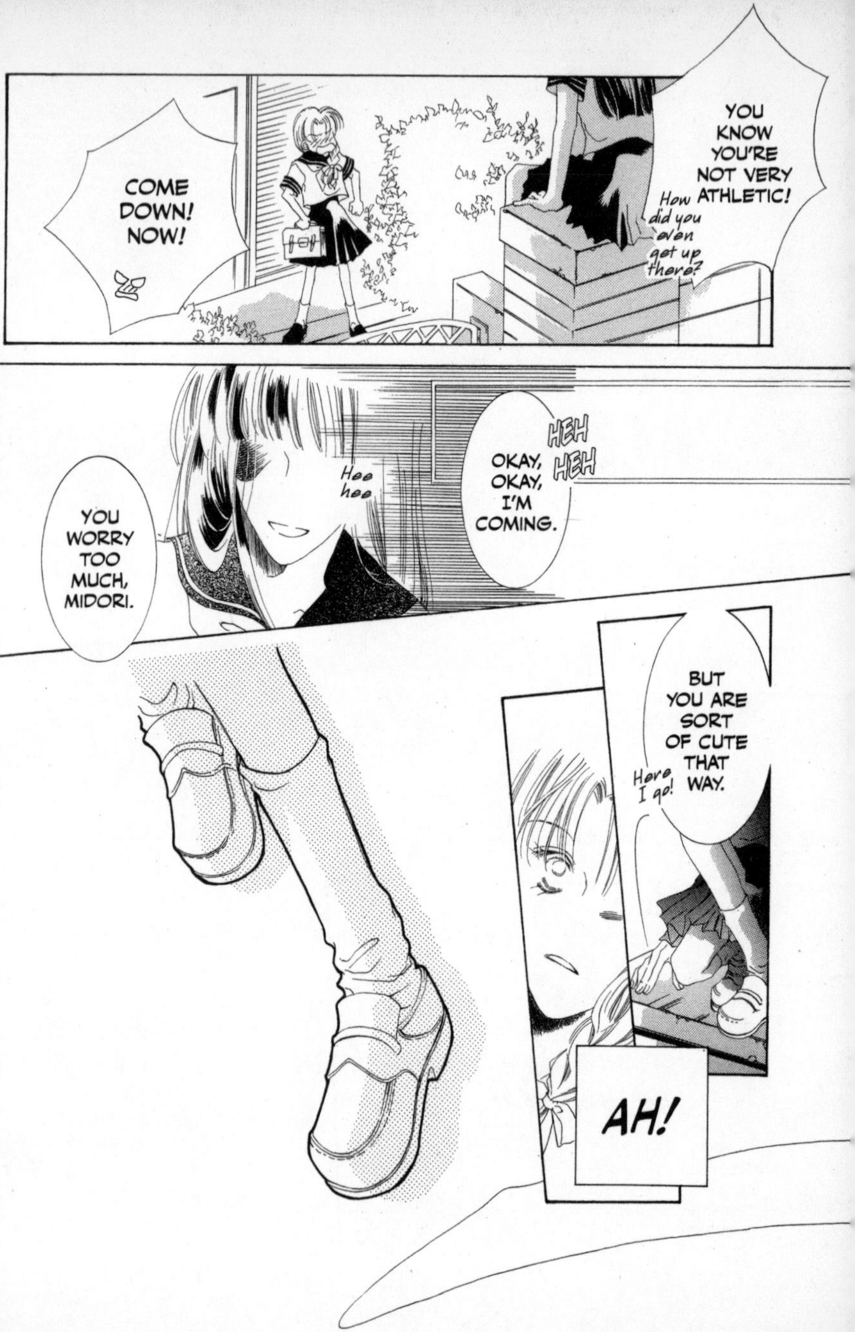
YOU KNOW YOU'RE NOT VERY ATHLETIC!
How did you even get up there?
COME DOWN! NOW!
HEH HEH
OKAY, OKAY, I'M COMING.
Hee hee
YOU WORRY TOO MUCH, MIDORI.
BUT YOU ARE SORT OF CUTE THAT WAY.
Here I go!
AH!

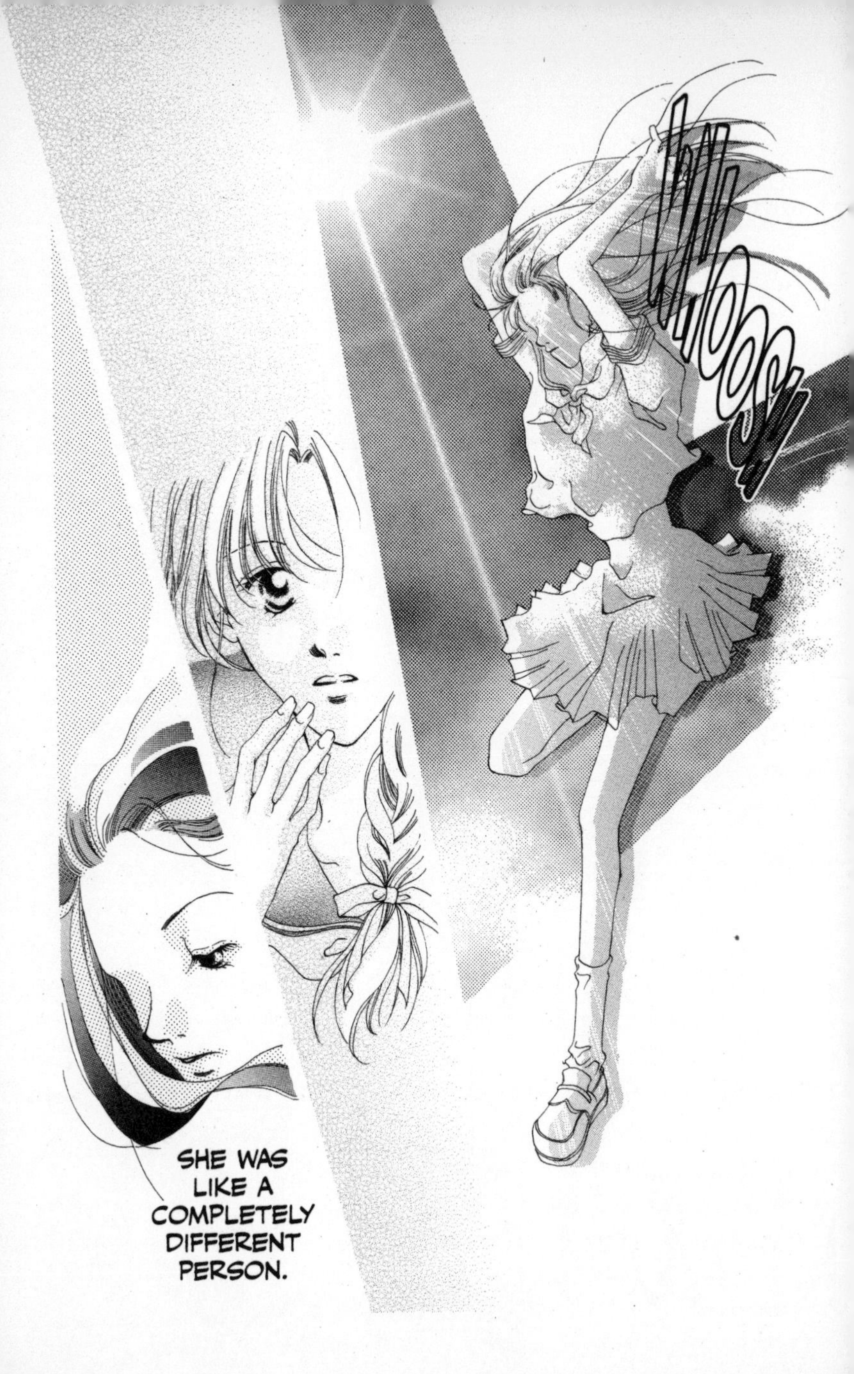
WHOOSH!
SHE WAS LIKE A COMPLETELY DIFFERENT PERSON.

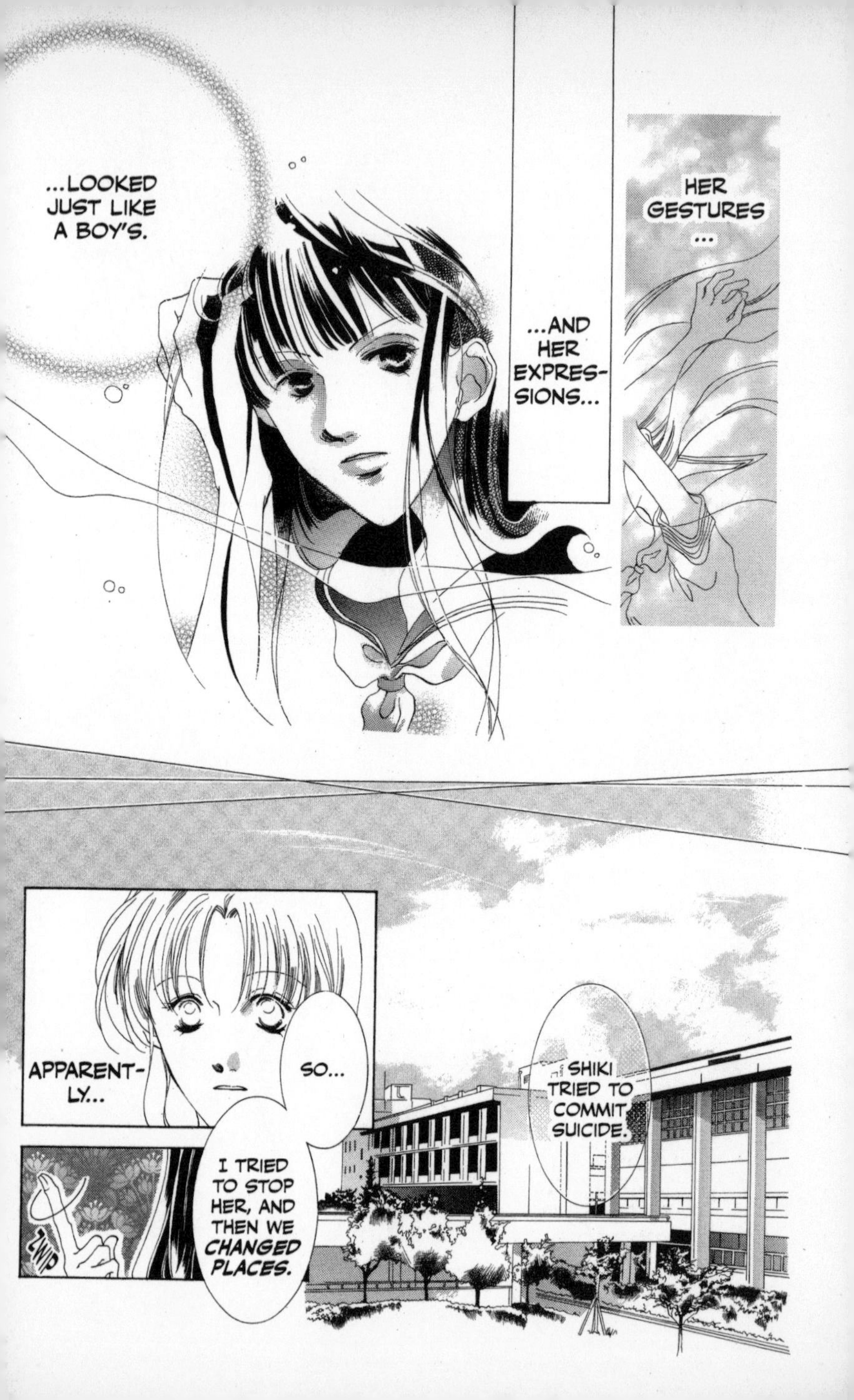
HER GESTURES ...
...AND HER EXPRESSIONS...
...LOOKED JUST LIKE A BOY'S.
SHIKI TRIED TO COMMIT SUICIDE.
SO...
APPARENTLY...
I TRIED TO STOP HER, AND THEN WE *CHANGED* PLACES.
ZWIP

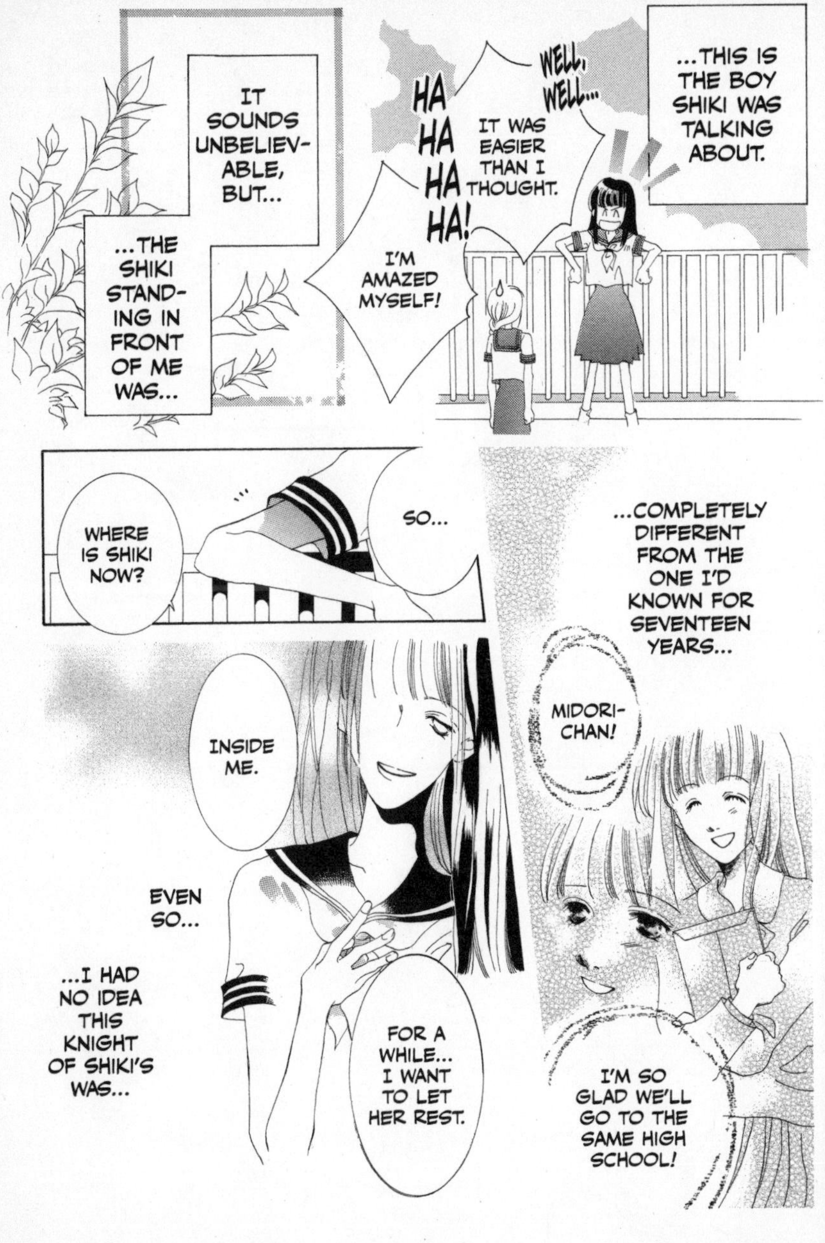
...THIS IS THE BOY SHIKI WAS TALKING ABOUT.
WELL, WELL...
IT WAS EASIER THAN I THOUGHT.
HA HA HA HA!
I'M AMAZED MYSELF!
IT SOUNDS UNBELIEV-ABLE, BUT...
...THE SHIKI STAND-ING IN FRONT OF ME WAS...
...COMPLETELY DIFFERENT FROM THE ONE I'D KNOWN FOR SEVENTEEN YEARS...
MIDORI-CHAN!
I'M SO GLAD WE'LL GO TO THE SAME HIGH SCHOOL!
SO...
WHERE IS SHIKI NOW?
INSIDE ME.
FOR A WHILE... I WANT TO LET HER REST.
EVEN SO...
...I HAD NO IDEA THIS KNIGHT OF SHIKI'S WAS...

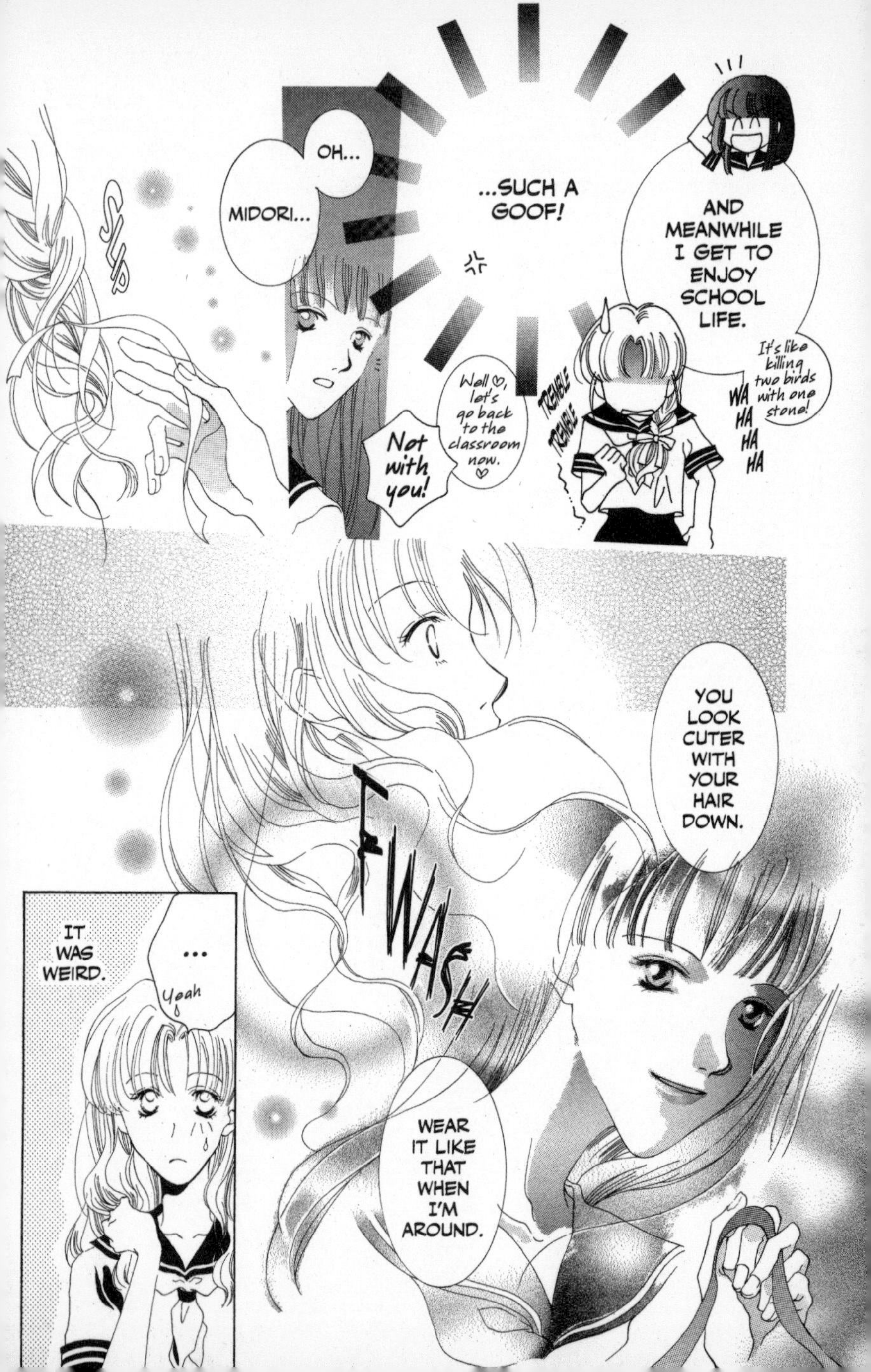
AND MEANWHILE I GET TO ENJOY SCHOOL LIFE.
It's like killing two birds with one stone!
WA HA HA HA
TREMBLE TREMBLE
...SUCH A GOOF!
Well♡, let's go back to the classroom now.♡
Not with you!
OH...
MIDORI...
SLIP
YOU LOOK CUTER WITH YOUR HAIR DOWN.
FWASH
WEAR IT LIKE THAT WHEN I'M AROUND.
...
Yeah
IT WAS WEIRD.

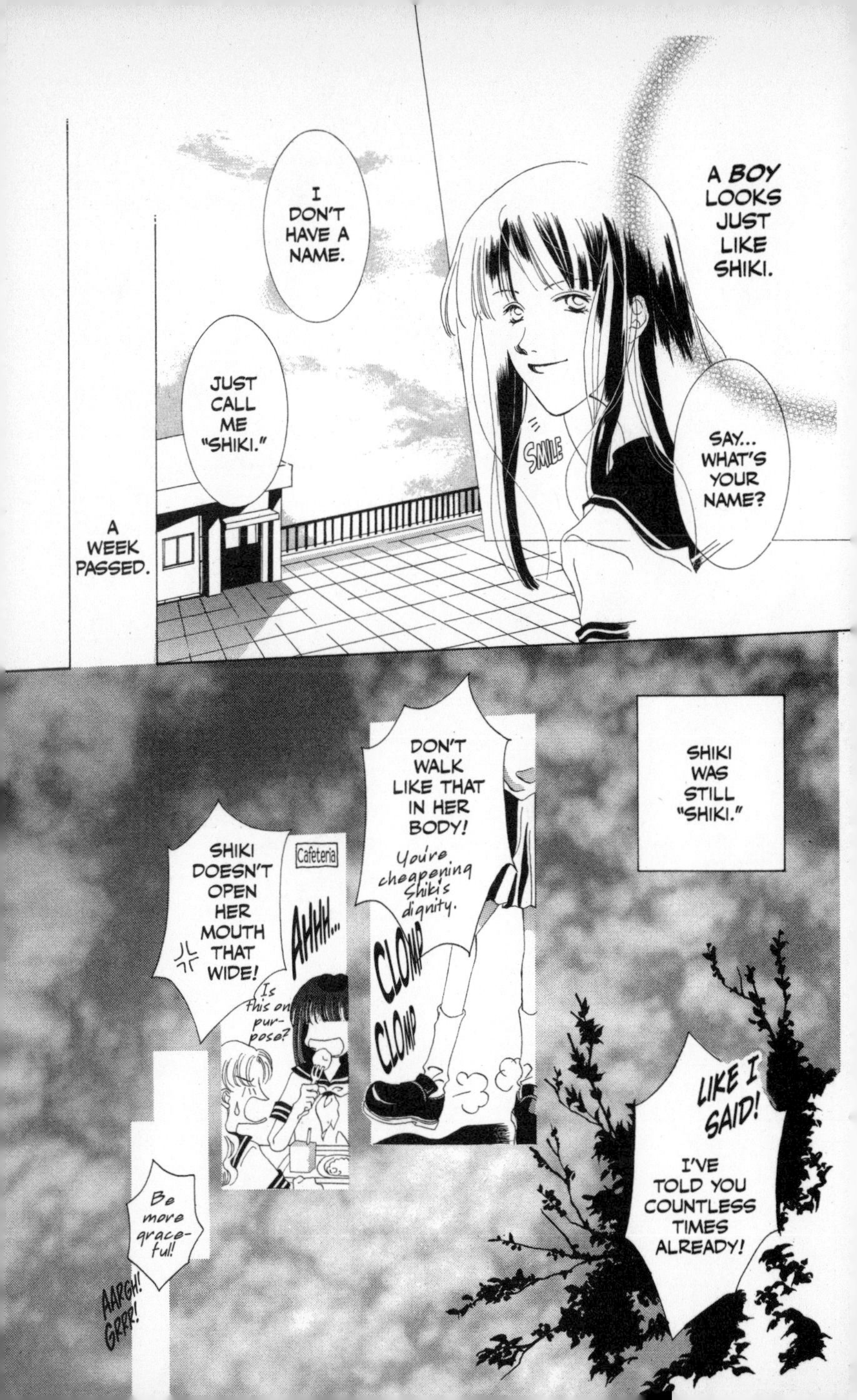
A BOY LOOKS JUST LIKE SHIKI.
SAY... WHAT'S YOUR NAME?
I DON'T HAVE A NAME.
JUST CALL ME "SHIKI."
SMILE
A WEEK PASSED.
SHIKI WAS STILL "SHIKI."
DON'T WALK LIKE THAT IN HER BODY!
You're cheapening Shiki's dignity.
CLOMP CLOMP
LIKE I SAID!
I'VE TOLD YOU COUNTLESS TIMES ALREADY!
SHIKI DOESN'T OPEN HER MOUTH THAT WIDE!
Cafeteria
AHHH...
Is this on purpose?
Be more graceful!
AARGH! GRRR!

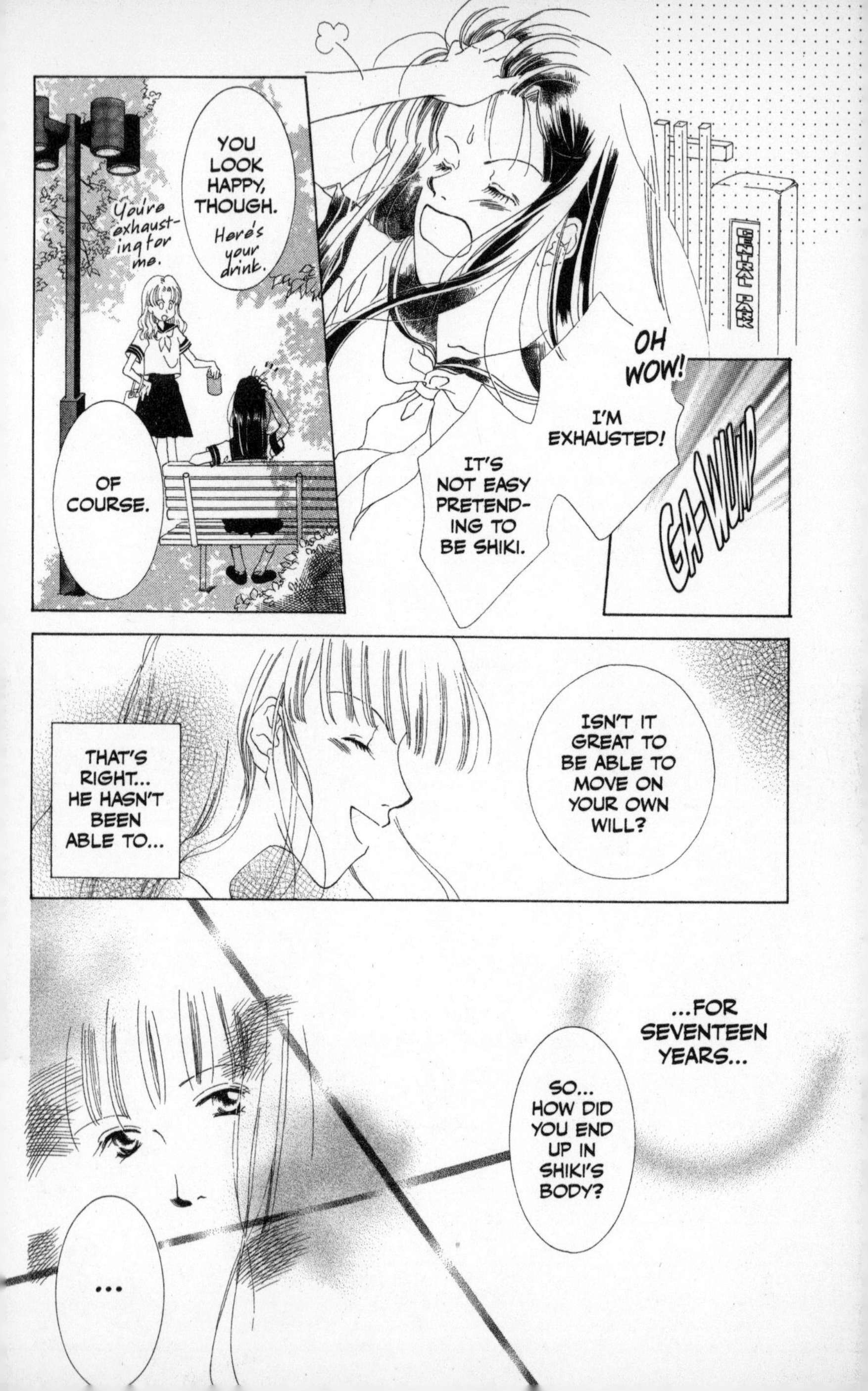
OH WOW!
I'M EXHAUSTED!
GA-WUMP
IT'S NOT EASY PRETENDING TO BE SHIKI.
CENTRAL PARK
YOU LOOK HAPPY, THOUGH.
Here's your drink.
You're exhausting for me.
OF COURSE.
ISN'T IT GREAT TO BE ABLE TO MOVE ON YOUR OWN WILL?
THAT'S RIGHT... HE HASN'T BEEN ABLE TO...
...FOR SEVENTEEN YEARS...
SO... HOW DID YOU END UP IN SHIKI'S BODY?
...

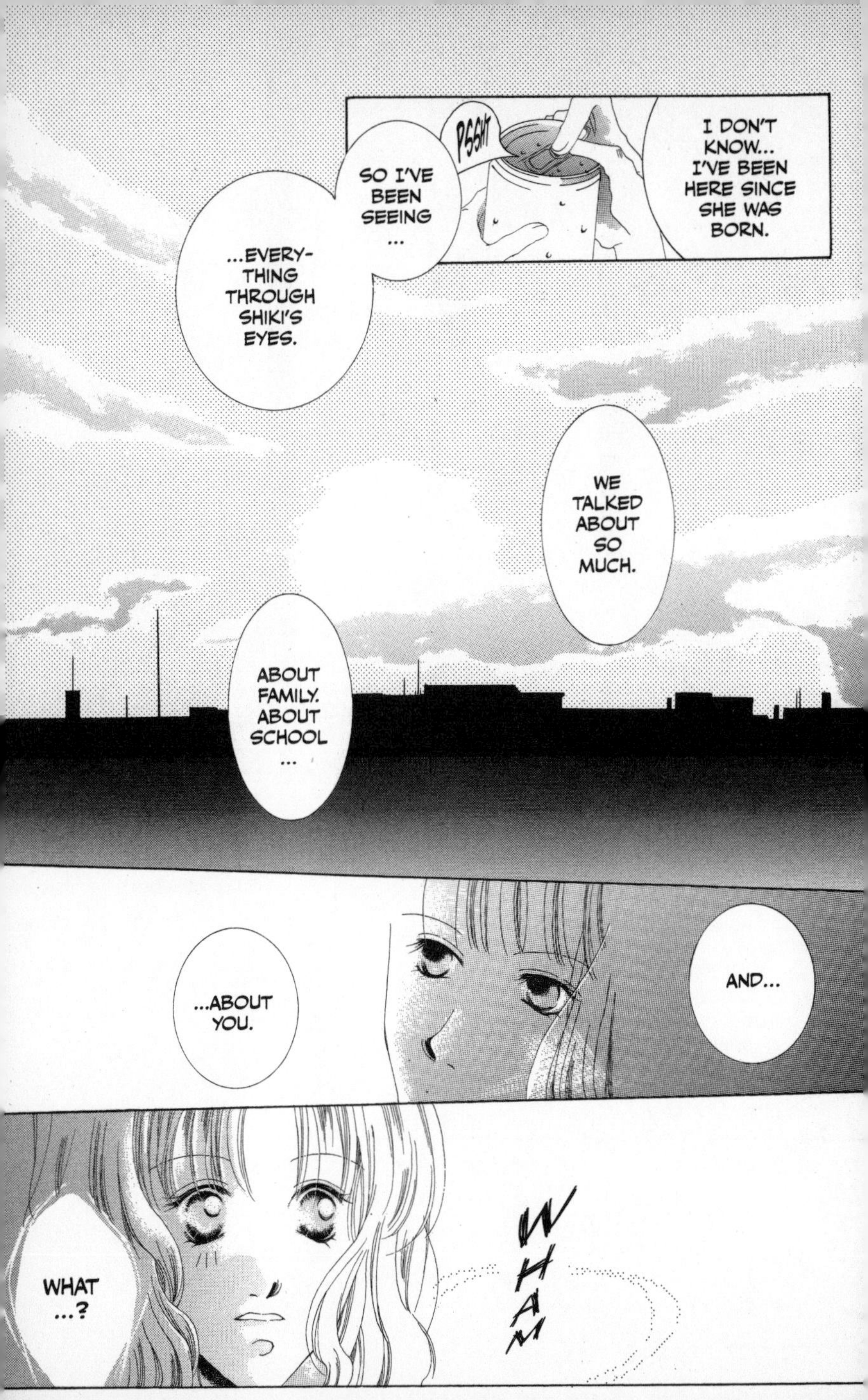
I DON'T KNOW... I'VE BEEN HERE SINCE SHE WAS BORN.
PSSHT
SO I'VE BEEN SEEING ...
...EVERY-THING THROUGH SHIKI'S EYES.
WE TALKED ABOUT SO MUCH.
ABOUT FAMILY. ABOUT SCHOOL ...
AND...
...ABOUT YOU.
WHAM
WHAT ...?

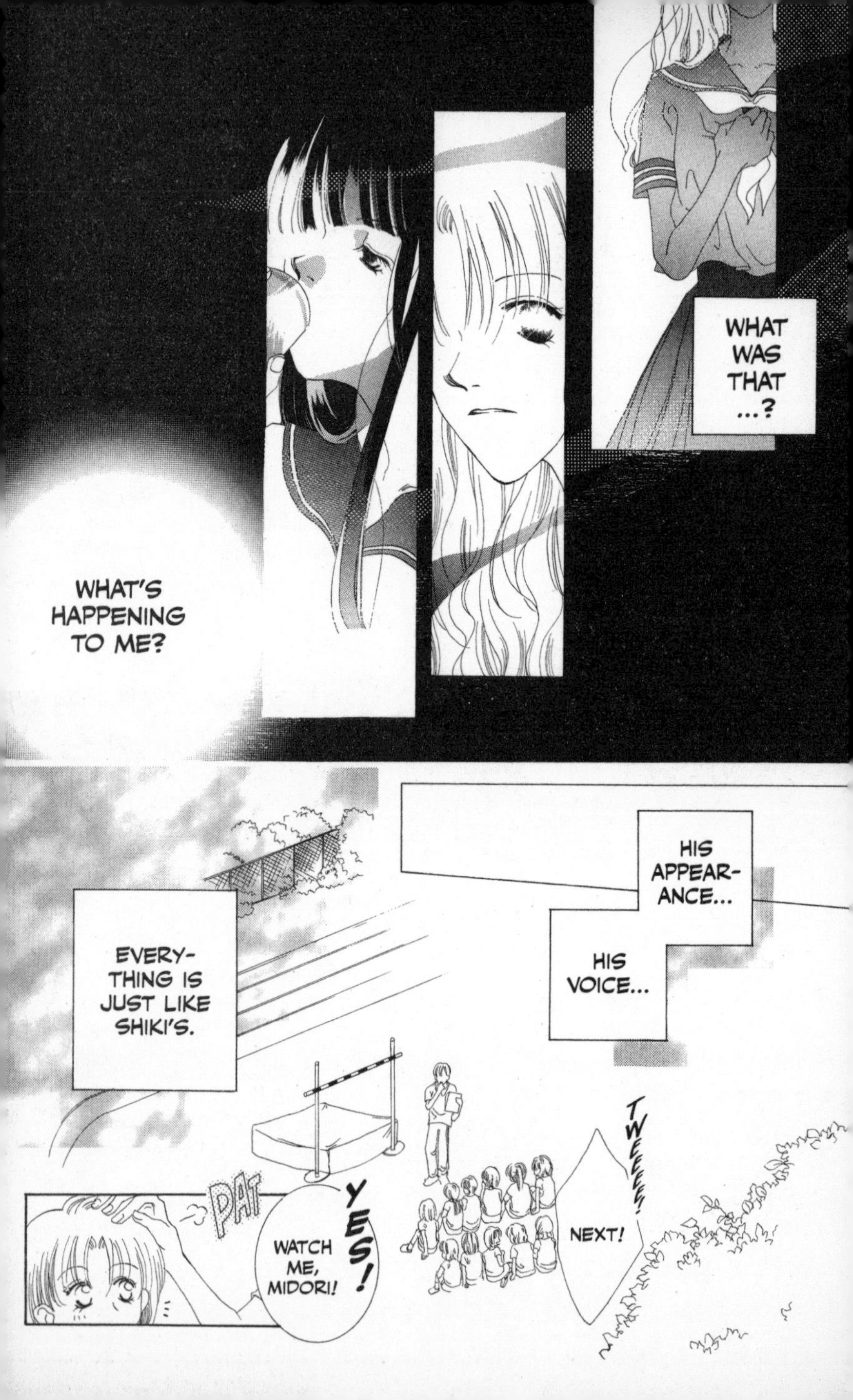
WHAT WAS THAT ...?
WHAT'S HAPPENING TO ME?
HIS APPEARANCE...
HIS VOICE...
EVERYTHING IS JUST LIKE SHIKI'S.
TWEEEE!
NEXT!
YES!
WATCH ME, MIDORI!
PAT

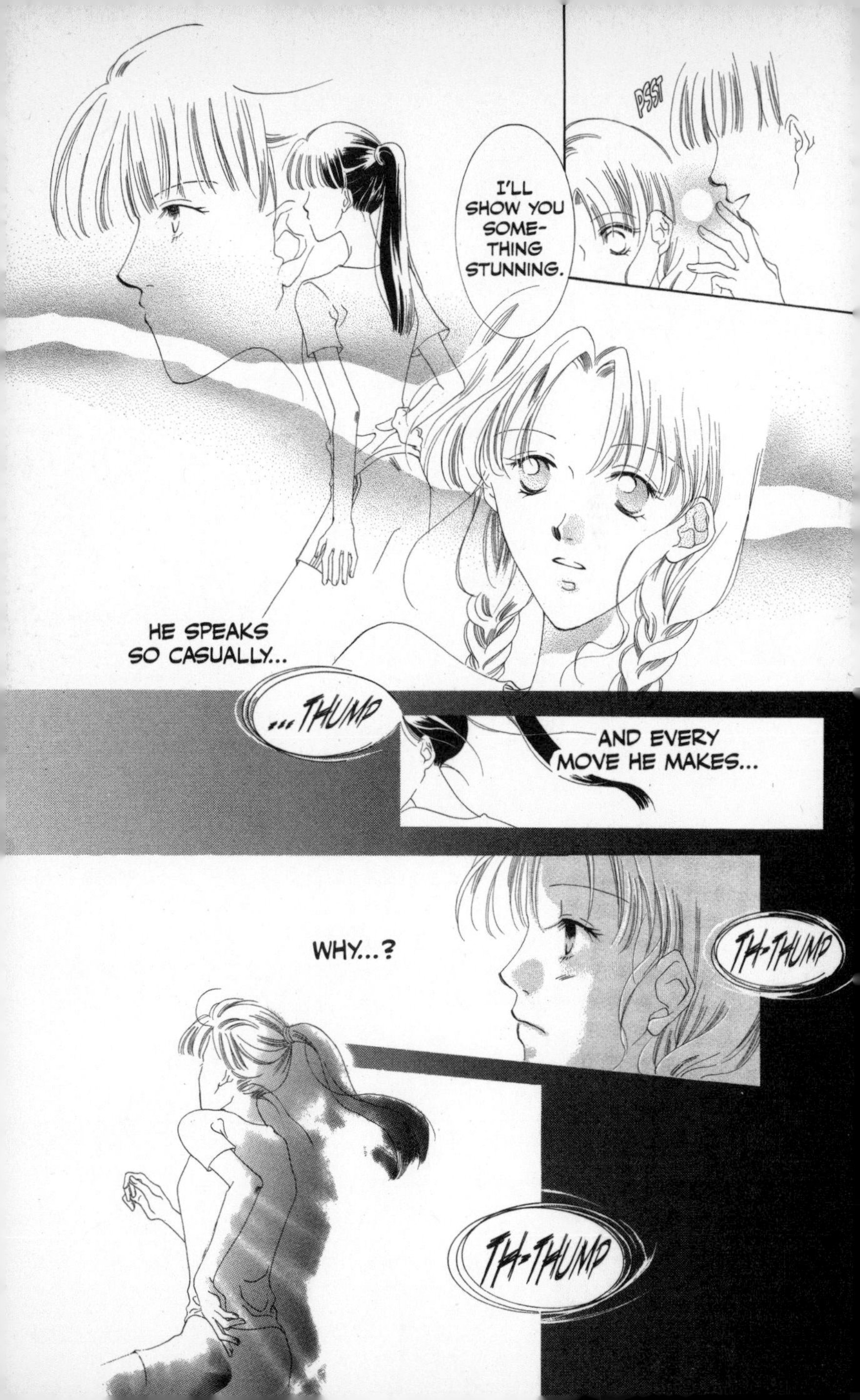
PSST
I'LL SHOW YOU SOME-THING STUNNING.
HE SPEAKS SO CASUALLY...
...THUMP
AND EVERY MOVE HE MAKES...
TH-THUMP
WHY...?
TH-THUMP

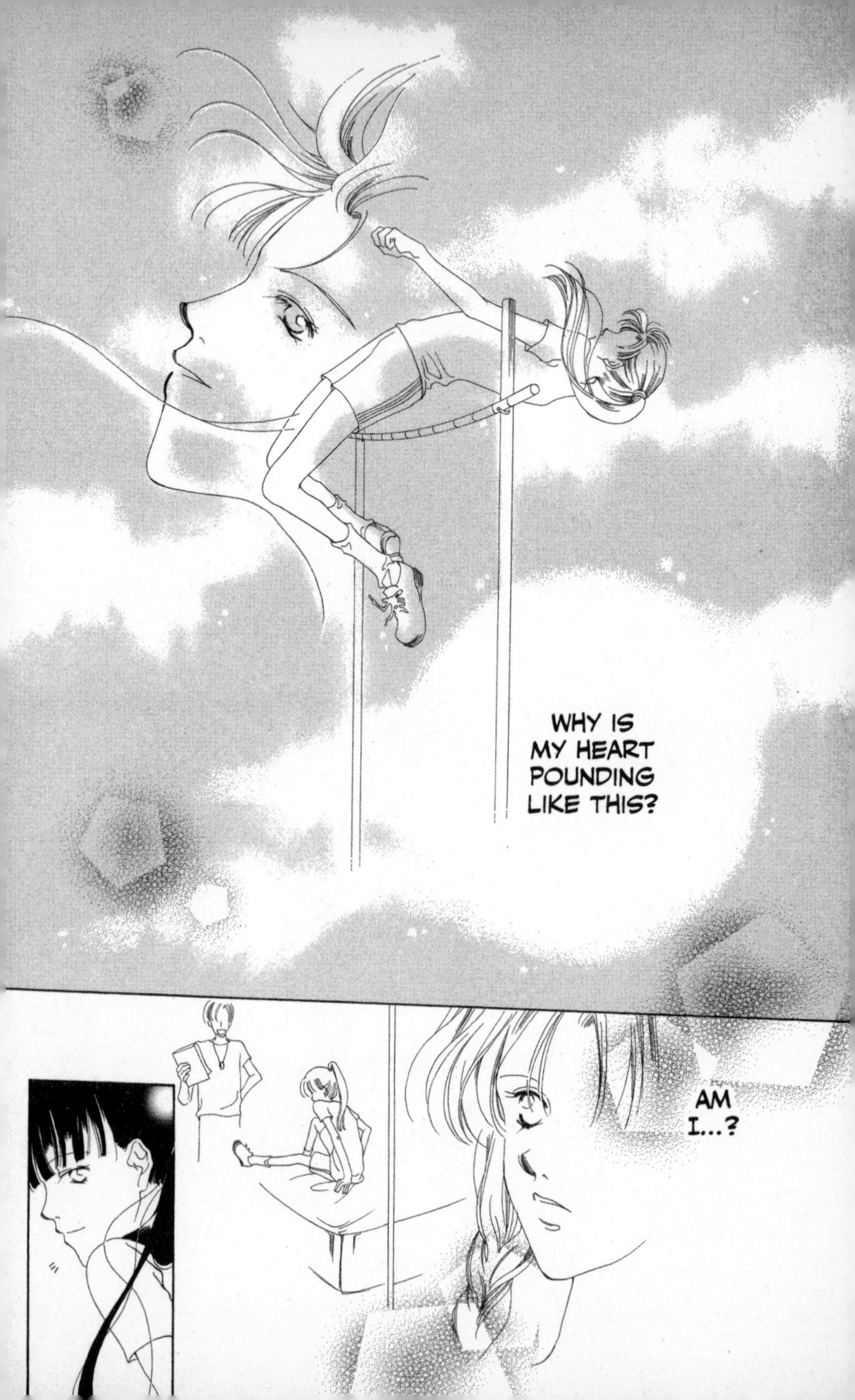
WHY IS MY HEART POUNDING LIKE THIS?
AM I...?

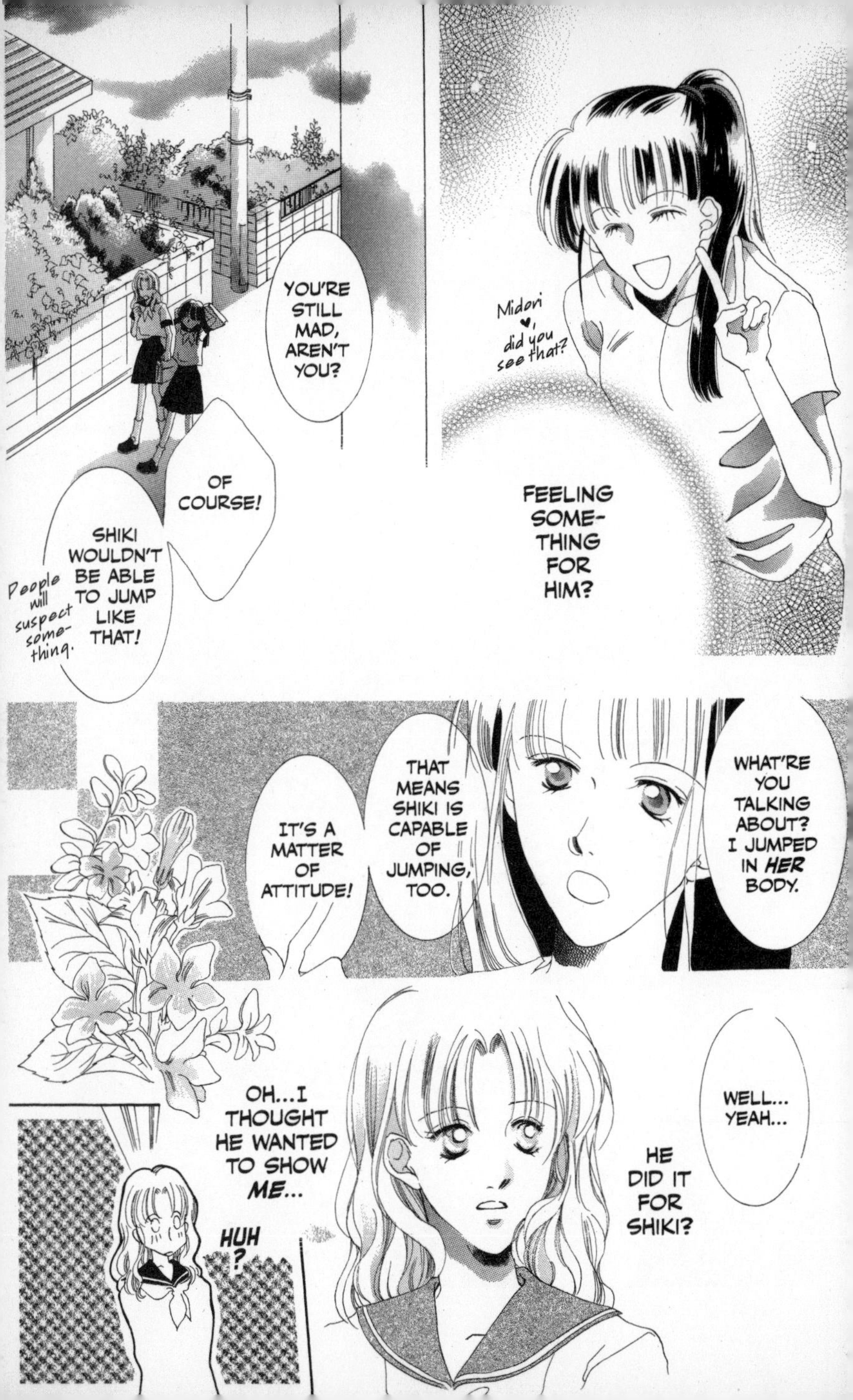
Midori ♥, did you see that?
FEELING SOMETHING FOR HIM?
YOU'RE STILL MAD, AREN'T YOU?
OF COURSE!
SHIKI WOULDN'T BE ABLE TO JUMP LIKE THAT!
People will suspect something.
WHAT'RE YOU TALKING ABOUT? I JUMPED IN *HER* BODY.
THAT MEANS SHIKI IS CAPABLE OF JUMPING, TOO.
IT'S A MATTER OF ATTITUDE!
WELL... YEAH...
HE DID IT FOR SHIKI?
OH...I THOUGHT HE WANTED TO SHOW *ME*...
HUH?

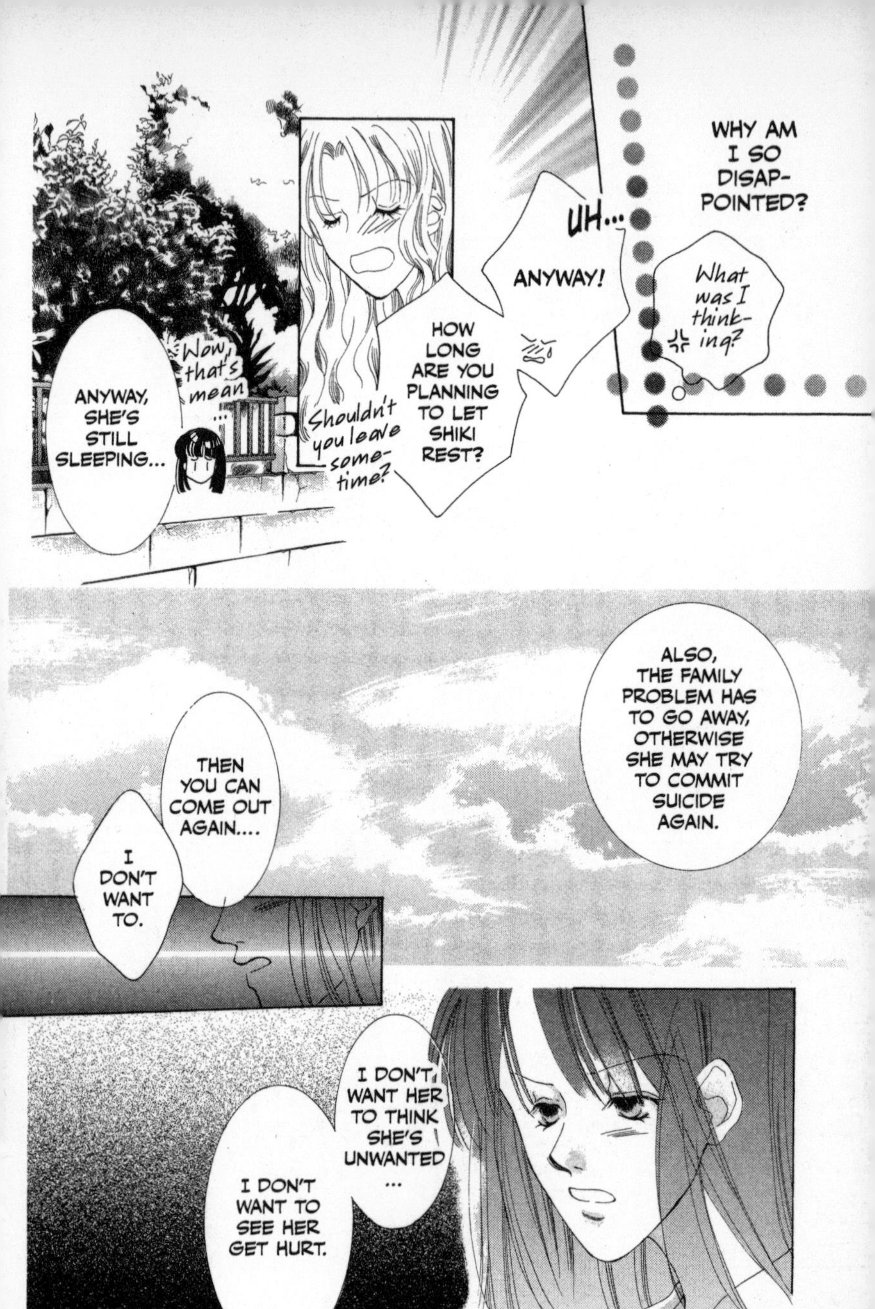
WHY AM I SO DISAP- POINTED?
What was I think- ing?
UH...
ANYWAY!
HOW LONG ARE YOU PLANNING TO LET SHIKI REST?
Shouldn't you leave some- time?
Wow, that's mean ...
ANYWAY, SHE'S STILL SLEEPING...
ALSO, THE FAMILY PROBLEM HAS TO GO AWAY, OTHERWISE SHE MAY TRY TO COMMIT SUICIDE AGAIN.
THEN YOU CAN COME OUT AGAIN....
I DON'T WANT TO.
I DON'T WANT HER TO THINK SHE'S UNWANTED ...
I DON'T WANT TO SEE HER GET HURT.

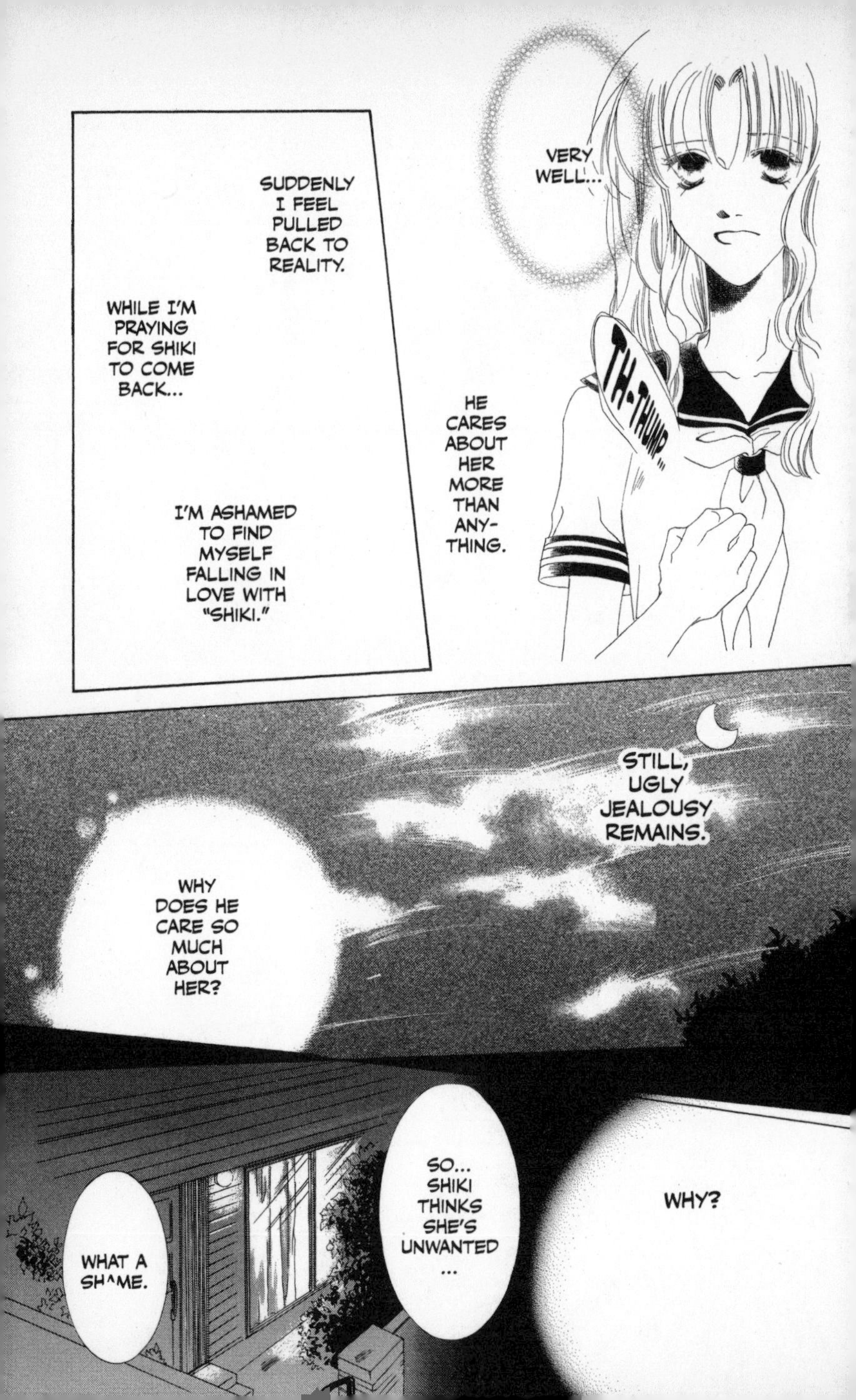
VERY WELL...
TH-THUMP...
HE CARES ABOUT HER MORE THAN ANYTHING.
SUDDENLY I FEEL PULLED BACK TO REALITY.
WHILE I'M PRAYING FOR SHIKI TO COME BACK...
I'M ASHAMED TO FIND MYSELF FALLING IN LOVE WITH "SHIKI."
STILL, UGLY JEALOUSY REMAINS.
WHY DOES HE CARE SO MUCH ABOUT HER?
WHY?
SO... SHIKI THINKS SHE'S UNWANTED ...
WHAT A SH^ME.

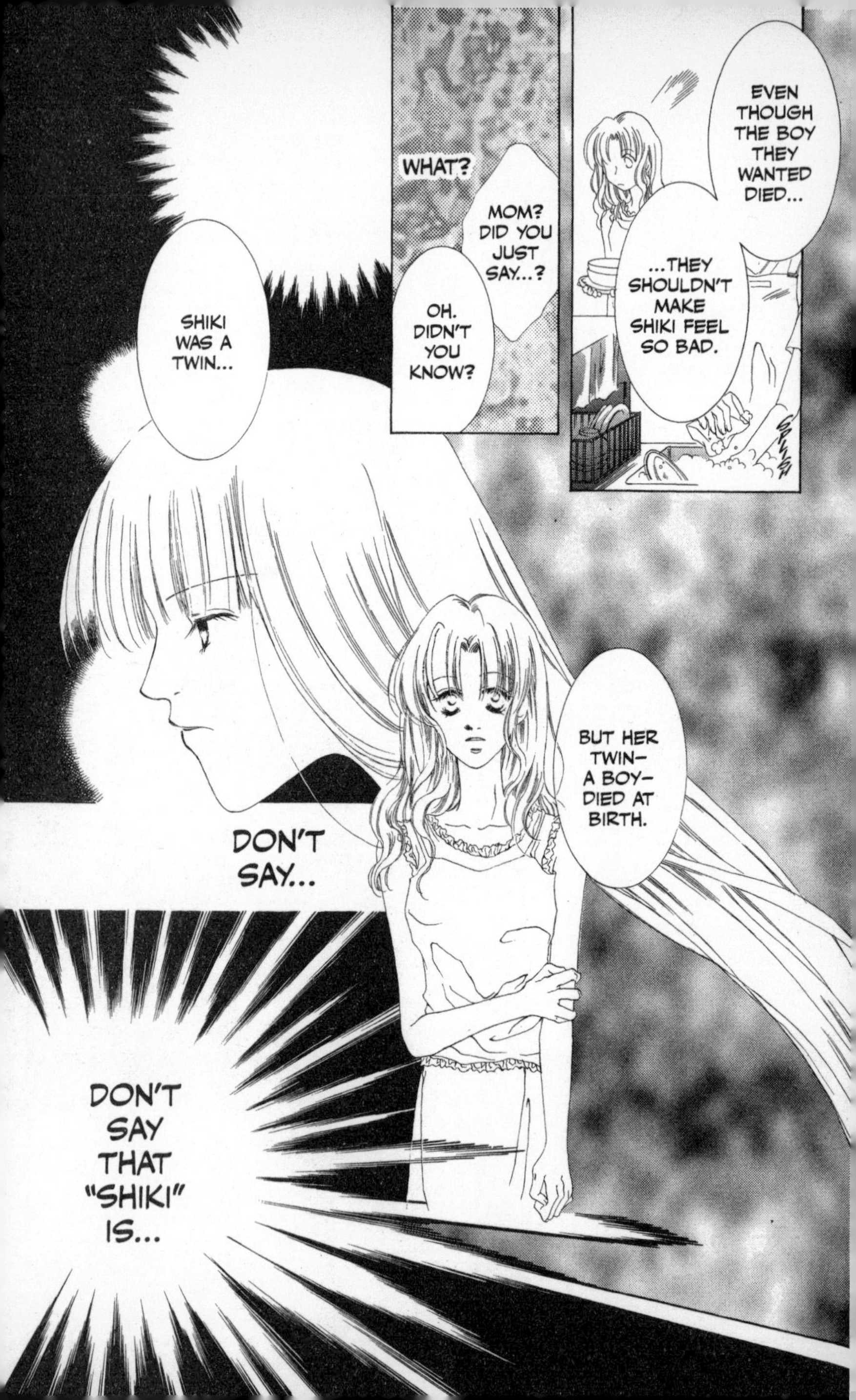
EVEN THOUGH THE BOY THEY WANTED DIED...
...THEY SHOULDN'T MAKE SHIKI FEEL SO BAD.
SPLISH
WHAT?
MOM? DID YOU JUST SAY...?
OH. DIDN'T YOU KNOW?
SHIKI WAS A TWIN...
BUT HER TWIN— A BOY— DIED AT BIRTH.
DON'T SAY...
DON'T SAY THAT "SHIKI" IS...

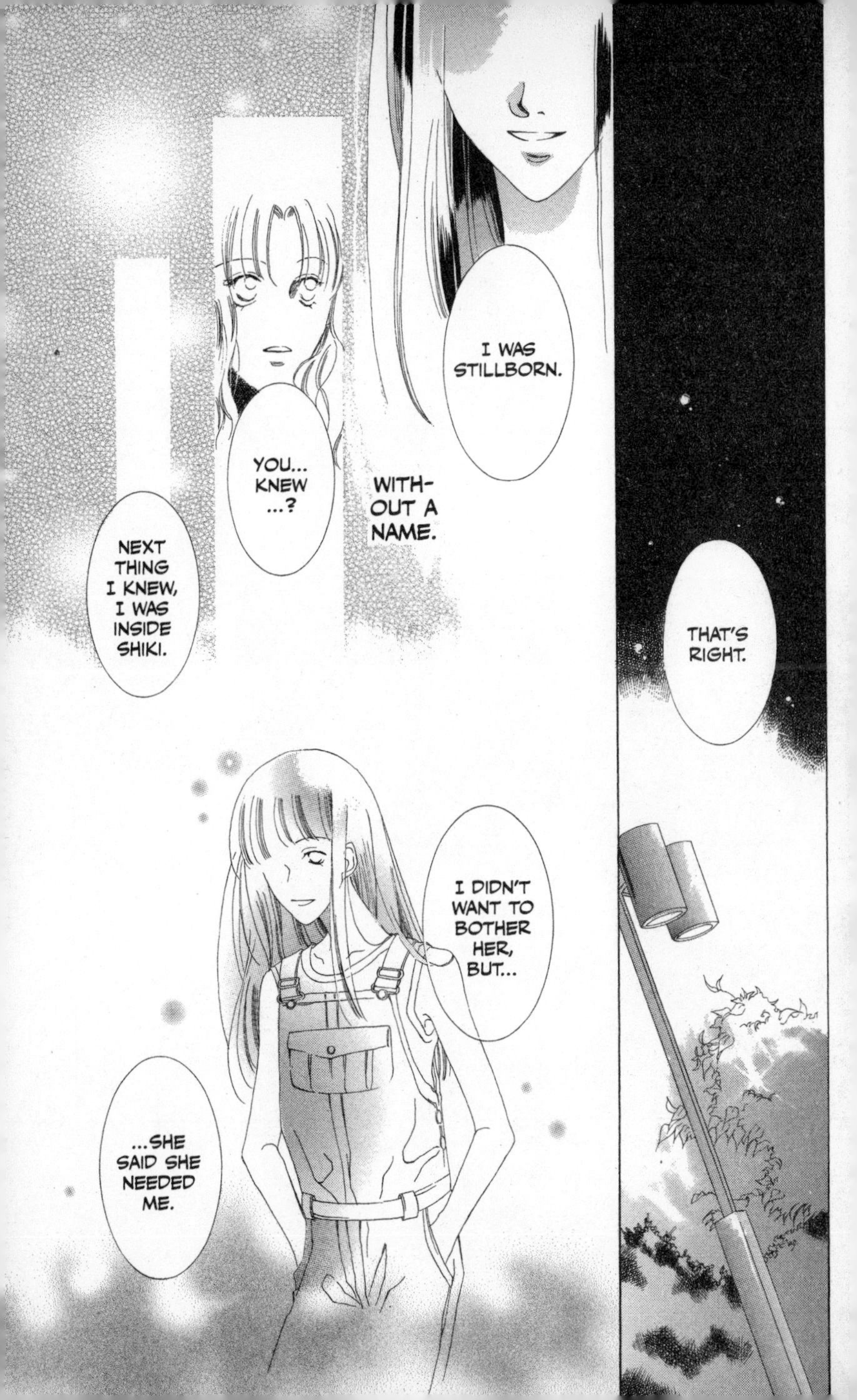
THAT'S RIGHT.
I WAS STILLBORN.
WITH-OUT A NAME.
YOU... KNEW ...?
NEXT THING I KNEW, I WAS INSIDE SHIKI.
I DIDN'T WANT TO BOTHER HER, BUT...
...SHE SAID SHE NEEDED ME.

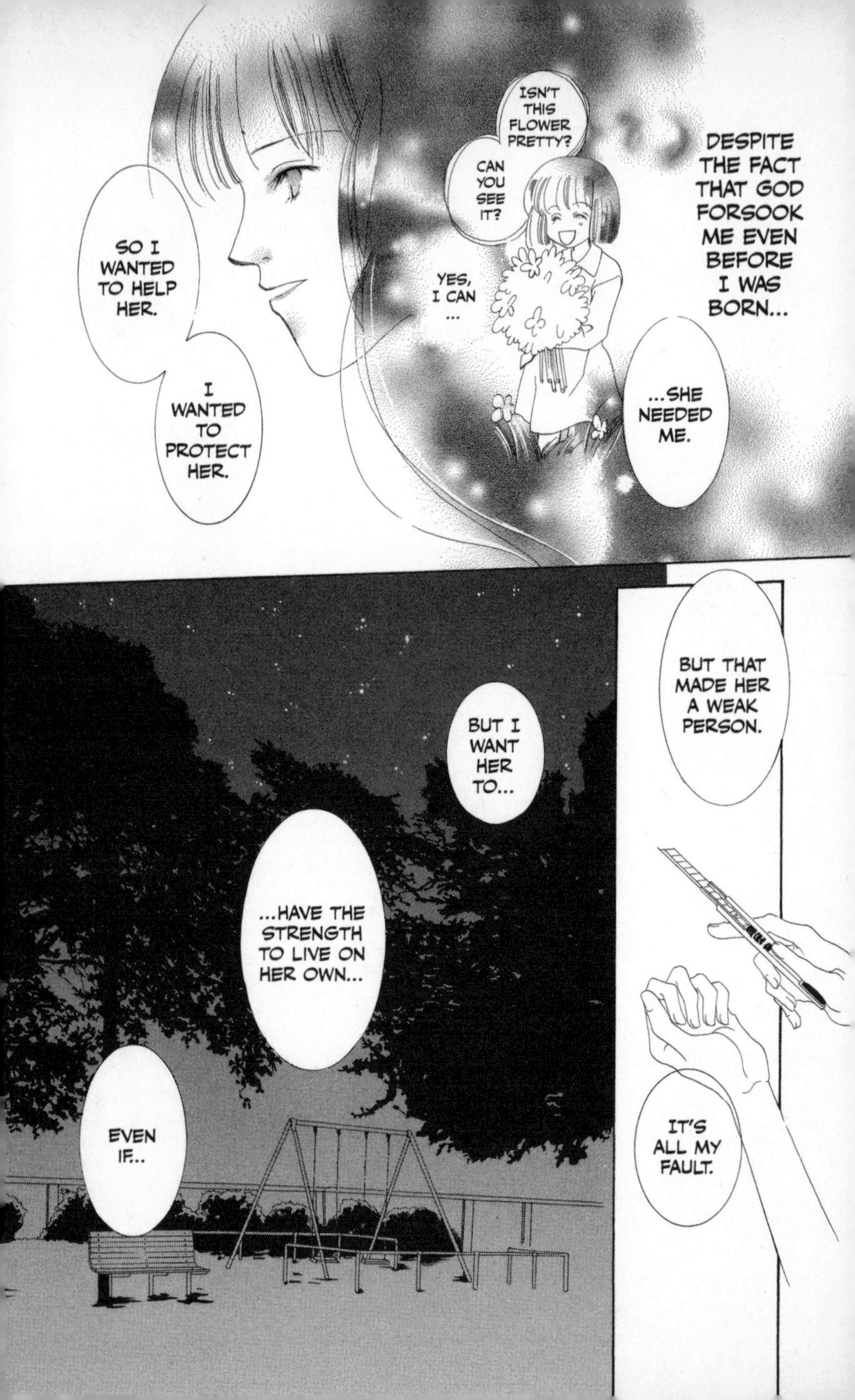
DESPITE THE FACT THAT GOD FORSOOK ME EVEN BEFORE I WAS BORN...
ISN'T THIS FLOWER PRETTY?
CAN YOU SEE IT?
YES, I CAN ...
...SHE NEEDED ME.
SO I WANTED TO HELP HER.
I WANTED TO PROTECT HER.
BUT THAT MADE HER A WEAK PERSON.
IT'S ALL MY FAULT.
BUT I WANT HER TO...
...HAVE THE STRENGTH TO LIVE ON HER OWN...
EVEN IF...

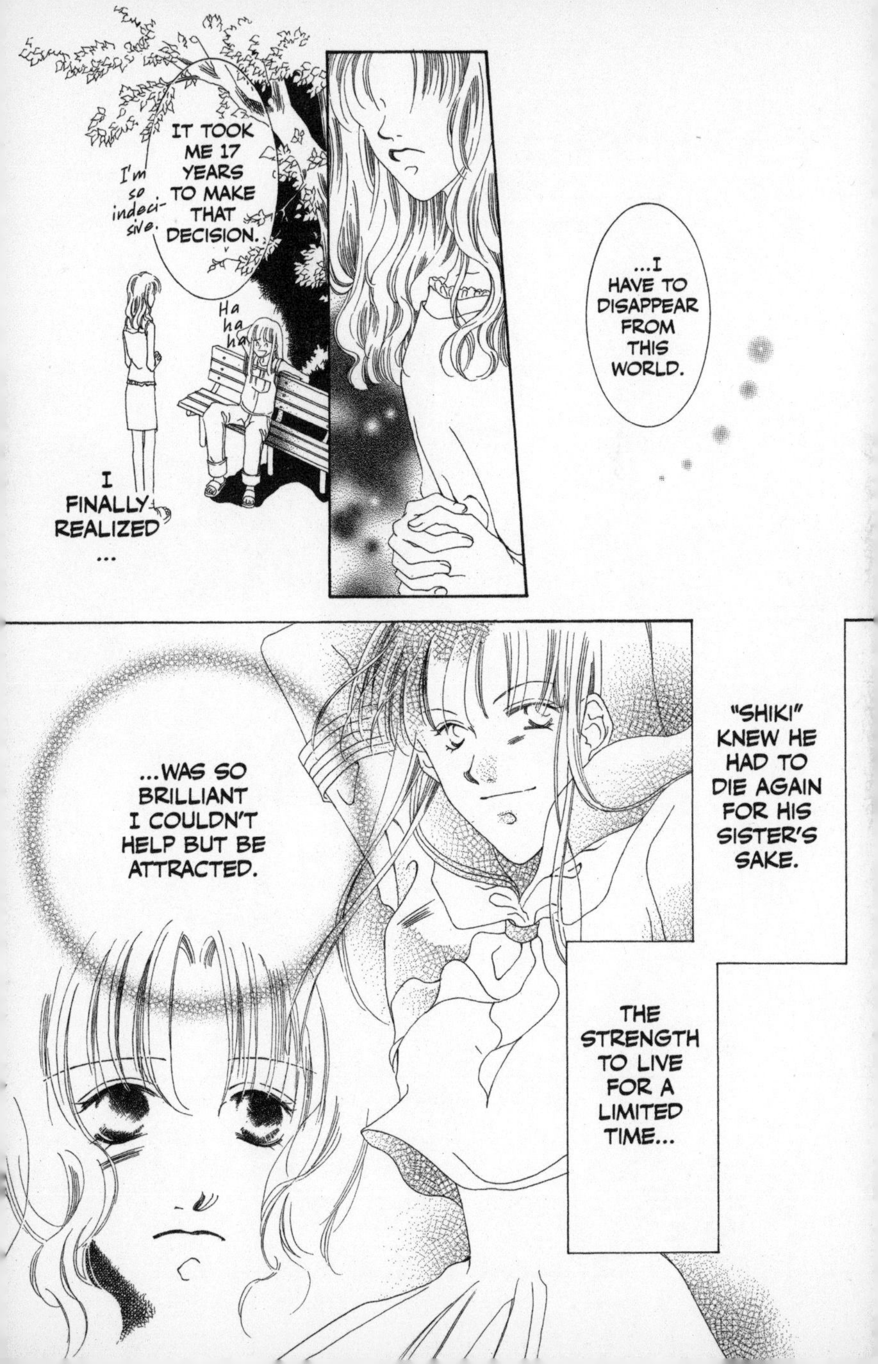

...I HAVE TO DISAPPEAR FROM THIS WORLD.
IT TOOK ME 17 YEARS TO MAKE THAT DECISION.
I'm so indecisive.
Ha ha ha
I FINALLY REALIZED...
"SHIKI" KNEW HE HAD TO DIE AGAIN FOR HIS SISTER'S SAKE.
THE STRENGTH TO LIVE FOR A LIMITED TIME...
...WAS SO BRILLIANT I COULDN'T HELP BUT BE ATTRACTED.

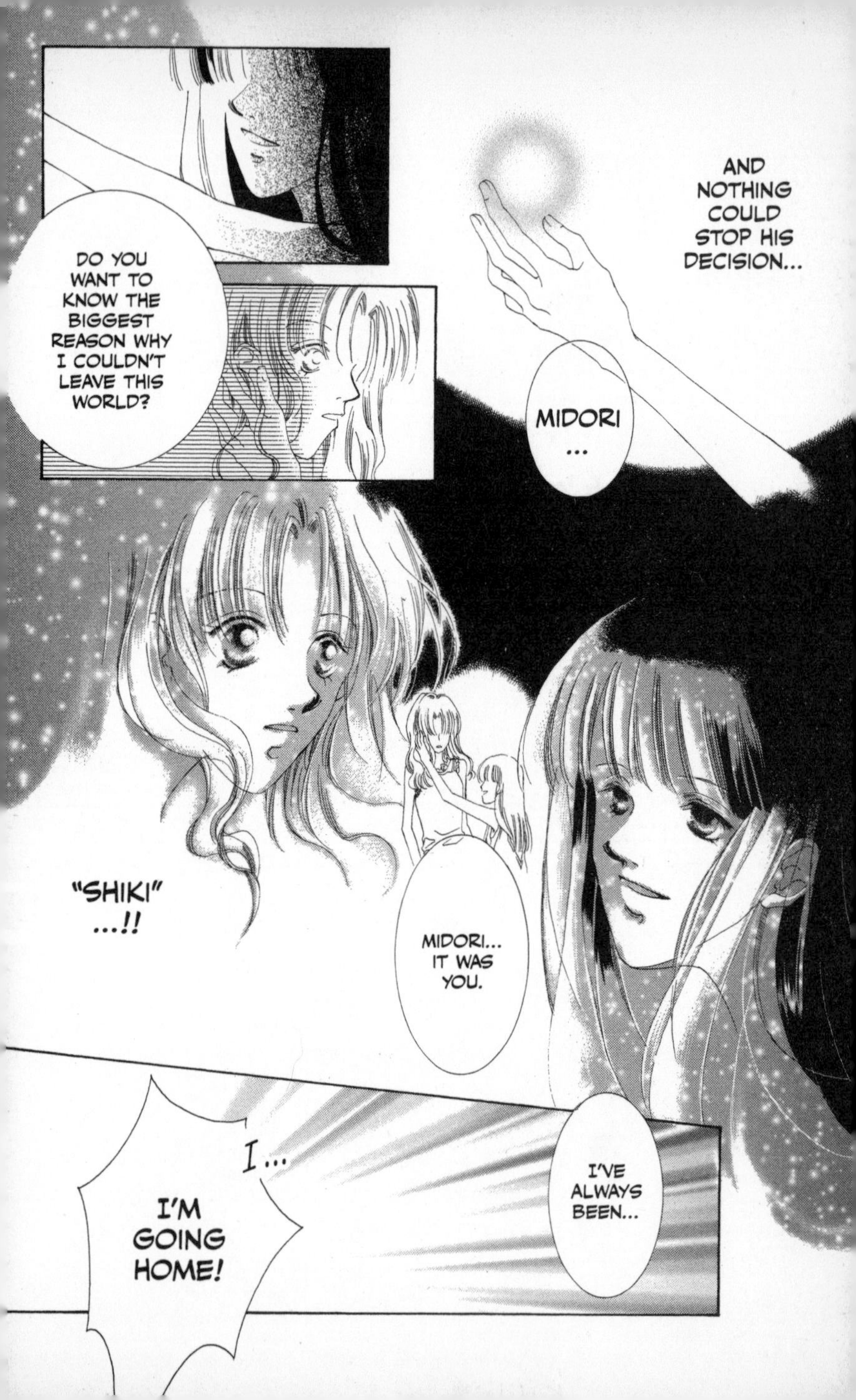
AND NOTHING COULD STOP HIS DECISION...
MIDORI...
DO YOU WANT TO KNOW THE BIGGEST REASON WHY I COULDN'T LEAVE THIS WORLD?
MIDORI... IT WAS YOU.
"SHIKI" ...!!
I'VE ALWAYS BEEN...
I...
I'M GOING HOME!

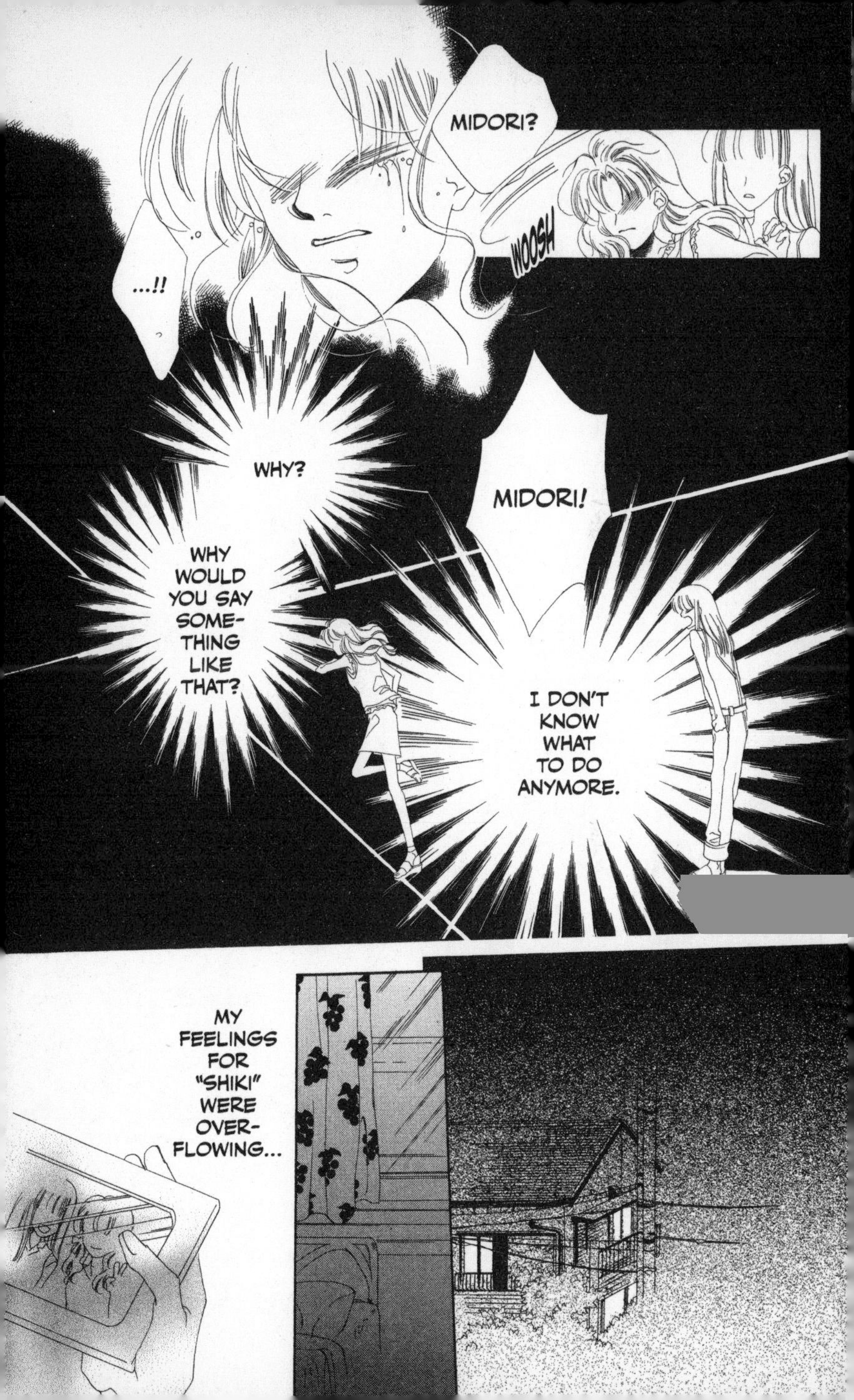
MIDORI?
WOOSH
...!!
MIDORI!
I DON'T KNOW WHAT TO DO ANYMORE.
WHY?
WHY WOULD YOU SAY SOME-THING LIKE THAT?
MY FEELINGS FOR "SHIKI" WERE OVER-FLOWING...

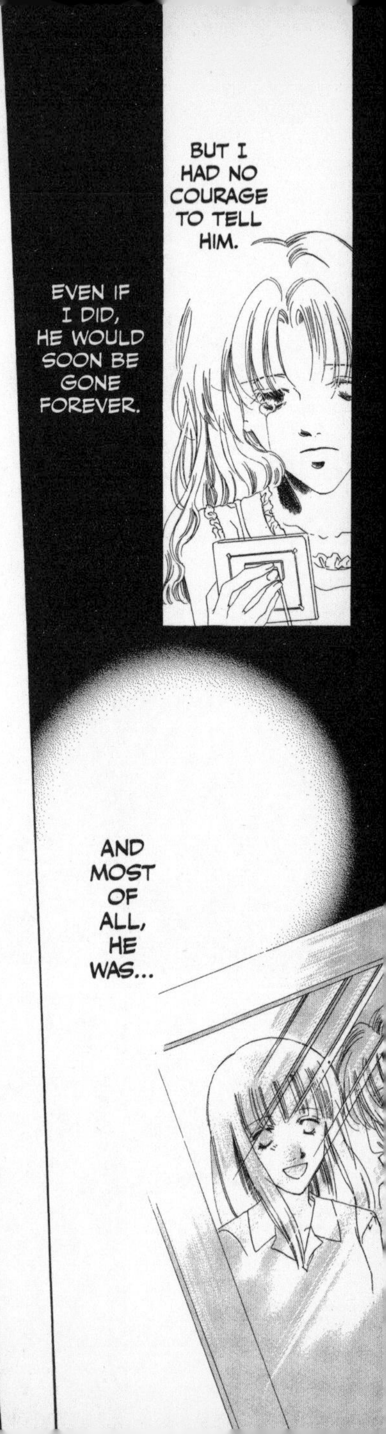
BUT I HAD NO COURAGE TO TELL HIM.
EVEN IF I DID, HE WOULD SOON BE GONE FOREVER.
AND MOST OF ALL, HE WAS...

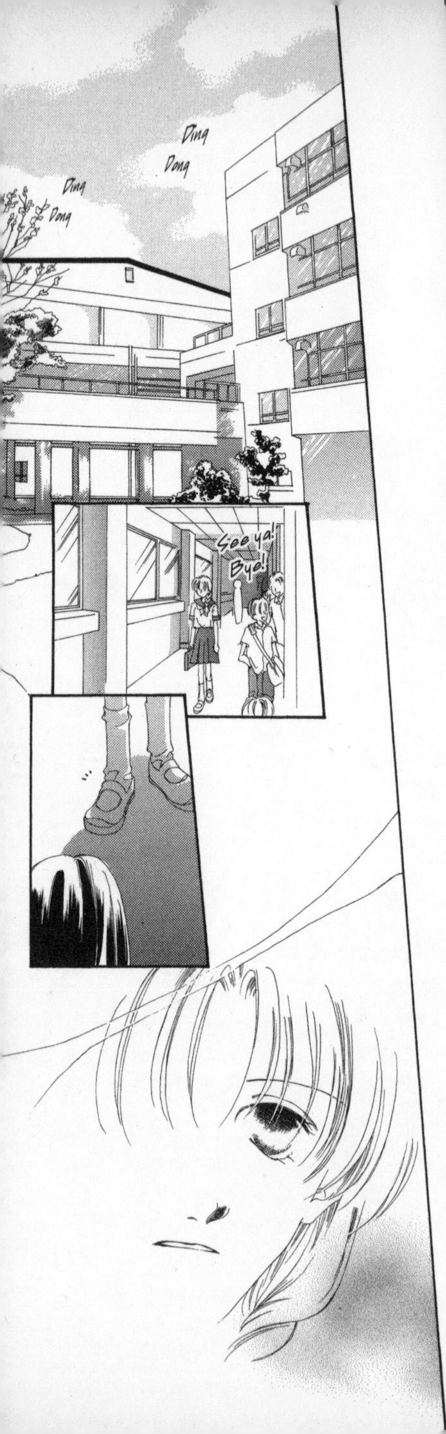
Ding Dong
Ding Dong
See ya!
Bye!
...

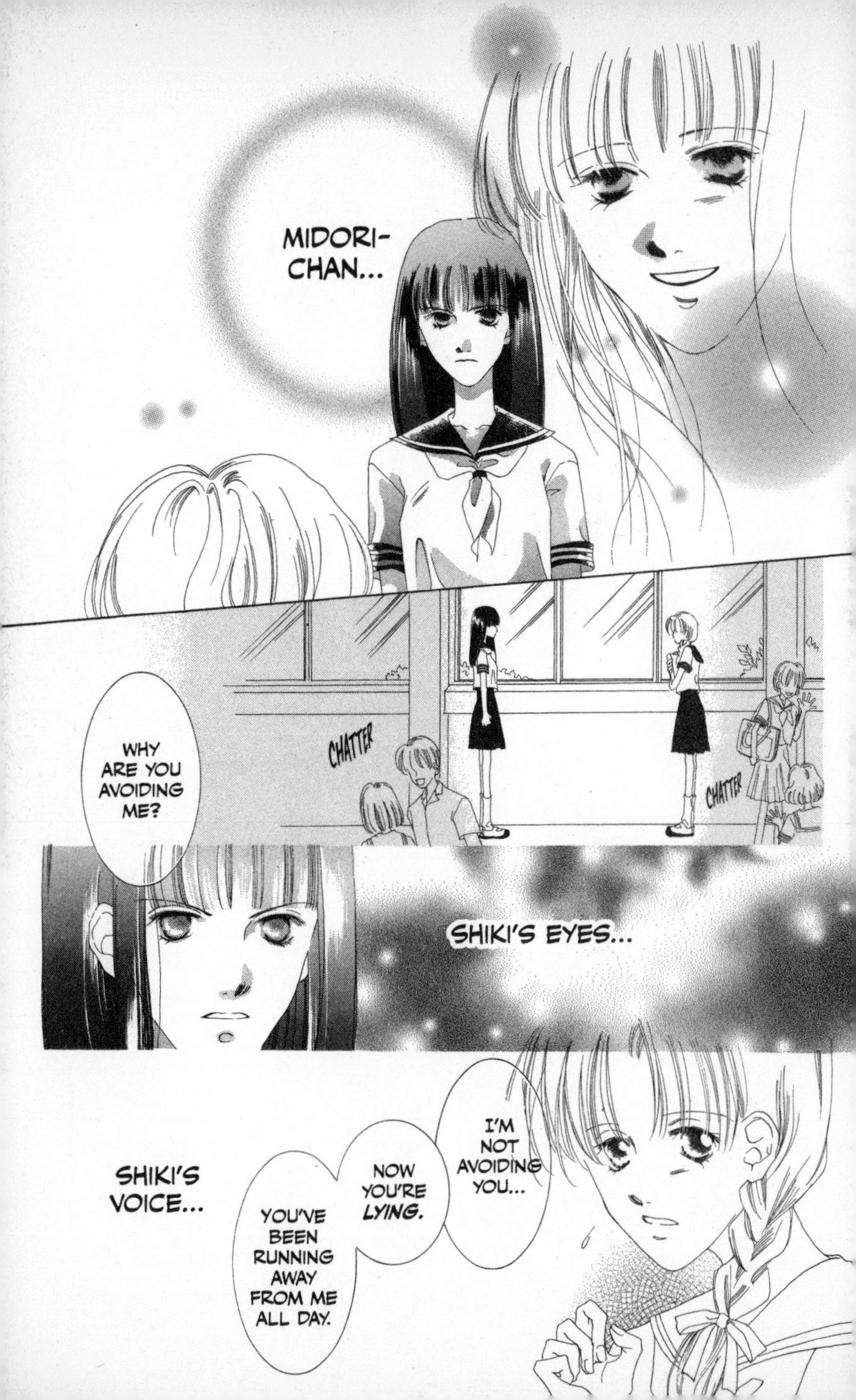
MIDORI-CHAN...
CHATTER
CHATTER
WHY ARE YOU AVOIDING ME?
SHIKI'S EYES...
I'M NOT AVOIDING YOU...
NOW YOU'RE *LYING.*
YOU'VE BEEN RUNNING AWAY FROM ME ALL DAY.
SHIKI'S VOICE...

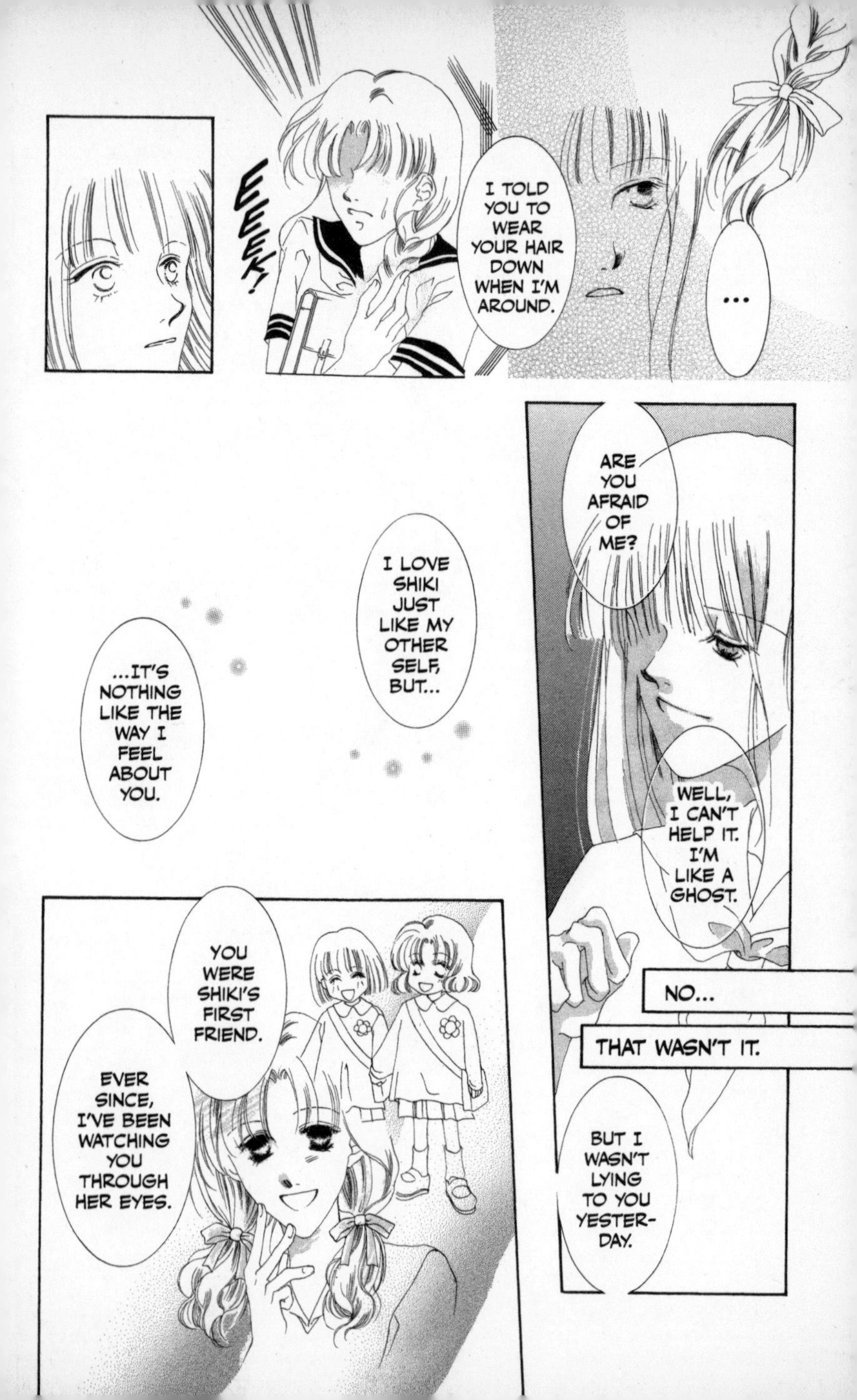
...
I TOLD YOU TO WEAR YOUR HAIR DOWN WHEN I'M AROUND.
EEEK!
ARE YOU AFRAID OF ME?
WELL, I CAN'T HELP IT. I'M LIKE A GHOST.
NO...
THAT WASN'T IT.
BUT I WASN'T LYING TO YOU YESTER-DAY.
I LOVE SHIKI JUST LIKE MY OTHER SELF, BUT...
...IT'S NOTHING LIKE THE WAY I FEEL ABOUT YOU.
YOU WERE SHIKI'S FIRST FRIEND.
EVER SINCE, I'VE BEEN WATCHING YOU THROUGH HER EYES.

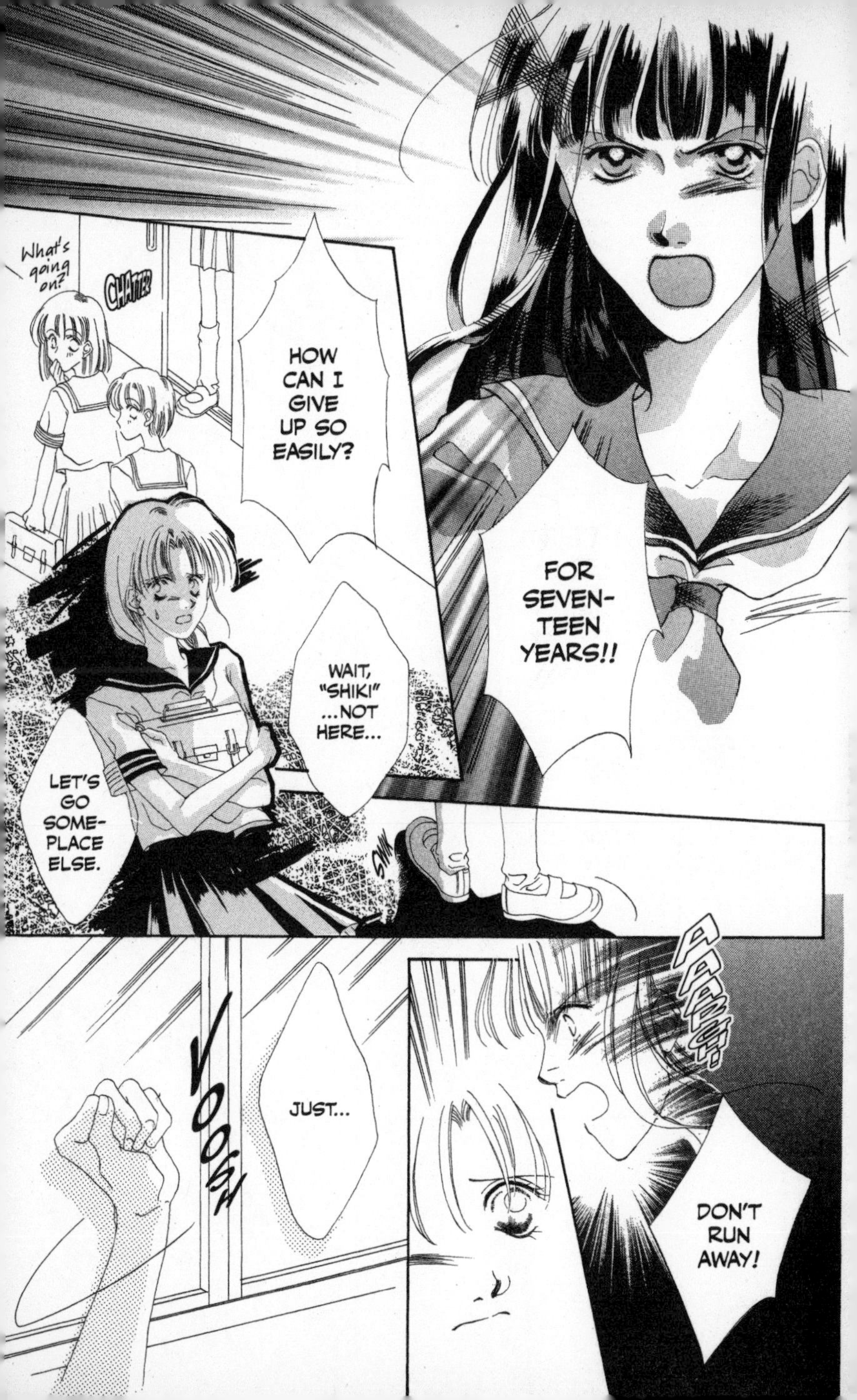
HOW CAN I GIVE UP SO EASILY?
FOR SEVEN-TEEN YEARS!!
What's going on?
CHATTER
WAIT, "SHIKI" ...NOT HERE...
LET'S GO SOME-PLACE ELSE.
SWIK
DON'T RUN AWAY!
AAAUGH!
JUST...
VOOSH

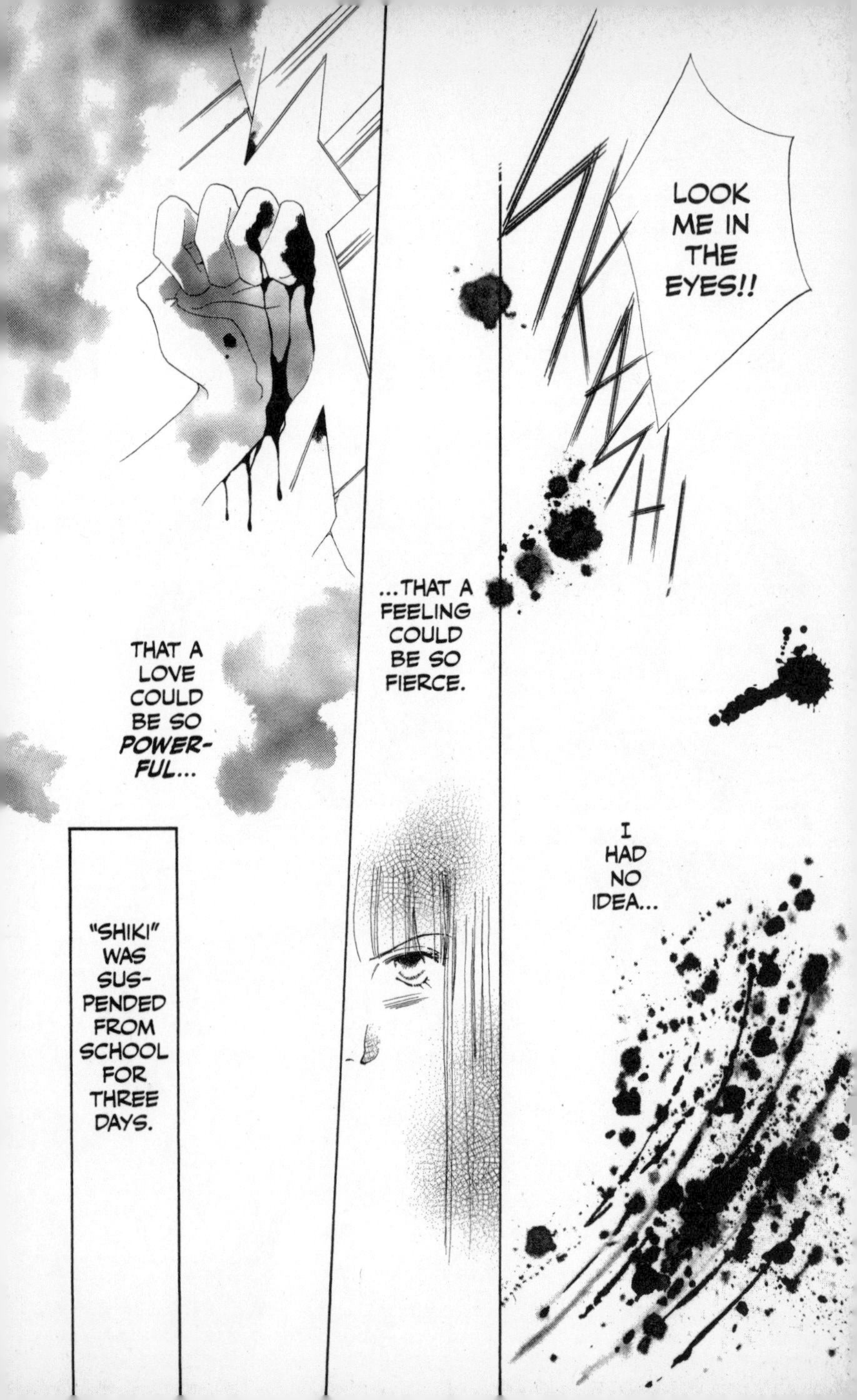
LOOK ME IN THE EYES!!
I HAD NO IDEA...
...THAT A FEELING COULD BE SO FIERCE.
THAT A LOVE COULD BE SO *POWER-FUL*...
"SHIKI" WAS SUS-PENDED FROM SCHOOL FOR THREE DAYS.

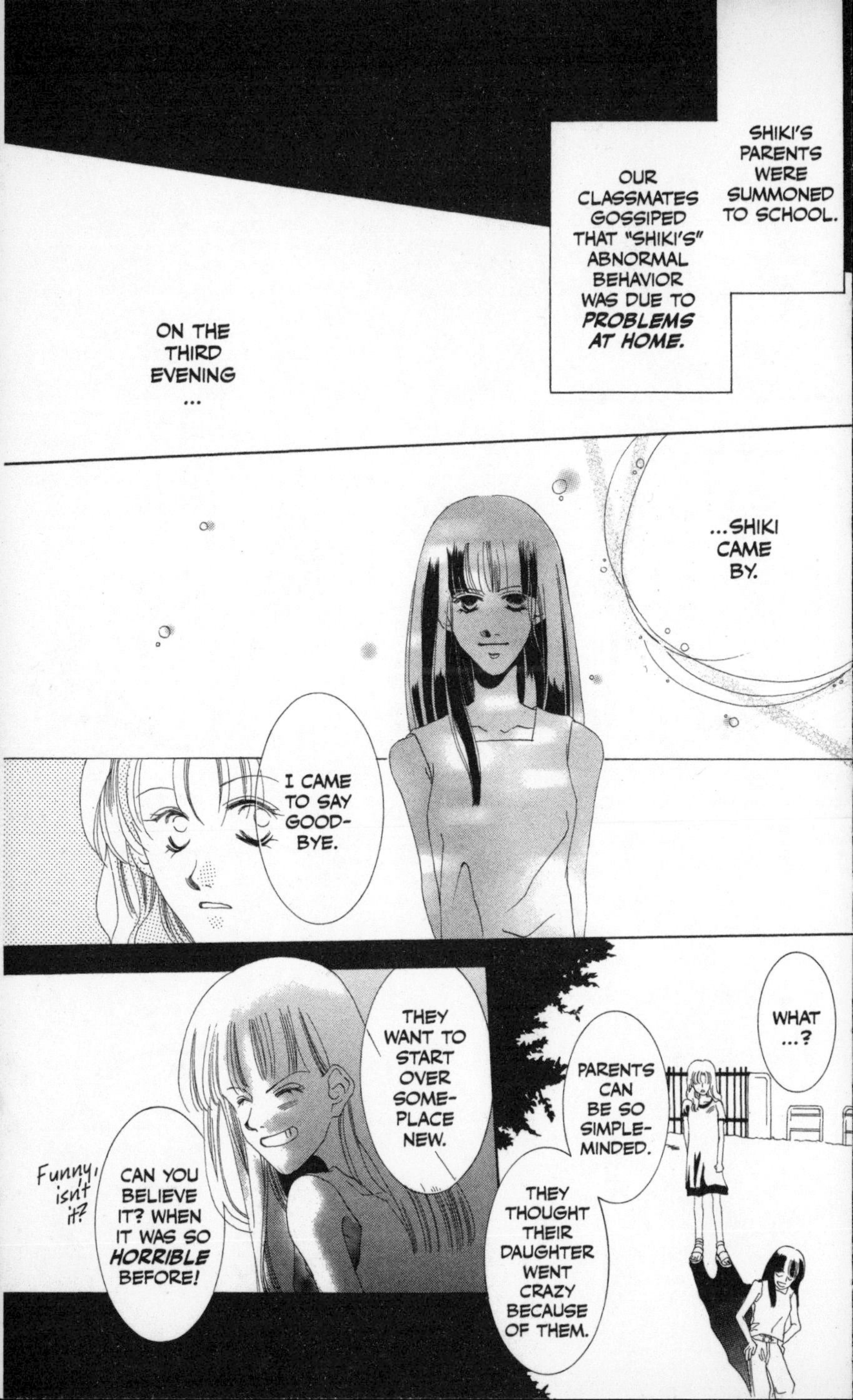
SHIKI'S PARENTS WERE SUMMONED TO SCHOOL.
OUR CLASSMATES GOSSIPED THAT "SHIKI'S" ABNORMAL BEHAVIOR WAS DUE TO *PROBLEMS AT HOME.*
ON THE THIRD EVENING ...
...SHIKI CAME BY.
I CAME TO SAY GOOD-BYE.
WHAT ...?
PARENTS CAN BE SO SIMPLE-MINDED.
THEY THOUGHT THEIR DAUGHTER WENT CRAZY BECAUSE OF THEM.
THEY WANT TO START OVER SOME-PLACE NEW.
CAN YOU BELIEVE IT? WHEN IT WAS SO *HORRIBLE* BEFORE!
Funny, isn't it?

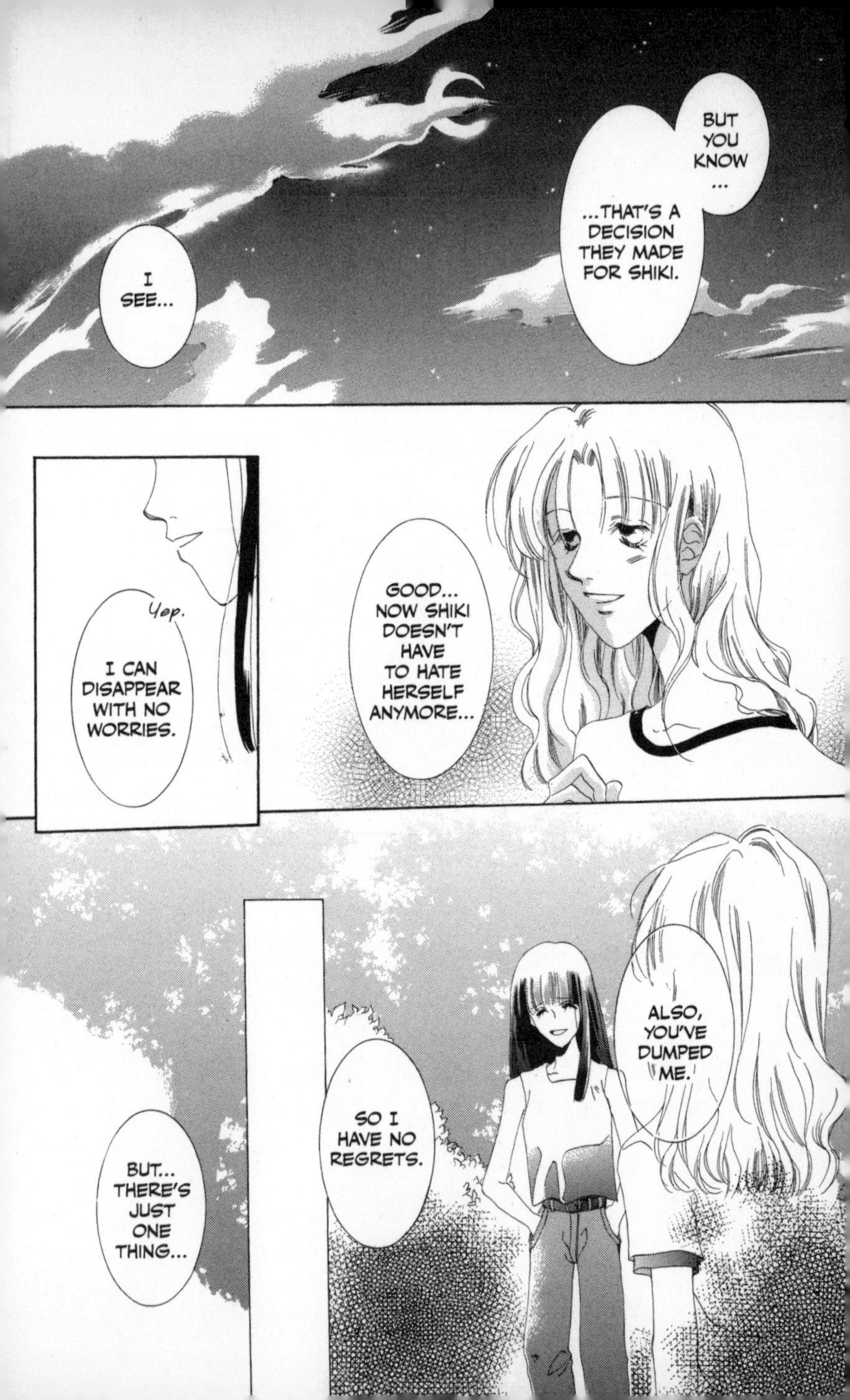
BUT YOU KNOW ...
...THAT'S A DECISION THEY MADE FOR SHIKI.
I SEE...
GOOD... NOW SHIKI DOESN'T HAVE TO HATE HERSELF ANYMORE...
Yep.
I CAN DISAPPEAR WITH NO WORRIES.
ALSO, YOU'VE DUMPED ME.
SO I HAVE NO REGRETS.
BUT... THERE'S JUST ONE THING...

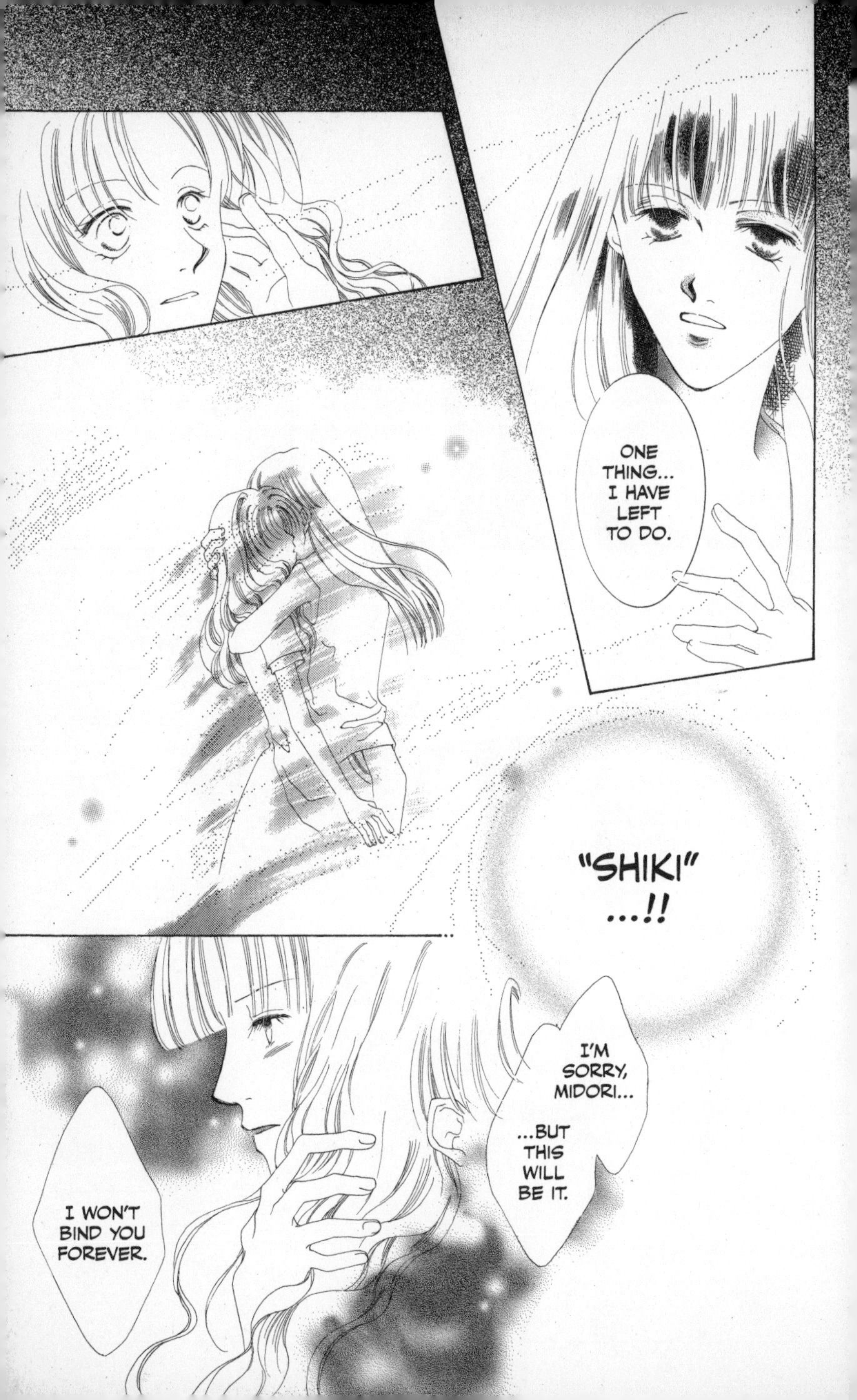
ONE THING... I HAVE LEFT TO DO.
"SHIKI" ...!!
I'M SORRY, MIDORI...
...BUT THIS WILL BE IT.
I WON'T BIND YOU FOREVER.

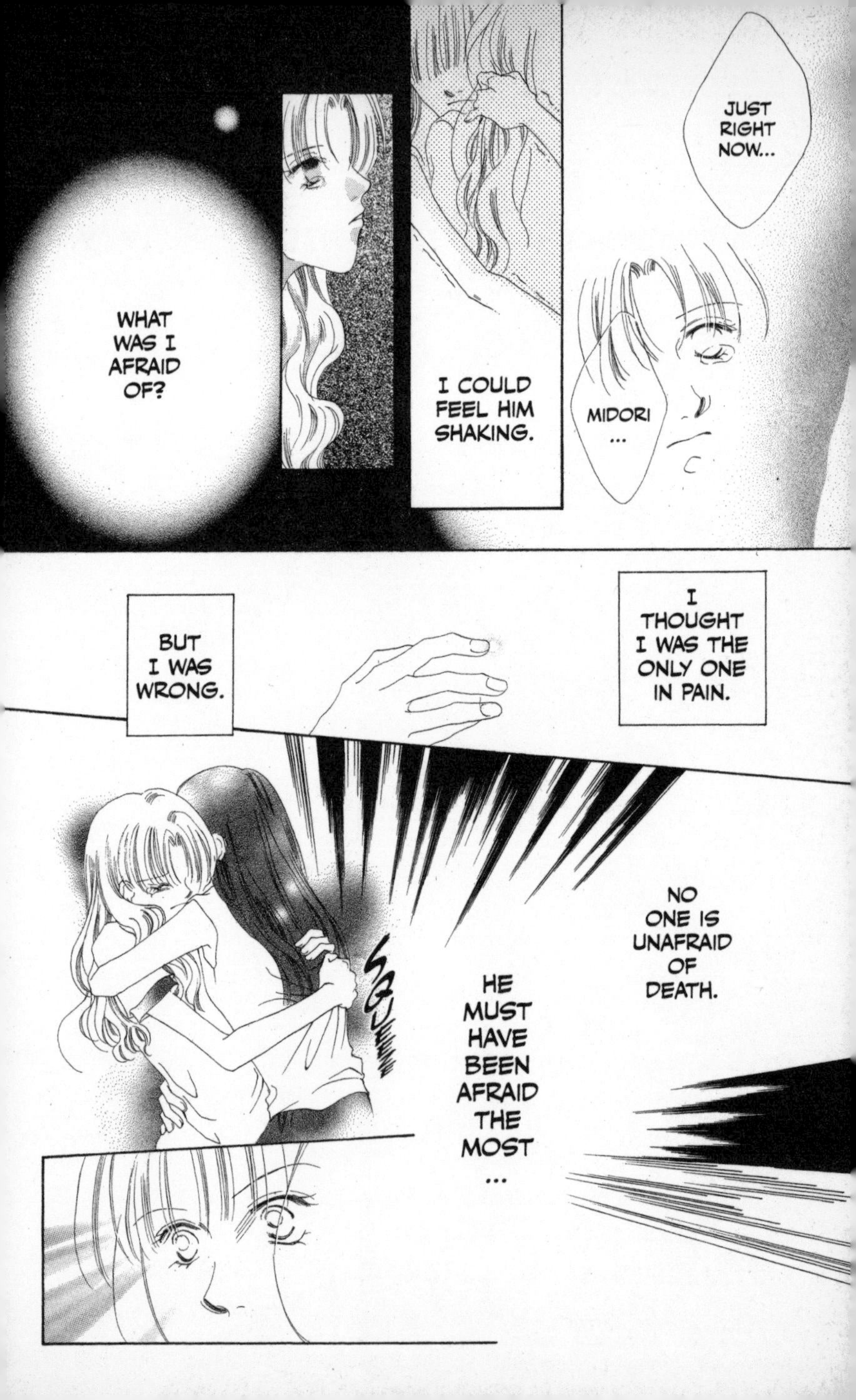
JUST RIGHT NOW...
MIDORI ...
I COULD FEEL HIM SHAKING.
WHAT WAS I AFRAID OF?
I THOUGHT I WAS THE ONLY ONE IN PAIN.
BUT I WAS WRONG.
NO ONE IS UNAFRAID OF DEATH.
HE MUST HAVE BEEN AFRAID THE MOST ...

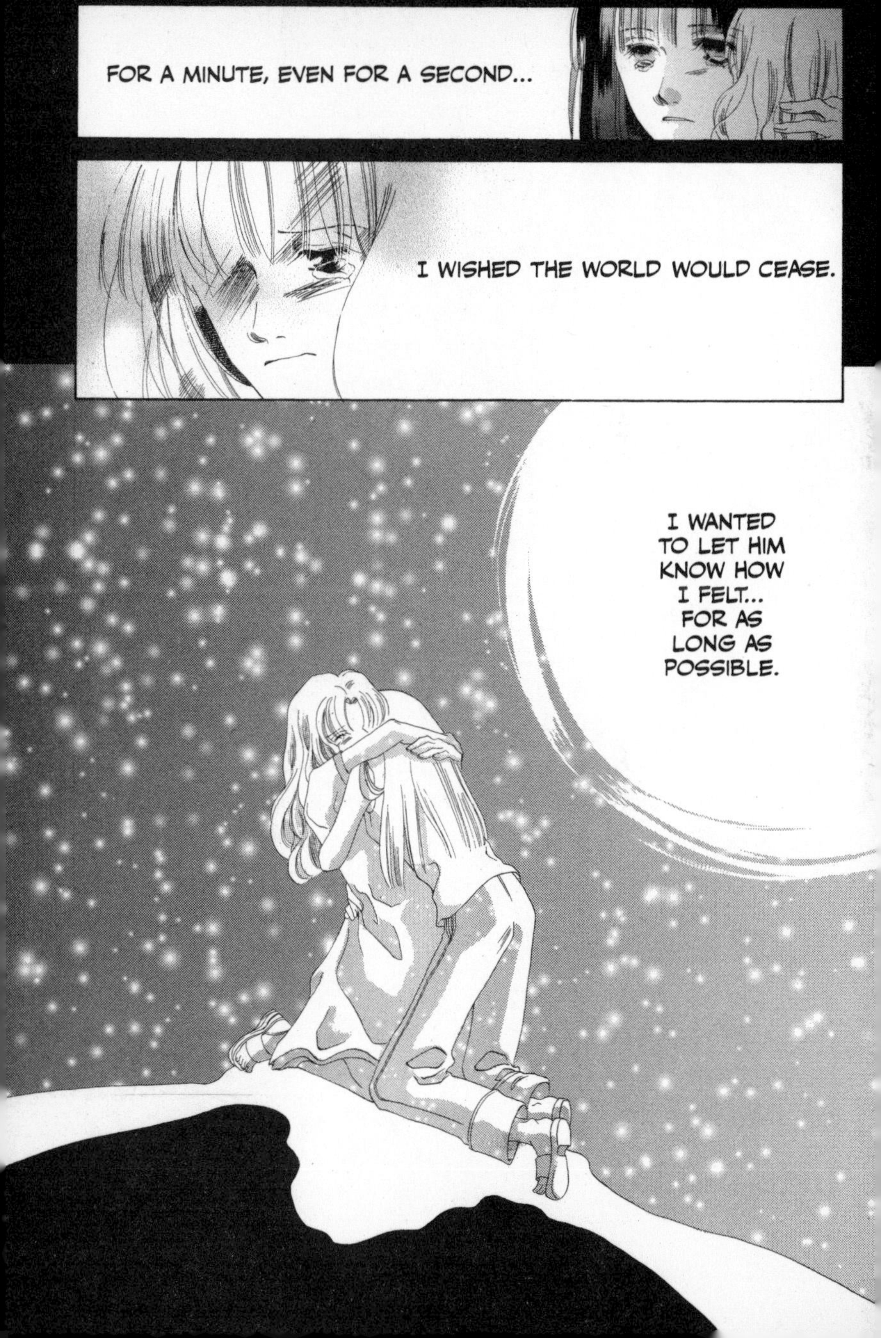
FOR A MINUTE, EVEN FOR A SECOND...
I WISHED THE WORLD WOULD CEASE.
I WANTED TO LET HIM KNOW HOW I FELT... FOR AS LONG AS POSSIBLE.

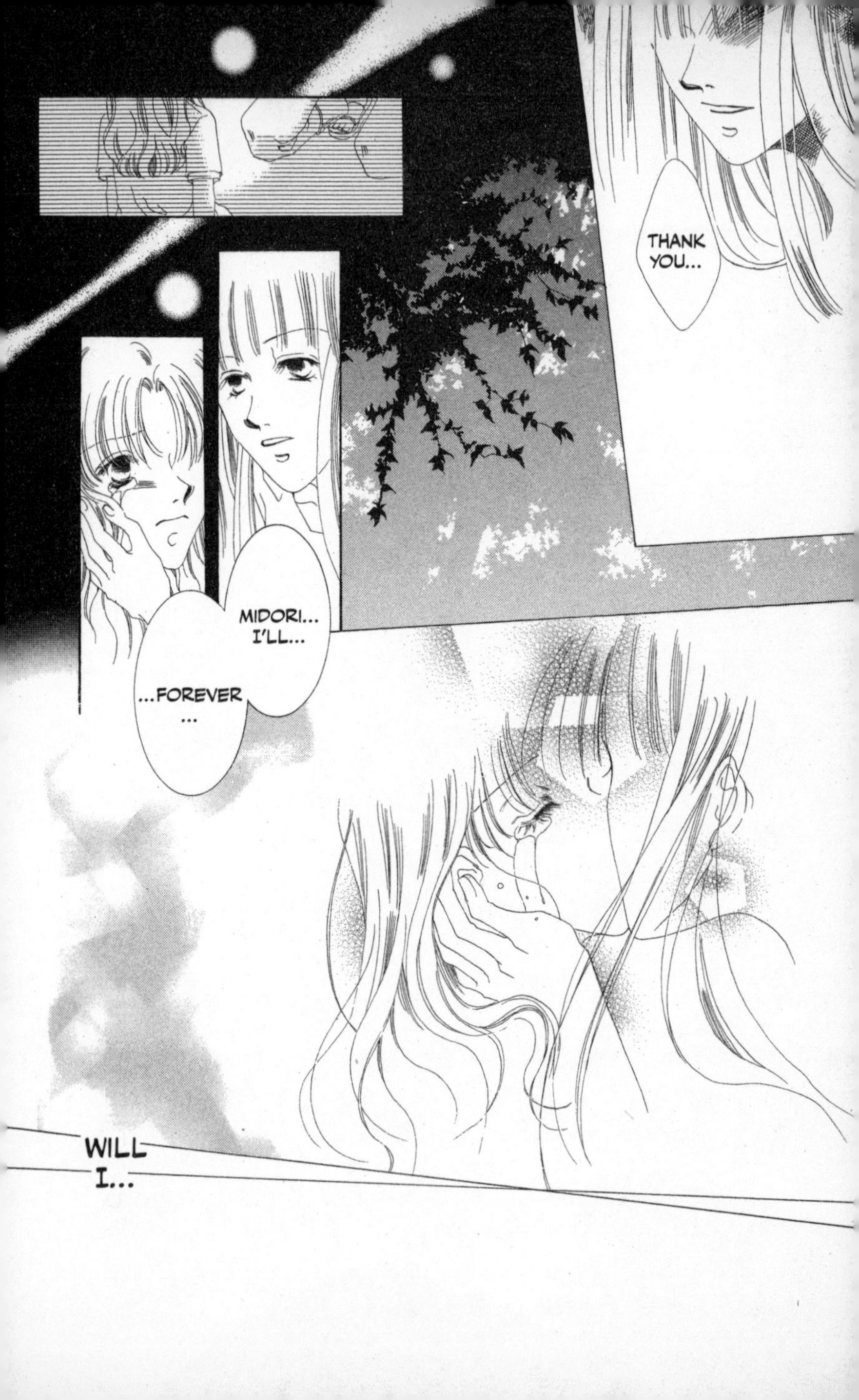

THANK YOU...
MIDORI... I'LL...
...FOREVER ...
WILL I...

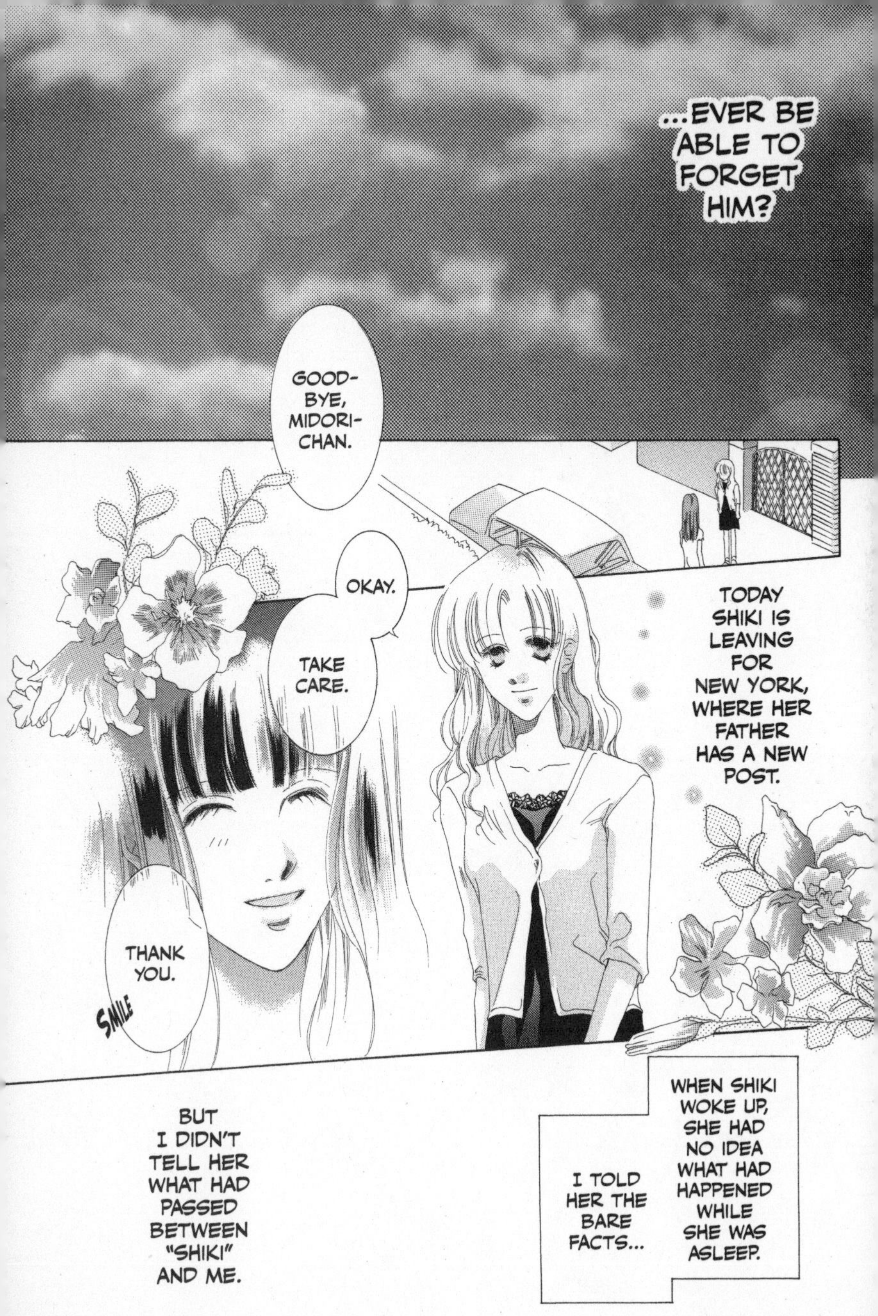
...EVER BE ABLE TO FORGET HIM?
GOOD-BYE, MIDORI-CHAN.
TODAY SHIKI IS LEAVING FOR NEW YORK, WHERE HER FATHER HAS A NEW POST.
OKAY.
TAKE CARE.
THANK YOU.
SMILE
WHEN SHIKI WOKE UP, SHE HAD NO IDEA WHAT HAD HAPPENED WHILE SHE WAS ASLEEP.
I TOLD HER THE BARE FACTS...
BUT I DIDN'T TELL HER WHAT HAD PASSED BETWEEN "SHIKI" AND ME.

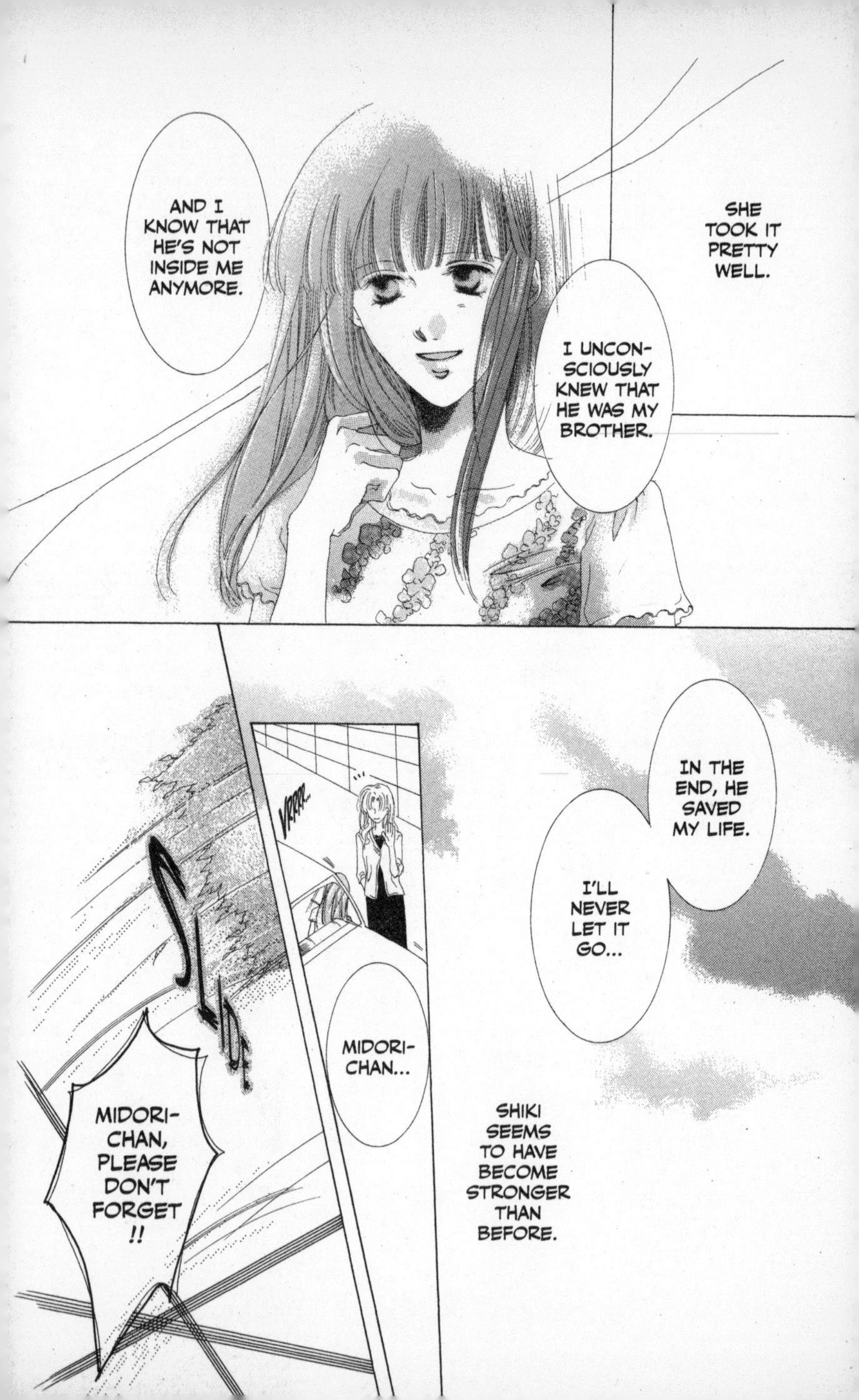
SHE TOOK IT PRETTY WELL.
I UNCON-SCIOUSLY KNEW THAT HE WAS MY BROTHER.
AND I KNOW THAT HE'S NOT INSIDE ME ANYMORE.
IN THE END, HE SAVED MY LIFE.
I'LL NEVER LET IT GO...
SHIKI SEEMS TO HAVE BECOME STRONGER THAN BEFORE.
VRRRR...
MIDORI-CHAN...
SLIDE
MIDORI-CHAN, PLEASE DON'T FORGET !!

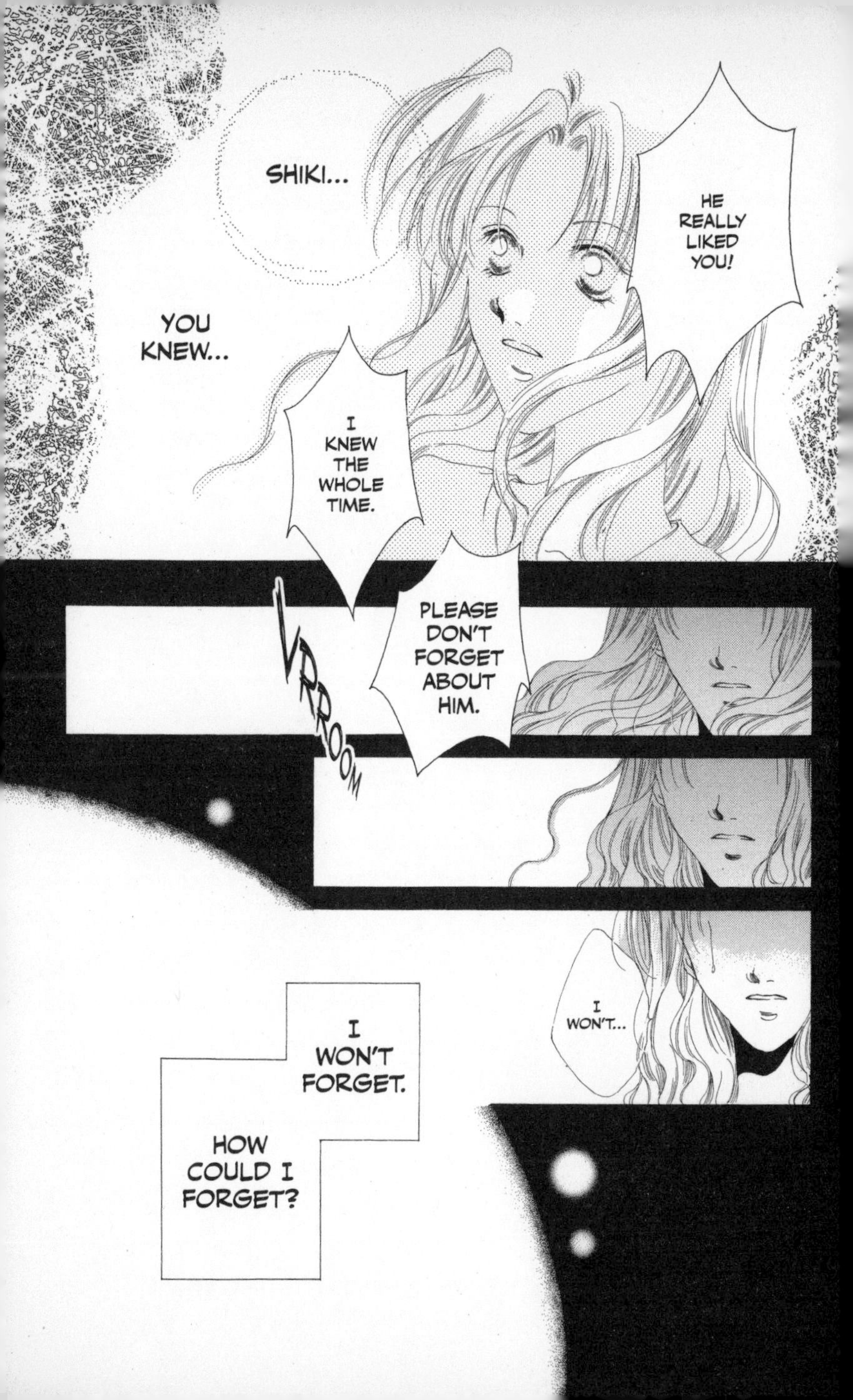
HE REALLY LIKED YOU!
SHIKI...
YOU KNEW...
I KNEW THE WHOLE TIME.
PLEASE DON'T FORGET ABOUT HIM.
VRROOM
I WON'T...
I WON'T FORGET.
HOW COULD I FORGET?

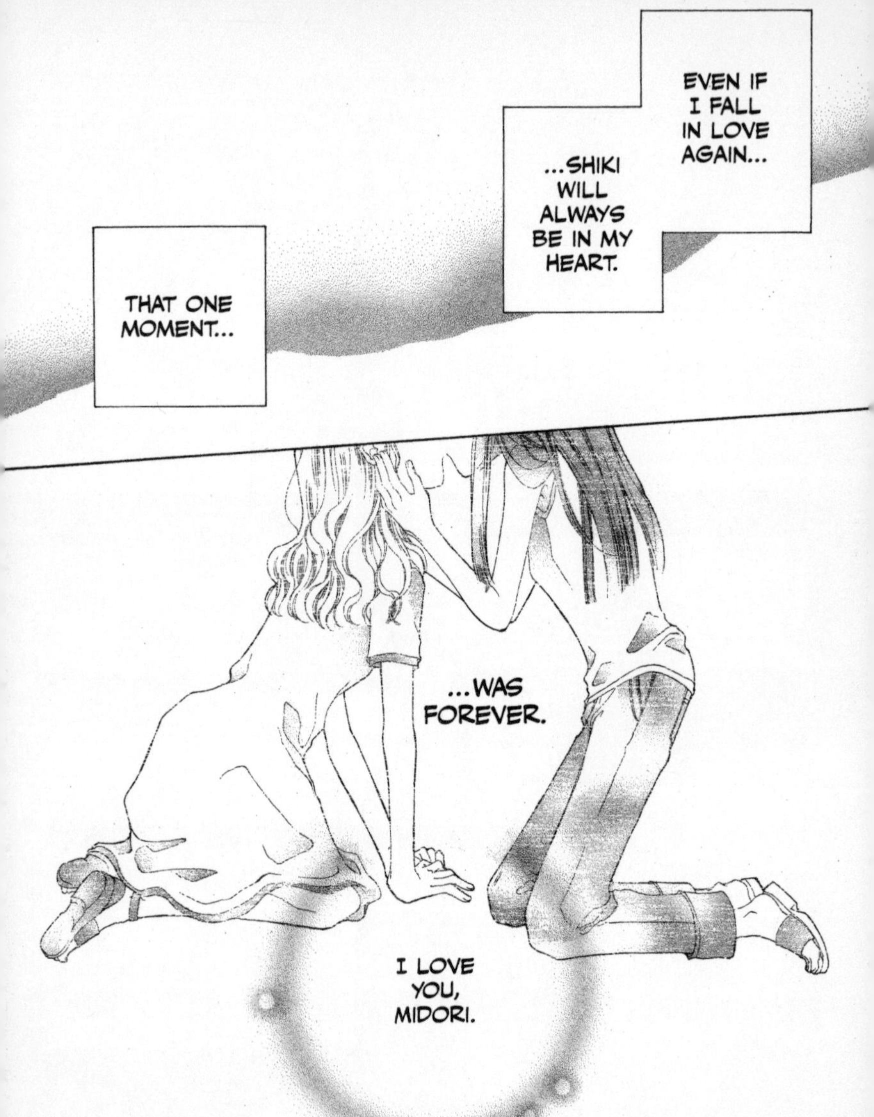
EVEN IF I FALL IN LOVE AGAIN...
...SHIKI WILL ALWAYS BE IN MY HEART.
THAT ONE MOMENT...
...WAS FOREVER.
I LOVE YOU, MIDORI.

A ROMANCE OF ONE MOMENT / THE END

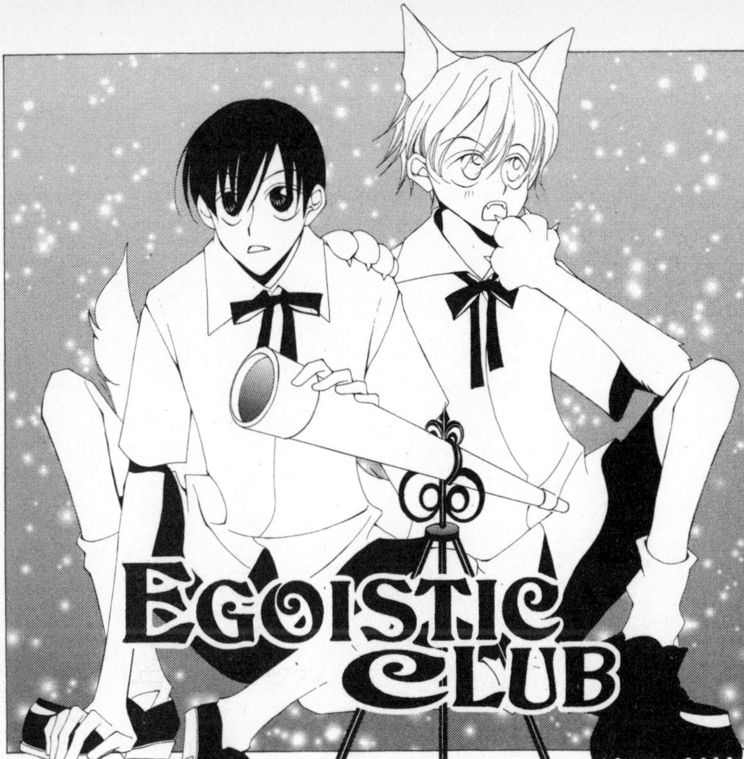
EGOISTIC CLUB

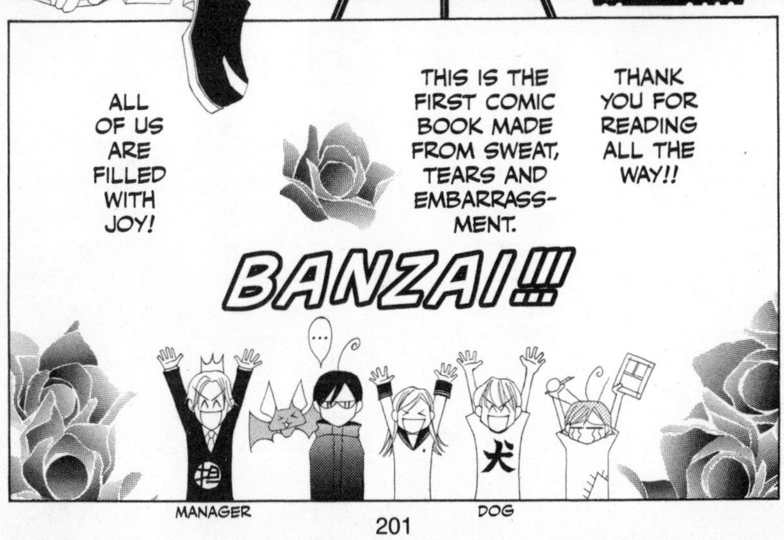
THANK YOU FOR READING ALL THE WAY!!
THIS IS THE FIRST COMIC BOOK MADE FROM SWEAT, TEARS AND EMBARRASS-MENT.
ALL OF US ARE FILLED WITH JOY!
BANZAI!!!
...
DOG
MANAGER

THE SUMMER OF 2000, HATORI HAD AN IDEA.

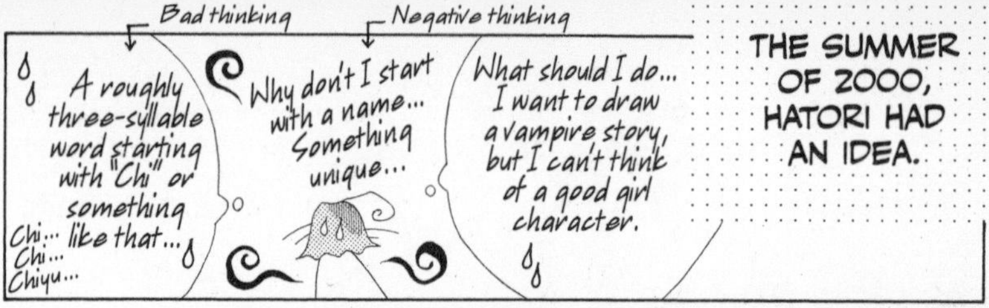
What should I do... I want to draw a vampire story, but I can't think of a good girl character.
Negative thinking
Why don't I start with a name... Something unique...
Bad thinking
A roughly three-syllable word starting with "Chi" or something like that...
Chi... Chi... Chiyu...

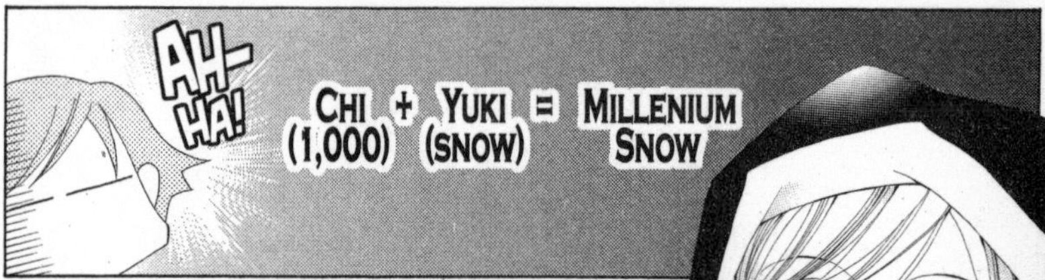
AH-HA!
CHI (1,000) + YUKI (SNOW) = MILLENIUM SNOW

THAT'S RIGHT! THIS STORY WAS BORN OF HER NAME.

SORRY IF I CONFUSED ANY OF YOU BY HAVING CHIYUKI BE SO ENERGETIC AFTER SHE WAS DISCHARGED FROM THE HOSPITAL, BUT IT WAS STILL THE SAME CHARACTER FROM MY POINT OF VIEW.

I tried to think of how her character would act after getting well.

I heard that some people actually have the name Chiyuki, and that surprised me. Personally, it's my favorite name.

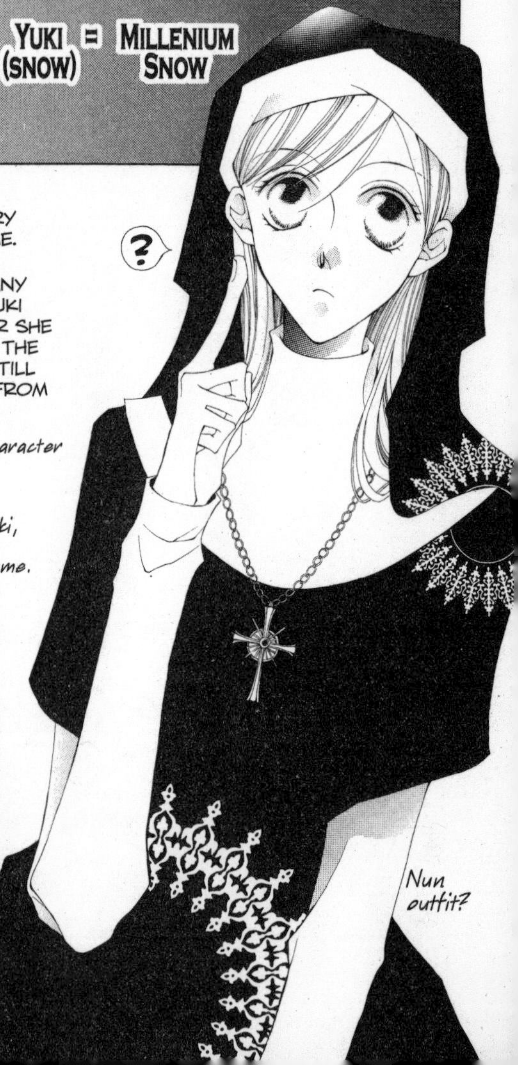
?
Nun outfit?

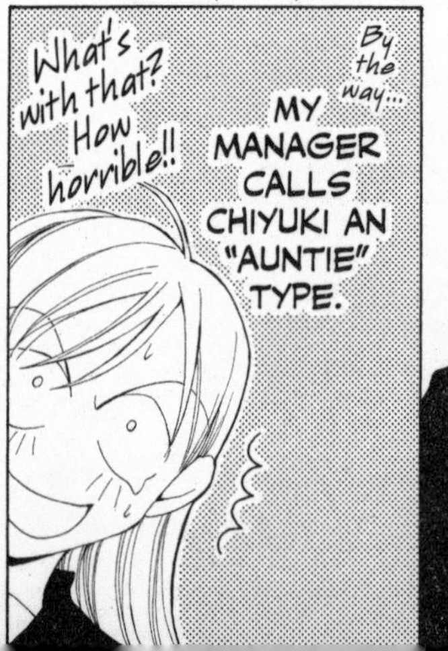
By the way...
MY MANAGER CALLS CHIYUKI AN "AUNTIE" TYPE.
What's with that? How horrible!!

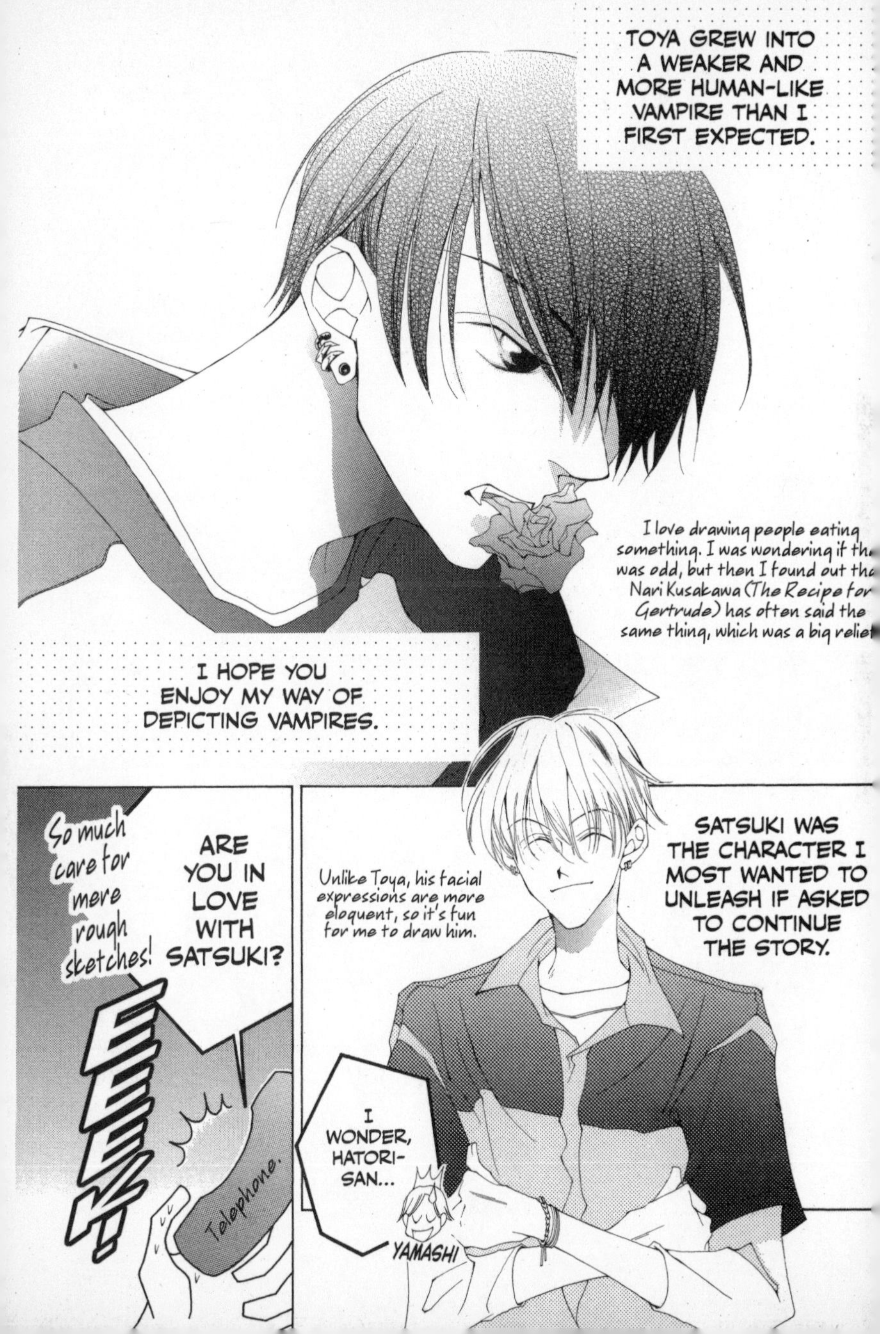
TOYA GREW INTO A WEAKER AND MORE HUMAN-LIKE VAMPIRE THAN I FIRST EXPECTED.
I love drawing people eating something. I was wondering if th was odd, but then I found out th Nari Kusakawa (The Recipe for Gertrude) has often said the same thing, which was a big relie
I HOPE YOU ENJOY MY WAY OF DEPICTING VAMPIRES.
SATSUKI WAS THE CHARACTER I MOST WANTED TO UNLEASH IF ASKED TO CONTINUE THE STORY.
Unlike Toya, his facial expressions are more eloquent, so it's fun for me to draw him.
I WONDER, HATORI-SAN...
YAMASHI
ARE YOU IN LOVE WITH SATSUKI?
So much care for mere rough sketches!
EEEK!
Telephone.

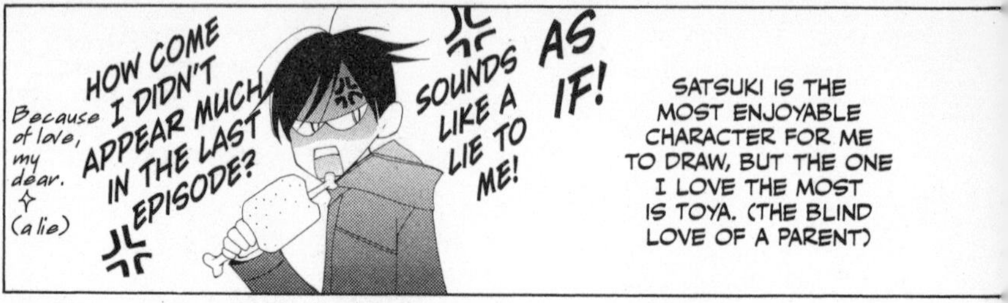
SATSUKI IS THE MOST ENJOYABLE CHARACTER FOR ME TO DRAW, BUT THE ONE I LOVE THE MOST IS TOYA. (THE BLIND LOVE OF A PARENT)
AS IF!
SOUNDS LIKE A LIE TO ME!
HOW COME I DIDN'T APPEAR MUCH IN THE LAST EPISODE?
Because of love, my dear. ✧ (a lie)

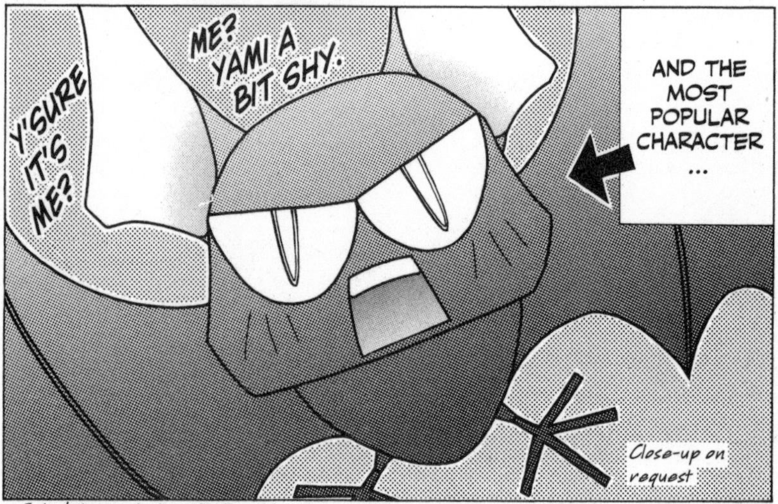
AND THE MOST POPULAR CHARACTER ...
ME? YAMI A BIT SHY.
Y'SURE IT'S ME?
Close-up on request

I don't know why he talks like this.

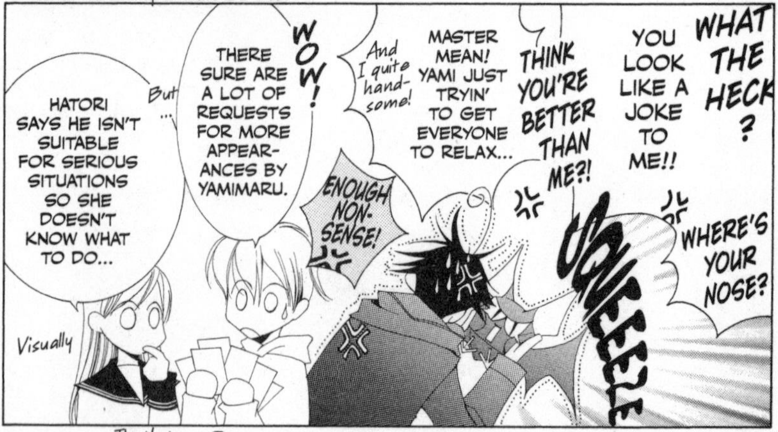
WHAT THE HECK?
YOU LOOK LIKE A JOKE TO ME!!
THINK YOU'RE BETTER THAN ME?!
MASTER MEAN! YAMI JUST TRYIN' TO GET EVERYONE TO RELAX...
And I quite handsome!
WOW!
THERE SURE ARE A LOT OF REQUESTS FOR MORE APPEARANCES BY YAMIMARU.
But...
HATORI SAYS HE ISN'T SUITABLE FOR SERIOUS SITUATIONS SO SHE DOESN'T KNOW WHAT TO DO...
WHERE'S YOUR NOSE?
ENOUGH NONSENSE!
Visually

That's true.

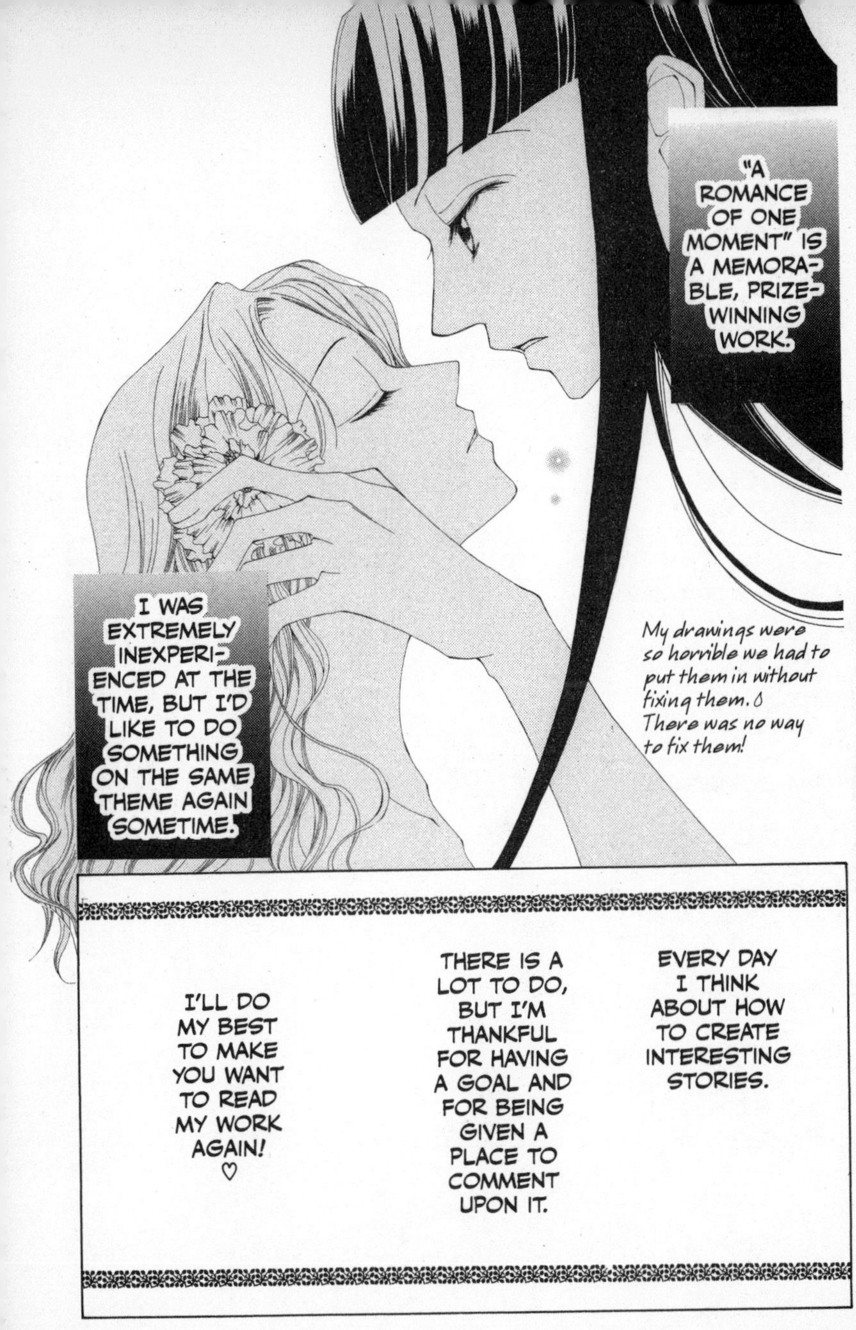
"A ROMANCE OF ONE MOMENT" IS A MEMORABLE, PRIZE-WINNING WORK.
My drawings were so horrible we had to put them in without fixing them. There was no way to fix them!
I WAS EXTREMELY INEXPERIENCED AT THE TIME, BUT I'D LIKE TO DO SOMETHING ON THE SAME THEME AGAIN SOMETIME.

EVERY DAY I THINK ABOUT HOW TO CREATE INTERESTING STORIES.

THERE IS A LOT TO DO, BUT I'M THANKFUL FOR HAVING A GOAL AND FOR BEING GIVEN A PLACE TO COMMENT UPON IT.

I'LL DO MY BEST TO MAKE YOU WANT TO READ MY WORK AGAIN! ♡

I READ ALL YOUR LETTERS WITH CARE.
PLEASE SEND ME YOUR COMMENTS ON THIS MANGA.

BISCO HATORI C/O SHOJO BEAT
VIZ MEDIA
P.O. BOX 77010
SAN FRANCISCO, CA 94107

Special Thanks!!

YAMASHITA
ALL THE EDITORS

*

EVERYONE
INVOLVED IN
PUBLISHING
THIS BOOK

*

FAMILY, FRIENDS

*

HIROMI KAMIYA
AZUMA SHIMAMURA
AYA AOMURA
RINA HASEGAWA

*

MECA TANAKA

*

NORIKO NAGAHAMA

*

AND ALL YOU
READERS!

2001.Nov.

Bisco.H

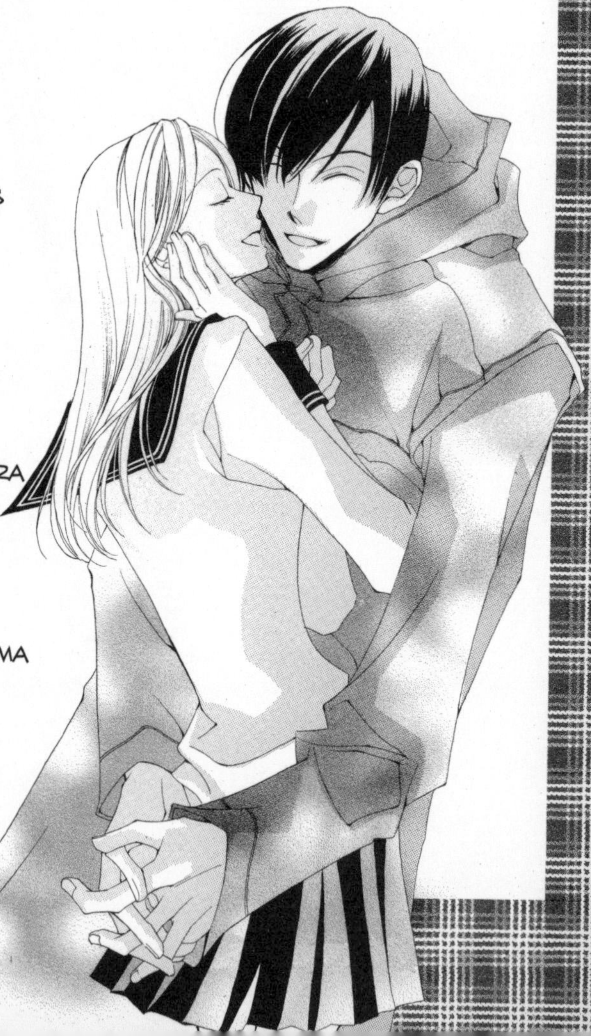

Glossary

While the appeal of the vampire needs no help to cross the language barrier, here are a few terms that could use a little extra explaining.

Chiyuki Matsuoka 千雪 松岡
The kanji in her first name mean "one thousand" and "snow."

Toya Kano トウヤ (冬哉) 叶
The first kanji in his last name means "winter."

Yamimaru 闇丸
The first kanji in his name means "dark" and the second is a common ending for boys' names.

Page 5, panel 1: Eika General Hospital
Eika means glory, prosperity, and other good things. It's a name of hope for a place often equated with despair.

Page 25, panel 7: Odaiba
An artificial island in Tokyo Bay that began as part of six fortresses built in 1853 to protect Tokyo from attack by sea. In the 1980s and early '90s Odaiba was rebuilt to be a showcase of futuristic living, but was largely abandoned when the economy collapsed. Today the district is a popular destination for tourists and Tokyo residents, with many shopping malls, a hot springs, a beach, a science museum, a giant Ferris wheel, and more.

Page 57, panel 5: Ume-konbu
Literally "plum-kelp," these are popular plum—and kelp—flavored Japanese snacks.

Page 93, panel 1: A big weed
Refers to the Japanese *udoka* (*Aralia cordata*), a large leafy tree that is more like an overgrown weed. It is sometimes used in Japan as a symbol for big idiots.

Page 138, panel 5: Ash
An indie Japanese band.

Page 141, panel 4: Koshi-hikari rice
A very popular, expensive brand of Japanese rice. *Koshi* means "surpass" and *hikari* means "bright."

Page 171, panel 2: "Shiki"
In the original Japanese, Shiki is spelled with kanji and "Shiki" is spelled with katakana.

Bisco Hatori made her manga debut with *Isshun Bkan no Romance* (*A Moment of Romance*) in *LaLa DX* magazine. The comedy *Ouran High School Host Club* is her breakout hit. When she's stuck thinking up characters' names, she gets inspired by loud, upbeat music (her radio is set to NACK5 FM). She enjoys reading all kinds of manga, but she's especially fond of the sci-fi drama *Please Save My Earth* and *Slam Dunk*, a basketball classic...

MILLENNIUM SNOW
VOL. 1
The Shojo Beat Manga Edition

STORY & ART BY
BISCO HATORI

Translation/RyoRca
English Adaptation/John Werry
Touch-up Art & Lettering/Gia Cam Luc
Design/Courtney Utt
Editor/Pancha Diaz

Managing Editor/Megan Bates
Editorial Director/Elizabeth Kawasaki
VP & Editor in Chief/Yumi Hoashi
Sr. Director of Acquisitions/Rika Inouye
Sr. VP of Marketing/Liza Coppola
Exec. VP of Sales & Marketing/John Easum
Publisher/Hyoe Narita

Printed in Canada

Published by VIZ Media, LLC.
P.O. Box 77010
San Francisco, CA 94107

Shojo Beat Manga Edition
10 9 8 7 6 5 4 3 2 1
First printing, April 2007

store.viz.com

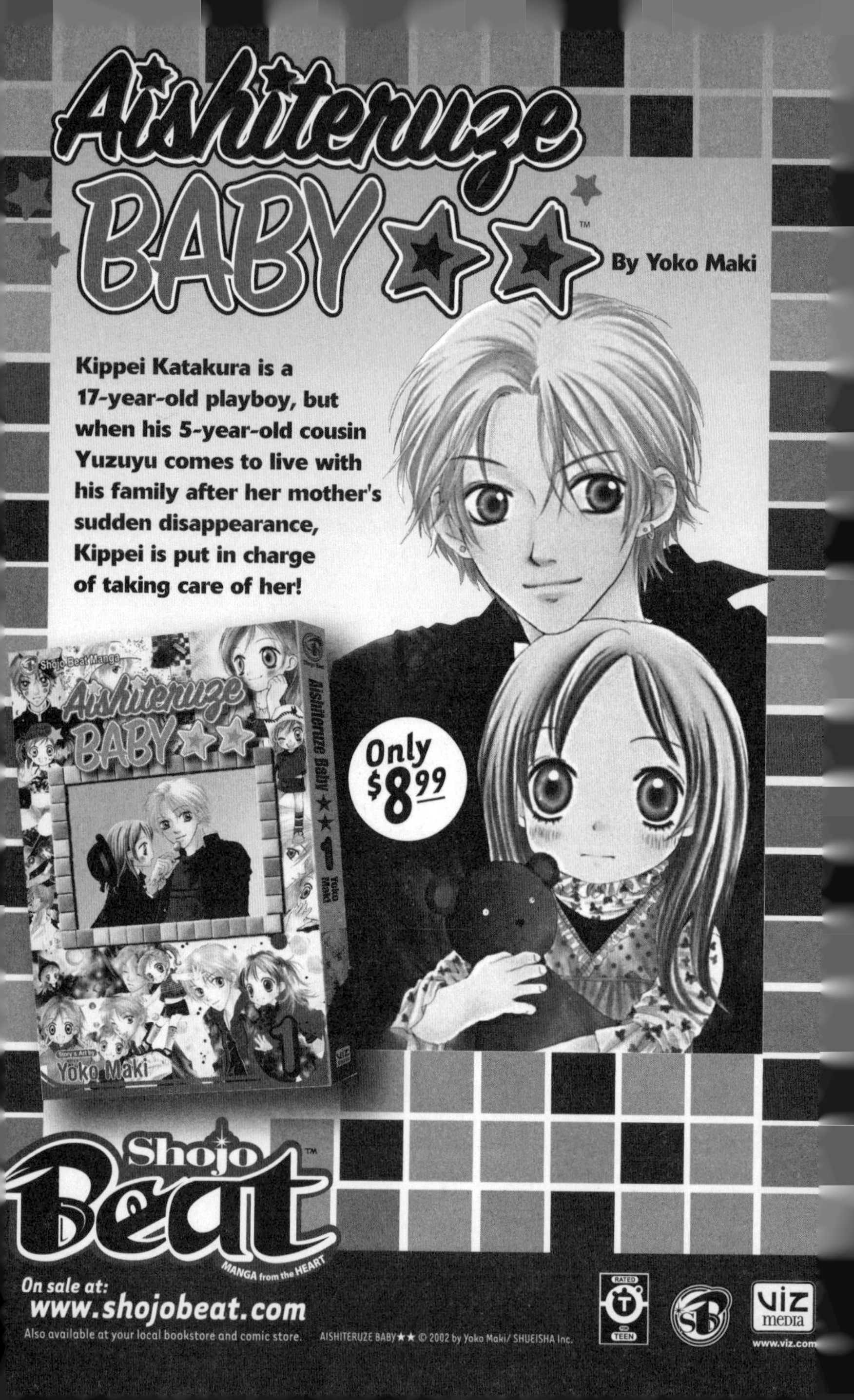
Aishiteruze BABY★★™
By Yoko Maki
Kippei Katakura is a 17-year-old playboy, but when his 5-year-old cousin Yuzuyu comes to live with his family after her mother's sudden disappearance, Kippei is put in charge of taking care of her!
Shojo Beat Manga
Aishiteruze BABY★★
Aishiteruze Baby ★★ 1 Yoko Maki
Story & Art by Yoko Maki
Only $8.99
Shojo Beat™
MANGA from the HEART
On sale at:
www.shojobeat.com
Also available at your local bookstore and comic store.
AISHITERUZE BABY★★ © 2002 by Yoko Maki/ SHUEISHA Inc.
RATED T FOR TEEN
VIZ media
www.viz.com

La Corda d'Oro™

by Yuki Kure

Ordinary student Kahoko couldn't be less qualified to participate in her school's music competition. But when she spots a magical fairy who grants her amazing musical talent, Kahoko finds herself in the company of some very musical—not to mention hot—guys!

Only $8.99